THE STATE AND MARKET IN INDIA'S SHIPPING

Nationalism, Globalization and Marginalization

THE STATE AND MARKET IN INDIA'S SHIPPING

Nationalism, Globalization and Marginalization

BALDEV RAJ NAYAR

MANOHAR
1996

First published 1996

ISBN 81-7304-178-4

Published by
Ajay Kumar Jain for
Manohar Publishers & Distributors
2/6 Ansari Road, Daryaganj
New Delhi 110 002

Printed at
Rajkamal Electric Press
B 35/9 G.T. Karnal Road Indl. Area
Delhi 110 033

For Nancy Ann

PREFACE

This study complements my earlier work on *The State and International Aviation in India: Performance and Policy on the Eve of Globalization*. I came to research on international aviation and overseas shipping not only because of their vital importance to economic welfare and national power, but also because of their relationship to key theoretical issues in comparative and international political economy. Initially, I had planned to do a single comparative study of the two sectors, because of my curiosity as to whether the nature of the international regime made any difference to state performance. As is known, it is often claimed that the international regime for aviation is authority-based while that for shipping is market-based. To the reader who is familiar with the earlier work on aviation, it will become obvious that the nature of the regime has had little impact on the final outcomes in the two sectors. Both sectors have witnessed the increasing marginalization of India in the world economy. And in both cases, regrettably, it is state policy that has to be faulted.

The study starts out in Chapter I with a broad perspective on the state-market relationship, both at the international and national levels. That chapter also summarily assesses the performance of India in tonnage acquisition for its merchant fleet, delineating the post-independence era into three periods, on the basis of quantitative data, for subsequent in-depth analysis. Chapter II looks at the global context in which national shipping functions, as also at the struggle of Indian shipping for rebirth and survival under the colonial state. Chapters III to VI examine India's performance in each of the three aforementioned periods after independence. The approach is analytical, not descriptive; it seeks to discover causes of outcomes, primarily in the state-market relationship. Chapter VII reviews the more recent attempt at restructuring the state-market relationship, and underlines the constraints under which

Indian shipping continues to operate. Finally, Chapter VIII provides a summary and conclusion for the study.

I owe a debt of gratitude to several colleagues, particularly Professors T.V. Paul, S.J. Noumoff, Jagdish Handa, and Filippo Sabetti, who read the manuscript in full or in part. I benefited enormously from their comments and critiques. In the field of shipping, my foremost debt is to Mr. B.V. Nilkund, chief executive of INSA in Bombay, who was always ready to help; he gave freely of his own time and provided full access to the resources at INSA. His selfless dedication to the cause of Indian shipping is most impressive. Dr. S.N. Sanklecha, the outstanding authority on Indian shipping, was always hospitable and welcoming. Dr. H.B. Desai allowed me to benefit from his wide knowledge of the subject by letting me spend a day with him in Baroda in 1992. I would like to thank the Shipping Division of UNCTAD and the Institute of Maritime Studies at the University of Wales, Cardiff, for the opportunity to do research there in May 1995. I am most grateful to Professor James Putzel at the London School of Economics for his help in setting up interviews at *Containerization International, Lloyd's Shipping Economist,* and P&O Containers in London. One can hardly thank enough Prem Malik, Administrative Director, Shastri Indo-Canadian Institute at New Delhi, for his invaluable help in research over the last two decades. Mr. Vijayakrishnan K. was very kind and generous in facilitating access to old committee reports in the parliament library. No words can be adequate for the generous and unstinted financial support provided by the Social Sciences and Humanities Research Council of Canada (SSHRC) over three decades.

It would have been difficult to proceed with research without the able administrative support of Helen Wilicka and Emilia Scognamiglio; Helen also proved to be an apt instructor in WordPerfect as did Michelle Marquis and Sami Khan. Phyllis Rudin, Reference Librarian, showed unusual enterprise and initiative in searching out UNCTAD and other government documents. My three daughters, Sheila, Kamala and Sunita, provided encouragement and moral support, and Sunita showed ingenuity in teaching me computer skills.

As always, my deepest debts are to my wife, in her own right a scholar of comparative religion. For 35 years, she has been a pillar of support in my academic endeavours. Her qualities of compassion, nobility of character, perpetual quest for truth, and devotion to family and research, have never shone brighter than now in her personal battle with breast cancer.

McGill University
April 15, 1996

Baldev Raj Nayar

CONTENTS

CHAPTER I

GLOBAL CHANGE, DEVELOPMENT, AND INDIAN SHIPPING

Economic development has in the half-century since the end of World War II proven to be a "great ascent" more in the steepness of the obstacles to be overcome than in the accomplishments actually made. True, the achievements of the "newly industrialized countries" are spectacular but, restricted as they are to only a small portion of the vast humanity in the developing world, their real significance lies in what can or ought to be accomplished, given the right mix of correct policy and favourable environment. Little wonder that the focus near the end of that half-century has come to lie on policy even as it was at the beginning. Meanwhile, massive changes have taken place in the global setting, the implications of which for economic development are uncertain.

In the wake of World War II, with the Axis powers decimated and defeated and the other major powers weakened, a new bipolar world was born, most of it presided over by the United States (US) as the new military and economic hegemon. The US fostered a "liberal international economic order" resting on the twin stools of GATT and the Bretton Woods system. The Soviet Union as the rival superpower, while "contained" territorially in its regional bloc, provided a military and, particularly, ideological challenge to American hegemony. In the interstices of the rivalry between the American and Soviet blocs there awakened politically the developing world, with high hopes of overcoming rapidly its economic backwardness, aided by some help from the two blocs.

A half-century later, the world stood transformed. Both the Soviet bloc and the Soviet Union had crumbled, with most of the successor states forthrightly opting for capitalism and democracy. The bloodless defeat of the Soviet Union resulted in a unipolar system with the US as the single military superpower. Meanwhile, the rise of Japan as an economic superpower and the increasing integration of Europe as a powerful economic unit have eroded further the economic domination of the US. Indeed, the erosion of American economic domination has been under way since the late 1960s, as symbolized in the collapse of the Bretton Woods system and the oil price shocks delivered by OPEC (Organization of the Petroleum Exporting Countries). However, economic power alone is not sufficient for political leadership or even political independence. For that reason, Japan and Europe not only remain within the political and military orbit of the US, but also exemplify their lack of capacity for managing international crises except under the leadership of the US. Such political and military dependence of Japan and Europe on the US has been well illustrated during the oil price shocks in the 1970s, the debt crisis in the 1980s, Iraq's occupation of Kuwait in 1989 and 1990, and the breakup of Yugoslavia in the 1990s.

For much of the developing world--notwithstanding the graduation of several Asian tigers to the status of "newly industrialized countries" (NICs) under the overarching military and political umbrella of the US--the last two decades of the half-century spelled economic turmoil, besides continuing poverty. The heavy debt burden, inflation, and economic stagnation made for balance of payments crises, which led to the imposition of structural adjustment programmes at the behest of the IMF and World Bank. With the loss of political leverage following the decline and collapse of the Soviet Union, the developing world could count for little help in its economic crisis from the developed world. In a cruel reversal of earlier expectations, the already-battered developing world, in fact, turned into a source of large capital transfers to the developed world by way of debt repayments.

Economic Globalization and The Developing World

In its efforts to grapple with the problems of national development, the developing world has confronted in the last quarter of the century a changed world economic system, characterized by heightened economic globalization, which poses new external challenges for it. As economic globalization has intensified it has come to loom large in the horizons of policy-makers, and adjustment to it has moved to the forefront of their economic agenda. Of course, economic globalization--also referred to as complex interdependence, international economic integration, or international division of labour--is nothing new on the international scene. Since the rise of states and markets during the "long" sixteenth century, the world has been on a course of increasing economic integration. This course has at times been interrupted by wars and recessions which were either accompanied or precipitated by mercantilistic policies, but the secular trend of a deepening economic integration of the globe is nonetheless manifest. Even as long ago as almost a century and a half, the stoppage of cotton exports from the US to England as a result of the American civil war had far-reaching effects on the agricultural economy of Egypt and India. But the pace of integration of the world economy accelerated with the launching of the "liberal international economic order" under the auspices of American hegemony after the end of World War II. In that sense, one can distinguish between an earlier "extensive" or "widening" phase in global economic integration and an "intensive" or "deepening" phase since World War II.

The intensification of international economic integration is evident in several new developments.[1] For one thing, there has been the growth in international trade, not only absolutely but also as a proportion of economic production which, in the three decades between 1960 and 1990, doubled from 10 per cent to 20 per cent. Even countries whose dependence on foreign trade was traditionally low have seen significant increases; thus, in the case of the US, the share of trade in its GDP doubled in two decades from 5.6 per cent during the second half of the 1960s to 11 per cent during the second half of the 1980s. Such expansion in international trade was accompanied by significant structural changes, with the proportion of manufactures in world exports rising from 60 per cent to 69 per cent between 1970 and 1990, while raw materials and agricultural products correspondingly declined from 28 per cent to less than 16 per cent.

Second, economic production has come to be increasingly organized on a global basis. This is manifest in the fact that 40 per cent of the world trade during the 1980s was managed within multinational corporations (MNCs). It is evident also in the spectacular increase in direct foreign investment. The total stock of direct foreign investment in 1990 amounted to $1100 billion, having multiplied twenty times since 1960. Wholly or partly foreign owned corporations were responsible for more than one-third of the world economic product. The increased economic globalization has resulted in new patterns of cooperation and competition among the multinationals; while relentless globalization has made for fierce competition, it has also brought about a pattern of "strategic alliances" among otherwise competing MNCs because of the tremendous costs of new technology, the development of which has been forced by competition in the first place.

Third, there has occurred the rapid internationalization of money markets, with the international money trade expanding six times during the 1980s, such that the daily volume was "more than fifty times as large as that of commodity markets".[2] Computer-based, instant satellite communications has resulted in a global capital market that functions round the clock.

Even as it may have the potential to advance human welfare, economic globalization also results in the transfer of disturbances from one part of the world economic system to other parts of that system, as abundantly conveyed by the oil shocks of 1973 and 1979 and also by the market crash of 1987. It also generates disturbances in national markets as the entry of economic agents from the outside, such as multinationals, affects the fortunes of local economic actors. The deeper economic integration of the world provides an apparent autonomy to the working of the global economic system, with its own laws of motion, even as it exercises an overpowering impact on national economies. National economies are increasingly buffeted by world economic forces and processes, which are not always amenable to effective national control. The consequence can be serious economic dislocations.

Such economic dislocations hold the potential for economic advancement and strengthening of economic capabilities, but also of weakening and erosion of capabilities, marginalization, and de-industrialization. The economic dislocations invariably make for gainers and losers. They consequently let loose struggles over shares in the economic product, which necessarily pull states into them, with the struggles then carried out in and between states, as well as in and between markets. In the conflicts so engendered, states--whether as national units, individually or jointly, or as constituted into a larger international system--and markets, whether domestic or global, have key roles. Both play multiple roles in economic conflict, for they are at once the arenas, the filters, the deciders, and the instruments through which such conflict is carried out, resolved or perpetuated. They are the arenas, for they serve as the sites for the conflict among economic units; they are the filters, for they determine which issues in the conflict will get on the agenda and at what level; they are the deciders, for they determine the outcomes in the conflict; and they are the instruments, for they serve as the policy tools in carrying out or resolving the conflict.

Because of their manifest crucial importance, states and markets deserve special attention in any consideration of the issue of how developing countries have attempted to cope with the challenges emergent from global economic change (see further below).

ISSUE-AREAS AND CASE STUDIES

The policy response in the developing world to changes in the world economic order can be studied at several levels. It can be studied at the level of the developing world as a whole, understandably differentiating several sets of countries since that world has experienced uneven development. Or, it can be studied in one or more of these sets or, again, in one or more individual countries within those sets. Each mode of study carries its own rewards and limitations in terms of the breadth or depth it makes possible.

Regardless at which level the study is carried out, the important question remains as to how one or more developing states have responded to the changes in the world economic order compared to their earlier posture. The policy response can be broken down into several parts: (1) How have developing states responded at the national level in terms of enhancing their capabilities relative to others within the existing world economic order (relational power)? (2) How have they responded at the global level in terms of changing the nature of the world economic order (meta power)?[3] (3) What policy instruments, or mix of policy instruments, have they employed in the achievement of these ends? In respect of each of these questions, an equally important supplemental query is: How effective have they been in achieving the desired ends? In other words, how effective has been their performance? While placed here at the end of this sequence of questions, the last one on performance can be accorded priority, indeed considered as the dependent variable, with policy response and the change in the global environment that transpires or compels it being regarded as the chief independent variables.

The issue of the response of a particular state or set of states in the developing world can be examined in several ways. It can be looked at from the perspective of the overall national posture towards the outside world, such as the policy of integration into the world system, or of delinking from it in order to enhance national autonomy. It can also be examined from the standpoint of economics by asking whether the policy is one of import substitution industrialization or of export oriented industrialization. Again, it can be investigated at the level of individual sectors, such as trade regimes, or monetary management, or technology markets. These areas are all undoubtedly important and therefore deserving of research.

The present study, however, seeks to focus more narrowly on an examination of the shipping sector in the larger issue-area of international transportation. This issue-area recommends itself for attention for several reasons: From the viewpoint of economics, international transportation is crucial to the whole process of global production, in so far as it brings together the various factors of production. Simply, no coördination of factors of production, no goods and services. Besides, transportation links production to consumption at the international level. International trade is contingent on transportation, for without transportation there can be no trade. For developing economies, the building of adequate capabilities in international transportation is necessary for structural change and diversification. It is essential also for the acquisition of new skills and for expanded employment. These capabilities are vital, too, to the balance of payments, inasmuch as they reduce economic transfers by way of invisibles to the developed countries. Beyond economics, the issue-area of international transportation is intimately linked to national security. Capabilities in this issue-area are recognized as constituting the second line of defence. In turn, shipping is of special importance within the issue-area since until the twentieth century it constituted almost the sole, and certainly the cheapest, form of international transport. Even with the increasing use of aviation for transport, shipping is responsible for the carriage of the overwhelming bulk of the world's cargo traffic by weight.[4] Historically, shipping has been critical to national power and has been referred to as the navy of supply.

The aim here, then, is to study the shipping sector in the wider issue-area of international transportation and to do so through a case study of India's policy response and performance in coping with the world economic order and changes within it during the twentieth century. By an examination of a single sector for a single country over a considerable historical period, it is hoped that what is lost in not having a broad comparative overview of several countries or blocks of countries is, possibly, adequately compensated by a closer investigation of a narrower area.

The choice of India for the case study stems from several considerations. In a sense, India invites examination because of the salience of the active role that its sophisticated elite played in international diplomacy during the 1960s and early 1970s to foster a new international regime that would assure the developing countries a fair and equitable share in world shipping. By its very activism in the past, it arouses the question as to how it has actually performed at home in building capabilities in this sector. Besides, India is a large country in terms of territory, population and resources that is located strategically athwart the main lines of maritime transport between the east and the west in the ocean that is named after it. Further, it is a country with a long, though interrupted, maritime tradition. Given its large size, its strategic location, and its vast skilled manpower, India's performance should be valuable in assessing the possibilities that are open to developing countries in shipping. If India with these advantages cannot assure for itself a fair and equitable share, what prospects can there possibly be for others?

Performance in the context of global economic change is premised on an adequate policy response. Since at a fundamental level policy response often focuses on the emphasis to be accorded to the state or market as policy instruments, a prior task is the examination of the relationship between the two.

States and Markets in Interaction

Politics and economics as specialized activities for the pursuit of power and wealth, respectively, have been evident in human society since the development of social differentiation in human groups above the level of tribes or folk societies. But the unique organizational expressions of these two activities in the modern era--indeed, these two organizational expressions are key elements in the very definition of the era as modern--are states and markets.[5] These two mighty innovations generated by Europe came to define European civilization over the last three centuries or so. They additionally enabled Europe to overpower physically the rest of the globe, and in turn diffuse the two social institutions across the globe either by force or by example. That process of building states and markets in areas outside Europe, and even in some parts of Europe, is a process that is still going on. Indeed, that is the very heart of the contemporary challenge for the developing world.

The two mighty innovations of Europe began their development in the sixteenth century. Although some interpretations, as in Marx and Polanyi, see the economy as the primary determinant, with the modern state viewed as an outgrowth of markets, others see the state as prior and determining. In the latter view, conflict among kingdoms led to the formation of the modern state,[6] with war activities between states and the consequent need for greater economic resources leading to the development of markets. Besides, in line with their prior and determining status, states have always kept markets subordinate to the higher interests of the state. Given the ambiguity of social facts, the dispute between these two contending views is unlikely to be resolved, but it is sufficient to note that, in the broad sweep of history, states and markets arose about the same time. Their rise was part of the birth of modernity in the world, while it in turn pushed modernity further. Having arisen together, the two social organizations, even as they have their separate spheres, are interacting forces, affecting each other. They are dialectically connected, even as they have their separate logics.[7]

The state exists in a world of other states, which are demarcated from each other territorially with defined boundaries, with each state sovereign over its people and claiming exclusive loyalty, monopoly of the legitimate use of violence, and sole responsibility for the protection of its territory and the welfare of its people. The key concerns of the state are security in relation to other states and legitimacy in relation to its population, at least the important groups within it.

Security is the primal interest of states, it is their very raison d'etre. Security requires power or capabilities, not only military but also economic, for military power rests on economic capabilities. Paul Kennedy succinctly articulates the connection: "It sounds crudely mercantilistic to express it this way, but wealth is usually needed to underpin military power, and military power is usually needed to acquire and protect wealth". There is a caveat, however; if too much is spent on security, the likely result would be economic weakness in the long term. The historical conclusion is nonetheless compelling: "The history of the rise and later fall of the leading countries in the Great Power system since the advance of western Europe in the sixteenth century... shows a very significant correlation *over the longer term* between productive and revenue-raising capacities on the one hand and military strength on the other".[8] Economic development or capital accumulation is thus essential for security; indeed, it is taken to be an imperative by the less developed countries.[9] Given the close relationship between capital accumulation and security, economic issues are not always, and cannot be, therefore evaluated in terms of economic criteria alone; strategic interests of the state are, and have to be, taken into account in the formulation of economic policy. To take a strictly economic view of such issues would be myopic and may put security at risk. In respect of security, the reference point for the state in regard to capabilities is other states; in other words, the state's view of capabilities is relative. States are interested not just in absolute capabilities but relative capabilities. For, relative capabilities are essential to the reduction of vulnerabilities in relation to other states, both military and economic.

Legitimacy refers to the tacit or explicit support of key groups in society. Such support may be obtained in return for protection afforded to groups or for the advancement of their interests. Protection is important since groups are likely to be in conflict in the pursuit of power and wealth. Since advancement of group interests revolves around material concerns, legitimacy also requires a capacity on the part of states to assure delivery of economic goods and services. Thus, legitimacy also demands capital accumulation.

Oriented to the twin tasks of security and legitimacy, the state has come to replace, in fact or in aspiration, other forms of political organization as the overarching political machinery for handling these tasks.

The market is a coordination mechanism for the exchange of goods and services on the basis of relative prices. Ideally, it is a self-regulating mechanism which brings together buyers and sellers on a competitive basis. Driven by the motive force of maximizing private gain, the market orders the overall productive system on the basis of demand and supply. Its key feature of competition between buyers and sellers serves as the driving force behind the noted efficiency of the system. The competition determines which economic actors will survive or flourish on the basis of their efficiency. Survival in competition on the basis of efficiency often rests on innovation in technique in production and distribution; indeed, technology has become an independent factor in production besides land, labour and capital, and a source of economic and political power in the world. The efficiency of the market system is believed to advance the absolute welfare of society, since everyone gains from it, at least over the long term, even if not in the same measure. This absolute advancement of economic welfare is based on the law of comparative advantage, where everyone contributes on the basis of one's endowment and benefits accordingly. The law, of course, entails a division of labour among economic actors, with specialization based on their capabilities.

Absolute gain for all, obtained through the market system resting on a division of labour, implies that there is a basic and ultimate harmony of interests among economic actors, and that the market system should accordingly be allowed to expand since all would gain--eventually even if not immediately. Similarly, it suggests that political boundaries ought not to be allowed to stand in the way of such market expansion, and that different political units ought to be brought within the compass of a single market economic system. That at least has been the liberal creed since Adam Smith, who saw markets, if left alone, to be self-regulating and socially beneficial. In *liberalism*, absolute gain emergent from the market system has priority (as against relative gain which is critical to states) while political boundaries are seen as an obstacle to the efficiency of markets (as against their being regarded as constituting the very definition of states).

Given that both states and markets are concerned with the economy, a principal issue has been as to what are the appropriate roles for markets and states in the economy. The issue arises because, even as states and markets have their separate logics, their operations affect each other and therefore are not likely to be left alone. Markets determine gainers and losers, and they decide the economic fate of different classes of producers, such as capitalists and workers. They do so not only in times of growth and expansion, but especially in times of economic crisis. Indeed, Marx saw social conflict, crises of overproduction and immiserization of workers to be structurally built into markets under capitalism, inevitably leading to economic collapse. Unlike Adam Smith, Marx saw not harmony but class struggle as the inherent consequence of markets under capitalism. The underlining of conflict among classes as an inevitable feature of capitalism has been the intellectual hallmark of *Marxism*. Regardless, through the differential impact they have on various groups, markets have a vital impact on political power. Their operations affect the material interests and welfare of different groups and classes, and therefore the legitimacy of government. Furthermore, importantly, markets also affect relative capabilities as between states in the international system and are therefore crucially linked to national security.

No state can therefore leave markets completely alone. States intervene to protect key groups that are important to their legitimacy, and therefore endeavour to regulate the economy in order to overcome "market failures". Keynes provided the theoretical rationale for state intervention and regulation of the economy, holding that, contrary to Marx, capitalism was fixable through such mechanisms rather than being fated for breakdown and self-destruction. States intervene and regulate the economy additionally to protect their economic interests in relation to other states, in so far as they are affected by its location in a competitive and conflictual international system. Such interests relate both to societal welfare and military security, and state intervention in the economy for their protection against external forces falls under the rubric of *mercantilism.*[10] State intervention in markets, whether stemming from legitimacy or security, may make for economic inefficiency, but the logic of states imposes its own political compulsions for it. Success in the endeavour, of course, would depend on national consensus over goals and the coherence of state institutions.

On the other hand, states may intervene in markets not just to overcome market failures, or for the mercantilistic protection of national interest, but for other reasons as well. They may take over the functions that the market performs in order simply to have access to the resources that markets provide. Indeed, some states may be predatory in relation to the economy. Or, states may, for reasons of ideology, appropriate entirely the functions which markets perform, as was the case with the Soviet Union. In such bureaucratic coordination of the economy, or "command economy", the economy assumes the form of a single firm run on the basis of superordinate-subordinate relations, with the state at the head of the firm issuing orders to those below as to how to carry out their functions in the productive and distributive processes. In other economies, the state may impose thoroughgoing licensing in respect of production and distribution, determining who shall produce or distribute what and how much and at what price.

Given the separate logics of economics and politics, such heavy intervention by the state often results in severe distortions in the allocation of the factors of production, and thus onerous costs, even if such costs do not become immediately apparent. Take, for example, the former Soviet Union, where Soviet planners had to administratively determine some 20 million prices,[11] which would otherwise have been automatically determined by the market on the basis of demand and supply. It has, however, simply not been within the competence of any group of planners so far to do such price determination effectively. The inevitable consequence of such market displacement is allocative distortions which make for economic inefficiency, and may even grind the economy to a halt. State intervention, often designed to overcome "market failures", can thus end up in "government failures".

Market economy and "command" bureaucratic economy are ideal types. Even among the advanced industrialized democracies what exists is not an unregulated market system, but a "mixed economy". State intervention in many of these states has gone beyond regulation of the market to encompass public ownership of firms as well as economic planning. The very rise of such a mixed economy is a result of the operation of politics within the modern state, especially the democratic state. In view of the political compulsions engendered by electoral politics, the modern state has intervened to protect vulnerable sections, to provide a welfare net for weaker groups, and to cope with the periodic disturbances that emerge from the functioning of markets, both internal and external. This profound modification of liberalism in practice, both domestically and internationally, inspired by the requirements of the state for the maintenance of social and political stability, has come to be conceptually characterized, following a distinction made by Polanyi, as "embedded liberalism".[12]

What is striking about the "mixed economy" or "embedded liberalism" of the advanced industrial democracies is that, despite state intervention, a delicate balance--no doubt, always in tension--has been kept between the state and market in economic management. The state has restrained itself from excessive intervention even as it has, in a process of constant and continuous readjustment, modulated this intervention on analysing what its effects are on the economy, now deepening it, now withdrawing from it. Economic policy reform therefore remains a perpetual item on the agenda of the modern state, and it has to do with the respective roles of state and market in the running of the economy. At one time, it may mean greater state intervention to overcome "market failures". At other times, it may mean limiting or shrinking the area of state interference in the economy, to remove restrictions imposed on the operation of the market and the private sector, to deregulate, to privatize the public sector, to shed its role as the owner and manager of economic enterprises--all this in an endeavour to correct "government failures".

Regardless of whether the state plays an expanded or shrunken role, it remains central to the functioning of the market in so far as it provides or must provide: the overall constitutional and legal framework for the operation of the market, the specification of property rights, and public investment in the social and economic infrastructure. In other words, the state undertakes or must undertake the provision of public goods that the private sector cannot or would not provide adequately--education, health, and the transportation network.

CHALLENGES FROM THE DEVELOPMENT OF A GLOBAL ECONOMY

There is an external dimension to economic policy reform as well, however, an understanding of which requires a little backtracking in history. As states and markets arose in the sixteenth century, they had somewhat contrary effects on the political and economic organization of the world. States tended to politically fragment the world, organized as they were on the basis of territoriality, legal sovereignty, and exclusive domestic jurisdiction. On the other hand, markets as they expanded tended to encompass several states within a single division of labour. They further tended to promote the integration of the several regional economies of the world. Such integration of the world took place not all at once, but gradually in an ever-expanding set of concentric circles until it brought the different regional economies within the single compass, though not in the same measure or depth, of a world economic system.

Though over a considerable period of time the integration of the world economy took place through physical force, especially in relation to the underdeveloped world during the age of imperialism, countries also took part in it willingly as they saw economic advantage in it, in absolute if not relative terms. They participated in it, and continue to participate in it, because there is economic advantage or, put another way, because there is some economic penalty in not participating in it.

Economically advantageous as it may have been or is to participate in the single world economy, the economic integration of the world has been based on economic specialization, which has tended to place countries in a hierarchical order. It has tended to divide the economies into "core" and "periphery", often through economic and military coercion during the successive stages of an expanding world economic system. The core economies have been the centres of autonomous growth and expansion, more advanced in technology, specializing in manufacturing and the production of higher value goods. In brief, the core economies have been the dynamic centres of economic power. On the other hand, periphery economies have stood at the other pole, largely rendered into a source of raw materials and a market for the manufactures of the core. The periphery economies were also rendered dependent on the core, with the core having the ability to transfer its economic disturbances to them and thus to condition their development. Indeed, in some cases, the economic agents of the core--the multinationals in the postwar period--came to exercise dominant control over periphery economies.

It has been the abiding contribution of dependency theory, rising in revolt against modernization theory, to link the location of societies in the hierarchy of the international economic system with the possibilities of national development. In contrast, modernization theory, which dominated western social sciences during the quarter century after World War II, had taken developing countries to be autonomous and rather closed systems, where the possibilities of development were largely a function of their social structure, institutions and political culture. Dependency theory was pessimistic about the prospects for development of the periphery as long as it was integrated into the world economic system, which drained its economic surplus. It therefore recommended breaking away from the world system in the cause of development. Of course, this radical recommendation masked a preference of the theory's proponents, often unstated, for socialism.

In its determinative prognosis, dependency theory was subsequently discredited with the rapid industrialization of Korea and Taiwan and their breaking out of the periphery precisely through, like Japan earlier in the postwar period, deepening their integration with the international economic system by way of a strategy of export-propelled growth. As a result, modernization theory felt vindicated in its emphasis on domestic factors and its assumption of a benign and growth-inducing international system. Still, while dependency theory as theory is no longer viable, its emphasis on the international system as a factor in national development is enduring. It is not without significance that all three countries made their industrial transition under the political and military umbrella of the US. Interestingly, China's adoption of an "open door" economic policy in the post-Mao period was based on a prior de facto strategic alliance with the US against the Soviet Union and on an understanding over access to the American market. Furthermore, the discrediting of dependency theory as theory does not dissolve the fact of dependence as a major aspect of existential reality in an asymmetrically divided world, which in turn has definite consequences for national development.

Economic dependence in a hierarchical world economy has implications for the welfare of the populations of the periphery states. If the economy is conditioned by outside forces, disturbances that are likely to be transferred to them from the more powerful economic centres would affect local populations adversely, bringing the legitimacy of the wielders of state power into question. Again, dependence within a global system of economic specialization makes periphery countries vulnerable in the world, not only economically but also politically, since to be less advanced and weak economically means to be weak and vulnerable politically in the interstate system. And for states what has mattered is not simply absolute gain within a world economic system but also relative gain in an interstate political system--relative gain as between core and periphery, but also as between different gradations of core and periphery. Known as "political realism" in international politics, this perspective, when translated into the economic sphere, has been referred to as "mercantilism", and has historically served as the action framework for countries that are less advanced and less autonomous. On the other hand, the core states, with the advantage of being economically advanced, have often insisted on liberalism as the disciplining framework for the world economic system which they dominate and benefit from. Indeed, one can quite legitimately maintain that liberalism is the mercantilism of the more advanced economic powers!

From the very dawn of the differentiation between the core and periphery in an increasingly integrating world economy, dependent states have intervened to modify their integration into the world economy so as to advance their national interests, whether in terms of their relative economic and political position in the international system, or the welfare of the local population. They have intervened to replicate, in whole or in part, in their own economies the economic structures of the core countries. Thus was inaugurated in one country after another "catch-up" industrialization, as if in a ripple effect. As against the core countries which, because of their initial economic head-start and therefore economic advantage, believed in free or liberal trade, or "outward orientation", the late industrializers adopted mercantilistic or protectionist policies to foster economic growth and development. In this fashion, they tended to cut down their integration in the world economy, for a shorter or longer period, at times with a view to subsequent re-insertion into the world economy on a more equal basis with the core countries, that is, coordinate with them rather than subordinate to them. In other words, they tried to disengage themselves from the world economy or to disassociate, or to delink from it, that is, they chose an economic strategy of "inward orientation" or "self-reliance". They did this in varying measure and through various techniques--tariffs and quantitative restrictions on imports. Some carried mercantilism to an extreme so as to set up national autarkic economies, as in the case of the Soviet Union and Maoist China.

There are costs also to excessive inward orientation, however, since countries adopting this economic strategy fail to take advantage of the opportunities and advantages that participation in the world economy provides. This specific strategy can introduce serious economic distortions and therefore inefficiencies since it limits taking adequate, if not the fullest, advantage of the particular endowment of the country through attempting to simply replicate the economic structures of the core. One consequence is the setting up of high-cost economies that produce goods of low quality which no one on the outside wants, making for serious balance of payments problems. States are consequently led to weigh carefully the relative advantages and disadvantages of participation in and withdrawal from the world economic system. The principal issue in economic policy reform for states on the external dimension therefore becomes the orientation of the national economy to the world economy. Should the posture be one of inward orientation or outward orientation, disassociation or association, delinkage or linkage, "closed door" or "open door", or some combination of the two? This is an issue that cannot be answered for all time and for all sectors. The answer would depend on the size of the economy, the nature of its endowment, its stage of development, and the capacity of its institutions. The issue would need to be constantly evaluated for the various sectors in terms of costs and benefits.

There is another aspect to the posture of states towards the world economy that goes beyond the issue of inward orientation versus outward orientation, which is relatively within their own jurisdiction and control. That aspect relates to *international regimes*, which as a concept refers to the overall framework of rules and norms governing the conduct of economic relations among states. The notion of international regime conveys the impression that it is an element that stands above the interests of individual states, something that is supranational and neutral in respect of their particular interests. However, in reality, international regimes are put in place, or existing regimes modified, by the economically powerful states, that is, the core states, precisely in order to serve their own interests. International regimes are thus an epiphenomenal reflection of the asymmetrical, hierarchical division of the world.

States which are at an economic disadvantage, because of the handicaps placed on them by existing international regimes, may consequently endeavour to change such regimes in order to serve their own interests beyond the issue of inward and outward orientation. Further, given their common weak position, similarly disadvantaged states may form coalitions to press for the modification of international regimes. Economic policy reform can thus also encompass the external policies of states addressed to bringing about changes in international regimes. However, real success is likely to elude such effort because of the lack of economic and political leverage, that is, lack of bargaining power, at the command of the weaker states. Even if successful in formal terms, the effort is likely to be undercut in practice by the more powerful if it impinges on their interests.

There is thus a vicious circle here: economic weakness requires but thwarts change in international regimes, which in turn perpetuates economic weakness. As a consequence, often the sole alternative left for the weak states is to work within existing international regimes which have been fostered and are sustained by the economically powerful and serve their interests. The only choice for them is to work within the constraints of the system and thus to reorder their own economies internally to fit in with the operative international regimes and, within the limits of these constraints, to advance their interests, barred as they are from changing the international regimes by their weakness. State elites in the developing world may go into sociological rage over this compulsion but that is how the world works.

With its attention to both internal and external aspects of development, the foregoing comprehensive analysis suggests that any study addressed to efforts of the developing countries to come to terms with the challenges of economic globalization must treat of their policy and its outcomes both in relation to expanding national capabilities (relational power) and changing international regimes (meta power), if not necessarily in the same measure.

INDIA'S PERFORMANCE IN SHIPPING

Increasing economic globalization--the pace of which accelerated after the oil price crisis in the mid 1970s--has confronted the developing world with enormous challenges of adjustment and adaptation. Such challenges are manifest already in many areas, not least in overseas shipping. Aware that the international regime of shipping has an enormous bearing on the opportunities available to them in the development of their merchant fleets, the developing world from the early 1960s onwards made shipping an important issue for the reworking of the regime in shipping at the United Nations Conference on Trade and Development (UNCTAD). Significantly, India played a leadership role in putting forward the demands of the developing world and in the negotiations to arrive at a new international regime that would assure a fair and equitable share in world shipping to the less developed countries.

Given India's leadership in voicing the demands of the developing world for a substantial role in world shipping, a more important question that emerges for investigation is as to what has been India's own record in building its merchant fleet. While international diplomacy for a more accommodative international regime may or may not be fruitful for acquisition of capabilities over the longer term, what is crucial from the perspective of the ends of wealth and power is the country's performance on the ground.

There are several measures for evaluating performance in the acquisition of shipping capabilities, but the most basic one is that of gross registered tonnage (grt), sometimes more simply called gross tonnage (gt). Although seemingly a measure of weight, grt is actually a measure of volume and refers to the closed-in space of a ship, with 100 cubic feet of such space being referred to as one ton. Another important measure is dead weight tonnage (dwt), which refers to the number of tons of fuel, supplies and cargo a ship is able to carry, with a ton equalling 2240 pounds. Both measures are used in describing and comparing world merchant fleets, but grt is the one that is more often employed in statistical collections for comparative purposes while dwt is the preferred term in the shipbuilding industry. There is no precise method for calculating the equivalence between the two, as one is a measure of volume and the other of weight, but a "rule of thumb" norm is to treat 100 dwt as equalling 60 grt.[13] The usual source of statistical data for comparative purposes is *Lloyd's Register of Shipping*, which covers vessels of 100 grt and over; until 1991 the date for coverage was July 1, but since then it is December 31. There can be variations in data among statistical collections because of differences in coverage; for example, the Indian official statistics are for vessels of 150 grt and over.

Table 1.1 sets out India's shipping tonnage capacity in grt for each year over the post-independence period. Overall, it suggests an impressive record of growth from a nominal tonnage at independence to a capacity of 6.55M (million) grt in 1992, which places India among the top 15 maritime powers of the world. Over the four decades from 1950 to 1989, India's tonnage grew fifteen-fold from 0.42M grt to 6.32M grt, at an average annual growth rate of 7.6 per cent.

Of course, the rate of growth has not been evenly spread over this entire period. If the data on tonnage were to be plotted on a graph, it would show the performance in respect of acquisition of shipping capacity to take the form of an "S" curve. Three distinct periods are evident. There is, first of all, the period from 1948 to around 1960, which is characterized by very slow but steady growth. The decade of the 1950s, which can be taken to be generally equivalent with the period as a whole, saw substantial augmentation in capacity with a respectable average growth rate of 6.8 per cent; the tonnage almost doubled over the decade. However, this growth took place from an extremely small base with the consequence that, even after a decade of growth, the total tonnage was far from reaching

TABLE 1.1: SHIPPING CAPACITY: NUMBER OF SHIPS (100 GRT AND OVER), TONNAGE (MILLION GRT), AND TONNAGE GROWTH (%)

	Indian Tonnage				Indian Tonnage		
Year	*No.*	*GRT*	*Growth*	*Year*	*No.*	*GRT*	*Growth*
1948	151	0.32	-	1970	399	2.40	7.14
1949	165	0,39	21.88	1971	397	2.48	3.33
				1972	412	2.65	6.86
1950	177	0.42	7.69	1973	430	2.89	9.06
1951	175	0.45	7.14	1974	451	3.49	20.76
1952	192	0.48	6.67	1975	471	3.87	10.89
1953	195	0.49	2.08	1976	526	5.09	31.53
1954	204	0.51	4.08	1977	566	5.48	7.66
1955	221	0.57	11.76	1978	591	5.76	5.11
1956	215	0.58	1.75	1979	601	5.85	1.56
1957	222	0.63	8.62				
1958	230	0.67	6.35	1980	616	5.91	1.03
1959	238	0.75	11.94	1981	620	6.02	1.86
				1982	644	6.21	3.16
1960	257	0.86	14.67	1983	677	6.23	0.32
1961	273	0.96	11.63	1984	710	6.42	3.05
1962	278	1.01	5.21	1985	741	6.61	2.96
1963	309	1.21	26.04	1986	736	6.54	-1.06
1964	347	1.45	19.84	1987	803	6.73	2.91
1965	354	1.52	4.83	1988	797	6.16	-8.47
1966	360	1.79	17.76	1989	834	6.32	2.59
1967	369	1.89	5.59				
1968	383	1.95	3.18	1990	855	6.48	2.53
1969	397	2.24	14.87	1991	890	6.52	0.62
				1992	871	6.55	0.46
				1993	886	6.58	0.46

Source: Lloyd's Register, *Shipping Tables 1991*, p. 31, and *World Fleet Statistics: December 1993*, p. 43. The figures for 1992 and 1993 are as at December 31; all the rest are as at July 1.

even a million grt capacity. The goal of the early shipping nationalists to acquire 2M grt capacity within seven or eight years from independence was thus nowhere near achievement even five years beyond the target date. Besides, notwithstanding Indian shipping industry's nominally breaking into new areas, such as tankers and bulk ore carriers, most of it remained confined to general or liner cargo and passenger service. As a result, much of the opportunity provided in the 1950s by large imports of PL-480 foodgrains and crude oil went unutilized by Indian shipping.

The succeeding two decades of the 1960s and 1970s were a different story, however, marking a long second period characterized by accelerated growth. Extending from 1960 to around the end of the 1970s, this period was the golden era of expansion of India's tonnage; capacity expanded almost eight-fold over the two decades with an average annual growth rate of 11.4 per cent. The 1960s featured a somewhat better record than the 1970s; indeed, they showed the highest growth rate of any decade in the post-independence period. Shipping capacity tripled over the period, growing at an average annual growth of 12.4 per cent. The tonnage crossed the one million grt mark in 1962 and the two million mark in 1969. The second half of the 1960s witnessed a severe economic crisis in the wake of two unprecedented droughts, but the crisis apparently did not harm tonnage expansion.

Even though their growth rate of 10.4 per cent was lower than that of the preceding decade, the 1970s saw the largest addition of tonnage for any decade, with the capacity increasing over two and a half times from 2.24M in 1969 to 5.85M grt in 1979. The difference of 3.61M grt represents the single largest absolute increase ever for any decade. Particularly noteworthy are the three years from 1974 to 1976, which saw a burst of expansion in tonnage, with capacity increasing by 2.20M grt; 1976 saw the largest increase for any single year, amounting to 1.22M grt. The subsequent three years saw continued growth but at a lower and declining rate.

After more than three decades of a consistent and literally unbroken record of growth, India entered its third period, stretching from 1980 to 1993, which was marked by stagnation and decline. There was hardly any growth in capacity over the period, with the average annual growth being a mere 0.84 per cent. For the first time in the post-independence period, two years saw the tonnage decline in absolute terms. There was a small decline in 1986 and a sharper one in 1988. Despite small increases in subsequent years, capacity in 1993 was below the level reached in 1985 and certainly that of the peak year in 1987. The high point in India's tonnage, which was reached in 1987, had not been eclipsed even by 1994. The early 1990s barely saw any expansion, the growth rate being only 1.02 per cent.

Although based on a single measure and therefore subject to refinement and elaboration on the basis of other criteria, the salient analytical puzzle that emerges from the foregoing analysis is the bifurcation in performance around 1980, with the earlier period marked by impressive expansion and the subsequent period by deterioration. More elaborately, three periods can be demarcated: (1) 1948-1960: slow but steady growth; (2) 1960-1980: rapid expansion; and (3) 1980-1993: stagnation and decline. The more important question is as to what is the explanation for the analytical puzzle. What key variables explain the variant pattern of performance?

There would seem to be two possible lines of explanation for the analytical puzzle. One line pertains to the external environment in an asymmetrically divided world, and seeks answers in the disparity in power, and therefore in bargaining, between the developing states and the developed states. In this line of argument, any developing state is likely to suffer the consequences of its inferior power in its relations with the developed world. The argument has considerable merit, and any explanation must come to terms with it. However, two possible objections can be raised. One, if the proposition is true, then why did it not preclude superior performance in the period before 1980? This is a valid objection, but that does not mean that the external environment was necessarily supportive of the better performance, which may have been achieved in spite of, and not because of, it. Two, the power hierarchy in the world has not prevented some developing countries in not only outperforming India, but also countries of the developed world. Again, while this objection is also valid, it does not tell us about the exact relationship of these developing countries to the developed world.

The contrasting line of explanation endeavours to find a solution to the analytical puzzle in terms of domestic structures.[14] This explanation can, in turn, be broken into two parts, one relating to the state and the other to society. A country's performance in building economic capabilities cannot be immune to the constraints of society, particularly those of underdevelopment, even though in the earlier period India did demonstrate a capacity to overcome such constraints. A critical variable in overcoming societal constraints is, of course, the role played by the state. Indeed, the state is the key actor, situated as it is at the intersection of the international system and society, with its principal responsibility being to respond to impulses from both. One decisive element with a bearing on performance is not only the relative roles accorded to the state and market in policy but also the timing of policy.

These alternative explanations need to be tested against the empirical data on policy and performance in the different periods since independence. The remainder of the study is addressed to that task.

Summary and Conclusion

Economic globalization confronts India as it does other developing countries with serious challenges in shipping as it does in other areas of economic activity. These challenges, however, are not narrowly economic but are strongly implicated in politics. Both states and markets are involved in the challenges emerging from the external environment as they are domestically in the adaptation of the developing countries to them. Depending on policy responses of the state, particularly in terms of the state-market mix in the management of the economy and its various sectors, globalization can make for economic advancement and the strengthening of economic capabilities, or it can result in marginalization and de-industrialization.

India's performance in the acquisition of capabilities in shipping over the period since independence displays discontinuities in terms of a decade of slow growth, followed by two decades of rapid expansion, and then a decade and a half of stagnation. It would seem that these discontinuities in performance are correlated with fundamental changes in the state-market equation in the management of the economy. There is evident a strong interplay of politics and economics in policy and performance. Nowhere is this more vividly manifest than during the colonial period, where political power was paramount in the shaping of the market.

NOTES

1. This part of the analysis draws on Mihaly Simai, *The World Economy of Our Age and the New Multilateralism: New Challenges for Hungary* (Budapest: Hungarian Scientific Council for World Economy, 1991), p. 30.

2. Simai, pp. 34-35.

3. The terms relational power and meta power are from Stephen D. Krasner, *Structural Conflict: The Third World Against Global Liberalism* (Berkeley: University of California Press, 1985), p. 14.

4. Couper states "three-quarters of international trade by weight, and over 65% by value, moves by sea". A.D. Couper, *The Geography of Sea Transport* (London: Hutchinson University Library, 1972), p. 73.

5. On the general theme, see Robert Gilpin, *The Political Economy of International Relations* (Princeton: Princeton University Press, 1987), chs. 1-2.

6. See Charles Tilly (ed.), *The Formation of National States in Western Europe* (Princeton: Princeton University Press, 1975), ch. 1.

7. Gilpin, p. 10. The attempt to reduce the interstate system to the single logic of the world capitalist system is challenged in David P. Rapkin, "The Inadequacy of a Single Logic: Integrating Political and Material Approaches to the World System", in William R. Thompson (ed.), *Contending Approaches to World System Analysis* (Beverly Hills, Calif.: Sage Publications, 1983), pp. 241-68.

8. Paul Kennedy, *The Rise and Fall of Great Powers: Economic Change and Military Conflict from 1500 to 2000* (London: Unwin Hyman, 1988), p. xvi.

9. I have dealt with this issue comparatively in "Political Mainsprings of Economic Planning in the New Nations: The Modernization Imperative versus Social Mobilization", *Comparative Politics*, VI, no. 3 (April 1974); see also its specific application to India in *The Modernization Imperative and Indian Planning* (New Delhi: Vikas, 1972).

10. Liberalism, Marxism and mercantilism are the three conventional approaches to international political economy. See Gilpin, chs. 1-2.

11. Charles E. Lindblom, *Politics and Markets: The World's Political-Economic Systems* (New York: Basic Books, 1977), p. 304.

12. John Gerard Ruggie (ed.), *The Antinomies of Interdependence: National Welfare and the International Division of Labour* (New York: Columbia University Press, 1983), p. 433.

13. Associated Chambers of Commerce and Industry of India, *Indian Shipping, Shipbuilding and Ship Repair Industries: Problems and Prospects* (prepared by G.B. Sundriyal; New Delhi: 1991), p. 8.

14. The seminal work on the two lines of explanation is Peter J. Katzenstein (ed.), *Between Power and Plenty: Foreign Economic Policies of Advanced Industrial States* (Madison: University of Wisconsin Press, 1978).

CHAPTER II

POWER AND THE SHAPING OF MARKETS: THE GLOBAL ORDER, IMPERIALISM, AND SHIPPING NATIONALISM

States and markets are interactive social organizations even as they have their own separate arenas and separate logics.[1] In some respects, shipping--or, more precisely, overseas shipping--seems like an exception to this general proposition. For one thing, shipping is often described as an international industry. Whether intended or not, such a description seems to convey the notion that, unlike other industries which are located inside the territorial boundaries of the state, and thus subject to regulation by it, shipping essentially operates on the open seas between the boundaries of states. Beyond that, the description also seems to underline the dominant role of the forces of the market rather than of the state. Take, for example, freight rates. They are, at least in bulk shipping, determined by the forces of demand and supply in the international market. Further, booms and recessions in the industry quickly spread throughout the world's shipping and affect the fortunes of the national merchant fleets. Besides, over 37 per cent of the world's fleet now sails under "flags of convenience",[2] indicating that they essentially operate outside the control of states.

Notwithstanding these known facets of the shipping industry, however, this chapter shall demonstrate the elemental role of states, and therefore of their relative power, in shaping the market in the case of the shipping industry as well. The chapter does this in two ways, but both with a considerable dose of history as a necessary cure for any misconception about shipping being largely immune from politics. One, it discusses the nature of the interaction between states and markets in the organization of the normative framework for the operation of the industry at the international level. Given the preponderance of the power of the United States in the twentieth century and therefore its enormous capacity to influence international processes, the discussion pays special attention to American state behaviour. Two, on a narrower scale, the chapter discusses the impact of imperialism--a more brutal form of the domination of powerful states over others--as well as of its nemesis, nationalism, on shipping and shipping policy in colonial India. Together, these two parts of the discussion serve to forcefully confirm the fundamental role power plays in the shaping of markets and dispel any notion that shipping is a sphere of economics alone.

Indirectly, the chapter also serves the essential purpose of providing for this study (1) an overview of the international context in which shipping in independent India has to function, and (2) the historical background on social and political forces during colonialism which had a formative influence on the subsequent development of shipping and shipping policy in post-colonial India.

THE NORMATIVE STRUCTURE OF WORLD SHIPPING

The term "international regime" is a recent concept which has been developed in the discipline of international political economy, and briefly refers to the overall framework of rules and norms in accordance with which activity is carried out between states in a given sector. More elaborately, regimes have been described as "sets of implicit or explicit principles, norms, rules, and decision-making procedures around which actors' expectations converge".[3] At one level, international regimes can be treated as autonomous and self-contained systems, governing conduct in one or another economic sector. At another level, they can be seen as related to the structure of power in the international system, though the precise nature of that relationship is a matter of contention in the discipline.

Three approaches to the question of the relationship of power to international regimes can be distinguished.[4] In political realism, international regimes are taken to be epiphenomenal. In this view, regimes are simply a reflection of the underlying distribution of power. In other words, at the base of the apparent consensual framework of norms and rules of an international regime lies a particular structure of power in the international system, which upholds that framework. That is to say, a dominant state or set of dominant states in a given configuration of power usually finds a particular normative framework more appropriate to serve its interests and is able, through coercion or consensus, to make it prevail in the international system. In this interpretation, then, international regimes last as long as the given balance of power lasts, only to be replaced by a new international regime consonant with the changed balance of power. As Susan Strange puts it: "All those international arrangements dignified by the label regime are only too easily upset when either the balance of bargaining power or the perception of national interest (or both together) change among those states who negotiate them".[5] What political realism does in its treatment of international regimes is to underline the centrality of power in the construction and maintenance of regimes, which may otherwise seem as purely economic or technical in nature.

In contrast to realism, the approach of institutionalism sees, notwithstanding the pervasive interstate conflict, the gradual but parallel emergence in the world of an international society centring on cooperation among states. In an increasingly interdependent world where elites are compelled to interact repeatedly, the institutionalists maintain, social practices or regularized patterns of behaviour develop. As these persist, they acquire a normative aura and come to act as constraints on the behaviour of leaders. A third approach, known as modified structural realism, endeavours to build a synthesis between the two approaches. While taking the state to be a rational, egoistic, utility-maximizing actor, this approach holds cooperation between states to be both necessary and possible. Utility maximization is not seen as a bar to cooperation but rather requires and induces it, for in the absence of cooperation the result would be suboptimal outcomes for most parties. Once patterns of cooperation are thus established to coordinate state behaviour, they tend to persist because of the functions they perform and in turn come to influence state behaviour.

While focusing on the short term may show the approaches of institutionalism and modified structural realism to be not without merit, a long-term perspective reveals the potent relationship between power and regimes. In a pioneering analysis of the changing regimes in shipping, Cafruny convincingly demonstrates the relationship of the rise and decline of hegemonic power to a succession of shipping regimes.[6] The emergence of Dutch maritime supremacy at the beginning of the seventeenth century, after the defeat of Spain by England, led to the inauguration of a liberal shipping regime, legitimized by an appropriate ideology of the freedom of the seas propagated by Hugo Grotius. The liberal regime proved premature and short-lived, however, for England refused to accept it, pursuing instead protectionist policies through a series of navigation laws. The end of Dutch supremacy over the seas at the hands of England in 1674 did not produce as yet a new hegemonic power, with the result that mercantilism characterized the shipping order.

The defeat of France in the first quarter of the nineteenth century--combined with Britain's rise as the first modern industrial power along with the technological breakthrough of steamship navigation in the second quarter--made Britain's position as a maritime power unassailable. As the ascendant hegemonic power, Britain fostered from the mid-nineteenth century onwards a liberal shipping regime, though perhaps more accurately it should be described as only a regime of private-ownership because of the cartelistic features that came to be associated with it. The decline of British hegemony by the beginning of the twentieth century led to most states pursuing protectionist policies in shipping as in other areas. The emergence of the United States (US) to hegemonic status after World War II brought into being in the immediate postwar period an international regime with two pillars. One pillar accommodated Europe's maritime interests by the re-installation of the regime that had prevailed before World War II in liner shipping, while the other sought to protect the interests of vertically-integrated American multinationals in the bulk carriage of oil and raw materials through the system of "flags of convenience" (FOCs). By the end of the 1960s, the decline of American hegemony, combined with American strength in container shipping which it pioneered as a technological breakthrough, led to a tougher posture in support of competition in liner shipping.

This brief review of the succession of international regimes in shipping since the beginning of the seventeenth century makes it abundantly clear that, first, regimes are not a permanent condition but change frequently, and, second, that the change is associated with the power and interests of dominant states. Rather than being self-contained systems of norms and rules for the conduct of international business and commerce, regimes are related to underlying structures of power and interests.

REGIME TYPES, AUTHORITATIVE ALLOCATION, AND THE UNITED STATES

What is the nature of the international regime in shipping? Any summary characterization of the regime can itself be a source of serious contention. Usually, international regimes are distinguished according to whether the direct or indirect allocation of resources and property rights is made by political authorities, or it takes place on the basis of the preferences and endowments of individual actors in the market. Employing this state-market dimension, Stephen Krasner draws a sharp contrast between the international regime for aviation and that for shipping.[7] The former is characterized as resting on authoritative allocation and the latter on market-based allocation. At times, he is constrained to acknowledge that competition is not perfect, given the pervasiveness of cartels in liner shipping and the vertical integration of bulk shipping within powerful multinational corporations. However, Krasner continues repeatedly nonetheless to characterize the existing international regime for shipping as market-based or competitive--unmodified by any further qualification[8]--sharply marked off from its polar opposite of authoritative allocation.

An ahistorical treatment of this nature is remarkable for simply taking the contemporary scene, even then selectively, as the point of departure for typology construction into unqualified polar opposites, apparently in an endeavour to delegitimize the concerns of the developing world about economic and political domination. The impact of such a treatment can be enormous, as it both follows and foreshadows a barrage of propaganda on behalf of the economic and political interests of the industrialized world, aimed against the aspirations of the less developed areas. However, the treatment is mistaken in several respects.

In the first place, it creates the false illusion that the division of labour and the hierarchy in maritime power in the shipping world is simply the consequence of the working out of autonomous market forces on the basis of the natural endowments of the actors, untrammelled by authoritative allocation. The reality is otherwise. The maritime power of both the United Kingdom (UK) and the US, two arch defenders of the marketplace in shipping and elsewhere, was built on the most thoroughgoing state intervention and mercantilism.[9] The shipping policies of the UK over the period from the mid-seventeenth to the mid-nineteenth century became a model of shipping nationalism later for others in Europe, the US and the developing countries. The subsequent turn to liberalism on the part of the UK was based on a conscious judgement that its established superior capabilities had outstripped those of its rivals to such an extent that there was more profit in competition than protection. One British parliamentary report had aptly observed: "In view of its great size, the British merchant marine stood to gain more from free access to foreign countries than foreign flags stood to gain from free access to British ports; and conversely a policy of mutual restriction would for the same reason have caused more harm to British than to foreign shipping".[10] That did not, however, mean an end to retaining the empire as a special preserve for British shipping.

Moreover, the advanced industrial states continue to play an active role in the nurturing of their fleets through a variety of interventionary and regulatory mechanisms that mould the market for the purpose. While protectionist measures of various kinds are fairly generalized throughout the western world,[11] it is the behaviour of the US that merits special attention because of the global reach of its power and the regime-transforming character of that power.

American shipping nationalism is not of recent origin. Before World War II, "in shipping, the most ardent nationalists were American". The US had "a legislative history of shipping nationalism and protectionist sentiments within the shipping industry as well as in Congress". Interestingly, "the American shipping industry developed under the wing of the government in a climate of Anglo-American hostility". The US Shipping Act of 1916 "provided a broad base for shipping nationalism", while subsequent legislation built on that base and expanded and intensified it.[12] The US has employed and continues to employ a vast armoury of policy instruments for the advancement of the interests of its merchant fleet and shipbuilding industry. Krasner acknowledges: "Among the industrialized countries, the United States has violated competitive practices more often than other nations".[13] Cafruny agrees: "Notably, the United States was the most significant violator" of proscriptions on protectionist measures over which there was a consensus among the advanced industrial powers.[14] The American armoury for the promotion of its shipping includes policy instruments in the three areas of protection, subsidy, and economic regulation.[15]

In the sphere of protection, the Merchant Marine Act of 1920, more commonly known as the Jones Act, makes mandatory the carriage of all water-transported goods between American ports only on ships built and registered in the US, and further requires that those ships be owned, controlled and manned by American citizens. This exercise of the privilege of cabotage applies not only to the coastal trade of the US and to that between the non-contiguous coasts of the mainland, but also to the ocean-traversing trade with its more distant offshore states and territories. In addition, the US provides protection for its shipping through unilateral cargo reservation, whereby government-impelled cargoes are reserved in various proportions for American bottoms. The interpretation of government cargo is quite broad, and includes goods that are covered by loan guarantees. All cargoes destined for the American armed forces abroad, cargoes supported by the US Export-Import Bank, oil imports for the Strategic Petroleum Reserve, and 75 per cent of PL-480 shipments are required to be shipped on American carriers. Besides, bilateral shipping agreements at different times with several countries, such as Argentina, Brazil and China as also the Soviet Union, have reserved 40 per cent or more of the bilateral trade for American ships.[16] Not without justification, European governments have regarded American requirements on cargo reservation as providing "a model for similar discriminatory practices abroad".[17]

When it comes to subsidies, the US record seems to have no peer, whether in the magnitude or in the scope of support, providing for cash subsidies, tax allowances, and loan guarantees. Samuel Lawrence matter-of-factly notes: "The United States, of course, maintains the most comprehensive programme with direct and indirect operating subsidies".[18] The US has undertaken every conceivable form of material support to national shipping. Most resolute in pursuing its national interests in the maritime arena, the American support of its shipping is of long standing, but was raised to new levels with the Merchant Marine Act of 1936 which, in the words of a leading American authority on shipping, "adopted a nationalistic and protectionist solution to the nation's shipping needs".[19] One serious study places the cost of subsidies for the 50-year period from 1936 to 1985 at over $35 billion in 1985 (constant) dollars--consisting of $26.6 billion for construction differential subsidies (CDS) and operating differential subsidies (ODS); $4 billion for costs of tax deferral under the capital construction fund (CCF); and $5 billion in support for training programs, maritime institutions, R&D, and the reserve fleet. The annual cost of such subsidies in the 1980s was about $3 billion.[20]

Further, since the Shipping Act of 1916 the US has, through a regulatory commission, regulated the activities of liner companies engaged in American trades on a scale unmatched by any other advanced industrial power. In 1966, Lawrence had observed: "The United States is the only nation in the world which has attempted unilaterally to enforce a comprehensive regulatory scheme over shipping serving its trade".[21] The issue is of deeper significance, for the US has arrogated to itself extraterritorial jurisdiction by extending its regulatory regime across the globe in what has been termed a "global unilateralism".[22] The assertion of American extraterritorial jurisdiction applies not just to the bilateral trades of the US, but also to the cross trades among other countries if the US feels that the regulatory policies of other states adversely affect free and open competition or the interests of American shipping. American representatives publicly threaten other states with reprisals if their policies discriminate against American shipping, even if the US is not involved in bilateral trade with them.[23]

On the other hand, where it has suited American interests, such as in the case of "flags of convenience", the US has allowed, indeed encouraged and planned, the practice of American ships to go outside the net of regulation altogether. In the process, there has been little compunction over the overthrow of what had been an integral element of the international regime--which required a "genuine link" between vessel ownership and vessel nationality--and the creation of an entirely new international regime in bulk shipping suited specifically for American interests.[24] Significantly, Cafruny refers to FOCs as "the joint project of the US government and the multinationals" and interprets the device "as a disguised form of mercantilism, an element of a competitive national shipping policy of a great power (or powers) willing and able to resort to such flags".[25] In view of the high costs of maritime labour in the US, the intent of American policy was to deprive competitors of their comparative advantage, initially among the traditional European maritime powers. Even as the device assured American primacy in bulk shipping, European powers "were compelled to adapt their business strategies and shipping laws to the dictates of the US-dominated regime".[26] The eventual consequence of the creation of the new regime in bulk shipping was to deprive the developing world of its comparative advantage in low-cost labour and to defeat its aspirations to have a role in bulk shipping.

There can be no doubt that the heavy involvement by the American state through protection, subsidies and regulation enormously distorts the operations of the world's shipping market. Given the example of the US, it would be difficult to argue with the position that "governments are so enmeshed in shipping affairs that it would be unrealistic to project any system which did not recognize their role,"[27] or to assume that shipping is an area of market allocation alone. What is amazing in respect of the US, however, is the glaring incongruence between its shrill and moralistic lecturing to all and sundry on the superiority of the freedom of the market and the simultaneous practice of protectionist measures on behalf of its own shipping industry. Lawrence Juda points up the "divorce between United States practice and United States rhetoric", and White agrees: "Unfortunately, U.S. maritime policies have largely been at odds with these [free market] principles".[28] In what to others appears as sheer hypocrisy, the US sees no contradiction between its rejection of the reform efforts by the developing world to regulate shipping cartels and its own protectionist and regulatory regime. It resolves the dilemma by the simple device of denying that it follows any discriminatory practices, and it is a testimony to American power that it can prevent discussion of them.[29] What is more, the US threatens others with unilateral reprisals if they attempt to do what it does for the protection of its own shipping, charging that they violate its conception of the free market.

Beyond the particular but important case of the United States, it is noteworthy that the actual market in world shipping has been dominated by quasi-monopolistic cartels of major shipping companies in liner shipping and by the vertically integrated operations of powerful multinational corporations in bulk carrier and tanker fleets. These features of the market situation represent strong barriers to entry. It cannot be maintained that they are simply consequences of the working of the market, having little to do with extra-market forces. For, both the American and British states have conducted periodic inquiries into the prevalent restrictive shipping arrangements and have decided to accept them, even as they have regulated them where they deemed it to be necessary. These arrangements have thus not been just a result of some autonomous market forces, but constitute an allocative framework that has been accepted by certain states because it was perceived beneficial to their overall economic and national interests. In the pursuit of those very interests, the same states have worked actively for the protection of that existing framework once the developing world began to challenge it.

It seems that typologies constructed in scholarship can have significant implications for practical affairs. If one makes only a dichotomous division, and characterizes an existing regime as only one or the other, then movements for changing the regime will be viewed differently than when it is delineated with greater discrimination. If, on the other hand, a typology along the state-market axis were to be sufficiently differentiated to take into account the existent reality by including, at least, an in-between category incorporating both types of allocation--as are evidently present in the shipping arena--the implications of scholarly analysis for public policy would be different. Considering the profoundly market-distorting nature of authoritative allocation within the present arrangements in shipping, the explicit recognition of it in typology construction would have served to cast in an entirely different light the efforts of the developing world to reform the shipping regime. It is noteworthy that such efforts at UNCTAD, partly owing their inspiration to the American regulatory model, did not approach anywhere near the degree of regulation and protection that the

American state practised unilaterally. They did not aim to create any international allocative authority, but only to foster within the existing framework norms of proper behaviour for shipowners--as evidenced in the words "code of conduct" in the title of the convention. The UNCTAD code did allow states to exercise cargo preference up to 40 per cent of the trade handled by liner conferences, but this was no novelty for the US.[30]

However, the US rejected the consensus worked out at UNCTAD. The issue for the US, it would seem, was not so much authoritative allocation versus market-based allocation, since it practised authoritative allocation itself, but American unilateralism. American protestations about the effect of the code on the freedom of the marketplace notwithstanding, it is not without significance that the code would have served to limit the existing broad coverage of reservation in respect of government-impelled cargoes, since it considered government cargo to consist only of military supplies for purposes of national defence. By rejecting the code, the US sought to have the best of all possible worlds: reservation of a broad segment of the market for itself in its own trades through authoritative allocation, and freedom of the marketplace in the trades of others. However, the characterization of the existing regime as market-based, whether by scholars or policy-makers, served to depict the efforts of the developing world one-sidedly as some novel and illegitimate invasion by authoritative allocation into some presumed ongoing market-based international regime.

In the light of actual practice among nations, the view of the international regime in shipping as one entirely based on allocation through the market is in serious error. Authoritative allocation played a major role in the building of merchant fleets and continues to do so in protecting and promoting them. However, it would be equally a mistake to view even the area outside authoritative allocation as representing the operation of a free market. For, well past into the second half of the twentieth century, the power of western states upheld a structure of world shipping which by design created powerful barriers to entry by newcomers, especially of the less developed areas.

THE RESTRICTIVE INSTITUTIONAL STRUCTURE IN LINER SHIPPING

While the restrictive nature of the market structure impinges on the less developed countries throughout the shipping industry, the liner shipping sector has been particularly important to them. The importance of liner shipping for them lies in two of its features. One, liner shipping is largely devoted to the carriage of manufactured or semi-manufactured goods. The incidence of freight levied on such goods by liner firms can have enormous significance for their export prospects. Since industrialization is a key goal for developing countries, anything that affects their export prospects is of obvious concern to them. Two, liner cargo is high-value cargo, and since freight rates are largely a function of the value of the cargo, the consequent total freight bill for its carriage looms large in the balance of payments of these countries. Cafruny points out that, while liner cargo constituted only about 20 per cent of world cargo by volume, it accounted for 80 per cent by value.[31] Similarly, a study on Indian shipping in the mid-1970s maintains that liner cargo represented 25 per cent of the country's foreign trade by volume but 75 per cent by value.[32] It is noteworthy that, in 1983, of the total US oceanborne foreign trade, liner cargo was 9.01 per cent by weight but 52.21 per cent by value;[33] earlier, in 1973, the corresponding figures were 8 per cent and 59 per cent, and in 1968 they were 11 per cent and 65 per cent, respectively.[34] These various figures on its economic value underline the centrality of liner shipping in overseas trade and, accordingly, in the calculations of decision-makers.

The market structure of the liner shipping industry has for more than a century been dominated by cartels, known as conferences; they were earlier, more forthrightly, also referred to as "rings". The conference system began in 1875, when British liner companies in the UK-Calcutta trade formed the Calcutta conference. The system then spread quickly, with established liner companies for one or more outward trade routes combining into conferences. By the beginning of the twentieth century, the entire liner shipping of the world had become cartelized under British leadership, marking an end to the brief period of shipping liberalism. Cafruny avers: "established in the context of the age of imperialism, conferences were originally the functional equivalents of formal colonialism: they represented an attempt (initially, by British shipowners) to maintain existing market shares".[35] For the developing world, however, they were not just functional equivalents of colonialism; rather, they were the very manifestation and instrument of imperialism, which in the ultimate analysis undergirded the system.

The most elaborate and thoroughgoing defence of the conference system in recent years has been offered by Gunnar Sletmo and Ernest Williams.[36] The two authors base their position not on economic theory, to challenge which is rather their primary aim, but on economic reality, paying particular attention to the specific features of liner shipping. Fundamentally, liner shipping is differentiated from the charter operations of bulk carriers and tankers by its being structured to provide scheduled services on fixed routes as a common carrier in a fluctuating market. For Sletmo and Williams, the dilemma for liner shipping lies in the "unique combination" of two characteristics that are built into it, that is, (1) the high proportion of fixed costs on the supply side, and (2) the smallness of the size of shipments relative to the capacity of the vessel on the demand side.[37] As they put it: "Scheduled services operate in markets where the typical unit of demand is small relative to the technical unit of supply, which is the ship's carrying capacity for a given voyage. This relationship between demand and supply is the core of the pricing difficulty that exists, not in transportation generally, but with respect to scheduled services in all kinds of transportation".[38]

Earlier, Sturmey had vividly portrayed the dilemma inherent in the very nature of liner shipping, given the high ratio of fixed costs relative to variable costs:

> For such [liner] services the direct or variable costs which can be attributed to the carrying of cargo or passengers may amount to no more than 10 or 20 per cent of total costs. This means that once a ship is on berth in a trade it will always pay the individual shipowner to carry cargo at from one-tenth to one-fifth of the rate required to cover total costs rather than sail with empty space. So long as the volume of cargo or the number of passengers is no less than the available space, both in aggregate and for individual sailings,

> there is no problem of rate-cutting. Where, however, the volume of space exceeds the cargo or passengers available then without an agreement all shipowners have an incentive to cut rates to the level of variable costs. While this will pay each shipowner in the short run so long as he is the only one cutting rates, it is clear that where there are competing shipowners all will be in the same position and all rates would quickly be cut to the level of variable costs. At such a level the shipowners obviously could not cover their costs and the regular services might cease.[39]

The likely consequence of the high ratio of fixed costs relative to variable costs in the liner industry is price volatility and firm bankruptcies and, therefore, market instability, all of which is no less damaging for shippers than it is for shipowners. There emerges therefore the need for coordination and rationalization among shipowners in respect of capacity, sailings and freight rates, and even pooling of revenues and profits. The mechanism of conferences, or agreements, among shipowners is engineered precisely to meet this need. The very nature of the liner shipping industry thus makes its economic survival dependent upon cartelization. In turn, cartelization enables shipowners to provide shippers with stability in service and rates. In this manner, the consequences of restraint on competition emerge as superior to those associated with free competition.

Sletmo and Williams therefore question the applicability of the American anti-trust doctrine to each and every industry without regard to its particular nature. Indeed, they hold it significant that legislative committees that have thoroughly investigated the working of the conference system since the early part of the century have, notwithstanding their misgivings about some aspects of its functioning, acknowledged its necessity in view of the need for coordination for the sake of market stability. Equally significant for them is the fact that the movement for a new international maritime order, generated by the developing world in the 1970s, wanted only reform of the conference system, not its overthrow; indeed, the movement favoured "closed" conferences.

It can be quickly conceded that there is a genuine need for coordination among shipping companies through the mechanism of conferences. However, what initially originates as a rational constraint on competition, for the sake of coordination, tends to become anti-competitive not only for shippers but also for liner companies, both inside and outside the conferences. As Daniel Marx had observed in the early 1950s, "the liner trades are governed by two conflicting tendencies; they tend either to develop and exploit a monopolistic position, or to suffer from the wastefulness of competition. Monopolistic excesses range all the way from petty abuses to unreasonable discrimination and fairly secure monopoly profits; whereas the competitive aberrations include the failure to rationalize sailing schedules, under-utilization, unfair methods of securing traffic, and occasionally cutthroat rate wars". His conclusion was that the dilemma was inescapable: "The disadvantages of competition can be lessened by increasing the monopoly power of the lines. This is the principal justification for the shipping conferences But the existence of conferences sufficiently strong to reduce the shortcomings of competition inevitably creates monopoly power, which may in turn be abused". Marx felt that the threat of abuse of monopoly power remained "sufficiently great to require some form of governmental supervision".[40] He therefore supported the American tradition of regulation of liner shipping in its trades.

Although differences exist among the 350 to 400 conferences, most of those outside the US trades have been "closed". As quasi-monopolies, their chief aim has been to eliminate price competition among the members and to bar entry of new competitors. The conference system has been attacked for its arbitrariness in the determination of what are essentially "administered prices", which were usually not made public. Invariably, given the quasi-monopoly position of the conferences, the initial aim of minimization of losses becomes transformed into the maximization of gains. The resulting high rates then often attract new competitors, generating a problem which the system was originally conceived to prevent--overtonnaging--necessitating, in turn, collusive action to kill competition.

The conferences attempt to retain their monopoly in the market by tying their clients through loyalty contracts in the form of dual rates--which privilege clients for their exclusive patronage--and deferred rebates, which are promised refunds but with their availability conditional on continued use of conference services. They endeavour to defeat new competitors by excluding them from membership and attempting to eliminate them from the market through the mechanism of "fighting ships", the sole function of which is to inflict losses on competitors by offering cutthroat rates. Deferred rebates and fighting ships have been the conference system's "two great predatory weapons".[41] Cargo allocation or assignment among the members has been arranged through mutual agreement over sailing schedules, which is a function of the bargaining strength of the members. The system has thus not been liberal, but only private, for the cartels "greatly restricted the workings of the marketplace".[42]

The closed membership of the conferences can be especially effective against the developing countries, given the limited resources of their lines. And the conferences were not reluctant to exercise this leverage, much to the detriment of the shipping of developing countries and the consternation of their decision-nakers. In no little measure, the subsequent adoption of measures of flag preference and the larger movement among the developing countries for the reform of the conference system through international regulation were provoked by the restrictive practices of conferences, dominated by western countries, especially Great Britain.[43] On the other hand, business and political leaders in western countries railed in chorus against what they characterized as flag discrimination by the developing countries, ignoring the whole complex of discriminatory and monopolistic practices of their own that strangled the shipping of the developing world.

As against the monopolistic tendency inherent in liner shipping, the competitive tendency, too, can manifest itself from time to time to limit the power of conferences. For, shipping is not only an international industry but a dynamic one, given to frequent change. The conference system can break down at times, and some new competitors may break through the restraints imposed even by closed membership. However, it would seem that the really crucial factor in moderating the monopolistic tendency of the conference system is *countervailing power*. One possible source of such countervailing power can be shippers, but for a variety of reasons shippers failed to organize into shippers councils until the 1960s. The other and more potent source of countervailing power has been the state.

This is evident most prominently in the US, where early on the Shipping Act of 1916 mandated open conferences in its trades, barred deferred rebates and fighting ships, and required filing of rates fixed by conferences in order to determine their fairness. However, the dominant maritime powers of Europe felt little need to place restraints on conferences, apparently because their economies benefitted materially from their already established position under the existing framework. Another source of countervailing power can be alternative means of cargo transport, such as air transport; the latter, however, did not arise on any significant scale until the early 1970s with the launching of jumbo jets. Still another source can be technological change which unsettles established patterns in the industry and weakens the conference system, such as has occurred with the containerization revolution in liner shipping.

Without employing the specific notion of countervailing power, Sletmo and Williams refer to a variety of developments in liner shipping--the rise of successful competitors from outside the framework of conferences, rival modes of transport, and technological change--to demonstrate that conferences are not the dangerous threat that the US Department of Justice is inclined to depict them as. So thorough and convincing is their defence of the conference system that one is led to wonder why decision-makers, particularly of the developing world, needed at all to be so exercised about the system's abuses from the beginning of the twentieth century onwards. The authors' argument gives the appearance that somehow the constraints on the conference system are inherent in it, and consequently states, particularly the US, are well advised to leave the system alone.

Curiously, in their eagerness to controvert the anti-trust orientation of the US Department of Justice, and to remove the constraining hand of state intervention in order to allow rationalization to occur in the north Atlantic trades, Sletmo and Williams ignore the implications of the monopoly power of conferences. To some extent, they are justified in doing so, for their work as the title of their book indicates pertains to the container age. By that time, the containerization of shipping had weakened the conferences, competition from the airlines for cargo was strong, and shippers were better organized to bargain. Besides, state intervention and mandatory regulation had, in certain areas, opened up conferences and outlawed their worst features. Indeed, the authors several times refer to the abuses of the system as only belonging to some past era.[44] However, it would seem that, if the purpose is to take adequate account of economic reality, one cannot rely on only a limited segment of time and ignore the abuses of the system that prevailed in the past, and which are likely to surface again in the absence of countervailing power from the outside.

It is precisely the situation of the absence of countervailing power that India as a colony faced before 1947. In that case, state power was lodged in the imperial power wherefrom the shipowners came and were able to count on it for support. On the other hand, shippers in the colony were helpless; being small-scale and dispersed, they could not afford to defy shipowners who had the backing of the empire. More importantly, the absence of countervailing power against the monopoly power of the imperial shipowners proved crushing for the maritime aspirations of local entrepreneurs. The sovereignty of the state, more importantly the exercise of that sovereignty, is thus fundamental to the survival of a national merchant fleet.

IMPERIALISM AND THE ANNIHILATION OF LOCAL SHIPPING

There exists a contentious debate around the question of the economic impact of imperialism.[45] In fact, it is an old debate[46] which manifests itself in new reincarnations, employing the particular conceptual paradigm and terminology of the time. Essentially, there are two opposing schools, consisting of (1) the nationalists, who single out the exploitation and underdevelopment that came in the train of colonial rule, and (2) the imperialists who emphasize what are perceived to be the beneficial results of imperialism and India's integration into the world capitalist system, especially the growth of new exports and the creation of a substantial industrial sector. However, it seems that so far the nationalists have made the stronger case not only because it is more forcefully argued but also because it is better documented. The cumulative record of foreign rule in India, as it emerges in the nationalist case, constitutes too massive and damning an indictment to sustain a respectable case for the imperialists. Still, since there is often sufficient ambiguity surrounding human affairs and their record, there are limits to completely demolishing any particular case in the social sciences.

It would seem, however, that there is little ambiguity in the facts as they pertain to shipping in India. British imperialism resulted in a thoroughgoing destruction of India's maritime capabilities and in the institution of an extreme "underdevelopment and dependency" instead. Indeed, shipping seems to have been an area marked for special intolerance of the existence or rise of local capabilities. While local entrepreneurs were tolerated though not encouraged in other industries, such as textiles, somehow shipping was considered central to the structure of imperialism and therefore local competitors were crushed.

THE ENTRENCHMENT OF BRITISH MONOPOLY

The maritime achievements of India's coastal peoples have been rightly celebrated by nationalist historians, such as Radha Kumud Mukerji and K.M. Panikkar.[47] They have served as a source of inspiration to entrepreneurs and decision-makers in the twentieth century. Although militarily the Indian Ocean had been dominated in the last millennium by a succession of external powers before the arrival of the British--the Arabs, the Turks, the Portuguese, and the Dutch--Indian maritime activity was of a high order. As one historian puts it: "Long before the Portuguese invaded the Indian Ocean, shipbuilders, shipowners, and sailors on the extensive littoral of the Indian peninsula had built up what was by all standards an impressive industry".[48]

India was at the centre of a world-economy organized around the Indian Ocean, the hinge that joined its eastern and western stretches. While this world-economy had many flourishing port cities, with quite a number of them on the east and west coasts of India, it was Surat on the upper west coast of India that was its hub, "situated right at the centre of the system", a major transhipment port and prominent in "navigation, trade, industry and credit".[49] The insulation of the Indian-Ocean world-economy was broken by the entry of Portuguese power, and in the sixteenth and seventeenth centuries it was incorporated into a larger world-economy under the hegemony of Europe. Initially, this incorporation "did not bring any essential change in the Indian Ocean economic system".[50] Indeed, European trade and shipping were simply added on to the existing system. Intercontinental trade between Europe and the Indian Ocean became no doubt a European monopoly, but "there existed within the region an, albeit at times uneasy, symbiotic relationship that allowed indigenous shipping to serve coastal and regional traffic".[51] The expansion of trade, and as a result sea transport, even had beneficial consequences for local enterprise. Certainly, "after a century of Portuguese 'dominance' Surat's merchants were more prosperous than ever".[52] At the beginning of the eighteenth century, its merchant fleet comprised more than 100 ocean-going ships.[53]

In the conflict among the European powers for domination of the Indian Ocean, the British finally emerged victorious. Their ascendancy on the sea led to the progressive and massive annexation of territory on the Indian subcontinent from the mid-eighteenth century onwards, eventuating ultimately in the establishment of the British empire in India. The initiation of empire had started a process of the decline of Indian shipping, resulting eventually in its annihilation. That outcome was, first and foremost, a function of the lack of political sovereignty, for the state was now in the control of a foreign power and was structured to serve its military and material interests. Technological change also fed into the outcome, but the failure in successful adaptation to it was fundamentally a consequence of the absence of political autonomy, for there was no lack of local enterprise and talent.

Most everywhere the growth of maritime power has, at least initially, taken place under the umbrella of protection and promotion of the state. In India's case, however, this umbrella was not available even before colonial rule, as some indigenous factors had impeded the growth of the shipping industry. One of these was the lack of institutionalized cooperation among the merchants and shipowners for the pursuit of commercial interest through combination, such as the joint stock enterprise, beyond the individual or family concern. More importantly, the fragmentation of political power into many states as also the absence of naval power, because of the land orientation of the state elites, had been a major handicap in the development of maritime power in the subcontinent. As Borsa puts it: "The ethos of the ruling class was oriented towards the land. The attitude of the Indian rulers towards the merchants was one of benign neglect. This left the merchants free, but did not afford them any protection. In quiet times, the freedom they enjoyed allowed them to prosper; but in troubled times, unable to protect themselves by joining forces and left alone by the state, they ran into difficulties and declined".[54]

The assertion of British naval hegemony in the Indian Ocean had enormous consequences: "Indian shipowners suffered most. Landbased merchants entrusted their goods to the English carriers, believing they were safer. The cooperation between Indians and the English continued, but the Indians had become by now the junior partners.... the colonial order was in the making in India before India became a colony".[55] Later, under British imperialism up to the mid-twentieth century, local efforts at building a merchant fleet invariably faced not only indifference and neglect but hostility from the colonial state that represented the interests of the metropolitan, rather than national, shipping. Even when the colonial state became less intolerant of Indian development of other industries, little was conceded to national shipping until the overthrow of colonialism.

The historian Frank Broeze divides the impact of British colonial rule on India's maritime industries into three periods: (1) from the foundation of the British empire in India in the mid-eighteenth century to the mid-nineteenth century; (2) from the mid-nineteenth century to World War I; and (3) the years between the two world wars. In the first period, with the establishment of British naval hegemony in the Indian Ocean, Indian trade expanded rapidly and new trade networks were opened to areas colonized by the British. Naturally, British shipping exploited the opportunities that its empire had opened up, and the balance between British and Indian shipping was transformed. However, Indian shipping was not yet completely marginalized; that would require the intervention of politics, for "in this first period no marked dualism existed between the technology and organization of Indian and British shipowners".[56] Although Indian vessels were not comparable in size and speed to the ocean-traversing European ships, the Indians proved adept at learning; "Indeed, it is remarkable just how quickly Indian (more so even than Arab and Indonesian) shipwrights and carpenters learned from European examples".

British shipowners in the region themselves depended on Indian shipyards, the most well-known of which was that owned by the Wadias. Hundreds of vessels were built from Indian teak to European design "and their best withstood the comparison with European ships with ease".[57] Indeed, the Royal Navy acquired a number of warships from the Wadias. Soon, ships built in India entered the overseas trade with Britain, and the Napoleonic wars compelled Britain to charter tonnage from India.

However, once the wars ended, "the employment of India-built and owned tonnage by the East India Company during the French Wars now suddenly opened the spectre of a formidable competition to the shipbuilders on the Thames who jealously guarded their collective monopoly over the shipping trade with Asia."[58] The British state responded to the pressures of the shipping lobby with the Registry Act in 1815, which prohibited the registration of ships built in India, thus barring in effect their sale to British shipowners. In addition, the same act held that Indians were no longer to be considered British subjects for the purposes of the Navigation Acts. That meant a drastic reduction in recruitment of Indian personnel, since the Navigation Acts mandated that no captains and no more than a quarter of the crew could be foreigners on British ships. This was a severe penalty for Indian ratings, known as *lascars*, since they tended to work as full crew.[59] Earlier, in 1811, the colonial government at Calcutta, soon to be followed by Madras and Bombay, doubled import duties on goods brought in other than British ships. While initially the chief targets of the measure were French and Dutch ships, before long they were granted exemption; on the other hand, Indian ships remained the victims of the practice until 1875.[60]

In 1823, the restriction on registration of India-built ships was eliminated, but it could be of little benefit to India-based owners since they had no sustained presence in England for registration. As the demand for India-built ships fell, shipyards fell into disuse. On the other hand, British shipowners were now allowed to send smaller size ships into the Indian Ocean, which enabled British shipping to enter India's coastal and regional trades. The restrictions on recruitment of Indian crew continued, however. Although sometimes humanitarian considerations were advanced for the restrictions, the real motivation lay elsewhere.[61] As has been pointed out on the basis of the testimony of John Forbes, a partner in an eminent British expatriate firm in India at the time: "The real reason for the lascars' exclusion, Forbes asserted, was the wish to make it virtually impossible for Indian shipowners to enter the trade with Britain and thus maintain the monopoly held by Britain's metropolitan merchant fleet. As no other legal means could be found to discriminate against Indian shipping, pseudo-humanitarian regulations had been adopted.... Forbes certainly touched on the heart of the matter: the interests of Britain's maritime industries and security were paramount". However, when the restrictions were repeated in new legislation in 1823, no reference to the welfare of Indian ratings occurred. Curiously, the restrictions on recruitment of Indians were not applied to local sailors from other British colonies in Africa and the West Indies, where apparently no threat was seen to British shipping. The restrictions on Indian crew were removed in 1849 with the abolition of the Navigation Acts, "but by then permanent damage had already been done".[62]

Imperialism thus, not surprisingly, placed British shipping and Indian shipping on an unequal footing. While British ships were free to operate in the coastal and overseas trades of India, Indian ships were effectively barred from the corresponding trades of Great Britain. Meanwhile, as British ships advanced in quality, Indian shipowners were placed at a disadvantage by the higher insurance rates required for Indian ships. Moreover, the British vessels now required higher skills to operate, the training for which was not available to local crews. The consequence was that even though local seafarers "could retain their position in traditional trades, elsewhere Europeans replaced them as masters and officers. In a very short period a process of de-skilling ('underdevelopment of skills') took place that relegated Indians firmly to the ranks of common ratings".[63] Imperialism thus proved destructive of Indian maritime capabilities in respect of all three requirements of ships, shipbuilding and seafarers.

In the second period from mid-nineteenth century to World War I, the new technology of steamships, combined with the discriminatory treatment in favour of British shipping, "soon caused the virtually complete absence of India in the areas of modern shipping, shipbuilding and seafaring above the rank of rating".[64] The commanding superiority of the new technology was reinforced by a British programme of mail subsides for a global imperial network. Other states could overcome the onerous disadvantage at which they were placed by providing protection for their national shipping, but this path was barred to India. As a consequence, "while the metropolitan core of the world made great progress, India's maritime industries declined by all standards.... Here one can observe a prime case of 'underdevelopment', a drastic deterioration of the relative position of the peripheral country. At the same time, it also constituted a marked example of 'dualism', with dynamic European technology now being far ahead, and moving even further ahead, of the largely traditional and, on the whole, stagnating methods of Indian sailing ship construction".[65]

In this new situation, there arose the virtual monopoly over India's coastal and overseas trades by two British shipowning firms--Peninsular and Oriental Steam Navigation Company, but usually referred to as simply P&O, and British Indian Steamship Navigation Company (BISN, or just BI). In 1914, near the end of the second period, the earlier cooperation and collaboration between the two was replaced by a merger even though each retained its separate identity and sphere of concentration, P&O in India's overseas trades and BISN in India's coastal and regional trades. P&O had been founded in 1837 and BISN in 1856, though not under precisely those names. The patronage of the colonial power was critical to their ascendance in shipping, for the "British rulers never disagreed with the opposition of the metropolitan British companies against the acceptance of the legitimacy of Indian steamshipping".[66] Massive mail subsidies from the British and Indian governments helped them establish their wide route networks. With both companies providing troop carriers for the empire, "state and company became mutually supportive, and in their respective spheres P&O and BISN became truly 'flagships of imperialism'".[67] As a consequence, both companies flourished and achieved a stranglehold in India's trades and the two together strode like a colossus in the Indian Ocean from the Suez to the Far East on the ruins of innumerable rivals who were eliminated in the process. The ascendancy of these shipping behemoths was fortified with the instituting of the conference system, which not fortuitously began in India with the Calcutta Liners

Conference in 1875. The decisive weapons in the destruction of their rivals were deferred rebating and predatory pricing.

The tie between company and state is vividly displayed in the career of Lord Inchcape (1852-1932), the redoubtable and ardent defender of Britain's imperial and shipping interests.[68] Born as James Lyle Mackay to a Scottish sea captain, Inchcape first came to India in the early 1870s to join the India office at Calcutta of the Scottish mercantile firm Mackinnon Mackenzie and Company. The latter had started BISN and served as its agents. Ambitious and industrious, he rose quickly within the firm, playing a crucial role in its growing prosperity. By 1894 he was the moving spirit and the real power in the firm. Even before then, he had in 1889 been elected president of the Bengal Chamber of Commerce, while in 1891 he was nominated to the Viceroy's legislative council and in 1892 appointed chairman of the Indian Currency Association. For a decade and a half from 1897 to 1911, he was a member of the India Council in Great Britain. In 1908, the Secretary of State for India recommended him to the cabinet, though unsuccessfully, for the viceroyalty in India. As chairman of BISN in 1913 and of P&O in 1914, he presided over the merger of the two companies, which together owned some 2 million grt. In 1922, he travelled to India again as chairman of the Indian Retrenchment Committee. He was made a viscount in 1924 and Earl of Inchcape in 1929. He was renowned for his scorn for Indian nationalism and shipping aspirations, and Indian shipowners had to bear the brunt of his fury.

THE STRANGLING OF INDIAN ENTERPRISE

The domination of BISN in India's trades did not put an end to the Indian quest for a role in shipping even though its bearers were not the traditional shipowners but modern industrialists and businessmen. There was no lack of enterprise, for between 1860 and 1925, a total of 102 shipping companies with a capital of Rs. 460 million are said to have been started.[69] However, most went into liquidation; as *Statesman* editor Sir Alfred Watson remarked before a legislative committee in the late 1920s: "Indian company after Indian company which endeavoured to develop a coastal service has been financially shattered by the heavy combination of the British interests".[70] Broeze agrees: "The basic cause of the lamentable position of Indian shipping was the formidable opposition they encountered from the major British companies.... Whenever a rival company was formed, they [P&O and BISN] engaged without hesitation in fierce rate wars that they with their accumulated reserves and large resources...could wage so much more successfully".[71] No modern state would have allowed such savage decimation of its entrepreneurial effort at the hands of foreign firms, but the colonial state shielded itself behind the ideology of laissez faire. However, as Professor K.T. Shah testified before a legislative committee: "Government elects to worship the overturned idol of 'laissez faire'".[72] Even as Indian companies were denied protection, mail subsidies enriched P&O and BISN.

The fate that Indian entrepreneurship met at the hands of British shipping interests is vividly illustrated by the story of the Tata Line, started by J.N. Tata, the venerable head of India's largest industrial empire at the time, and later the founder of the modern steel industry in India. Tata found that P&O was charging excessive freight rates for exports of yarn from his textile mills even as it gave secret rebates to collaborator firms, with the result that he was being priced out of the Far East markets. He repeatedly tried to get P&O to lower the freight rates, but to no avail. He then endeavoured to mobilize the cooperation of two foreign firms which, however, left him in the lurch after a year of stiff competition; indeed, they joined up with P&O, with the combined cartel raising the rate first to Rs. 13 and again to Rs. 19 per cubic ton.

Frustrated, Tata determined to set up his own shipping line. No doubt, he saw economic benefit in protecting his yarn exports, but "patriotic motives of founding the nucleus of a modern Indian merchant marine fired his zeal".[73] Similar motives were to inspire his subsequent decision to pioneer the steel industry. The task was daunting in either case: "It indeed required a good deal of courage to fight the P&O which had immense resources and was firmly entrenched in the trade. But Shri Tata did not lack courage".[74] Tata entered into an agreement with Nippon Yusen Kaisha of Japan to start a new line called the Tata Line as a joint venture, with both parties bearing equal risk. Tata travelled to London and chartered two ships for the purpose. The new company charged Rs. 12 per ton as against P&O's rate of Rs. 19. A rate war followed, with P&O

and its fellow members in the cartel lowering the rate to Rs. 1.50 and making "the unusual offer of carrying cotton to Japan free of charge".[75] These lower rates were offered on a deferred basis. In addition, P&O spread rumours that Tata's ships were not seaworthy, increasing its insurance rates.

Struck by the cutthroat competition, Tata complained "bitterly" to the Secretary of State about the underhanded practices of P&O and its ring members: "With scores of liners, English and foreign, plying in these waters which our petted and much glorified Anglo-Indian Company can afford, and perhaps find it good policy to tolerate, it is only jealous of a small enterprise like ours, and while it can lovingly take foreigners and possible future enemies of England to its bosom, it discards the poor Indian for whose special benefit it professes to have come to India and from whose pocket it draws the greater part of its subsidy".[76] His memorandum had little effect. Undercut by the deferred rebates, Tata lost the battle; as his biographer sadly acknowledged, "For once Mr. Tata was beaten".[77] With the Tata line crushed, P&O immediately raised the rate to Rs. 16 a ton.[78]

A fate similar to that of the Tata line befell the Swadeshi Steamship Company that had been founded in 1906 by the South Indian nationalist leader Chidambaran Pillai for service between Tuticorin and Colombo. It was heavily invested with the symbolism of economic nationalism, paralleling the rise of the militant phase in nationalism in the political sphere. The very name of the firm, using the nationalist slogan Swadeshi [national, indigenous], was provocative for the British as was its flag bearing the title of the national song Vande Matram. But "the B.I., as could be expected, hit hard. A fierce rate war ensued and the B.I. began to carry passengers even free. Political and other pressures were freely used to break the Indian venture. Government officials were secretly asked not to travel by the Swadeshi ship and for some time the Swadeshi ship was allowed to leave Tuticorin only after the B.I. ship left".[79] In this case, while the company survived BISN's attempt to crush it through a rate war by rallying nationalist passengers and traders, the colonial state sent its founder to jail on political grounds; the company then languished and finally disappeared.[80] Another shipping company established in eastern Indian in 1905 was the Bengal Steamship Company. It flourished initially, but then a freight war launched by BISN destroyed it: "The B.I. cut the passenger rate to the ridiculously low figure of eight annas and sometimes they took passengers free also. As an added attraction, passengers were given free handkerchiefs!"[81]

The case of the Tata line is instructive not only for the indifference of the government to its fate but also, not unrelatedly, the cynical recognition of power by P&O. The same P&O that was intolerant towards Indian competition had a sharply different posture towards Japanese and European shipping lines, with which it was ready to reach an accommodation. Broeze comments insightfully:

> The decisive difference, however, was that British shipowners always could be certain that, while Japanese shipowners were ultimately supported by their government, no such help would come forward for Indian shipping. On the contrary, all mail subsidies were granted to the P&O and BISN, and no native infant shipping company could hope either to share in them or to be protected from the chilling winds of unfettered competition that the government's convenient and ideologically correct commitment to free enterprise allowed to be unleashed. Thus, with the tacit but no less significant support from the Indian government, which contrasted sharply with the protectionist anti-British coastal reservation acts that during the same period were passed in Canada and Australia, or for that matter Britain's own Navigation Acts that for two centuries from 1651 had constituted such a powerful support for her fleet, the leaders of the British companies could feel justified in their denial of legitimacy to their Indian rivals.[82]

The fate of the Tata Line stood as a chastening lesson to Indian entrepreneurs who dreamed of venturing into shipping. However, they refused to be intimidated, and countless new attempts were made even if only to be vanquished on the rocks of the rate wars. Such was the pattern that lasted until the end of World War I. Indeed, for a decade before the end of the war no one had dared to start a shipping enterprise. Then in 1919 another group of visionaries started a new venture that in retrospect dazzles the imagination for its sheer daring and determination. The product of their labours, Scindia Steam Navigation Company, named after the Maharaja Scindia of Gwalior, became in due course the nucleus of independent India's modern merchant fleet. But before that could happen, the enterprise went through more than a quarter-century of harsh conflict and struggle, with its survival constituting the stuff of legends. Indeed, the history of Indian shipping between World War I and Indian independence in 1947 became essentially the story of Scindia's struggle to survive, defying the insuperable obstacles set against it.

The "Saga of Scindia" and the Rise of Shipping Nationalism

Worthy of admiration as Scindia's struggle may have been, its survival was not entirely the outcome of the ingenuity and grit of its entrepreneurs, enormously skilful undoubtedly though they were. It was also a consequence of the changed economic and political context in India. World War I saw the expansion of local industry and, relatedly, the consolidation of a national capitalist class and the accumulation of capital in its hands from huge wartime profits. These new elements provided both the base and the desire for diversification away from traditional industries, such as sugar and textiles. In the political arena, the end of the war saw the intensification and transformation of the nationalist movement. Mahatma Gandhi transformed the movement from an intermittent gathering of the narrow urban-based, English-educated middle class into a mass movement, which encompassed that middle class plus the rich and middle peasantry of the rural areas, even as it was supported financially by the newly consolidated capitalist class. It was this confluence of factors that proved critical in facilitating the survival of Scindia. The leaders in the shipping venture themselves were not unaffected by the nationalist movement. They may not have been without the profit motive, but no profit motive alone could have withstood for a moment the terror that BISN's name struck in the hearts of those who aspired to be shipowners, and they were all familiar with the fate of past efforts at the hands of BISN. They were moved by patriotism, and they took their effort to be an expression of nationalism in the economic sphere. Nationalist leaders, in turn, looked at Scindia with awe and admiration for its grit and determination, and rose to support it to the extent that they could under foreign rule.

Remarkably, notwithstanding its hallowed place in the history of shipping nationalism in India, Scindia was in its immediate origins a result of fortuitous circumstance. An Indian businessman of boundless curiosity and energy, Walchand Hirachand, was travelling from Delhi to Bombay by train. During the journey, he heard from a fellow passenger that, with the war ended, the Maharaja Scindia of Gwalior was anxious to sell for Rs. 2.5 million the hospital ship s.s. *Loyalty* (earlier *Empress of India* of the Canadian Pacific line) which he had purchased to assist the British war effort. Alighting at the Bombay VT railway station on February 17, 1919, Walchand headed straight for the harbour, rather than going home first, to inspect the vessel even though he knew nothing about ships or shipping. Impressed, but cognizant that shipping was not a matter of a single ship and would require a large capital investment, he proceeded to Narottam Morarjee, a respected textile magnate with enormous financial prowess, to discuss the venture. Narottam agreed to support it, and the next day Walchand met two other businessmen and the four of them formed an initial partnership to arrange the purchase. On March 27, 1919 a company was registered with an initial share capital of Rs. 45 million, which until then was the largest amount of capital raised by any company in the market; even the Tata Iron and Steel Company had a smaller subscription.

THE SHIPPING TRIUMVIRATE

In the trials and tribulations of the company under colonial rule, its fortunes rested on the triumvirate consisting of Walchand Hirachand, Narottam Morarjee, and Mansukhlal Atmaram Master. All three had origins in Gujarat and possessed the proverbial Gujarati acumen for business, though Walchand's family had settled in Maharashtra two generations earlier. All three were innocent of any knowledge of shipping, though they were extremely quick learners. All three were fired by patriotic zeal, though they did not overtly participate in politics. All three were born in the last quarter of the nineteenth century and grew to maturity during the rise of nationalism under the aegis of the

Indian National Congress, which was founded in 1885; they identified with it and supported it financially.

The key figure in the group was, of course, Walchand Hirachand (1882-1953), a self-made man who had been very successful in the construction business, where he undertook daunting engineering projects. However, at the time that he was instrumental in founding Scindia, his entrepreneurial achievements in industry still lay in the future, for in addition to making money in sugar he went on to pioneer in aircraft manufacture, automobile production, and shipbuilding. Although coming from a devout but reformist Jain family, he was personally indifferent to religion. He was driven by a passion to make India over into an industrialized country, believing deeply that economic independence was essential to political independence. He detested the country's subjugation and endeavoured to undermine colonialism through its economic regeneration. He was no believer in foreign investment and wanted industry in the country to be owned, controlled and managed by Indians. He was always insistent on Indians being treated as equals in personal or business interactions.

An entrepreneurial genius and a born manager of men, Walchand turned into success most everything he touched. A man of action and iron will, with formidable talents, he had as his foremost characteristic "supreme self-confidence which was at once the inspiration of his followers and the despair of his adversaries".[83] In shipping, his extraordinary energy and dynamism were most of all directed to the success of Scindia, in an effort to destroy the myth cultivated by the British that India was not a seafaring nation and was incapable of running a shipping company in the modern world. His own achievements stood as a refutation of the myth. He was not reticent about the unfair practices of British shipping and of its accomplice, the colonial state, which strangled Indian shipping. Where his other business friends were inclined to caution so as not to provoke those in authority, he was outspoken, blunt and pugnacious, and "he gave the British shipping interests few moments of peace. Sharp of tongue and quick of wit, he revelled in verbal combats with those in power and the leading lights of British business in India and raised wherever he went a storm of controversy".[84] In his educative role towards his compatriots, he held that shipping was no ordinary business but one vital for the country's economy and security; indeed, "it was his compelling advocacy that brought the support of the political leaders of the country fully to the issue. It is to him that India owes the creation for the first time of a national shipping consciousness in the country".[85]

Narottam Morarjee (ca. 1877-1929) was critical to the initial survival of Scindia because of his standing in the financial community, which was essential for the mobilization of capital. That standing is sufficiently reflected in his being one of the founder directors of the Tata Iron and Steel Company. Narottam was made the first chairman of Scindia on its founding and continued in that position until his death in a car accident in 1929, when Walchand took over to stay on as chairman until 1950. A newly formed firm, Narottam Morarjee and Company, fully owned by him alone but sharing profits with the other three partners, was appointed as managing agents for Scindia. Narottam was inclined more towards caution and moderation though he was no less committed to the struggle against British hegemony in shipping. He was close to the leaders of the nationalist movement, and Mahatma Gandhi was a frequent guest at his house. In a tribute to him, Gandhi declared that Narottam had initiated Scindia "as much through patriotism as through ambition".[86]

Mansukhlal Atmaram Master (1884-1970) was Narottam's loyal assistant with a law degree and a lawyer's skills. He became the general manager of Scindia at the company's founding. As "an energetic, patriotic and intelligent young man", he provided invaluable assistance to Walchand and Narottam. He excelled at discerning their aims, while "his unstinted devotion to both men was only equalled by his prodigious loyalty, which they in their turn rewarded with confidence, affection and trust beyond reckoning".[87] Through study and application, he soon acquired mastery over the intricacies of the shipping business, and emerged as the technocratic spokesman and defender of Scindia and Indian shipping. He was particularly skilful in negotiations, for

> He had a unique talent for building up his case on solid proofs and presenting it in a systematic way. He was an adept at recognizing his opponent's line of attack, relying on that other's own previous statements, and turning the whole

> thing back on him. How often British officials would frankly confess, "Young man, you've left us with nothing to say; you've got a marvellous gift of the gab!" .... Respectful, reasonable, armed at the critical moment with a swift power of repartee, Master is able to expound the subjects under analysis by obtaining a smooth acceptance of the essential points, and ramming home the conclusions which must follow; and he employs such speech as reinforces the above.[88]

Master represented Scindia in high-level discussions and negotiations right up to Lord Inchcape in the industry and the Viceroy in the government, and was a member of Indian delegations to international conferences. He was a prolific publicist, with a selection of his published writings between 1947 and 1969 alone adding to 1500 pages. Master was a sharp and meticulous analyst of shipping policy and a stout and indefatigable advocate of India's shipping interests against what he saw as the depredations of foreign shipowners, particularly British. His educative role assumed a new salience after his retirement from Scindia in 1951. He was a passionate supporter of an expanded national merchant fleet, and took every opportunity to educate the public and decision-makers. His writings are marked by lucidity and packed with factual data; they are largely critical of the diffidence of national decision-makers and of their ideological predilection for state ownership.

THE WAR BETWEEN "THE GIANT AND THE DWARF"

With these three at the helm, Scindia swung into action even though traders and agents had been intimidated by BISN into not cooperating with it, not only in India but also along the way in Europe. On April 5, 1919, within less than 10 days of the founding of the company, s.s. *Loyalty*, in a daring assertion of defiance with its own flag with a traditional Indian symbol, sailed from Bombay for London with a group of dignitaries among its passengers, including Walchand and Narottam. That day has been considered an historic day in India's maritime development, and since 1964 has been celebrated annually as national maritime day. Significantly, though unrelatedly, Gandhi launched his first nationwide strike the next day after the ship sailed as part of the non-cooperation movement against colonial rule. The ship's sailing and arrival in London aroused the anger of British shipping interests; at their behest, travel agents and shippers refused to cooperate in securing passengers or cargo for the return journey. Even though this was his first visit to a western country, Walchand rose to the occasion. He rented another room in the hotel, and turned himself into a booking agent and lined up passengers. Failing to obtain cargo enough even for ballast, he purchased 1500 tons of iron and cement for the purpose with the intent to sell it in India.

One aim in Walchand making the trip was to purchase more steamships for a well-rounded shipping line. Overcoming wartime statutory restrictions, he was after strenuous and persistent effort eventually able to buy six ships following an undertaking that he would not purchase any more British ships.[89] While in London, Walchand got adequate warning about the future struggle that awaited Scindia. Lord Inchcape refused even to see him, for "Inchcape did not acknowledge the notion and strength of Indian nationalism, and like his deputy Currie and his British agents in India regarded the entry of Scindia into imperial waters as an unacceptable intrusion into his domain".[90] The persistent Walchand was finally able to get a meeting with Inchcape's deputy, Sir William Currie, who warned him:

> Your intrusion into our field we consider as downright piracy. We have built up this sea transport business by years and years of infinite toil and devotion; and if you fancy that you can rob us of it by shameless bluster and a fat purse, you are grossly mistaken. The sooner you remedy your mistake, the better. Otherwise you will go the way of your predecessors.[91]

Persuaded by the fact that it did not have a sufficient fleet to provide a regular service in overseas trades, Scindia finally decided to operate nearer home and enter the coastal cargo trades, focusing on the India-Burma trade, with Burma then being part of India. BISN immediately threatened shippers with cancellation of their deferred rebates should they cooperate with Scindia. Meanwhile, the government denied the Scindias the opportunity to bid for transport of coal between Calcutta and Rangoon, while port authorities placed obstacles in Scindia's operations, particularly delaying the departure of its ships until after BISN's had left port.[92] Several nationalist-minded shippers were defiant, but their cargo was not sufficient for the Scindia vessels. With an intrepid management at the helm, Scindia ingeniously combined trading with shipping through establishing affiliate trading companies of its own and bought rice for transport by its ships. It carried cargo to smaller ports not frequented until then, and innovatively transported sugar from Java to the west coast. When stevedoring and bunkering firms refused to service Scindia ships on BISN's prompting, Scindia started its own subsidiary for the purpose. It even brought in a Norwegian expert to develop plans for a ship repairing and building yard, though these had to be given up for the time being because of his sudden death.

Foiled in its attempt to crush Scindia, BISN then resorted to its ultimate weapon of a rate war, bringing down the rate for the Rangoon-Bombay trip from Rs. 18 per ton to Rs. 6 even though the operating cost was about Rs. 14.[93] While BISN and P&O were flush with funds Scindia had few resources to meet this onslaught. It suffered huge losses, and its capital base shrunk into half.

Facing doom, Scindia was still determined to survive and, with the country in the grip of nationalism under Gandhi's leadership, it adopted the strategy of mobilizing nationalist support. The nationalist leadership and press rallied behind it, and pressed for a national mercantile marine built on the basis of reservation of India's coastal trade entirely for it. Thus, just as imperialism was critical to the domination of British shipping, so was political nationalism to the assertion of shipping nationalism in India; indeed, "it is doubtful that Scindia could have survived, if it had not been for the rising tide of political nationalism".[94] Lord Inchcape, who was in India at the time as chairman of the government's Retrenchment Committee, could personally see the limits which nationalism placed in his path in attempting to eliminate Scindia. For, "although the collapse of the steamer rates was drying up its capital, the Scindia Company neither relaxed its policy of clashing with his companies, nor showed any signs of doing so. On the contrary, it showed a tendency towards taking greater and greater advantage, for the purposes of its private war, of the anti-British climate engendered by the Non-cooperation Movement in the country. And when he saw all this, his canny Scotch mind began to think of playing a fresh kind of game".[95]

Inchcape then resorted to a new stratagem and, in Scindia's parlous financial condition, made a tempting offer that would have been difficult to refuse--to buy out the firm. Under the offer, each share of Scindia would be exchanged for Rs.12.50 in cash and Rs. 12.50 in BISN's interest-bearing tax-free preference shares; besides, the directors would get Rs. 1000 per month for ten years while the managing agents would be given a large sum in settlement.[96] The Scindia directors, however, summarily rejected the offer, resolving that "nothing which should make the company lose its existence shall be acceptable",[97] but they agreed to open negotiations with a view to entering the relevant conference. A special meeting of eighty of the important shareholders with a majority of the shares was called to win their support for the position. At the meeting, Narottam gave a stirring speech, concluding:

> It lies not in my mouth to tell you that, should you regard these matters from the angle of temporary and personal gain, and sell the Company, it will be a blow to our country's prestige, with a probability of unwelcome repercussions in India's industrial life, and that our first duty is to adopt the national viewpoint and prevent these things. You are all thoughtful men. You are all capable of deciding whether the good of the individual, or the good of the nation, is the more important. What can I say, in such a context, to men such as yourselves?[98]

All except one favoured the stand of the directors.

During the negotiations of the directors with Inchcape, Walchand developed the suspicion that his colleagues may waver and get enticed into acceptance of the offer. To stiffen their spine, he let the nationalist newspaper *Bombay Chronicle* know that "all the hopes I've cherished up to now, are likely to go up in smoke. I shall not be able to hold up my head any more. The nation's interests are going to be murdered". At that, the newspaper promptly published a stinging editorial the next day warning Scindia's directors against selling the company, and asked them to contemplate "the judgement the country and posterity would pass" on them. At the next meeting, Inchcape chastised them for going public on what was to him a private business deal. The exchange that followed revealed vividly the different perspectives that the antagonists brought to the issue. Fearing that the silence of his two colleagues meant acquiescence in the accusation, Walchand responded:

> Everything is fair in love and war. You and we are now at war. In war, such tactics are necessary. In particular, when a heartless company like yours, with no thought for the rights and wrongs of it, launches murderous attacks on a newly-born Company like ours, whatever tactics we may fight you with, will be considered proper. We have nothing to regret. Since you refer to the question of clean and straightforward tactics, and decent behaviour, I must ask you--Who started the present rate war? Was it not you? As if this war, and your tactics in it, are clean and straightforward! Noble Lord! Your henchmen in the Burma rice trade affairs are trying to drive us out of there, fighting us with all sorts of tricks and harassing us in all sorts of ways. But I tell you to your face that until foreigners like your henchmen, who have come to these lands to loot the people, are driven out, I will not think twice before using not only our present tactics, but still more venomous ones. So long as you people do not give up your devilish policy of plundering and oppressing us, I shall continue to keep alight the flame of discontent which will burn you up. My aim is to leave no stone unturned to break up your imperialism in the industrial field. We can rightfully sail our own ships freely over the seas of our native land, and we will sail them. For this we do not want your grace and favour.

At this, Inchcape exploded:

> Native land! Whose native land! Whose sea! We are all sons of the British Empire. We people have as much right as you, to travel along the coast of India. So long as the British Empire lasts, no power on earth can stop us coming here. The way you people are now carrying on, is the way pirates carry on. We look on the Scindia Company, which

> has trespassed into our maritime field, as pirates. That's what you are--pirates!

Similar words had been uttered to Walchand by Inchcape's deputy in 1919 when Inchcape had not deigned even to see him. At that time, Walchand had been stunned by the novelty of the remarks, but now he retorted: "Who are the pirates? We--or you? Our home waters--do they belong to you people, coming from beyond the seven seas, or to us who were born and bred in this land? I see! *You* are the owners, and *we* are the thieves, the pirates! Excellent!"[99] The session broke up, but that was not the end of the affair.

Baffled by the turn of events, Inchcape subsequently broached the subject of Scindia with a fellow member on the Retrenchment Committee, Sir Purshottamdas Thakurdas, an eminent businessman who was perceived in nationalist circles as a collaborator of the British. The latter informed him: "These men are of an intensely nationalistic type, with fiery views. They have the power to translate their views into action, and a full share of determination. What they say, they will perform". Purshottamdas nonetheless thought that they would not be unreasonable but wondered whether "you yourself will be reasonable enough to permit them to occupy their legitimate place in the Indian economy". At that, Inchcape shouted, "I will beat them down if they are stubborn",[100] even as he had meanwhile come to realize that he now confronted men made of sterner stuff than what he had encountered earlier. Inchcape's presence in India while the country was in the throes of nationalism, as also the colonial state's increasing sensitivity to it, could not have been without its impact on him.

Narottam had disapproved of what seemed to him as lack of adequate restraint in Walchand's behaviour, at which Walchand excused himself from future sessions. When told of that, Purshottamdas warned Narottam:

> It will prove dangerous to keep him out of it. You have not sized up Lord Inchcape properly. He's a deep and crafty one, that old Scot. It is not the case that he means what he says, nor that he says what's in his mind. He has something very different up his sleeve. To know what this is, the opponent has to possess the same scheming brain as he's

> got. In my view, the only one among you who has it, is Walchand. Inchcape is a dyed-in-the-wool imperialist, of the old generation with expansionist attitudes developed in the reign of Queen Victoria, self-centred, egotistic and individualistic. To meet the tactics of a man like that, you need a dyed-in-the-wool nationalist, like Walchand.[101]

At the next session at Inchcape's residence, only Walchand spoke for Scindia in a show of unity among the directors. With Scindia struggling for survival, he then made a move remarkable for its sheer audacity: "No matter how bad the situation in which we find ourselves, we have no intention of selling the Company and leaving a clear field for you. The Scindia Company is not for sale; on the contrary, we are prepared to buy your B.I. Tell us your price. You want to end the dispute, don't you? So sell us the B.I. Then the quarrels between us will be settled for ever". Years later, he confessed that there was little money to buy BISN with, but that he had behind him "the irresistible force of the growing nationalism of a country impatient and anxious to obtain its freedom. It is this unshakeable faith both in my cause and in my country that make me talk and act in a manner which the 'live and let-live wallahs' fail to appreciate, much less to imitate". Inchcape dismissed the suggestion as impertinent, and exclaimed: "Have we cherished the B.I. and raised it to such heights, in order to sell it?" To that, Walchand responded: "In that case, my Lord, have we tenderly cherished the Scindia Company, and are we watering it with our blood, in order to sell it? When you talk of buying the Scindia Company, don't you think you are being quite obviously impertinent to us?"[102]

Both sides then recognized that they were engaged in a suicidal war. After further bargaining, they reached an agreement that Walchand called a "slavery bond" because of its one-sided and restrictive nature, but which Scindia accepted under the compulsion to survive. With that, a truce was called on March 14, 1923. Briefly, the resulting ten-year agreement which was to last until 1933 allowed Scindia the right to carry cargo, but no passengers, along the coasts of India, Burma and Ceylon--and only along these coasts, thus excluding it from overseas trades. It prohibited Scindia from acquiring additional tonnage for a year beyond its existing seven steamships of a total 29,126 grt. Further, it barred Scindia from exceeding a total tonnage of 75,000, and required it to space out the possible acquisition of some seven additional steamers of 5000 grt each over the years 1924 to 1927.

In the years following the agreement, Scindia felt victimized by the clause that excluded it from carrying passengers. More crucially, it contended that BISN continued to engage in rate-cutting and employed deferred rebating to drive Scindia into ruin even as the railways and port authorities under colonial rule favoured BISN. It petitioned the colonial state and the British government and tried to mobilize the nationalist movement in favour of reservation of coastal traffic for national shipping. While appearing to sympathize with Scindia's plight, the colonial state refused to act to mitigate it.

Thwarted, Scindia agreed to replace the agreement with BISN by a new tripartite agreement in 1933 with BISN and its protege Asiatic Steam Navigation Company, which only marginally improved its situation. For its part, BISN needed stability, for it could not ignore the rising nationalist sentiment for coastal reservation or, more importantly, the graver threat emerging from the increasing intrusion of Japanese shipping into India's coastal trade. Under the new agreement, Scindia could now increase its tonnage to 100,000 grt and carry passengers on two out of four India-Burma routes. While the agreement provided for cargo allocation according to specified percentages among the three companies at the major ports and the fixation of freight rates jointly by them in writing, it still barred Scindia from India's external trades.[103] Nationalism was able to prevent the extinction of Scindia, but was not powerful enough yet to assure it a place on an equal footing with the British companies. The seven-year agreement provided little respite for Scindia, for it had to continually struggle for survival against the forces unleashed against it and other Indian shipping companies by BISN and its allies through deferred rebating and rate discounting. Relations between Scindia and its British rivals dipped in 1937. Scindia asked for rights to half of the coastal trade and entry into the overseas trades, with Walchand warning BISN "to realize in its proper implications, the temper of the public in India". Knowing that these concessions would be at its cost, BISN was reluctant to agree. Before the resulting deadlock could be resolved, World War II intervened.[104]

By 1939, Scindia had pushed its tonnage to almost the maximum allowed--98,812 grt--distributed among 23 ships, including 5 passenger ships; together with its affiliates, it controlled 120,000 grt. The entire Indian shipping at the time consisted of 132,000 grt out of a world total of 70 million grt, and after two decades of strenuous effort had a share of 25 per cent in the coastal trade and none at all in the overseas trade.[105] When World War II started, the colonial state commandeered most of Scindia's fleet while allowing much of the British fleet in India to operate commercially as if to entrench it even further in India's trades.[106] At the end of the war, because of wartime losses, the Scindia fleet stood reduced to 15 vessels with a total capacity of 69,934 grt, much of it aged and desperately in need of repairs and replacement. Unlike British shipping, there was no help from the colonial state for it. Meanwhile, the agreement, which was originally to operate until 1939, lasted until 1950 when new legislation reserved the coastal trade of independent India for Indian shipping.

SCINDIA'S LINKAGE WITH NATIONALISM

In order to protect Scindia and other Indian shipping interests, Walchand and his associates, particularly Master, engaged in a massive public relations campaign to cultivate nationalist leaders and to educate and mobilize public opinion. They produced innumerable pamphlets and briefing papers, newspaper articles, and book-length analyses to support their position. Their campaign was based on the fundamental premise that success in economic endeavour required political support.

In response, a galaxy of political leaders, which is a virtual roll call of all the heroes of the nationalist movement, ardently supported Scindia's cause. Indeed, Sardar Vallabhbhai Patel underlined the "parallel between the illuminating history of the Scindia Company and the annals of another great institution in India viz. the Indian National Congress".[107] The protective interest of the nationalist leaders in Scindia was evident in their pressing for statutory reservation of coastal trade for national shipping. Although enthusiastically supported by nationalist leadership, such legislation was repeatedly thwarted by the

British bureaucracy; finally, the Government of India Act of 1935 barred any legislature in India from enacting laws favouring Indian shipping as against British shipping.[108] As Calcutta's *Capital* had so perceptively observed, "The brutal truth is that on such an issue argument is subordinate to power".[109]

Foremost among Scindia's political backers was Mahatma Gandhi, who wrote articles on the subject in his periodical *Young India*, in which he declared himself to be "an out and out protectionist", and castigated the British for building their prosperity "upon the ruin of India's commerce and industry. The cottage industry of India had to perish in order that Lancashire might flourish. The Indian shipping had to perish so that British shipping might flourish". He disputed the British logic on treating coastal reservation as flag discrimination, asking: "What is equality of rights between a giant and a dwarf?" Gandhi singled out the importance of shipping among Indian industries by including it in his "eleven points" of demands on the Viceroy in 1930 as a condition for cooperation with the colonial government.[110]

As British shipping interests screamed discrimination on the question of coastal reservation, one of Gandhi's senior colleagues, Motilal Nehru, sharply underlined in 1928 the necessity of state action to reverse the plight to which Indian shipping had been reduced at the hands of colonialism:

> How can we fight? You have made us helpless; we cannot do it; we cannot compete with you now; Why, Because you have consolidated your position to such an extent that it is not possible for us with our meagre resources without legislative help to hold our own against you.... It is like offering battle to your helpless victim whom you have deprived of all arms and strength and then you roll up your sleeves and say 'stand up and I will fight you'. We simply want to be put on our feet and no more. It is not that you have any right of preemption upon India. You know how you got it and how you have kept it so far; and now that we are asserting our rights in various directions, is it for you to say, 'Oh, this is discrimination'. Discrimination is there from the beginning; and we are now trying to get out of discrimination by, what you may, if you are so pleased, call in a

> loose sense, counter-discrimination. Why should the people of the country not resort to it?[111]

During the same year, another colleague, Lala Lajpat Rai, reminded the supporters of British interests: "If we had the power in our hands--the power of public purse and the political power--we would have established this industry long before today on a safe basis in the same way as Japan did, as Australia did, and as Chile did--and as other nations have done".[112]

The opening of the new building of the Scindias in 1938 became the occasion for a virtual competition among the nationalist leaders to demonstrate their identification with and support of Scindia. It was particularly appropriate that the building was opened by Sardar Patel, a friend of Indian business generally, who admired Scindia for having survived "the efforts to throttle it and annihilate it in a variety of ways". He expressed his opposition to "the domination of the foreigners" and the Congress party's determination "to flush out these foreign vested interests".[113]

Scindia had hitched its fortunes to the wagon of nationalism at a time when the colonial state was powerful. It was unsuccessful in getting coastal trade reserved for Indian shipping. However, its insistent campaigning and its equation of national interest with its own survival enabled it to survive where others before it had been vanquished at the hands of P&O and BISN.

SCINDIA'S MULTIFACETED LEGACY

As independence approached, new Indian shipping companies opened services and in due course the public sector assumed a dominant role, but Scindia remained a symbol of India's determination to enter the community of maritime powers. Its major contributions lay in three areas.

First and foremost, through assuring its own survival, it established the nucleus of a merchant fleet for independent India. It successfully introduced modern shipping with modern management under Indian control. Its shrewd and capable leaders, with little experience to go on, quickly acquired expertise in the intricacies of shipping to challenge the established British firms with a strong maritime tradition, and managed to survive against their hostility and that of the colonial bureaucracy. But it did more through its creation of a nucleus of a merchant fleet. It provided an example for others to follow and, when they were threatened by British shipping interests, it rushed to their protection and threw a protective umbrella over them. There are several instances to this effect.[114]

In 1933, the owner of the Bengal-Burma Steam Navigation Company, with only two ships, made a desperate appeal to Scindia for a loan of Rs. 350,000 to save it from being taken over by BISN in its weakened state following a rate war. Scindia quickly made the loan and saved it from being absorbed by BISN. In 1934, four small companies serving the trade between Karachi and ports on the Malabar coast became the target of a rate war by BISN with a view to their liquidation. Even though a partial member of the Indian coastal conference, Scindia refused to join in the rate war; instead, it strenuously opposed it and led a delegation to the Viceroy to intervene to protect the companies. An arbitration award allocated 85 per cent of certain of the west coast trades to the companies. The award affected Scindia's annual revenues adversely to the extent of Rs. 0.5 million, but Scindia accepted it "willingly and proudly". Again, in 1936, two other companies on the west coast--Indian Cooperative Navigation and Trading Company, and Ratnagar Steam Navigation Company--also became the victims of a rate war at the hands of a British shipping company, and appealed to Scindia for help, which was promptly provided. These actions of Scindia's led to charges of expansionism by British firms and the colonial state. Walchand reacted vigorously:

> Indian shipping is in its early stages of growth and vitality. It has to struggle against the strangling competition of powerful non-Indian rivals not only for expansion in its home waters, but even for its very existence. The wiping out of any Indian shipping venture or its absorption by non-Indians has always been and will always be a serious menace to the development of an Indian merchant navy. It is therefore enlightened self-interest--if not true service--to stand by an Indian shipping concern and prevent it from falling under the axe of the outsiders. It is these broad considerations which have guided hitherto the policy of the

> Scindia Company in its relation to the other Indian shipping companies on the coast. I am sure that you will agree with me that it is the only sound policy which can give true national shipping the strength it needs to live and grow in spite of the deadly onslaughts of powerful outsiders and without even the semblance of support from the government of the country.[115]

In its eagerness to strengthen the hands of Indian shipping, Scindia was instrumental in establishing in 1930 the Indian National Steamship Owners Association, with Walchand as president and Master as secretary. It became the preeminent lobbying organization of Indian shipowners, and continues to this day in that role under the name of Indian National Shipowners Association (INSA).

A second achievement of Scindia, beyond its vessels physically forming the nucleus of a merchant fleet, was the training of Indian talent for maritime activity and providing it with employment opportunities within the limits of its capacity. Britishers had hitherto monopolized all positions other than ratings in India's coastal shipping. Scindia endeavoured to employ Indians as officers and engineers, and to explode the myth fostered by British shipping and colonial interests that Indians were neither fit nor eager to enter these positions. Scindia opened a school for training technical personnel, and followed the practice of getting its foreign employees to train Indians with a view to replacing them. Its supporters in the legislature, even though they failed to get the colonial state to agree to the reservation of the coastal trade, were able to make it bend some on assigning the *Dufferin* as a training ship for developing local talent. Later, this ship became the core of the complex of training facilities established after independence. Scindia took an active role in the governance of the training ship, and provided jobs to Dufferin graduates. It thus played a major role in initiating the re-skilling of Indians and building maritime capabilities. In conformance with its pioneering thrust, Scindia oversaw in 1950 the first modern ship to go overseas completely officered and manned by Indians.

Finally, a crowning accomplishment of Scindia's and a tribute to the vision of its founders was the establishment of the country's first modern shipyard. The founders actively pursued the idea of building a shipyard within months of setting up the firm, but the death of the Norwegian advisor and the subsequent struggle for survival postponed its effective consideration. Not until the mid-1930s was the idea revived, but they found the colonial state uncooperative in allowing it to be situated in Bombay or Calcutta; even the outbreak of the war failed to elicit its assistance. Finally, the Scindias settled on the less important port of Visakhapatnam on the east coast. The shipyard's foundation stone was laid in 1941 by Congress president Dr. Rajendra Prasad, who referred to "the melancholy meanness" of the British attitude towards Indian shipping.[116] As work proceeded briskly on the project, Japanese bombing of the port led to the government ordering closure of the shipyard in 1942 and moving its men and machinery for repair work to Bombay. It was not until 1946 that the shipyard was moved back to Visakhapatnam. On March 14, 1948, independent India's first prime minister, Jawaharlal Nehru, launched the first modern ship built in India. Unfortunately, in view of its losses and the lack of financial assistance from the state, the shipyard came first under majority ownership of the state in 1952 and ultimately under its full ownership in 1956. By the time, the shipyard was transferred to state ownership, it had built eight modern ships of 8000 tons each.

SUMMARY AND CONCLUSIONS

The international regime for shipping has often been described as a liberal or market-based one. That characterization understates the element of power operative in the regime. In the first place, the present regime does not represent some natural order, but comes at the end of a succession of regimes, the formation and maintenance of which have been integrally related to power. Further, power continues to manifest itself in the behaviour of states in the protection and promotion of their merchant fleets. Power thus has been fundamental to the world shipping order and to the behaviour of states in shipping.

As a phenomenon of power, imperialism in its heyday destroyed India's maritime capabilities and thwarted their development. In turn, imperialism gave birth to its nemesis, nationalism. As imperialism weakened in its conflict with nationalism, the nationalist shipping firm of Scindia seized the opportunity to survive. The countervailing power of nationalism as against imperialism was paramount in the survival of Scindia. Through its multifaceted activities, Scindia then made an unenviable contribution to India's mercantile marine capabilities. Beyond that, its leaders actively contributed to consciousness-raising among the public about the importance of the merchant fleet. Still further, as independence approached, Scindia was instrumental in restructuring the thinking on the part of the state about shipping policy and in charting out goals which in due course became an integral part of official thinking in the future.

NOTES

1. Robert Gilpin, *The Political Economy of International Relations* (Princeton: Princeton University Press, 1987), p. 10.

2. UNCTAD, *Review of Maritime Transport 1993*, pp. 20-22.

3. Stephen D. Krasner, "Structural Causes and Regime Consequences: Regimes as Intervening Variables", in Stephen D. Krasner (ed.), *International Regimes* (Ithaca, N.Y.: Cornell University Press, 1983), pp. 1-21 at p. 2.

4. These are dealt with more extensively in Baldev Raj Nayar, "Regimes, Power, and International Aviation", *International Organization*, vol. 49, no. 1 (Winter 1995), pp. 139-70, in which the various proponents of the three approaches are cited.

5. Susan Strange, "Cave! Hic Dragones: A Critique of Regime Analysis", in Krasner (ed.), pp. 337-54 at p. 345.

6. Alan W. Cafruny, *Ruling the Waves: The Political Economy of International Shipping* (Berkeley: University of California Press, 1987).

7. Stephen D. Krasner, *Structural Conflict: The Third World Against Global Liberalism* (Berkeley: University of California Press, 1985), pp. 196-226.

8. Witness the following in Krasner: (1) "Thus, in international shipping, developing countries confronted a market-oriented regime in an institutional environment, which provided them with only limited leverage" (p. 211); (2) "The market-governed and predominantly commercial nature of the international regime for shipping...." (p. 215); (3) "In all areas of shipping, the Third World has challenged prevailing market-oriented principles and norms" (p. 224); (4) "Most of the world's shipping continues to be governed by market-oriented behaviour" (p. 225). Krasner, *Structural Conflict*.

9. On state protection for shipping in the western world, see S.G. Sturmey, *British Shipping and World Competition* (London: The Athlone Press, 1962), chs. II-V, VIII and IX; and Cafruny, chs. 2 and 8.

10. Cited in Cafruny, p. 49.

11. For a summary statement on subsidies provided by the different states for shipping, see UNCTAD document UNCTAD/SDD/SHIP/3 dated May 8, 1995, pp. 19-25; for an earlier statement, see the document TD/B/C.4/301 dated August 25, 1986, pp. 5-13.

12. Cafruny, pp. 75, 85 and 130.

13. Krasner, p. 209

14. Cafruny, p. 26.

15. Lawrence J. White, *International Trade in Ocean Shipping Services: The United States and the World* (Cambridge, Mass.: Ballinger Publishing Company, 1988), pp. 29-39. Kilgour terms the three pillars of US maritime policy as subsidies, cargo preference, and cabotage; see John G. Kilgour, *The U.S. Merchant Marine: National Maritime Policy and Industrial Relations* (New York: Praeger, 1975), ch. 3.

16. White, pp. 30-33. Bilateral agreements of the US have not been confined to these countries. Note the following observation: "by 1979 the FMC [Federal Maritime Commission] had

approved nineteen equal access and pooling agreements between the United States and Argentina, Brazil, Chile, Colombia, and Peru.... United States participation in bilateral cargo-sharing has not been limited to Latin American trades. The FMC has approved pacts with South Korea, the Philippines, and some ports of India and Bangladesh. Intergovernmental bilateral agreements have been concluded with the Soviet Union (1972) and People's Republic of China (1980)". Cafruny, pp. 164-65. Note, however, the irony of "American delegates using UNCTAD committee meetings to plan bilateral deals with foreign shipowners even as they made speeches against bilateralism". *Ibid.*, p. 164.

17. S.A. Lawrence, *International Sea Transport: The Years Ahead* (Lexington, Mass.: Lexington Books, 1972), p. 45.

18. Lawrence, *International Sea Transport*, p. 22.

19. Samuel A. Lawrence, *United States Merchant Shipping Policies and Politics* (Washington, D.C.: The Brookings Institution, 1966), p. 49.

20. White, pp. 69-84. An earlier, well-documented assessment is in Gerald R. Jantscher, *Bread Upon the Waters: Federal Aids to the Maritime Industries* (Washington, D.C.: The Brookings Institution, 1975).

21. Lawrence, *United States Merchant Shipping*, p. 16.

22. Cafruny, pp. 239-40 and 275.

23. See the statements by (1) James Joseph Carey (Federal Maritime Commission), "The Federal Maritime Commission and Shipping Nationalism", in Lawrence Juda (ed.), *Shipping Nationalism and the Future of the United States Liner Industry: The UNCTAD Code and Bilateralism* (Wakefield, Rhode Island: Times Press, 1984), pp. 81-85; (2) Robert A. Ellsworth (Federal Maritime Commission), "The Impact of Rising Nationalism on the U.S. Merchant Marine", in *ibid.*, pp. 125-29; and (3) Jeffrey Shane (Deputy Assistant Secretary for Policy and International Affairs, U.S. Department of Transpor-

tation), "United States Policy Options in an UNCTAD Code World", in *ibid.*, pp. 135-40.

24. On the origins of flags of convenience, the involvement of American leaders in organizing them, and the US defence of them, see Rodney Carlisle, *Sovereignty for Sale: The Origins and Evolution of the Panamanian and Liberian Flags of Convenience* (Annapolis, Maryland: Naval Institute Press, 1981), and Cafruny, ch. 4.

25. Cafruny, pp. 279 and 91.

26. Cafruny, pp. 112-113.

27. Lawrence, *International Sea Transport*, p. 53.

28. Lawrence Juda, *The UNCTAD Liner Code: United States Maritime Policy at the Crossroads* (Boulder, Colorado: Westview Press, 1983), p. 49; and White, p. 111.

29. One keen student of the subject noted in the late 1960s that "The United States Government does not regard itself as a practitioner of flag discrimination" and that "The US tone in the 'Informal Intergovernment Shipping Talks' held in Washington in June 1959 with the OEEC countries has served to discourage any subsequent public discussions of the problem in international meetings". He concluded: "In the area of flag discrimination, there appears to be an incongruity between the regulatory and the promotional elements of US shipping policy. From the simple viewpoint of consistency, it seems that the United States Government should abandon its international efforts at combatting flag discrimination in foreign countries if it is going to continue its cargo preference programme. On the other hand, a phase-out of cargo preference would permit the Government to continue in clear conscience with an effective programme for discouraging flag discrimination". See Philip Earle Franklin, *The Economic Impact of Flag Discrimination in Ocean Transportation* (Ph.D. dissertation; Washington, D.C.: American University, 1968), pp. 129, 336, and 239.

30. Note: "Yet despite opposition to the UNCTAD Liner Code the fact is that the US Government itself has engaged in cargo reservation practices of its own". Lawrence Juda, "The Reagan Administration and United States Maritime Policy", *Journal of Maritime Law and Commerce*, vol. 19, no. 3 (July 1988), pp. 323-48 at p. 335. Interestingly, even as President Carter expressed his opposition to the UNCTAD code in a letter to the US Congress, he called for a more thorough implementation of American cargo preference legislation on government-impelled cargoes. Juda comments: "The Carter Administration like others before it saw no contradiction in opposing cargo sharing involving privately generated cargoes and cargo preference in relation to government generated cargoes." Juda, *The UNCTAD Liner Code*, p. 53.

31. Cafruny, p. 53.

32. Indian Institute of Foreign Trade (IIFT), *Role of Shipping Policy in the Export Strategy of India* (New Delhi: IIFT, 1977), p. 53.

33. Based on data in White, p. 11.

34. Gunnar K. Sletmo and Ernest W. Williams, Jr., *Liner Conferences in the Container Age: U.S. Policy at Sea* (New York: Macmillan, 1981), p. 24.

35. Cafruny, p. 277

36. Sletmo and Williams, Jr., *Liner Conferences in the Container Age: U.S. Policy at Sea.*

37. Sletmo and Williams, pp. 9 and 263.

38. Sletmo and Williams, p. 9.

39. S.G. Sturmey, *Shipping Economics: Collected Papers* (London: Macmillan, 1975), p. 12.

40. Daniel Marx, Jr., *International Shipping Cartels: A Study of Industrial Self-Regulation by Shipping Conferences* (New York: Greenwood Press, 1953), pp. 267 and 299. Interestingly, Marx had come to the same conclusion as the Alexander Committee in the US in 1914, which had noted: "the disadvantages and abuses connected with steamship agreements and conferences as now constituted are inherent, and can only be eliminated by effective government control". *Ibid.*, p. 295.

41. Sturmey, *British Shipping and World Competition*, p. 340.

42. Cafruny, p. 21.

43. Olav Knudsen, *The Politics of International Shipping: Conflict and Interaction in a Transnational Issue-Area, 1946-1968* (Lexington, Mass.: Lexington Books, 1973), p. 62.

44. Note the following in Sletmo and Williams: (1) "The threat of predatory pricing practices was a reality in the early history of conferences when 'fighting ships' were at times used to duplicate the services of independent operators in order to drive them out of the market. Such predatory practices are illegal with or without conferences" (p. 208). (2) "Whatever barriers to entry may have existed in liner services appear to have fallen or to have been seriously eroded" (p. 209). (3) "conferences...have not succeeded in maintaining whatever barriers to entry they may have enjoyed in the past" (p. 210). (4) "liner conferences today do not enjoy any significant degree of market power in U.S. trades" (p. 218). (5) "recent developments in liner shipping, including containerization and the advent of major state-owned fleets on the maritime scene, have greatly reduced the relevance of previous studies in competitive practices. As a result of the weakening of conferences in the last decade, competitive practices are in a state of flux.... predatory or coercive behaviour by conferences in U.S. trades is a thing of the past" (pp. 219-220). (6) "the market power of conferences has been weakening.... actual or potential competition from other lines...has increased greatly over the past few years" (pp. 220-21). (7) "their wings have been progressively clipped over the last couple of decades" (p.234). (8) "Shippers are not only becoming more vocal, but better

organized and more demanding.... several of the most important checks on conference power are steadily growing stronger" (p. 236). (9) "Many of the questions he [Daniel Marx] raised have been resolved since he wrote his classic study" (p. 314).

45. See Morris D. Morris, Toru Matsui, Bipan Chandra and T. Raychaudhri, *Indian Economy in the Nineteenth Century: A Symposium* (Delhi: Delhi School of Economics, 1969).

46. See Martin Deming Lewis, *The British in India: Imperialism or Trusteeship?* (Boston: D.C. Heath, 1962).

47. See Radha Kumud Mukerji, *Indian Shipping: A History of the Sea-Borne Trade and Maritime History of the Indians from the Earliest Times* (Bombay: 1912), and K.M. Panikkar, *A Survey of Indian History* (London: Meridan Books, 1947).

48. Frank Broeze, "Underdevelopment and Dependency: Maritime India During the Raj", *Modern Asian Studies*, vol. 18, no. 3 (1984), pp. 429-457 at p. 432.

49. Giorgio Borsa, "Recent Trends in Indian Ocean Historiography 1500-1800", in Giorgio Borsa (ed.), *Trade and Politics in the Indian Ocean* (New Delhi: Manohar, 1990), pp. 3-14 at p. 5.

50. Borsa, p. 8.

51. Broeze, p. 432.

52. Borsa, p. 8.

53. Borsa, p. 8.

54. Borsa, pp. 11-12.

55. Borsa, p. 12.

56. Broeze, p. 433.

57. Broeze, p. 433.

58. Broeze, p. 435.

59. Broeze, p. 435.

60. N.G. Jog, *Saga of Scindia: Struggle for the Revival of Indian Shipping and Shipbuilding* (Bombay: Scindia Steam Navigation Co., 1969), p. 10.

61. Besides such concerns, the Parliamentary Select Committee referred to the delegitimizing impact on colonial rule: "The native sailors of India to the disgrace of our national morals, on their arrival here, are led into scenes which soon divest them of the respect and awe they had entertained in India for the British character. The contemptuous reports which they disseminate on their return cannot fail to have very unfavourable influence on the minds of our Asiatic subjects, whose reverence for our character, which has hitherto contributed to maintain our supremacy in the East, will be gradually changed for most degrading conceptions". Cited in Jog, p. 11.

62. Broeze, p. 438.

63. Broeze, p. 438.

64. Broeze, p. 441.

65. Broeze, pp. 442-43.

66. Broeze, p. 457.

67. Broeze, p. 444.

68. This brief review of Inchcape's career is drawn from Jog, pp. 12-13, and G.D. Khanolkar, *Walchand Hirachand: Man, His Times and Achievements* (Bombay: Walchand & Co., 1969), pp. 66-70.

69. T.S. Sanjeeva Rao, *A Short History of Modern Indian Shipping* (Bombay: Popular Prakashan, 1965), p. 76; Broeze, p. 443, and Jog, p. 13.

70. Jog, p. 13, and Rao, p. 74.

71. Broeze, pp. 443-44.

72. Cited in Broeze, p. 446.

73. Rao, p. 68.

74. Rao, p. 68.

75. Cited in Rao, p. 69.

76. Rao, pp. 69-70; Jog, pp. 14-15.

77. F.R. Harris, cited in Rao, p. 70.

78. Jog, p. 15.

79. Rao, p. 72.

80. Khanolkar, pp. 59-60.

81. Rao, p. 74.

82. Broeze, p. 446.

83. Rao, p. 78.

84. Rao, p. 79.

85. Rao, pp. 79-80.

86. Jog, p. 1.

87. Khanolkar, p. 185.

88. Khanolkar, pp. 185-86.

89. Jog, p. 26.

90. Broeze, p. 448.

91. Cited in Khanolkar, p. 73.

92. Jog, p 27, and Khanolkar, pp. 176 and 179.

93. India, Commerce Department, *Report of the Reconstruction Policy Sub-Committee on Shipping* (New Delhi: Government of India Press, 1947), p. 12

94. Broeze, p. 457.

95. Khanolkar, p.183.

96. Jog, p. 32, and Khanolkar, p. 184. One retrospective statement puts the offer on purchase of shares at four times their market value; see the speech by Scindia chairman Dharamsey M. Khatau, in *Eastern Economist*, February 25, 1955, p. 317.

97. Jog, p. 32.

98. Khanolkar, p. 187. For a slight variation on the speech, see Jog, p. 33 and Rao, p. 85.

99. Khanolkar, pp. 189-90.

100. Khanolkar, pp. 192-93.

101. Khanolkar, pp. 193-94.

102. Khanolkar, p. 196.

103. Jog, p. 90, and Khanolkar, pp. 265-66.

104. Broeze, pp. 452-53.

105. *Report of the Reconstruction Policy Sub-Committee on Shipping*, pp. 37 and 42.

106. Jog, p. 122.

107. Cited in Jog, p. 1.

108. Jog, p. 86. For a fuller treatment of Indian attempts for coastal reservation under colonial rule, though fruitless in the end, see Rao, pp. 92-123.

109. Jog, p. 67.

110. Jog, pp. 67 and 84; Rao, p. 118.

111. Rao, p. 112.

112. Rao, p. 114.

113. Jog, pp. 111-18.

114. Jog, pp. 93-102; Rao, pp. 86-89; and Khanolkar, pp. 267-99.

115. Jog, p. 96.

116. Jog, p. 132.

CHAPTER III

THE ERA OF SLOW GROWTH, 1947-1960: THE MARKET-STATE RELATIONSHIP IN TRANSITION

From a long-range perspective, the period from 1947 to 1960 represents what might fairly be considered the era of slow growth in India's expansion of shipping capacity. On the other hand, this assessment may legitimately be contested, for during that period India's tonnage more than doubled, expanding from 0.32M grt in 1948 to 0.75M grt in 1959 at an annual growth rate of 8.2 per cent. Yet, these figures can be somewhat misleading since the starting base was extremely small. For three decisive reasons, the characterization of the period as representing slow though steady growth seems valid.

First, the government had in 1947 accepted as national policy the achievement of the goal of a share of 50 per cent for Indian shipping in the country's overseas trades within five to seven years, in addition to 100 per cent share of the coastal trade. To that end, it had accepted the target of 2M grt at the latest by 1954. In actuality, by that date India had acquired only one-fourth of the tonnage target; the decade of the 1950s ended with capacity at only 0.75M grt. Even for the accomplishment of half the targeted tonnage, the country had to wait until 1962. Second, the country's decision-makers repeatedly acknowledged that the targets for tonnage acquisition that the planning machinery established were exceedingly modest; however, achievement still fell short of even the modest targets. Third, the share of Indian shipping in the country's overseas trades remained at abysmally low levels; at the end of the decade it had reached only about 10 per cent, and even in the coastal trade foreign shipping continued to have a considerable role. It could be maintained that the goal of 2M grt initially accepted as part of the national consensus on shipping was unrealistic. It is true that the rapid recovery and enormous advance of the traditional maritime powers in expanding shipping tonnage after the end of World War II was not within India's means and capabilities, but the initial goal was technically not unreasonable from the viewpoint of India's capacity.

The key theoretical rivals in any explanation for the slow growth are the international system and domestic structures. In this instance, both were implicated, and in substantial measure in that the impact of neither can be ignored in the outcome. Still, although the external environment was restrictive and placed limitations on the opportunities for Indian shipping companies on international routes, yet the real determinants for the slow growth in shipping capacity lay nearer at home. In one respect, the slowness of growth is a surprise, for shipping now had a state that was sympathetic to national aspirations for an expanded merchant fleet. Indeed, the state itself shared these aspirations and there was evident a consensus over the extent of expansion necessary. However, it is the thesis of this chapter that the slow growth was related to the fact that in some key respects the policies of the state were in transition, with the state unsure about their direction. The lack of policy clarity created uncertainty among major actors, even as the state had to function under severe constraints related to the situation of underdevelopment. In exploring this thesis, the chapter looks at (1) the dialectics between goals and constraints in development as well as the initial consensus on goals; (2) the perils of negotiating with foreign shipping from a position of weakness; (3) the interaction between the state and private sector before the planning era; (4) the crises in planning under the constraints of underdevelopment; and, finally, (5) the conflict between the state and private sector, leading to the unravelling of the consensus.

THE DIALECTICS OF DEVELOPMENT: GOALS AND CONSTRAINTS

In considerable measure, economic performance rests on the nature of the state and its policies. The state is fundamentally the ensemble of institutions with overall responsibility for the integration and adaptation of society. In their endeavour to foster the adaptation of society to its environment, states establish and modify institutions and policies that structure and organize economic and political activity towards that end.

Through establishing institutions and enacting policies, states have the aim of "decreasing uncertainty, reducing transaction costs, and thereby facilitating economic activity".[1] How successful a state is in fostering the adaptation of society to its environment depends on the nature of state power, which can be considered to consist of two analytically distinct elements--autonomy and capacity. The element of state autonomy involves the ability of the state to define goals or preferences, where "the degree of consensus within the state is a key determinant of its ability to define preferences independently of leading economic interest groups". The element of state capacity, on the other hand, involves the ability of the state to implement goals on which a consensus has been reached, where the key determinants are "the effectiveness and cohesiveness of government institutions".[2]

The defining characteristic of former colonial societies at independence is their economic underdevelopment. At the point of departure of their colonial masters, the economies of these societies are largely agricultural, integrated with the metropolitan economies in order to serve colonial interests, while their populations mostly live at subsistence levels. For the successor post-colonial state, some economic goals or preferences can be conceptualized as already given, flowing out of the very condition of underdevelopment. These goals are summarized in the term development, revolving essentially around industrialization. In aiming for development, post-colonial states are not guided by some frivolous motivation of prestige to emulate the advanced countries. Rather, situated as they are in a world that is part developed and rich and part backward and poor, they have little choice but to focus on development. They are impelled to choose development by considerations both of national security in relation to the outside world and of political legitimacy among socially mobilized populations internally.[3] There is thus considerable consensus among new states that have emerged from colonialism on the basic goal of transformation of their agricultural and backward economies to industrial and advanced economies. Often, because of the drastic disparity between the developed and underdeveloped societies, new states tend to aim high in their push for development.

The same condition of underdevelopment that sets up the goal of development for post-colonial societies, however, also imposes constraints on their states to break out of that condition and to achieve the desired goal. A backward economy caught in a low-level equilibrium trap suffers not only from the scarcity of resources required for investment but also from the lack of appropriate institutions to foster development. There thus issue out of the condition of underdevelopment both the goal and the constraints. New states evolve institutions and policy in the context of the dialectics between the goal and constraints, and in the nature of the case there is a transitional period of trial and error, tension and conflict, until a settled policy regime and institutional arrangements are arrived at. In this period of transition, in the meantime, economic actors may face uncertainty, which understandably is likely to affect investment and performance adversely.

THE INITIAL CONSENSUS ON GOALS AND ITS LIMITATIONS

On August 15, 1947, colonial rule ended and power passed to a composite national government, centred around the Congress party, with Jawaharlal Nehru as India's first prime minister. However, prior to that event, Nehru had been inducted in September 1946 as head of an interim government in the rush to the withdrawal of colonial power. Although the Congress party inherited a colonial state that was largely intact, the party itself had led a genuine national liberation movement. It was a movement sustained over nearly three-quarters of a century, turning into a mass movement and mass organization in the 1920s under the leadership of Mahatma Gandhi. A series of mass agitations brought ever-widening circles of political support for the nationalist movement. Millions took part in popular agitations, hundreds of thousands went to prison in the cause of the movement, and thousands got killed for it. Independence had not come easy to India. The last of the major agitations, the Quit India movement of 1942, turned violent as the British in a final bid to crush the nationalist movement made a preemptive attack. But that agitation shook British rule to its roots, a development which was kept secret through wartime censorship. "India attained independence through revolution", says an American scholar, and "the mid-war Quit India movement climaxed India's nationalist revolution, which overthrew a powerful, effective regime".[4] Meanwhile, World War II weakened Great Britain, loosening its hold on the colonies.

The Congress party was, however, not just committed to achieving political independence, but importantly to industrialization as well. Indeed, the aim of industrialization goes back to the beginnings of the Congress party, long before the Soviet revolution. During the liberal phase of the Congress party, the political leadership took industrialization through large-scale industries to be a self-evident proposition, and "by the end of the nineteenth century, the demand for rapid industrialization of the country along modern industries had assumed national proportions".[5] In one interpretation, the transformation of the nationalist movement from moderation to militancy during the first quarter of the twentieth century resulted, not simply from disappointment at the pace of political reform, but also from a sense of betrayal of the trust reposed in the colonial authorities that they would bring about the industrialization of India on the pattern of Great Britain. Indeed, it was not just that Britain was perceived as doing nothing to assist in industrialization, but it was seen as deliberately thwarting such development.[6] Subsequently, the national scene became dominated by political struggles, but industrial and other leaders put forward plans for the country's industrialization.

If the leadership at the helm of the new state shared a consensus on the aim of industrialization, it was helped in arriving at a consensus on goals in regard to shipping by the report of a committee set up under the aegis of the former colonial state. However, the establishment of that committee by the colonial state was not unrelated to the course of the nationalist movement. The first among the plans for the country's development during the pre-independence period was put forward by Dr. M. Visesvarayya, a great visionary engineer, who in 1934 advocated the rapid industrialization of the country through a ten-year programme, designed to increase industrial production five-fold. In 1938, the Congress party appointed the National Planning Committee, with Nehru as its chairman, to work out a development plan. It did a lot of useful research work on planning, but it could not complete its work and did not submit a final report as Nehru, the inspiration behind the setting up of the committee, went to jail after the outbreak of

World War II. However, with its many meetings and publications, the path-breaking endeavours of the committee had enormous educative value in making Indians plan-conscious. It also evoked imitation, as business groups cooperated to develop the 15-year Tata-Birla plan, with industrialization as its major thrust. Even the colonial state moved in this direction, partly perhaps to pre-empt nationalist activity in planning.

During the war, the colonial state appointed a Postwar Reconstruction Committee to plan for development after the war. In recognition of the importance of shipping, this committee set up a Reconstruction Policy Committee on Shipping, among the members of which were Walchand Hirachand and M.A. Master. There was apparent some contrition on the part of the colonial state after decades of neglect. A preliminary statement recognized that, in the light of the size of the country and its vast coastline along with its strategic location, "India possesses a distressingly small number of deep sea ships", and further that "the vulnerability of India's position has been revealed by the stress of war time conditions". Walchand presented an extensive analysis of the condition of shipping and spelled out the desired goals at the first meeting of the committee in 1944;[7] his proposals were to find substantial echo in subsequent recommendations. To investigate the subject in depth, the committee established in November 1945 the Reconstruction Policy Sub-Committee on Shipping under the chairmanship of Sir C.P. Ramaswami Aiyar. The Aiyar committee brought forward its report in March 1947. Unusual among government reports for its lack of bureaucratic language and written in a vigorous style, its text of 47 pages provided an incisive analysis of the shipping scene. Part lament over the fate Indian shipping had met in the past, part condemnation of British colonial policy for its role in that fate, part formulation of a national shipping doctrine, and part agenda-setter for the future, the report was a landmark analysis of the desperate condition of India's shipping.[8] For the next two decades, the report became a constant reference point to measure achievement, and on that account alone deserves serious consideration.

Aiming for Maritime Power: Pointing to the strategic location of the country in the Indian Ocean and its large volume of trade, the committee in its report took the position that "India is a great maritime country", which deserved to "have a large and powerful navy both of supply and of defence". Sadly, for it, however, India had neither, and it immediately linked their absence to state policy: "Every maritime country has...its own national shipping policy. India alone is a glaring exception to this universal rule" (p.1). Underlining the critical role played by the state in the development of other maritime fleets, it observed: "India continued to remain a glaring exception to the recognition of the responsibility of the State to develop the National Merchant Marine. It took no action. Indian shipping did not grow--could not grow" (p.10). Frequently using the word "tragedy" to describe Indian shipping's parlous condition, the committee stated: "It is however a tragedy that what other maritime countries in the world did to build up their national shipping India did not do" (p.3). The consequence was that India has "practically no share of [its] very large overseas trade.... Indian shipping has practically no footing in India's overseas trades.... Indian shipping is conspicuous by its absence in the overseas trades of India" (pp.31,38). Instead, British shipping controlled "the entire carriage of the trade between India and the United Kingdom", hauling over 95 per cent of UK exports to India and over 99.5 per cent of Indian exports to the UK (p.31). Even in its coastal trade, Indian shipping had a share of only 25 per cent (pp.37,42). In sum, "only meagre and insignificant share of the trade is carried by national shipping" (p.42).

No doubt, the committee was emboldened by the imminent end to colonial rule, but its report was nonetheless brutally frank in analysing the root cause of the condition of Indian shipping: "India had no national government. India had therefore no national shipping policy" (p.3). It charged that "the Government of India have more or less been pursuing a policy of indifference during the last 25 years" (p.21). It reiterated that point by noting that "the main obstacle to the development of an Indian Mercantile Marine is", apart from the dominant position of British India Steamship Navigation Company (BISN), "the utter indifference and unconcern of the Government of India to protect Indian shipping from the relentless and powerful opposition" (p.19). Its indictment, however, went further than the simple avoidance of positive action by the colonial state to assist Indian shipping. For, at bottom, there lay the state's complicity in the destruction of Indian shipping in favour of British shipping: "the Government of India missed not a single opportunity to extend its patronage during this last century to this British Company [BISN] and thus encouraged it in every way to act against the national economic interests of the country" (p.11). In its account of discrimination on the part of the colonial state, it referred to the award of generous mail contracts exclusively to BISN, the denial of the right to Indian shipping companies to even bid for carriage of government cargo, and the penalization of government employees if they travelled by ships not belonging to P&O (pp.11-12).

In a devastating assessment of British policy, the committee underlined that it was "a tragedy" that the state took no effective action when Indian shipping was wiped out by the "ruthless freight wars", "ruthless rate-cutting", and "ruinous competition" (pp.11-12,14). In this manner, "British shipping thus continued to raise its edifice on the ruins of Indian shipping" (p.12). The committee summed up the relationship of British domination and policy to the condition of national shipping thus: "Its history has been, for the National Shipping Companies, a sad story of ceaseless struggle and sacrifice; for the people of the land it is a painful chapter of bitter disappointment at the lack of response from the Government of India to their demand for stability and expansion; and for the Government of India it is a tragic tale of broken promises, unredeemed assurances and neglected opportunities" (p.10). Further, "owing to the powerful position of the British Company and the utter indifference of the Government of India to give Indian shipping the protection that it urgently needed, it was able to decide whether any Indian steamships shall ply for traffic at all on any route and that it was within the B.I.'s power at any time to force them into liquidation and bankruptcy" (p.15). It underlined that BISN, by virtue of its dominant position and "its powerful financial resources and the ruthless freight wars, wiped out one Indian shipping company after another from the coastal waters of India" (p.11).

The committee's powerful recommendations matched the desperate state of Indian shipping. Situating the country's problem in the international context in which it functioned, it warned: "The world is progressing. India alone is standing still. The Government of India will have to watch with the utmost vigilance how other nations are adding to their fleet and capturing international trade" (p.27). Its key message was that "India must build up her own national shipping to carry her own cargo in the overseas trades. All other considerations are subsidiary to this main objective which Government should have to keep in view" (p.32). Its point of departure for national policy was exceedingly simple: "India should adopt a national shipping policy similar to the policies adopted by the important maritime countries of the world" (p.46). Consequently, consistent with accepted international norms, the entire coastal trade ought to be forthwith reserved for national shipping (p.29). In respect of overseas trades, it pointed out: "The principle, which is strongly emphasised in the modern world of shipping, is that a country should carry in her own national bottoms at least 50 per cent of her maritime trades" (pp.29,46).

Following from that general principle, the committee was insistent that India should achieve its share of 50 per cent in the overseas trades rapidly, within the relatively short time frame of five to seven years (p.39). In some respects, influenced by the trend of the times, it took an expansive view of what India's share in the trades ought to be. More precisely, it recommended that "hundred per cent of the purely coastal trade of India, seventy five per cent of India's trade with Burma and Ceylon and with the geographically adjacent countries, fifty per cent of India's distant trades and thirty per cent of the trades formerly carried in axis vessels in the Orient should be secured for Indian shipping in the next five to seven years" (p.46). Some elements of the aim were particular to the time. The larger than half the share in the adjacent trades could be ascribed to either an overly broad conception of India's interests in the region, or a recognition of the weak capabilities of the other states in the region and a desire to preclude further entrenchment of British shipping in the trade. The desire to have a share in the Far East trades grew out of the immediate postwar situation, where European and American shipping companies were asserting dominance in the trades vacated by the axis powers. Subsequent policy in independent India readily shed these extraneous elements. The core aim was the total reservation of the coastal trade and half of the external trades for Indian shipping, and the committee saw this as consistent with internationally accepted principles. Even though India has not articulated a shipping doctrine as such, this central aim lies at the heart of it. The committee applied the same criteria of India's legitimate share to the carriage of passengers by ship. Converting these general aspirations on cargo and passenger shares into shipping capacity, the committee estimated that a tonnage of 2 million grt would be required, and it urged that "the Government of India should do all that is possible to ensure that this 2 million tons is acquired before the end of the 7 year period" (p.40).

As to how to proceed in the acquisition of the necessary tonnage, the committee was not completely averse to giving a trial to the government's preference for negotiations with the British government. It, however, reminded the decision-makers that "India has rather a bitter experience of the efficacy of a policy of negotiation for the purpose of national tonnage". Regardless, it was certain that "the policy of negotiations alone cannot develop national shipping", and it urged that "Like other important maritime countries of the world, the Government of India will have to take a militant view of their responsibilities and obligations towards national shipping" (p.40). It reminded the government that Indian shipping had received no protection "whatsoever", and asked "with all the emphasis at our command" for it to "be prepared to adopt all measures, including financial assistance for the development of Indian shipping" (p.41).

In terms of institution-building, the committee recommended the establishment of an Indian Shipping Board, on the model of the US Maritime Commission, as an independent body to serve as "the spear-point of policy locally and internationally", to regulate the shipping industry, and to administer aid and subsidies (pp.32-33,46). It favoured construction subsidies to shipowners for ships built in India and wanted every possible encouragement to Indian enterprises to increase tonnage (pp.42-43). In all this, "the one fundamental fact that should weigh [is] that Indian tonnage must be enabled, within a very short time, to carry a very substantial portion of India's overseas trade and a fair portion of the carrying trades of the world" (p.33).

On the question of what constituted Indian shipping, the committee took a strongly nationalist view. This question had arisen earlier in the 1930s when a rate war had developed between the Bombay Steam Navigation Company and two Indian shipping companies. At that time, Bombay Steam Navigation claimed that it was just as Indian as the Scindias because it included Indians among its shareholders and directors. Walchand Hirachand referred the matter to Mahatma Gandhi for advice. Gandhi took the position that "only those concerns can be regarded as Swadeshi whose control, direction and management either by a Managing Director or by Managing Agents are in Indian hands". He, however, did not object to the employment of foreign capital or of foreign talent, "but only on condition that such capital and such talents are exclusively under the control, direction and management of Indians and are used in the interests of India".[9] That position was heartily adopted by the capitalist class, and was endorsed by the committee on shipping. Although there were two dissenting notes, the committee had by majority decided that the term "'Indian shipping' should denote shipping *owned, controlled* and *managed* by the nationals of India" (p.28).

Even though the committee had been initially appointed by the colonial authorities, its report was remarkable for the thrust it gave to national self-reliance in the shipping sector. It constituted a ringing affirmation of the nationalist position, articulated forcefully between the two world wars. For that reason, the committee has subsequently often been referred to as the National Shipping Policy Committee, notwithstanding its colonial origins, while its report has been described as the *magna carta* of Indian shipping.[10]

The Limitations of the Report: The report of the committee on shipping had been eloquent on the determination of national goals in reference to the place of the country in the international maritime environment. However, it did not directly confront the question of the mechanism to be employed for the organization and coordination of economic activity in the industry. It did not raise the question of whether the tonnage targeted should be achieved by the market or the state, that is, by the private sector or the public sector, or both. Though it went unstated, the fundamental presumption was that the economic system would continue to be organized basically by the private sector. In so far as economic activity in the private sector was concerned, the committee set its face against any restrictions on its growth, for "the crux of the problem lies in the fact that Indian enterprise needs every possible encouragement to increase Indian tonnage" (pp.42-43). While it was not averse to the state seeing that small companies are not ousted from the market, it saw absolutely no justification for "even considering the question as to what limitations and restrictions can be usefully imposed on Indian shipping companies in their growth from infancy to early adolescence and then to full manhood". It reminded the government that "in none of the maritime countries of the world is there any legal or other bar against the expansion of tonnage owned by its nationals" (p.43). The committee may not have realized it, but in taking that position it was running counter to an important trend in the country's political economy, which would become a source of considerable contention in the subsequent two decades.

Although the nationalist movement was united on the goal of industrialization and the Indian capitalist class was a quiet ally of the movement, there was no consensus on the state-market relationship in the organization and coordination of economic activity. Indeed, there was some apprehension in the business community about this aspect, and with adequate cause. It is true that from the turn of the twentieth century, the nationalist movement had emphasized Swadeshi as against foreign industry, and under Gandhi's leadership it had further made Swadeshi the centrepiece of the Congress party's economic platform.

However, in the late 1920s, a younger and more assertive group within the Congress led by Jawaharlal Nehru pressed for socialism as the appropriate ideology for the party. While the Congress party refused to endorse socialism, under Gandhi's persuasion it accepted, in order to prevent the alienation of the leftist group, a wider role for the state. In 1931, the Congress party at its Karachi session passed the Resolution on Fundamental Rights and Economic Policy, which declared: "The State shall own or control key industries and services, mineral resources, railways, waterways, shipping and other means of public transport". The Karachi resolution became a landmark in the evolution of the party's economic policy, and a reference point subsequently for assessing performance of the government. Later, the National Planning Committee under Nehru's chairmanship, although it did not issue a final report, was in agreement on state ownership and control of defence industries, while "regarding other key industries, the majority were of opinion that they should be state-owned, but a substantial majority of the committee considered that state control would be sufficient".[11] After independence, policy on state ownership evolved with the changing configuration of political power in the state. Until the debate on it was finally settled, it was a source of uncertainty for the capitalist class, shipowners not excluded.

From Committee Report to National Consensus: The committee on shipping submitted its report to the interim government in March 1947, a time when India was in the midst of momentous convulsions and decisions about the political future of the country. Within less than four months after the submission of the committee's report, notwithstanding its other distractions the government endorsed its recommendations in an historic resolution, published on July 12, 1947, about a month before independence and accession to full power. The resolution promised a new departure by fully endorsing the view that "India like other important maritime countries must adopt a dynamic policy with regard to her shipping". Expressing agreement with the committee's recommendation on the desired cargo shares for India in the various trades, and implicitly with the tonnage requirements to achieve those shares, it assured the shipping industry that "it is the intention of the Government of India to assist Indian shipping as far as possible in this direction". It, however, favoured opening negotiations with the British government and shipping interests to see "how Indian aspirations could best be met". While taking the committee's conception of Indian shipping as that owned, controlled and managed by Indian nationals as "the ideal one and should be the ultimate objective", the government decided that an Indian shipping company was one that had at least 75 per cent of its capital owned by Indians and all of its directors Indians. The government also accepted the recommendation on setting up an Indian Shipping Board.[12]

India had thus on the eve of its independence developed a fairly mature national consensus on shipping, the core elements of which were: (1) reservation of the entire coastal trade for its shipping; (2) a share of half of the external trades; and (3) self-reliance in the ownership, control and management of its shipping. India had rejected the domination of its trades by foreign shipping as well as the adverse imbalance in its share in those trades; equally, it refused to become a base for "flags of convenience". India's conception of its merchant fleet was that it would be national and that it would have its rightful share in the trades. Curiously, this consensus was silent on the relationship between market and state. That was apparently the result of the government at the time being a national, not a single party, one in which issues bearing on the market-state relationship were seen as disruptive, particularly when the new state was waiting to be born. For its part, the shipping industry took the government's promise on assistance as an indication of its eagerness to help the shipping companies within the existing market framework.

THE PITFALLS OF NEGOTIATING FROM WEAKNESS: DISAPPOINTMENT AND DISCRIMINATION

The goal of building a merchant fleet of 2M grt within a matter of five to seven years was certainly an ambitious one, for only five countries at the time had more than 2M grt; even France had less than 2M. Apart from physically acquiring the tonnage, the ambitious goal meant that India would need to have few or no barriers against its participation in the external trades unlike the earlier situation when it was completely barred from them. Scindia's exertions to change that situation in the 1930s had come to nought by the lack of responsiveness on the part of BISN and the colonial state.

Consequent to receiving the report of the shipping committee, the government opened negotiations with the British government with a view to obtaining a fair share of the India-UK trade. At the suggestion of the British government that the matter be settled through negotiations between British shipowners and Indian shipowners, the Indian government despatched a five-member delegation to London under the leadership of Walchand.[13] When negotiations started on July 16, 1947, at the P&O headquarters, there seemed to be no common ground between the two sides. The Indian side took as its mandate the achievement of the goal of 2M grt and was eager to explore how British shipowners could assist in reaching it, particularly through the allocation of a fair share in the India-UK trade.

The British side, however, would have none of it. Sir William Currie, chairman of BISN and P&O, underlined Britain's "difficult economic situation, which requires us to maintain maximum exports, including our shipping services". He opposed any general debate or negotiations about cargo shares between nations "as a matter of principle", indeed remarking that "we British shipowners cannot accept in principle the validity of your aspirations". Instead, he favoured only discussions on concrete proposals between shipowners within the relevant conferences.[14] The Indian delegates were told bluntly to first obtain the required tonnage before laying claims for a share in the overseas trade.[15] At that, the meeting broke down, with Walchand declaring that British shipping interests "are determined to continue their domination in future as in the past over India's overseas trade".[16]

Any progress towards a greater share in India's external trades now depended on action in India. As it moved towards independence on August 15, 1947, the breakup of the subcontinent into two states, along with the breakdown of law and order and the massive movement of refugees that followed it, overwhelmed the government, forcing it to focus its immediate attention on the survival of the new state. However, there had been in the meantime some movement on the shipping scene. Notwithstanding the difficulties in obtaining ships from the UK and US, India had been able to quickly expand its tonnage from 98,286 grt at the end of the war to 249,261 grt by the end of colonial rule.[17] With independence on the horizon, India Steamship Company, which changed from tramping to liner shipping, established regular India-UK/Continent services from Calcutta in 1946 and was joined by Scindia from Bombay in 1948. Scindia opened regular services to the US in March 1947. With independence, the two liner companies of India Steamship and Scindia were admitted to the India-UK/Continent conference but only as associate, and not full, members; they could attend conference meetings but were not allowed to vote in them. They were further restricted to operating no more than eight ships each whereas they wanted the right to run 17 ships each; further, they were barred from employing chartered vessels.[18]

The lack of voting power soon emerged as significant when a new development in 1949 threatened the future of India's two liner companies. As Indonesia asserted its independence, following the outbreak of war between the Dutch forces and the nationalists, the Dutch shipowners in the area were left with considerable capacity but little cargo. Until then India had not been important for them, but now they asked in compensation for a bigger share in the Indian trade. On their request being denied, they launched on what has been called "the Dutch freight war", in which the rates per ton were reduced drastically from 90 shillings to 1s 6d. In the process, considerable havoc was inflicted on India's two shipping lines. To put an end to the freight war, the British-dominated conference offered 45 per cent of the trade between India and the Continent to the Dutch shipowners, while conceding only 8 per cent to the Indian lines. The generosity of the British lines to the Dutch shipowners at the cost of India was motivated by the larger need to protect British shipping's interests in relation to the participation of the Dutch lines in Britain's trades in Europe.[19] The Indian lines protested against the humiliating treatment only to be told that they did not have any voting rights. In other words, India was without rights in its own trades, while foreign shipping lines arrogated to themselves the right to allocate shares in them. With the political backing of the Indian government, the Indian lines were eventually able to settle the issue to their minimum satisfaction.[20]

Effective April 1950, the two Indian lines were accepted as full members by the India-UK/Continent conference, but the number of ships that each could deploy was restricted to twelve, far below what they wanted, though they were now free to employ chartered ships.[21] However, this did not mean an end to restrictive and discriminatory practices against Indian companies. Indeed, the entire period of the 1950s was marked by obstructionism on the part of foreign shipping, particularly British shipping, through denying Indian lines membership in the conferences en route between India and the UK/Continent. Literally in every year of the 1950s, the chairmen of Scindia and of India Steamship at their annual shareholders' meetings dealt with the subject of Indian lines being barred from picking up cargo at Colombo, Aden, or Sudan on their way to the UK/Continent through denial of membership in the relevant conferences. Similarly, they could not carry traffic to these ports on the way back to India from the UK or Continent. Being thus barred meant uneconomic operation of their vessels as they could not fill up empty space. Again, Indian lines were denied membership in the conferences between Western Italy and Burma, Ceylon or Pakistan.[22]

What rankled the Indian lines most was the disparity in treatment meted out to them and that received by foreign lines in the Indian trades. As late as 1958, chairman Ramaswami Mudaliar of India Steamship was still angrily referring to such treatment:

> Year after year, in these addresses, I have referred to the unsuccessful applications for membership to various conferences which Indian lines have made. Indian lines have not been admitted to the conference of lines trading from ports like those of Ceylon, Burma, Egypt and other ports on our direct route, to the ports of the United Kingdom or the Continent. But the Indian trade is a happy hunting field for shipping of numerous foreign countries.... I venture to state, with due deliberation, that the shipping lines of certain European countries are readily accorded by the conference the privilege of calling at several Indian ports irrespective of the volume of traffic or the number of lines that are already serving these ports. A solid front of opposition is presented to a reasonable demand by the Indian lines of serving the wayside ports. When this attitude is combined with the deliberate policy of accusing Indian lines of resorting to flag discrimination on the flimsiest of flimsy grounds, an intolerable situation arises and a determined effort is needed to remedy this state of affairs.[23]

The next year, he expressed his frustration again that negotiations had led nowhere. Further, he was distressed at the impudence of the British-dominated Colombo conference when it extended its coverage to all of Ceylon in order to prevent Indian lines from calling at the other ports on the excuse that they were not members of the Colombo conference. He commented with sarcasm on these actions as "a supreme example of the freedom of the seas and non-discrimination of flags which some of the lines constantly speak of". Finally, in an act of defiance, he announced that the Indian lines considered the Colombo conference's decision "as adding insult to injury and they have now both definitely declared that they will call at all the Ceylon ports including Colombo as necessity demands and that they will not be bound by any rules of that Conference" except for freight rates.[24] His counterpart at Scindia, Dharamsey Khatau, reiterated the determination of the Indian lines to stand up to the conferences and warned that "unless Indian shipping can make its voice felt in the various conferences that govern the different trade routes of the world and thus influence the various freight rates, India's trade with the world is bound to suffer".[25]

Although the Indian lines had the sympathy of the government in their predicament, it would seem that the government was rather timid in dealing with the restrictive practices adopted by the conferences against their interests. It even meekly suggested to the Indian companies that it did not have a quid pro quo to use in bargaining with British companies in according a better treatment to the Indian lines.[26] There is no doubt that another country, like the US, would have found the situation intolerable and acted swiftly.

India did not adopt any cargo preference measures, perhaps because the limited size of the fleet did not provide adequate incentive for the adoption of this means. It was perhaps also immobilized by the fragmentation of decision-making within the government between the departments that advocated shippers' interests as against those of the shipowners. Besides, the government was apparently kept on the defensive by the constant barrage of propaganda launched by the traditional maritime powers, particularly Britain, about flag discrimination. The chairmen of the two Indian lines drew a pointed contrast between the scrupulous behaviour of the Indian government and the restrictive practices of the foreign governments which had brought their shipping companies to their present status. Further, they underlined the disparity between the rhetoric and practice of the foreign lines, stating that "far more important and inexplicable is the fact that no reference is made to the restrictive business practices which are resorted to by some of the shipping companies which have established themselves in the past".[27]

The evidence is clear on the point that the discriminatory restrictive practices of foreign shipping lines were certainly a factor in the low share of Indian lines in the country's trades during the 1950s. However, it would seem that the real source of the weak performance of the Indian lines lay in their failure to build an adequate tonnage.

THE STATE AND PRIVATE SECTOR BEFORE PLANNING

The period between the end of World War II and the beginning of economic planning was a tumultuous era. Even before the war formally came to an end, the colonial state released the Congress party leaders from incarceration. Soon negotiations began in order to bring colonial rule to an end. In September 1946, an interim government was installed with Nehru at its head. A few months later, the Congress party's political antagonist with its demand for the partition of the subcontinent, the Muslim League, entered the interim government, making for a thoroughly stalemated polity. In early 1947, Finance Member Liaquat Ali Ḳhan, representing the Muslim League, cleverly struck a severe blow to the Indian capitalist class with his "soak-the-rich" budget; with his own socialist inclinations, Nehru could hardly object. The heavy taxation disrupted the financial markets. Meanwhile, outside the corridors of government, virtual civil war prevailed across north India. Finally, on June 3, 1947 the various parties agreed to the partition of the country. Within less than two and a half months, the two states of India and Pakistan were born out of the colonial state. What had been an integrated economy was now disrupted by being divided into two separate ones.

The partition was followed by the breakdown of law and order and the movement of millions of refugees between the two countries. It also resulted in a 15-month war between the two successor states over Kashmir. To ward off the threat of complete disintegration, India also brought about a quick merger into the new state of the 562 princely states, many of which had aspirations for sovereignty. The political engineer of the merger project was Sardar Vallabhbhai Patel, a friend of the capitalist class and the powerful leader in control of the Congress party organization. From the birth of the new state until Patel's death near the end of 1950, India was virtually governed by a duumvirate consisting of Nehru and Patel. Patel's aversion to Nehru's socialism and the division of the Congress party into roughly equal groupings behind each leader, meant no drastic change in economic policy and a continuation of the economic status quo, which lasted into the early 1950s.

In shipping, the end of the war had been followed by a return of the commandeered ships back to the shipping companies. The Indian shipowners took to expanding their fleets with gusto, partly to meet the pent-up demand from the war and partly in expectation of an enlarged Indian mercantile marine. Even before independence, the interim government had attempted to facilitate the expansion of the merchant fleet through negotiations in London. However, that effort ended in failure because of British refusal to cooperate in achieving the target of 2 million grt. When the talks collapsed, the Indian government informed the British Secretary of State for India that it had substantially accepted the recommendations of the committee on shipping. It further let it be known that, without losing any further time, it was "pledged to give fullest possible assistance to Indian shipping companies in their endeavour to obtain within the next few years the legitimate share in the coastal and other trades".[28] At the time, government policy proceeded on the assumption that the responsibility for the development of national shipping basically lay with the private sector, while the state was obligated to assist it in the achievement of the agreed targets.[29]

About two and a half months after independence, the Commerce Minister, C.H. Bhabha, who had responsibility for shipping, made a series of important announcements on government policy at a conference of shipping interests on November 3, 1947. First, he declared that the government had accepted the reservation of coastal shipping for national shipowners and the target of two million tons for the national merchant fleet. Second, he went on to commit the government to expeditious action on the implementation of these two aims as also on rectifying weaknesses, such as scarcity of trained personnel, and undertaking such measures as were necessary to protect Indian shipping at home and abroad. Third, he signalled a more active role for government, which seemed to mark a fundamental departure from the earlier policy of sole reliance on the private sector. He revealed that the government intended to promote the development of shipping through the mechanism of joint ventures between state and private sector. In such joint ventures, which were to be called shipping corporations, the state would hold 51 per cent of the equity while the remainder would come from private companies or the public.[30]

Apart from the expressed hope of attracting a greater inflow of private capital into shipping, the underlying rationale for the move to establish this type of mixed enterprise or mixed economy was to combine the presumably large resources of the state with the technological and managerial expertise of the private sector in order to accomplish the goal of enhancing the share of India's shipping in its trades. As Bhabha explained:

> Very few of the shipping companies in this country have the resources to buy a sufficiently large number of these ships, and it has been increasingly borne in upon the Government that if at the present stage of the development of shipping companies in this country, Government have to rely on private enterprise, the growth and development of our mercantile marine will be disappointingly low. The Government of India have, therefore, come to the conclusion that their new shipping policy must be broad based on the active cooperation of the State with enlightened private enterprise, in an endeavour to secure for India her rightful place among the maritime nations of the world.

He further expanded on the allegedly large resources of the state and their implications for the growth of Indian shipping:

> As the resources of the state were very great, it would considerably help the cause of Indian shipping, if corporations were started where the state and the enlightened private enterprise could work together for running shipping services.[31]

Bhabha felt that the shipping corporations would, apart from helping in the greater mobilization of capital, facilitate in eliminating unhealthy competition among Indian shipping companies and in preventing the rise of private monopolies. With this, Bhabha entered an area which the committee on shipping had basically left untouched. He warned that "we must be on our guard against any hurried moves or any false steps taken in a huff", but made it clear that "we must make the basic foundations of our shipping industry secure from attack both from within and without and it is only a cooperative structure, based on the active guidance and cooperation of the state, that can withstand such an attack".[32]

Apparently, Bhabha's plan on the shipping corporations drew its inspiration from Nehru's economic philosophy; it is difficult to see how it would have had Patel's blessing since he was close to the Scindia house, the dominant Indian shipping company at the time. Notwithstanding the fact that the country was engulfed by a multitude of daunting problems associated with the partition, radicalism was very much in the air and shipping could not have escaped its impact. Indeed, during the same month as Bhabha spoke, the Congress party resolved to establish "an economic structure which will yield maximum production without the creation of private monopolies and the concentration of wealth" as "an alternative to the acquisitive economy of private capitalism and the regimentation of a totalitarian state". Two months later in January 1948, the Congress party's Economic Programme Committee, chaired by Nehru, dropped what was for the business community a bombshell by asking that defence and key industries, public utilities, and all industries which were large scale or monopolistic in nature be reserved for public ownership, while all consumer goods industries be set aside for cooperatives in the cottage or small-scale sector. Faced with a crisis of production, however, the government, also headed by Nehru, demurred from accepting all these recommendations.

As a compromise between the party's ideological aims and the requirements of the economic exigency, the government--which was a composite national, rather than a party, government at the time--issued its Industrial Policy Resolution in April 1948 to calm business fears and to lend stability to the economic environment. It assured business that there would be no nationalization for ten years. It further made a tripartite division of the industrial field to demarcate the roles of the public and private sectors. There was first (1) an exclusive monopoly sector for the state in arms and ammunition, railway transport, and atomic energy. This exclusive state monopoly sector was supplemented by a second (2) reserved public sector, where in six fields--coal, iron and steel, aircraft manufacture, shipbuilding, telephone and telegraph manufacture, and mineral oils--the establishment of new undertakings was left to the state. Finally,

(3) the rest of the industrial arena remained with private enterprise. But this was not without qualification, for the state reserved the right to "progressively participate" as well as "intervene" even here if performance of private enterprise was not satisfactory. An illustrative list included 18 basic industries the "planning and regulation" of which by the state was considered "necessary in the national interest".[33] That list included air and sea transport, which meant stricter government regulation of the shipping industry in the future. However, shipping was not yet in the state or public sector. There was also no threat of nationalization even though the state may increasingly enter the industry.

The proposal by Bhabha to set up two or three shipping corporations, symbolizing the state's new interest in the shipping industry, met with a rather cold reception from the shipping community. The latter preferred that the government provide the private shipping companies with loans on easy terms for the purchase of vessels as also operational subsidies, rather than muscle into the arena through majority ownership. The government, on the other hand, was unwilling to take the path of providing easy finance or subsidies.[34] Through the mechanism of the corporations, the seeds of rivalry between the private sector and public sector were thus sown early in the country's development, though a full-blown conflict was still a few years away.

Partly perhaps owing to its nationalistic past, Scindia was the only company to offer cooperation, while the rest of the private sector chose to remain aloof. In 1950 a joint venture under the name of Eastern Shipping Corporation was established, with the government holding 74 per cent of the equity while Scindia contributed the other 26 per cent and served as managing agents for the corporation. Notwithstanding its entry into the shipping industry, and even that with the cooperation and collaboration of private enterprise, the government in general displayed at this stage a protective interest in the private sector. It basically saw its own role as supplementing private effort. It chose not to operate in trades where the private sector was already functioning, and proceeded to service only those routes where the private sector had not entered or did not wish to enter.[35] The Eastern Shipping Corporation was, in line with its name, allocated routes in the eastern trades, chiefly Australia, Far East, Japan, and Malaya.[36]

Anxious for India to enter overseas services, Bhabha had met Scindia chairman Walchand in December 1947 and asked that Scindia open passenger services from Bombay to the UK, apparently promising all possible support and assuring him that the state would compensate it for any losses incurred. Scindia complied quickly, and cargo-cum-passenger services were introduced in February 1948.[37] Already, in 1946, India Steamship Company had established regular services between Calcutta and the UK. Scindia introduced regular services between India and the US in 1947. In 1948, Great Eastern Shipping Company was established with the specific aim of concentrating on tramp shipping. However, in none of these cases was financial assistance from the state forthcoming by way of operational subsidies or grants. Indeed, after five years of operating the India-UK passenger services at a loss, Scindia suspended them when the state refused to provide any compensation.

Although Bhabha referred to the state's resources being "very great", it is difficult to know what precisely he had in mind, for the leadership at the head of the state at the time was coming to the realization that its resources were rather limited. Even otherwise the state was institutionally handicapped to move with despatch. The government was unable to match its words with action. Even Bhabha's promise of quick action on the reservation of coastal trade for national shipping had to wait until 1950 to be placed on the statute book while its actual implementation took even longer; indeed, the last foreign ship left the coastal trade only in August 1952. The target of two million tons was to encounter serious and prolonged difficulties, precisely because of the limitation of resources at the disposal of the state.

One element in the state attempting to assume a more active role in shipping was the perception in the government that private capital was shy, that the private sector was not forthcoming with adequate investment, and that private enterprise was in general lacking in dynamism. This was a perception not specific to shipping alone but was at the time held in relation to the larger private sector as a whole, and was influential in policy formation. Perhaps government expectations of the capacity of the private sector were exaggerated, but the latter's performance in shipping seems to have been a remarkably creditable one, especially considering the difficult economic and political situation and the almost insuperable problems in acquiring ships from either the US or the UK.

The Indian merchant fleet had emerged from World War II reduced and aged. On January 1, 1946, it consisted of 42 vessels with a total tonnage of 98,286 grt. By April 1, 1951, when the First Five Year Plan began, its capacity stood at 97 ships with a total tonnage of 386,229 grt, a figure almost four times larger than in 1946 (see Table 3.1). Over this period, the total tonnage added was 333,048, while 45,105 was discarded, resulting in a net addition of 287,943.[38] What this level of performance indicates is that the picture of slow growth belongs

TABLE 3.1: SHIPS AND SHIPPING TONNAGE, 1946 to 1951

	Tonnage at Start of Year		*Tonnage Added*		*Net Tonnage Added*	
Year	*No.*	*GRT*	*No.*	*GRT*	*No.*	*GRT*
1946	42	98,286	18	90,940	18	90,940
1947	60	189,226	14	65,297	12	60,035
1948	72	249,261	17	86,242	12	83,229
1949	84	332,490	14	42,065	6	32,142
1950	90	364,632	6	27,864	2	2,014
1951	92	366,646	6	20,640	5	19,583
1951	97	386,229	75	333,048	55	287,943

Source: M.A. Master, *So I Rest on My Oars: Collection of Writings and Speeches, 1947-1970,* edited by K.V. Hariharan (Bombay: M.A. Master Memorial Trust, 1977), 1, p. 230. The figures are for January 1 except for 1951, where the first set of figures is for March 31 and the second set is for April 1.

more appropriately to the planning period in the 1950s. Certainly, in the face of this performance, it could not be maintained that the private sector did not show adequate enterprise, dynamism or eagerness in expanding the tonnage. For, the expansion was the result almost entirely of private enterprise, with the entire contribution of the public sector as represented in its joint venture standing at only two ships for a total tonnage of 14,433 grt.

What is more, with no subsidy, no loans, and no financial assistance, the private sector spent over Rs. 220 million out of its own resources to acquire the tonnage as against the state's investment of Rs. 4.5 million.[39] Master fought hard to dispel the notion that the private sector was not dynamic, but to no avail. For, in the meantime, the belief that the private sector was unwilling to invest had assumed the proportions of a myth through endless repetition. For instance, as one example, the Committee on Public Undertakings observed in 1965: "In the postwar years the growth of India's shipping tonnage was slow and private companies were reluctant to invest in shipping industry to the extent required. Government, therefore, considered that State participation was necessary to inspire confidence in private Indian companies and encourage them to expand".[40]

Planning Under the Constraints of Underdevelopment

At independence, India had already arrived at a national consensus on its vision for a mercantile marine. The consensus aimed for nothing short of complete self-reliance in merchant shipping. It involved reserving the coastal trades and securing a share of half of the country's external trades, and towards these ends developing a merchant fleet with a tonnage of 2M grt, owned, controlled and managed by Indians. Highly valued as the goal of national self-reliance in shipping was, as more generally that of industrialization, its achievement encountered severe constraints. Fundamentally, these constraints stemmed from the country's condition of underdevelopment, chief among them the scarcity of resources and the multitude of claims on them. In its state of underdevelopment, the country simply lacked the financial resources to acquire tonnage adequate enough to match its ambitious targets. This constraint in financial resources was particularly marked in the area of foreign exchange, which was crucial to the purchase of ships abroad, given the lack of sufficient shipbuilding capacity at home. The requirements of capital for a fleet of two million tons were simply massive. Indeed, overwhelmed by the massive challenge India's decision-makers soon seemed to some to have developed "a defeatist mentality".[41]

In the conflict between its valued goals and the scarcity of resources, the new state often tended towards oscillation between bravely expressing its determination to push for an expanded tonnage under Indian ownership and throwing open its doors to foreign shipping in India's trades. What is apparent here is the paradox of over-ambition in national self-reliance, where the attempt to achieve highly ambitious objectives leads back to the very foreign dependence, to overcome and avoid which was the goal to begin with. This element is well illustrated by the state engaging early on in a clumsy manoeuvre to attract foreign capital in shipping, even as its leaders were espousing radical ideas on economic policy. To many that smacked of hypocrisy, but more importantly it left the national shipping community aghast and outraged.[42] Apparently with a view to making a rapid entry into India's overseas trades, the government approached British shipping interests for assistance, the very interests that had in the past thwarted the growth of Indian shipping. Observers believed that the underlying cause was "the stress of extreme dearth of capital sources".[43]

Apart from the aim to overcome the capital constraint, there may also have been at play an attitudinal element of aversion and hostility towards the Indian private sector on the part of some sections of the political elite, stemming in part perhaps from the sentiment for socialism among the left wing and in part perhaps from the residual deference towards, and nostalgia for, the former colonial masters. At any rate, as Master points out:

> some people occupying responsible positions in the Government have often remarked that there was no need to give priority to the raising of capital needed for the expansion of Indian shipping. They coolly tell us that British shipping has been meeting all the needs of India now and will meet them in the future. They are obsessed with the idea that replacing British ships by Indian ships for the carriage of India's overseas trades will only mean transfer of profits from British capitalists to Indian capitalists.[44]

If this perception is correct, it provides an indication of the bias that the private sector had to struggle against and live with. It did not make for a climate that encouraged local enterprise.

Active negotiations began at the end of 1949. Sir William Currie, P&O chairman, informed his shareholders on May 31, 1950 of the plan of British shipping interests, in response to the Indian request, "to create two joint Indo-British companies in which we were prepared to accept a minority shareholding and for which we would provide experienced management. These companies would operate ships under the Indian flag, both of them engaging in the coastal trade and each engaging in addition in one overseas trade in collaboration with our existing lines".[45] Since the negotiations occurred before the reservation of coastal trade for Indian shipping, the plan would have meant allowing the British companies to continue their presence in the coastal trade without giving up too much in the overseas trades.

Indian business strongly opposed the move. In reaction, the government asked if business "would want a postponement of the development of Indian shipping until we are in a position to build up the industry ourselves without external aid". The Federation of Indian Chambers of Commerce and Industry, the representative body of Indian business, responded by declaring that "even a stop-gap arrangement for the expansion of Indian shipping till this ideal is reached with the help of foreign shipping interests, will be detrimental to the growth of national shipping".[46] Although the government's consideration of the proposal seemed to have reached an advanced stage, it was forced to drop the issue in view of the strong opposition.[47] However, the move caused considerable uncertainty in the shipping community. Reportedly, another attempt on similar lines was made to treat a British owned and controlled company as an Indian shipping company, but was turned down on the intervention of Sardar Patel, the deputy prime minister.[48]

The scarcity of resources during the period was not just financial, but also institutional as well. The legacy of colonialism, its policy of laissez faire and the neglect of national shipping to the benefit of British shipping, meant the absence of an institutional framework for the promotion of national shipping. An appropriate institutional framework had thus to be evolved by trial and error over a period of time. The new state had to work out policies and administrative arrangements on loans, subsidies, and allocation of foreign exchange, and this took a considerable period of time. Meanwhile, the shipping sector had to countenance a conflict of considerable duration over demarcation of roles as between the state and private sector, the prolonged nature of which did not serve the cause of aggressive expansion of capacity.

Partly for ideological reasons--for socialism and the planning associated with it were for long a basic goal with Nehru--and partly for instrumental reasons to manage scarce resources efficiently to achieve the desired goal of industrialization, a Planning Commission was set up in 1950. Underlying the planning approach conceptually is a *rational actor model* of political economy, where a group of key decision-makers in the state set priorities among the goals that they seek, assess the resources that are available, and finally allocate the resources among the priority goals.[49] This initial planning of tasks is followed by a continued process of evaluation of the results to see if changes in priorities or allocation of resources are necessary. In this fashion, the irrationality and chaos of the market is sought to be replaced by the rationality of planning by the state.

The ultimate impact of establishing the planning commission was to lead to a "command economy" encompassing both the public sector and the private sector, even if within the framework of a democratic polity. The move towards a command economy through centralized economic planning served to place the determination of the pace of expansion of the private sector firmly in the hands of the state. Gradually, through a regime of physical controls, the state came to determine the structure of the shipping industry and its development. What tonnage was to be acquired and in which branches, and how finance for it was to be raised, were matters for decision by the planning commission, not simply by private enterprise. A licensing system was installed under which the addition and reduction of capacity had to receive the prior sanction of the state. The key to the control of private sector activity, besides the direct management of the public sector, was the allocation of finance, foreign exchange, and routes.

Although allocations of finance and foreign exchange to shipping companies were ultimately made by the ministry of finance on the recommendation of the ministry of shipping, the larger framework of development of shipping over the medium term was, in the first instance, determined by the planning commission in the context of the overall plan for the economy as a whole. The planning commission decided, after discussions with the various ministries and sectoral bodies, on the acquisition and retirement of tonnage in the different branches of shipping, keeping in view the resources available and the priority to be accorded to the various economic sectors over a given five-year period. Tonnage acquisition therefore took place through the filter of the constraints of financial and foreign exchange resources as seen by the planning commission.

The rationalistic view of planning posits it as a superior mechanism for coordination of economic activity compared to the working of the market in the achievement of national goals. However, since no set of decisions-makers can fully divine the working of the economy or the consequences of their actions, in actual practice the planning process encounters frequent crises, breakdowns or disequilibria. The ensuing process of crisis management approaches less the rational actor model than the *bureaucratic politics model,* where decisions result from bargaining among different agencies of varied influence and power. Even the initial determination of priorities is not immune from this bargaining process, however.

In the determination of priorities, whether in the context of crisis or otherwise, the planning commission has ranked the shipping industry rather low and not recognized it as being part of the "core" of the plan. It has therefore often applied the axe liberally to the demands for allocation of finance for shipping. In the ideological context of the time, the honour of constituting the core of the plan belonged to basic industries such as steel. Despite the consciousness-raising done by Scindia in the period before independence and the lobbying activity of the shipowners after independence, shipping had not been designated as belonging to the core sector. The shipping lobby made a strong, and what it believed to be a convincing, case that more foreign exchange could be earned and saved, and quickly, by spending foreign exchange on shipping than on other industries. It requested that shipping should be treated as a special case, with its foreign exchange earnings being put in a separate account to be used for purchasing ships abroad. The planning commission, however, would not accept the argument on the ground that the country's foreign exchange earnings constituted a single pool, and allocations from it had to be determined on the basis of overall sectoral priorities.

While the planning commission determined the physical targets on tonnage, there was little settled consensus in the government on policy for the promotion of shipping through evolving an effective overall strategy that integrated ship acquisition and the obtaining of cargo for the acquired vessels. The lack of consensus over matching policy with targets stemmed from the fragmentation of decision-making concerning shipping among several ministries and the difficulties in arriving at a coordinated policy. Although there seemed to be a notional consensus on the importance of promoting national shipping, the pertinent ministries had different priorities when it came to concrete measures for its advance. For, the concerned ministries represented different societal and sectoral interests, even though in some cases these interests were in the period under consideration only latent and not fully manifest and organized. Indeed, at times, there could be little agreement even within the same ministry; as two knowledgeable authorities pointed out, "Even the two wings under the same Ministry--Railways and Shipping --do not cooperate--but they very often clash--in promoting the shipping policy laid down by the Cabinet of the Union Government".[50]

The ministry of railways understandably sought to protect the interests of the railways as against shipping. Since that ministry wielded strong influence within the government--given its responsibility for the far-flung and massive state-owned railway network and its status as the largest single employer in the country--the consequence of its safeguarding its own interests was stagnation in coastal shipping as allocation of traffic between coastal shipping and the railways was so arranged as to favour the latter. Similarly, the ministry of commerce represents the interests of exporters and shippers, who are far more numerous and influential than the small group of shipowners. As another powerful and strategic ministry within the government, commerce has been successful in having the interests of its clients often prevail over those of the shipowners. All attempts to adopt a policy of reservation of cargoes for national shipping have foundered on the opposition of the ministry of commerce, in turn backed by the lobby of exporters and shippers. At the same time, the ministry of finance, as the strongest of the ministries with its responsibility for balancing the government's budget, has been averse to any programme of subsidies. These three ministries are powerful, and their occupants are members of the cabinet. This has not often been the case with shipping, which has not been considered an important enough portfolio for inclusion in the cabinet and has been in a weak bargaining position. If at times it has been under the charge of an influential leader, it has been more an accident. In any case, the status, orientation and abilities of the individual at the head of the ministry of shipping, representing the interests of shipowners (including the public sector), have been significant in the bureaucratic politics over determining policy.

A major part of the decade of the 1950s saw shipping under the charge of Lal Bahadur Shastri. He served first as Minister of Transport and Railways and then as Minister of Transport and Communications from 1952 to 1958, though with a short break in that period when, in 1956, he resigned in an unusual principled gesture of assuming moral responsibility for a serious railway accident. Although private sector shipping was under pressure during the 1950s, it held Shastri in remarkably high regard, not only in retrospect but also during his tenure as transport minister. For his part, within the limits of the framework of the government's overall economic policy, Shastri was understanding of the problems of the private sector, appreciative of its enterprise and contribution, and ready to sincerely attend to its grievances, even as he was ready to remind it of its responsibilities. His successor, S.K. Patil, was also favourably inclined towards the private sector, but his tenure was not long. However, the period in office of Patil's successor, Dr. Paramasiva Subbarayan, saw the initiation of policies which seemed to overturn the existing framework and were increasingly viewed as discriminatory in favour of the public sector at the cost of the private sector. Thus, individual preferences of the leaders at the helm have played an important role in the determination of policy.

As against the image of planning as a rational process, the actual course of planning has been marked by crises. In the ensuing crisis management, the bargaining power of different ministries and individual preferences of ministers have had a significant role. At times, the resulting compromises have tended to move the planners towards solutions which it was the very purpose of planning to avoid, such as inviting foreign capital to compensate for the inadequacy of resources. This is illustrated by the course of the planning process in relation to shipping during the 1950s.

FIRST PLAN'S MODEST SCOPE AND RELIANCE ON PRIVATE SECTOR

The First Five Year Plan, covering the period 1951-1956, was a hurried affair and represented less an effort to launch fundamental changes in the economy or to initiate a process of rapid growth, but more to bring some measure of rehabilitation to an economy that had been physically exhausted under the stresses and strains resulting from World War II and the partition of the country. It was a modest plan, limited in its aims, size and the demands that it made on the population. It was also moderate in its policy stance. In formulating the plan, the planners were throughout torn between what was desirable and what was feasible under a democratic system, but opted for feasibility over desirability. While recognizing the need over the long run for a larger role for the public sector and reorienting the private sector to fit in with a planned economy, for the present they admitted that "the productive capital in industry and in services essential to it is so small compared to the needs of the country that in the further accumulation of it, the two sectors can well supplement each other and need not necessarily expand at the expense of the one or the other".[51]

In line with the overall orientation of the plan, the goals for shipping--about which there had been no consultation with the industry--were also modest. They did not aim to make either substantial advance towards the target of 2 million tons or to keep up the momentum built up before the planning period. The plan envisaged a total tonnage of about 600,000 grt by 1956, of which 322,202 would be in coastal shipping and 283,505 in overseas shipping. The former target was deemed essential for implementing the policy on coastal reservation, while the latter was regarded necessary for "fuller participation" in overseas trades. The overall target represented an increase of only 55 per cent over the tonnage at the beginning of the plan, not some multiple of existing capacity. It compared poorly with the increase of 293 per cent over the preceding five-year period between January 1, 1946 and April 1, 1951.

Apart from aiming to expand the tonnage in the public sector, the First Plan recognized the necessity of providing financial assistance to the private sector companies because of the tight capital market situation that had prevailed for several years. The government outlay for shipping was placed at Rs. 149 million. In addition to making a generous provision of Rs. 44 million for the public sector's Eastern Shipping Corporation, the plan allocated Rs. 40 million to coastal shipping and Rs. 65 million to overseas shipping with a view to providing loans to private sector companies. The private sector was expected to supplement these loans with Rs. 20 million and Rs. 22 million in the two arenas from its own resources. In return for providing loans, the plan required the government to maintain "a continuous watch" on private firms to see that they charged coastal freight rates and passenger fares that were reasonable and that they set aside funds for renewal and renovation.[52]

The government in 1951 started a programme for providing loans, marking a departure from the practice of the colonial state. There was, however, disappointment and concern at the slow pace of the utilization of loans and consequently in the acquisition of tonnage. The private sector found neither the rates of interest nor the other terms to be attractive. The government then announced in November 1953 more favourable terms. Loans were then made available up to 85 per cent of the purchase price at interest rates of 2.5 per cent for overseas shipping, and up to 80 per cent and at interest rates of 4 to 4.5 per cent for coastal shipping. The policy change had "a magic effect on tonnage acquisition" in the private sector.[53] Such, indeed, was the enthusiasm for the loans that the government increased the outlay for them in the First Plan to Rs. 263 million. However, the change in policy had come too late in the life of the plan to assure its success. A total of Rs. 241 million was sanctioned for loans but only Rs. 161 million had actually been drawn by the end of the plan.[54]

The accomplishment in tonnage acquisition fell well short of the target of 600,000 grt. At the end of the plan on March 31, 1956, the merchant fleet consisted of 120 vessels with a total tonnage of 495,714 grt (81 coastal ships of 237,060 grt and 39 overseas ships of 258,654 grt).[55] Only by including ships under construction could the plan target be said to have been achieved. It is obvious that the First Plan represented a sharp slow down from the pre-planning period. The shortfall was particularly severe in respect of the target in coastal shipping. Coastal shipping provides an example of the lack of coordination between target setting and shipping policy. Tonnage expansion was affected by government failure to work out an adequate policy on allocation of cargo as between carriage by rail and sea, and on timely promulgation of economic freight rates for shipping.[56] As ship operators found coastal shipping unremunerative, they shifted vessels out of coastal shipping to overseas shipping.

In general, the First Plan represents a period of missed opportunities in shipping. India could achieve a share of only about 5 per cent in its overseas trades, while the share in the trade with the adjacent countries, which can be considered an extension of the coastal trade, was 40 per cent. Apart from the outflow of valuable foreign exchange because of the continuing poor share in the overseas trades, India was unable to avail of the opportunities provided by the large food imports. This failure stemmed from the government's unwillingness to provide economic freight rates for Indian vessels, whereas American ships were subsidized by their government. Even in coastal shipping, because of lack of coordination in the government, foreign oil companies were allowed to transport oil and oil products in their own vessels.

SECOND PLAN'S "BIG PUSH" AND THE STRAIN ON THE CONSENSUS

Unlike the First Plan, the Second Five Year Plan was a bold and ambitious one, designed to give industrialization a "big push" and bring about fundamental structural changes in the economy. Patterned after the Soviet model, its centrepiece was the programme to create a complex of heavy industries designed to make India self-reliant in the production of capital goods in order to make economic growth a self-sustaining process. Its broad outline was heralded in March 1955 in the "plan-frame" developed by the economic planner P.C. Mahalanobis.[57] Although subsequent debate made for some revision, the basic strategy embodied in the Mahalanobis model survived intact in the Second Plan as finally approved.

The formulation of the Second Plan took place in a different political environment from that of the First Plan, one marked by a sharp turn to radicalism. In the initial years after independence, power in the national government had been divided between Nehru and Patel, the acknowledged leaders of the left and right wings of the Congress party, respectively. Patel's death near the end of 1950 resulted in the ascendance of Nehru and the left wing within the party. As Nehru consolidated his leadership, both party and government moved sharply to the left. In the period immediately before the formulation of the Second Plan, Nehru made it clear that he rejected capitalism as a path, for the fundamental reason that "a system which is based purely on the acquisitive instinct of society is immoral", the days of which were numbered in any case. More positively, he declared:

> The picture I have in mind is definitely and absolutely a Socialistic picture of society. I am not using the word in a dogmatic sense at all. I mean largely that the means of production should be socially owned and controlled for the benefit of society as a whole. There is plenty of room for private enterprise there, providing the main aim is kept clear.[58]

The Second Plan was meant to launch the stage of transition to socialism. The key mechanism in this transition was the public sector, which was designed to grow both absolutely and relatively (in relation to the private sector) so as ultimately to reduce the private sector to simply an appendage of the national economy. As Mahalanobis authoritatively expressed it: "The public sector must be expanded rapidly and relatively faster than the private sector for steady advance to a socialist pattern of economy".[59] Changes in economic policy followed, heralding a new era of rapid advance for the public sector and the installation of a tight regulatory regime of physical controls over the private sector. The year 1956 marked a turning point; not only was the Second Plan launched in that year, but also a new Industrial Policy Resolution adopted.

Industrial Policy Resolution of 1956: The resolution of 1956, which replaced that of 1948, distinguished similarly among three categories of industries, but the industries included were different. In the first category (1) were industries of basic and strategic importance and public utilities, the development of which was henceforth "the exclusive responsibility" of the state, with all new units in the future reserved for it. Encompassing 17 items, the category included shipbuilding. The second category (2) included industries which were to be "progressively state-owned and in which the state will therefore generally take the initiative in establishing new undertakings". However, here private enterprise was also "expected to supplement the effort of the state", and to have "the opportunity to develop in this field, either on its own or with state participation". Significantly, among the 12 items included in this category was sea transport. Finally, the third category (3) comprised all other industries; these were generally "left to the initiative and enterprise of the private sector", but the state reserved the right "to start any industry even in this category".[60]

The result of the change in the place of shipping in industrial policy was to sharply elevate the role of the state, for shipping was now envisaged to be increasingly state-owned even as the private sector was to be allowed to exist in a supplementary status. The shipping industry was seriously concerned at the new role accorded to the state. It was even haunted by the spectre of possible nationalization, as had happened in the case of the aviation industry. One journal commented: "This apprehension cannot be considered as altogether without foundation.... This threat cannot be ruled out in the case of shipping".[61]

However, Transport Minister Shastri tried to calm the industry's fears by underlining the pragmatic nature of the government's approach, by declaring his own aversion to making a distinction between the public and private sectors, and even pledging that "it is not our intention that shipping in public sector should run in competition on routes on which existing private shipping companies had established themselves".[62] His successor, S.K. Patil, who was equally sensitive to private sector concerns, also provided the assurance that "there should be no sense of competition between the private sector and the public sector, so far as shipping goes. The very conception, the very idea of competition is dangerous". Indeed, he deemed the private sector to have priority, telling the shipowners: "The public sector in shipping is just in the position of your younger brother, and I assure you will always remain the elder brother".[63] Although for the time being there was no immediate threat to the position of the private sector, the state did expand the public sector presence in shipping. The state in 1957 assumed full ownership, control and management of the Eastern Shipping Corporation, thus burying the earlier policy of mixed enterprise. Meanwhile, in 1956, it also started the new Western Shipping Corporation as a means to enter the western trades.

Pruning the Plan: Of greater concern to the private sector for the moment was what it believed to be the injustice done to the shipping industry in the Second Plan's allocations. Initially, the Mahalanobis plan-frame had proposed a target of 1.5 million grt.[64] By this time, the government had come to consider the 2M grt goal of the Aiyar committee on shipping as impractical. But there then began a process of pruning which drastically reduced that target. Keeping in view the financial constraints facing the planning commission, a study group of the Consultative Committee of Shipowners in 1955 asked for a target of 1.05M grt. Transport Minister Shastri considered the target "well-balanced and capable of attainment" though he personally preferred a higher target, for "there can be no two opinions about the imperative need for a far more rapid pace of tonnage expansion, specially in the overseas trade". In the parliament, however, there was sentiment for a higher target, and it proposed increasing it to 1.2M grt.[65]

Finally, the planning commission set the target at only 900,000 grt with an outlay of Rs. 370 million, which came "as a rude shock to the country" and "brought about a degree of gloom in shipping circles". Shastri was also disappointed, but observed that "there is, however, no help because the limitations of finance cannot be got over".[66] The logical implication of the reduced target was that there could be no leapfrogging to India's aspiration to acquire a 50 per cent share in the overseas trades. Apart from its disappointment over the overall targets, the private sector felt that there was inadequate recognition of the contribution made by it, while undue favour was being shown to the public sector on nothing but ideological grounds. There was particular anger at being excluded from the tanker trade, which was allocated to the public sector despite the fact that the private sector had pioneered in it.

With the reduced target, the chief aims that the Second Plan sought to accomplish in shipping were to: (1) build up adequate tonnage to cover all the requirements of coastal trade; (2) increase the share of Indian ships in the overseas trade; and (3) establish a nucleus for a tanker fleet. The breakdown of the targets in tonnage was: coastal 412,000 grt; overseas 405,505; tramp 60,000; tankers 23,000; others 1000. Even in its own words, with this capacity Indian vessels would "carry about 12 to 15 per cent of the country's overseas trade and 50 per cent of her trade with adjacent countries as against the present proportions respectively of 5 and 40 per cent".[67]

It had been expected that the plan would provide Rs. 550 million. Instead, the final figure was Rs. 450 million, but the real availability of new funds was only Rs. 370 million, for the rest was simply a carry-over from the First Plan. Of the total, Rs. 200 million was for direct investment in the public sector's Eastern Shipping Corporation and the yet to be established Western Shipping Corporation. The remainder was meant to assist the private sector with loans, which was to be supplemented by Rs. 100 million from the private sector's own resources. Even then it was anticipated that "the amount allotted in the plan will not be sufficient for achieving the full target of an additional 3 lakh [300,000] tons during the plan period".[68] In view of the rising prices of ships, this was an understatement.

Foreign Exchange Crisis: Within twelve months, the entire provision meant for five years was exhausted, yet only about half of the required additional tonnage could be acquired with it. The other half still remained to be procured. Foreign exchange was critical for the remainder, since the order book of the country's only shipyard was already full. Even if the shipyard had been able to oblige, it would still have been a burden on the balance of payments as 80 per cent of the value of a ship built by it was based on imports. The order books of the foreign shipyards were also full at the time.

Then, suddenly, in 1957 the country was faced with a major balance of payments crisis, which led to a ban on the release of foreign exchange for purchase of ships. The private sector came forward with several proposals to overcome the foreign exchange constraint in respect of shipping. A major suggestion was that the foreign exchange earnings of Indian shipping be put in a special pool reserved for purchasing ships from the international market. This was not acceptable to the planning commission. Nor was the industry's demand--later endorsed by the National Shipping Board--to recognize shipping as part of the "core" of the Five Year Plan. Recognition as part of the core of the plan would have allowed the industry continued access to foreign exchange for purchase of vessels. Instead, the government asked the private sector to rely on its own mechanisms to obtain the foreign exchange necessary for purchase of ships, such as deferred payments or self-financing. Through these more costly arrangements, the private sector purchased another 136,968 grt, which its supporters took to be indicative of the dynamism of private enterprise.[69]

Apart from the question of foreign exchange, where his hands were tied, Shastri was very accommodating towards the private sector in its straitened circumstances, and initiated two major policies which became institutionalized subsequently. One was to establish a non-lapsable revolving fund to provide loans to the private sector for purchase of ships. Later termed as the Shipping Development Fund, it drew on grants and loans contributed by the government as well as repayments on loans extended by it to the industry. The other initiative was to establish a "Shipping Coordinating Committee", which came to be to be known more by its telegraphic code name "Transchart", for channelling government cargo to Indian shipping.

Shipping and Foreign Exchange: Regardless of the potential that these two mechanisms may have had for addressing the problems of the shipping industry, they could do little to relieve the immense crisis of foreign exchange. The paradox was that the inadequacy of shipping tonnage, and therefore the small share of Indian shipping in overseas trades, itself played a significant role in the foreign exchange scarcity. A statement by the Minister for Shipping in parliament in April 1962 revealed that India's overall share in the overseas trades was 10 to 11 per cent, while in the liner trades it was 25 per cent.[70] Other observers dissented, maintaining that, at the end of the Second Plan, Indian shipping had a share of about 9 per cent, at any rate less than 10 per cent, of the overseas trades.[71] Nor was coastal shipping without a foreign presence. While the transport ministry claimed that 100 per cent of the coastal trade was carried by Indian shipping, a detailed analysis in 1960 showed that, of the total coastal trade of about 5.6 million tons, as much as 43 per cent was carried by foreign ships.[72] Not only had the state signed away its traffic rights to the oil multinationals on the coastal movement of petroleum products, but shortage of tonnage necessitated chartering of foreign ships.

The consequence of inadequate tonnage capacity was that huge payments for freight charges had to be made to foreign shipowners. There was a strong imbalance in the foreign exchange earnings of national and foreign shipowners. Transport Minister Shastri informed the Lok Sabha in 1958 that the annual freight bill was Rs. 1500 million; of this, the Indian share was Rs. 160 million, while the remaining Rs. 1340 million went to foreign shipping. Considering that foreign companies had to incur expenses within India to earn the freight, one authority put the outflow at Rs. 800 million.[73] Especially serious was the foreign exchange drain from freight paid for foodgrain imports. From the end of World War II to March 1959, India had imported 32.5 million tons of foodgrains; it had paid a freight charge of Rs. 2290 million, out of which Rs. 2125 million (93 per cent) went to foreign shipping. Prime Minister Nehru expressed his dismay at the large amounts that were being transferred out of the country on account of freight charges. He confessed, while inaugurating the National Shipping Board in 1959, "I have been not merely alarmed but horrified that these vast sums of money have gone just on freight", and thought it would have been better to have used some of these funds for building the country's own tonnage. The Estimates Committee commented that "the current drain on foreign exchange" on account of freight for food imports could have been avoided through proper planning by spending on tonnage acquisition a part of what was being paid out for freight.[74]

In the face of the large outflow of foreign exchange on account of freight charges, Indian shipowners insistently faulted the government's wooden policy on employment of Indian capacity. Their complaint against the government had two aspects. One related to the lack of coordination within the government in channelling cargoes to Indian vessels. The other, more important but not unrelated, aspect concerned the government's unwillingness to provide Indian shipowners economic freight rates that would make it profitable for them to operate their vessels. On the other hand, the Indian government insisted on paying only the lowest going price on the world market. Finance Minister Morarji Desai told shipowners in his usual blunt language, "as it is, it is impossible for me to accept this demand of economic freight rate". He pleaded helplessness: "Howsoever much I would like to see that all our foodgrains are brought by our own ships, I would be forced to the necessity of taking the help of other shipping if you insist on this, because it is impossible for me to do what you are asking me to do, with the finances that are at our disposal". More generally, he sought to educate them about the limits on the government's ability to help: "Ultimately for Government it is all a matter of capacity. The desire is there.... But the question of capacity limits this desired fulfilment".[75]

His cabinet colleague, Transport Minister Subbarayan, even as he urged Indian shipowners in 1960 to purchase large numbers of ships to carry future PL-480 food imports, also told them: "It is not possible for this department to agree to pay a higher rate of freight than the rate for which shipping can be arranged in the world market". Curiously, perhaps only for tactical reasons to silence Indian shipowners, a new concept was also beginning to be favourably received within the government at the end of the 1950s, that it would constitute flag discrimination to pay higher freight rates to Indian vessels or even to accord preference to them for carriage of government cargo.[76]

Indian shipowners screamed that it was sheer fantasy to expect them to compete with foreign companies which had amassed huge reserves and were receiving subsidies from their governments or operating vessels flying flags of convenience. Significantly, in 1959-60 alone, Panamanian and Liberian vessels had carried 3.29 and 2.75 million tons of Indian cargo, respectively. Indian shipping suffered doubly from the employment of foreign vessels; first, it was deprived of the import cargo by the foreign vessels and, second, these vessels took away export cargo by offering throw-away rates rather than take ballast. The Indian shipowners also reminded the government that it should not forget the central objective to develop a national mercantile marine, which was being undercut through the employment of foreign vessels.[77]

On the other hand, the government in its situation of financial stringency proved unwilling to bend, even though its practice was from the national perspective a less advantageous solution for the long run. Indeed, it exerted considerable pressure on conferences not to increase freight rates or even to roll back freight rate increases, so that exports were not adversely affected. Similarly, when conferences threatened levying a surcharge on cargoes to Indian ports because of delays there stemming from labour problems, the government was successful in having them desist from the move.[78] Such actions were not particularly appreciated by even the Indian lines, for they affected not only their revenues but ultimately the expansion of their tonnage. These actions confirmed for Indian shipowners the notion that the government had little understanding of the problems of the shipping industry. At the same time, the actions provide an illustration of the cross pressures from shippers and shipowners, under which the government had to make decisions.

If the government was not too understanding of the viewpoint of the shipping industry, the problem was compounded by a lack of adaptability on the part of the shipping industry. Certainly, the government could not afford to pay the high freight rates of liner shipping for the carriage of bulk supplies of food and fertilizer. The industry, on the other hand, was dominated by the two liner companies, Scindia and India Steamship. Rather than take to tramp shipping themselves, the two companies were insistently critical of the government. They were too attached to the British model with its focus on liner shipping, and were not up on more recent developments in trade and shipping. Perhaps because of its nationalist halo, Scindia showed particular rigidity. A new tramp shipping firm, the Great Eastern Shipping Company, had come into existence in 1948 and was expanding; it was the first carrier in India to acquire an oil tanker in 1956. However, instead of being praised for its efforts, it was attacked for them. There thus developed a fissure within the shipping industry itself. Scindia chairman Khatau declared in 1955:

> There is recently apparent in some shipping circles an interest in tramp tonnage as a basic constituent of a well-planned national mercantile marine. The futility of this approach will be realized if the history of the subject is borne in mind.... It is thus abundantly clear that it would be prejudicial to an early growth of a national marine if India today proceeded to encourage tramp tonnage as a matter of definite policy, particularly as bulk cargoes of coal and ores, regularly shipped from India, are generally low-rated and their normal destinations are countries from which we do not obtain dry cargo in substantial quantities.... Tramps are a dying breed.

On the other hand, Great Eastern's chairman, A.H. Bhiwandiwalla, complained:

> Owing to ignorance and apathy on the part of Indian shipowners, as well as the Government in this country, about the importance of tramping business and its requirements, we had to face not only lack of cooperation, but actual hostility and obstruction, in the form of numerous restrictions that were placed on our "freedom of the high seas".... In view of the prevalent bias against tramp shipping, the Government has been influenced and swayed by the liner interests and prejudices, and conditions for the creation and growth of the tramp fleet in this country have not been established.... The Government restrictions on letting out Indian ships on time-charter to foreigners have acted as a restrictive influence on expansion of Indian tonnage and foreign exchange earnings without doing an iota of good to the country.[79]

Perhaps the problem both between the liner and tramp owners, and between the government and shipowners, could have been resolved, given some willingness to understand each other, but it ran into the larger problem within the polity at the time of lack of rapport and cooperation between business and government, which manifested itself in a variety of areas and issues. Regardless, the dilemma for the government was severe. Its resource scarcity constrained it from providing Indian shipowners with what they called economic freight rates, while its foreign exchange crisis constrained it from letting them purchase additional vessels abroad. On the other hand, lack of capacity made for the outflow of foreign exchange through freight charges paid to foreign shipping, worsening the crisis. In these exiguous circumstances, governments's thoughts once again turned to entertaining the possibility of allowing entry of foreign capital into shipping. This only brought into the open the conflict between the government and the shipowners. The occasion for precipitating the conflict was the bringing forward of the Merchant Shipping Bill, which otherwise was a momentous development in laying down the institutional framework for shipping.

THE STATE AND PRIVATE SECTOR ON COLLISION COURSE

The primary purpose of the Merchant Shipping Bill was to establish India's own shipping register and the institutional framework governing the operations of shipping companies and ships, for hitherto Indian ships were technically on the British register and were largely governed by British legislation. The Bill was a voluminous and comprehensive undertaking, attempting to consolidate earlier legislation and to emulate British legislation. Little wonder that it lent itself to controversy. After it was introduced in parliament in February 1958, the Bill became a source of contention between the shipping community and the government. Without an appropriate preamble, the Bill was regarded as a dry affair and lacking in inspiration, especially compared with the stirring purposes outlined in the corresponding US legislation. Also, it was criticized for not providing for a National Shipping Board, which had long ago been recommended by the committee on shipping to serve as an apex body determining shipping policy. Most importantly, what the Indian shipowners found particularly objectionable were the provisions on the definition of what constituted an Indian ship.

A forewarning of the Bill's provisions on the issue had come in August 1957 when the Minister of State for Shipping, Raj Bahadur, had stated, in relation to participation by foreign capital in Indian shipping, that "at any rate, partnership on the basis of 51:49 can always be considered". The shipping community was stunned, for it had assumed that the standing policy of the government continued to be that announced in the resolution of July 12, 1947. That resolution had required 75 per cent of the ownership of capital and all directorships to be vested in Indians as a condition for being considered a national shipping company. The minister now announced that those requirements "are not mandatory and in suitable cases, exemptions can be given". Apparently, Raj Bahadur seemed to treat shipping on par with other industries, but he was not unaware of the serious implications in the case of shipping. For, he also observed in reference to the forthcoming Indian Merchant Shipping Bill: "If we allow foreigners to register, it might not be entirely free from danger at a time of crisis. It may prove to be a double-edged sword. There may even be a positive disadvantage because shipping is the life-line of a nation".[80] If the shipping community was confused, it was not to blame; it wondered why in the light of such implications was the government willing to facilitate majority ownership for foreigners.

PRIVATE SECTOR'S PYRRHIC VICTORY

The introduction of the draft Bill in February 1958 came as a "shock" to the industry,[81] for it allowed a ship to be regarded as Indian as long as foreign ownership did not exceed 31 out of 64 shares of a ship. Another provision which the industry found objectionable entitled a ship to be considered Indian if it was owned by a firm registered under the Indian Companies Act, even if the firm was under foreign control and management. No other government action had aroused the shipping community to such anger as these provisions. Believing them to be an "invitation to suicide", the shipping interests resorted to "a raging and tearing campaign...in the press, on the platform and wherever an opportunity for educating and rousing public opinion was available".[82] In their view, shipping was a strategic industry and could not be treated like other industries. As the chairman of Bharat Line warned:

> Difficulties of foreign exchange are perhaps sought to be covered by broadening the definition of an Indian ship. I am afraid this is really asking for trouble both in times of peace

> and war, and in the result we shall probably lose more than we gain. If there is shortage of funds at the moment, this is not the way to cover it. Better go slow and build firm, than move fast and repent at leisure.[83]

All the big names in shipping entered the noisy campaign, with Sumati Morarjee (daughter-in-law of Narottam Morarjee) playing a major role in her dual status as a director of the Scindias and president of the Indian National Steamship Owners Association. The Bill influenced M.A. Master to come out of retirement to join the opposition. Among others in the campaign were the chairmen of Scindia (Dharamsey Khatau) and India Steamship (Ramaswami Mudaliar) and C.H. Bhabha, former minister for commerce.[84]

There were few supporters for the government's unpopular position except for S.N. Haji who, ironically--during a life-time of service in the management of Scindia's--had been a stout defender of the interests of Indian shipping under the colonial state. Haji had in 1928 moved the bill in the central legislature for the reservation of coastal trades for national shipping. Having retired from Scindia, he was now seeking participation by American capital in a new venture.[85]

Recognizing the unpopularity of its stand, the government relented, promising to be guided by the resolution of 1947, which, however, it regarded as flexible. When the Bill was considered by a joint select committee, its earlier objectionable provisions were replaced by one that recognized a ship as Indian if it was owned by Indian citizens or by a company with its main office in India and with at least 75 per cent of its equity owned by Indians. This was accepted by the government. Transport Minister Patil attempted further to assuage the shipping community with the assurance that he would not permit entry of foreign capital in shipping even to the extent allowed; he bravely declared that if the achievement of tonnage targets was "to be done at the cost of inviting foreign capital in a vital industry like national shipping, I would rather remain without that shipping than endangering our shipping by inviting capital from outside".[86] Still, the government got away with the right to change the minimum requirement on foreign share in equity. Five years later it raised the limit on foreign participation from 25 per cent to 40 per cent.[87] However, unlike

1958, in the changed circumstances the shipping industry stayed quiet. Strangely, while anxious to get foreign capital, the government incorporated a provision in the Bill which required that disputes over ships mortgaged abroad had to be settled in Indian courts, thus providing little incentive for foreigners to loan funds for purchase of ships.

Although the government bent to the opposition and withdrew the unpopular provisions, its initial move had not been without justification. When the joint select committee recommended an amendment to the Bill requiring a ratio of 75:25 between national and foreign ownership, there were ten minutes of dissent, a majority of which favoured a ratio of 60:40 instead. The dissenters regarded the opposition by shipowners as based on a hangover from the colonial era. They felt that the country must achieve the target of 2M grt by the end of the Third Five Year Plan in 1966 and therefore ought to welcome foreign capital since the achievement of that target was not within the means of the country.[88] One journal addressed "the crucial issue squarely":

> To put it in plain terms, have we enough foreign exchange to purchase the balance of the tonnage that we need to reach the target of 900,000 tons by the end of the period of the present Plan?.... The alternative to the acceptance of foreign capital for financing part of the development is to call a virtual halt to the expansion of shipping.... It is a fundamental weakness in the case of the opponents of foreign participation that they have failed to look beyond the second Plan. It is these cumulative considerations which have impelled the Government to change the definition of Indian shipping.[89]

In addition to reverting to the original definition of Indian shipping, the government accepted to amend the Bill to provide a preamble setting out the aim of the state to "foster the development" of a national mercantile marine "in a manner best suited to serve the national interest", and gave statutory recognition to the Shipping Development Fund. The amended Bill also instituted a National Shipping Board as an advisory body, which the Minister of Transport Patil described, at its inauguration in 1959, as the highest policy making body for shipping and promised that government would give its proposals the highest attention.[90] The government's responsiveness to the advice of the Board in the period since has, however, failed to live up to that promise.

While the private sector may have won the battle with the government over the definition of Indian shipping and to block the entry of foreign capital into shipping, it proved ultimately to be only a pyrrhic victory. For, the private sector soon ended up losing in the larger war to obtain a more accommodative posture on the part of the government towards it.

THE UNRAVELLING OF THE CONSENSUS: EMERGENT TIDE AGAINST THE PRIVATE SECTOR

In 1958, Shastri left the ministry of transport for commerce; the shipping community's sense of loss was palpable, for it felt that Shastri was always willing to listen to the genuine grievances of the community even if limited by the overall policy framework. His successor, S.K. Patil, a leader close to business, was also believed to be sympathetic to the demands of the shipping community. Despite its differences over planning targets and other issues, the shipping industry was comfortable with these two leaders in office, and it had indicated in public and private its happiness with them. The shipping industry had a lot to be grateful for. Shastri had instituted the Shipping Development Fund to provide loans on easy terms, extended a special development rebate to Indian shipowners to mobilize resources for investment, and established Transchart to channel government cargoes to Indian shipping. Besides, the industry had been able to get a special exemption from the imposition of wealth tax. The private sector was also allowed to participate in shipping services flowing out of bilateral agreements with the Soviet Union and other members of the bloc. Although the government did not have a cargo reservation policy, its preference and rhetoric, though not implementation, had by the end of the 1950s settled on a division of liner cargo between India, the other trading state and third states in the ratio of 40:40:20--precisely the formula subsequently adopted by UNCTAD.

There was also some support in political quarters that the private sector should be treated on a fair basis relative to the public sector. The Estimates Committee had in the mid-1950s recognized the important contribution that the private sector had made, and urged that the industry's demands for easier terms and conditions for loans "should be considered sympathetically by Government and every encouragement given to the shipping industry". It wanted a reconsideration of the question of operational subsidies to the private sector and to treat such subsidies as a measure equivalent to the practice of indemnification of the public sector against losses.[91]

However, new trends were set in motion for a greater thrust for the public sector once Dr. P. Subbarayan succeeded to the office of transport minister in September 1959, although omens were not altogether lacking earlier. For the shipowners, the new flow of pronouncements from New Delhi marked a complete reversal of earlier policy and "cast a gloom" over them.[92] First, Subbarayan bluntly reported that he was not bound by the commitments made by his predecessors in the past. He declared that it was "no longer feasible to keep the two sectors in completely separate water-tight compartments", and that henceforth the public sector would enter the lucrative trades in competition with the private sector, even as he ominously warned: "the sooner the private shipowners recognize this fact, the better it will be for the continued cooperation of the two sectors".[93] Second, he preempted the oil tanker trade for the public sector, and asked the private sector to "appreciate this position and leave this field completely to the public sector without demur".

It would seem, however, that Subbarayan's position was not idiosyncratic but reflected a wider trend more generally on the economic scene, verging on ideological orthodoxy, to accord the public sector the dominant role. His views had a larger institutional base as is evident from the immensely influential 38th report of the Estimates Committee in 1959. This committee acknowledged that government policy since 1947 had been to depend on the private sector for advance in shipping, with the state providing it assistance. However, in its view, the Industrial Policy Resolution of 1956 marked a sharp point of departure, so that "the policy of the Government as envisaged in 1947 has been more or less reversed and the responsibility for the development of Indian shipping now rests squarely on the public sector". The earlier supplementary role envisaged for the public sector was therefore not acceptable any more to the committee. Asking for a redefinition of the role of the public sector in shipping, it stressed:

> while the principle of filling the gap and playing a supplementary role might have been in keeping with the policy of Government a decade ago, it does not take into account the fact that the role of Government in the field of shipping has since undergone a change and that it is no longer to play the supplementary role, but the main role itself.[94]

In this evident reversal of policy, the public sector entered into trades that were earlier operated only by the private sector, chief among them the India-UK/Continent trade. In regard to the coastal trade, which it also now entered, the government maintained that the private sector had agreed to the new role taken on by the public sector, a claim that was disputed by the private sector.[95] If the government had, indeed, been "actuated by the desire to see a rapid growth in coastal shipping", as was suggested by some observers,[96] that hope for long remained unfulfilled. Meanwhile, not only the private sector but even the respected chairman of the National Shipping Board, G.L. Mehta, expressed concern at the new menacing trends; Mehta hoped that the public sector would only supplement, and not supplant, the private sector.[97]

The reversal of policy came at a difficult time for the private sector, for the late 1950s were marked by a slump in world shipping. The resulting decline in freight rates made the predicament of the shipping companies precarious. Ordinarily, the slump in world shipping ought to have provided an opportune time to buy secondhand ships for a fleet that was so deficient in capacity. However, without a sympathetic state policy on economic freight rates and cargo preference, the private sector was shy in making new purchases, especially when the financial results of private companies were adverse. That shyness only confirmed the government's belief that the private sector lacked dynamism and necessitated a more active advance by the public sector.

Meanwhile, the Second Plan was fairly successful in achieving its modest targets though not in the manner intended. The overall accomplishment was a tonnage of 0.86M grt as against the target of 0.90M grt; the achievement of 0.55M grt in overseas shipping was higher than the target of 0.49M grt while that of 0.31M grt in coastal shipping was far below the target of 0.41M grt. Despite the fact that the Second Plan ended when seven years had passed the deadline of 1954 set by the Aiyar committee on shipping, however, not even half of the target of 2M grt had been achieved.

SUMMARY AND CONCLUSIONS

India started with high ambitions in the area of shipping. However, it was stymied in its efforts to expand vigorously in this direction. There were, no doubt, elements in the international environment that blocked the rapid expansion of services by Indian shipowners. Besides the restrictions placed on the capacity that Indian lines could operate on the direct services between India and the UK/Continent, there was obstructionism on the part of conferences en route. Important as these elements were in impeding the growth of Indian shipping, however, the really important factors blocking growth were located within the country. These largely stemmed from the structure of underdevelopment inherited from colonial rule. That structure placed severe constraints on rapid growth, chief among them being the scarcity of resources. The lack of adequate financial resources, particularly of foreign exchange, prevented the achievement of the ambitious targets. The same constraints of underdevelopment led, in order to preserve foreign exchange, to a rigid regime of licensing and controls which made decisions on purchase and sale dependent on the prior approval of the state. Additionally, weak capital markets made private firms dependent on government for loans for adding to capacity.

The constraints of underdevelopment were compounded by the lack of a settled policy framework over the period. Partly this can be seen as a function of transition from the colonial to post-colonial state, which involved the creation of new institutions to promote shipping as against the earlier policy of neglect. But it was also partly a function of the ideological orientation of the new leadership in charge of the state. In the eyes of the leadership, the explanation for India's poverty and underemployment lay in capitalism, and their eradication required a socialist regime. The shipping arena during the period was marked by a transition from a situation where assets and operations were completely vested in the private sector to one in which the public sector would become dominant. Paradoxically, the private sector which had played an historic role in opposing imperialism, and had-been supported by the same leadership that was now in charge of the state, was no longer considered worthy of sympathetic treatment. It is understandable that in the situation of transition and the uncertainty that necessarily went with it, progress towards the achievement of the ambitious targets would have been slow. Additionally, state controls over freight rates, especially in coastal shipping, and release of foreign exchange inhibited rapid advance.

NOTES

1. Michael McFaul, "State Power, Institutional Change, and the Politics of Privatization in Russia", *World Politics*, vol. 47, no. 2 (January 1995), pp. 211-43 at p. 214.

2. McFaul, p. 215.

3. I have dealt with this issue in Baldev Raj Nayar, "Political Mainsprings of Economic Planning in the New Nations: The Modernization Imperative versus Social Mobilization", *Comparative Politics*, VI, no. 3 (April 1974); reprinted in Norman W. Provizer (ed.), *Analysing the Third World* (Cambridge, Mass.: Schenkman Publishing Company, 1978), pp.460-85. See also Baldev Raj Nayar, *The Modernization Imperative and Indian Planning* (New Delhi: Vikas, 1972).

4. Francis G. Hutchins, *India's Revolution: Gandhi and the Quit India Movement* (Cambridge: Harvard University Press, 1973), pp. 1-2.

5. Bipan Chandra, *The Rise and Growth of Economic Nationalism in India: Economic Policies of Indian National Leadership, 1880-1905* (New Delhi: People's Publishing House, 1966), pp. 65-89.

6. Alok Sheel, "Peasant Nationalism in India in the Gandhian Era", in Amit Kumar Gupta (ed.), *Agrarian Structure and Peasant Revolt in India* (New Delhi: Criterion Publications, 1986), pp. 67-92.

7. See India, Commerce Department, *Report of the Reconstruction Policy Sub-Committee on Shipping* (New Delhi: Government of India Press, 1947), pp. 53-57. See also G.D. Khanolkar, *Walchand Hirachand: Man, His Times and Achievements* (Bombay: Walchand & Co., 1969), pp. 550-60.

8. See India, Commerce Department, *Report of the Reconstruction Policy Sub-Committee on Shipping.* The other members of the committee were: K.C. Neogy, M.A. Master, Abdul Halim Ghuznavi, and W.L.A. Radcliffe. Subsequent references to this report are included within parentheses in the text.

9. Khanolkar, p. 293.

10. See the chapter on "Magna Carta", in N.G. Jog, *The Saga of Scindia: Struggle for the Revival of Indian Shipping* (Bombay: Scindia Steam Navigation Co., 1969), pp. 135-141.

11. Jawaharlal Nehru, *The Discovery of India* (New York: John Day Company, 1946), p. 403.

12. For the text of the resolution, see India, Lok Sabha, Estimates Committee (1956-57), *Sixty-Fifth Report: Ministry of Transport: Shipping* (New Delhi: Lok Sabha Secretariat, 1957), Part II, pp. 56-58.

13. The other members were M.A. Master, Surji Vallabhdas, Hoshang Dinshaw, and Sir B.P. Singh Roy.

14. Khanolkar, pp. 568-72.

15. Jog, p. 141.

16. Khanolkar, p. 573.

17. The figures are for January 1, 1946 and January 1, 1948. See M.A. Master, *So I Rest On My Oars: Collection of Writings and Speeches, 1947-1970,* edited by K.V. Hariharan (2 volumes; Bombay: M.A. Master Memorial Trust, 1977), vol. I, p. 230.

18. Jog, p. 178; Master, I, pp. 16 and 351.

19. Master, I, pp. 136 and 454; and Master, II, p. 378.

20. Master, I, pp. 16, 329, and 352.

21. Master, I, p. 352.

22. On the Indian grievances, see *Eastern Economist,* January 9, 1953, p. 71; January 1, 1954, pp. 29-31; January 15, 1954, p. 96; January 7, 1955, pp. 25 and 33; February 25, 1954, p. 315; January 6, 1956, pp. 31-32; February 24, 1956, pp. 305-307; January 9, 1959, pp. 197-99; December 11, 1959, p. 961. See also *Economic Weekly,* February 27, 1960, p. 389.

23. *Eastern Economist,* January 9, 1959, pp. 197-99.

24. *Eastern Economist,* December 11, 1959, p. 961.

25. *Eastern Economist,* February 27, 1960, p. 389.

26. Master, I, p. 440.

27. *Eastern Economist,* January 1, 1954, pp. 30-31. See also *ibid.,* January 9, 1953, pp. 71-72; February 20, 1953, pp. 305-307; January 6, 1956, pp. 31-32.

28. Master, I, p. 690.

29. India, Lok Sabha, Estimates Committee (1958-59), *Thirty-Eighth Report: Ministry of Transport and Communications: Department of Transport* (New Delhi: Lok Sabha Secretariat, 1959), p. 3.

30. Jog, pp. 142-43.

31. Cited in Master, I, p. 691.

32. Jog, p. 143.

33. Baldev Raj Nayar, *India's Mixed Economy: The Role of Ideology and Interest in Its Development* (Bombay: Popular Prakashan, 1989), pp. 180-85.

34. T.S. Sanjeeva Rao, *A Short History of Modern Indian Shipping* (Bombay: Popular Prakashan, 1965), pp. 151 and 164.

35. Rao, p. 164.

36. Rao, p. 164.

37. Master, I, p. 15.

38. For the statistical data, see Master, I, p. 230.

39. Master, I, pp. 212 and 229.

40. India, Lok Sabha, Committee on Public Undertakings (1964-65), *Third Report: Shipping Corporation of India Ltd., Bombay* (New Delhi: Lok Sabha Secretariat, 1965), p. 1.

41. Master, I, p. 194.

42. Jog, pp. 146-47.

43. Rao, p. 167.

44. Master, I, pp. 439-440.

45. Master, I, pp. 296-97.

46. Master, I, p. 297.

47. On the episode, see Master, I, pp., 64-65, 193 and 330.

48. Master, I, p. 133, and Master, II, p. 333.

49. On the rational actor model and bureaucratic politics model, see Graham T. Allison, *Essence of Decision: Explaining the Cuban Missile Crisis* (Boston: Little, Brown and Company, 1977).

50. M.A. Master and C.H. Bhabha, "Development of Shipping: A Policy for Expansion--Need for Larger Coastal Fleet", in Master, I, pp. 228-40 at p. 238.

51. India, Planning Commission, *First Five Year Plan* (New Delhi: 1953), pp. 32-33.

52. *First Five Year Plan*, p. 408.

53. Rao, pp. 152-53, 172-73 and 205.

54. Master, I, pp. 564 and 569-79.

55. Master, I, p. 570.

56. For one analysis of this aspect by the industry, see the chapter on "Too Late, Too Little", in Jog, pp. 164-76.

57. P.C. Mahalanobis, "Draft Recommendations for the Formulation of the Second Five Year Plan 1956-1961", in India, Planning Commission, *Papers Relating to the Formulation of the Second Five Year Plan, 1955* (Delhi: Manager of Publications, 1962), pp. 29-55.

58. Jawaharlal Nehru, *Planning and Development: Speeches of Jawaharlal Nehru, 1952-56* (New Delhi: Publications Division, n.d.), p. 17.

59. Mahalanobis, p. 39.

60. Nayar, *India's Mixed Economy,* p. 199.

61. *Eastern Economist,* February 10, 1956, p. 196.

62. Rao, p. 165; and *Eastern Economist,* September 7, 1956, p.367.

63. N.P. Mehta, "The National Shipping Policy: Relative Roles of Private and Public Sectors in Indian Shipping Development", *Indian Shipping,* vol. 12, no. 5 (1960), pp. 11-19.

64. Mahalanobis, p. 46.

65. Master, I, pp. 47-48, 215 and 300.

66. Master, I, pp. 47-48, 215 and 300; and Croesus, "Second Thoughts on Shipping Targets", *Eastern Economist,* September 23, 1955, p. 489.

67. India, Planning Commission, *Second Five Year Plan* (New Delhi: 1956), pp. 480-83.

68. *Second Five Year Plan,* p. 482.

69. Master, I, pp. 255 and 301.

70. Rao, pp. 183-84.

71. Master, I, p. 161.

72. Jaya Chamaraja Wadiyar, "Indian Shipping Under the Five-Year Plans", *Eastern Economist,* November 4, 1960, pp. 828-832. See also Master, I, pp. 48 and 295.

73. Master, I, p. 77.

74. Master, I, pp. 91, 163, 170 and 303.

75. See the text of speech by Finance Minister Morarji Desai at the annual INSA meeting on May 11, 1961, *Indian Shipping,* vol. 13, no. 5 (1961), pp. 7-11.

76. Master, I, pp. 102, 144-45, 155, 161, 163, 170 and 201.

77. Master, I, p. 164, and *Eastern Economist,* February 24, 1961, p. 556.

78. Rao, p. 175.

79. *Eastern Economist,* February 25, 1955, p. 315, and *ibid.,* December 7, 1956, pp. 871-74.

80. India, *Lok Sabha Debates,* August 8, 1957, pp. 7549-7550.

81. Rao, p. 169.

82. Jog, p. 148.

83. C.R. Srinivasan, in *Eastern Economist,* August 1, 1958, pp.163-64.

84. On the case of the shipowners against the definition of Indian ship in the draft bill, see Indian National Steamship Owners Association, *"Indian Ship": Why Shipowners Oppose Indo-Foreign Combine for Shipping* (Bombay: INSOA, 1958).

85. Rao, p. 170.

86. Rao, p. 171; and Master, I, p. 77.

87. Jog, pp. 148-49.

88. *Eastern Economist,* August 29, 1958, pp. 286-87.

89. "Storm Over Shipping", *Eastern Economist,* July 18, 1958, p.72.

90. *Indian Shipping,* vol. 11, no. 4 (1959), p. 3.

91. India, Lok Sabha, Estimates Committee (1956-57), *Sixty-Fifth Report,* Part II, pp. 29 and 32. See also Master, I, p. 58.

92. Croesus, "Shift in Shipping Policy", *Eastern Economist,* July 22, 1960, p. 138; and Master, I, pp. 158-72.

93. See the text of the speech of Dr. P. Subbarayan at the annual INSA meeting on June 22, 1960, *Indian Shipping,* vol. 12, no. 6 (1960), pp. 14-17.

94. India, Lok Sabha, Estimates Committee (1958-59), *Thirty-Eighth Report,* pp. 4-5. See also Rao, p. 166, and Master, I, pp. 688-89. For an early trenchant critique of the report, see N.P. Mehta, "The National Shipping Policy: Relative Roles of Private and Public Sectors in Indian Shipping Policy Development", *Indian Shipping,* vol. 12, no. 5 (1960), pp. 11-19.

95. Rao, p. 166.

96. Rao, pp. 166-67.

97. *Indian Shipping,* vol. 13, no. 7 (1961), pp. 11-13.

CHAPTER IV

THE GOLDEN AGE OF RAPID EXPANSION, 1960-1980: THE STATE IN COMMAND

The period of the 1960s and 1970s constitutes the golden age of rapid expansion of the merchant fleet. As against the 0.75M grt in 1959, tonnage crossed the 1 million grt mark in 1962 and the 2 million mark in 1969. By the end of the 1970s, it stood close to 6 million grt. By the mid-1970s, India had emerged as the largest maritime power in the developing world, and the largest also between Europe and Japan. Besides, starting only with an entirely liner cargo fleet, India had diversified into bulk carriers, oil tankers, and offshore vessels. It was truly a tremendous achievement.

However, tonnage is only a simple and rough indicator of performance in the area of shipping, even though eminently useful as a starting point. A fuller appreciation of performance and evaluation of policy would require taking into account other dimensions as well. These dimensions would certainly include the actual share of the fleet in the country's trades, the diversification of the fleet, the technological status of the fleet, and the financial health of its shipping enterprises. If some of these dimensions are taken into account, a considered assessment of the period would have to take note of the important fact that around 1975 Indian shipping entered into a major crisis which lasted through the 1980s. The Indian industry did not recover from the aftermath of the crisis until after 1993, and even then with serious imbalances and technological deficiencies. Strictly in terms of tonnage, the momentum built up over the period from 1960 to 1975 nonetheless continued to expand the fleet as vessels ordered earlier joined it. However, in its exploration of the determinants of the rapid expansion, this chapter essentially applies to the period from 1960 up to the mid-1970s.

Although the international environment was, no doubt, favourable for the rapid expansion of the country's fleet and adequate note needs to be taken of it, fundamentally the expansion during the period was state-driven. The chapter therefore largely focuses on (1) the state, paying attention to the leadership and its vision as well as its capacity to implement the vision, (2) the overall strategy for expansion, and (3) the specific measures adopted to assure the three basic essentials of an expanding fleet--ships and finance for their acquisition, cargo for the ships to transport, and trained manpower to operate the ships.

State Power, Autonomy and Capacity

As discussed before, state power is a key determinant in the success of a state in guiding the economic development of a country. In turn, state power consists of two analytically distinct elements--state autonomy and state capacity. State autonomy relates to the ability of the state to formulate its preferences or goals independently of the preferences of the chief economic interest groups. This ability is a function of the degree of consensus within the state. On the other hand, state capacity relates to the ability of the state to implement its chosen preferences, and it is a function of "the effectiveness and cohesiveness of government institutions".

THE HIGH WATERMARK OF STATE POWER

In regard to the period under consideration, the first third of that period was characterized by remarkably high state autonomy and state capacity for an underdeveloped country. This high degree of state power up to the mid-1960s rested on a tripod of factors--the personal charisma of India's first prime minister, Jawaharlal Nehru, who served in that office for 17 years; the institutional charisma of the ruling Congress party, acquired through the struggle for national liberation from colonial rule over two-thirds of a century; and the administrative "steel frame", manned by a group of generalists who had been recruited through a highly competitive examination system which weeded out all except the best and brightest. This tripod of factors had enabled the Indian state to survive the traumas of partition, war with Pakistan, the integration of princely states, the massive agitations for linguistic states and the administrative reorganization of the states on a linguistic basis, and to go on to consolidate a polity based on parliamentary rule and to undertake a broad-front programme for restructuring economy and society. By 1960, the new state had put in place most of the policies that set the basic framework for the development of the economy, especially industry, for the next quarter century. This was no less true of the shipping sector than of the rest of the economy.

Nehru himself was deeply conscious of the importance of shipping even as he was personally fascinated by ships as much as he was by airplanes. As a statesman with a strong awareness of history, he recognized the strategic role of a merchant fleet in the country's economy, its defence and its place in international politics. In a message in 1938 on the occasion of the opening of Scindia House, he had expressed his impatience at waiting to see Indian ships carry the Indian flag around the world, and stated with regret: "I have no doubt that if India had been a free country and in a position to control her own destiny, we would have developed long ago a National Mercantile Marine worthy of our country whose ships would have ploughed the oceans of the world". Nehru made it a point to be present at landmark occasions connected with shipping. In 1948, he took the time to launch the first modern ship built in the country at the Scindia shipyard. Four years later, in a speech on the occasion of the silver jubilee of the training ship *Dufferin,* he averred: "It is patent that a country like India must have a sufficiently developed mercantile marine.... a mercantile navy for this country is quite essential. It does not require any argument. The only possible argument that one can advance is in relation to the pace of its growth".[1]

The economic implications of the lack of an adequate merchant fleet apparently weighed heavily on Nehru. While inaugurating the National Shipping Board in 1959, he expressed his horror at the outflow of vast amounts of foreign exchange on account of employment of foreign ships. For him, it would have been preferable to have spent some of that money on the purchase of ships and prevented the outflow.[2] Until then, the development of shipping in India had been oriented, following the British model, towards liner shipping, neglecting both bulk carriers and oil tankers. Nehru's concern would soon find expression in a dramatic move to expand in the areas that had been hitherto ignored. Such consciousness and concern about the importance of shipping at the highest level of government had implications for formulation and execution of policy all down the line in administration.

Again, Indian shipping was fortunate to have during much of the 1950s a leader such as Lal Bahadur Shastri in charge of the portfolio as part of his larger responsibilities for the ministry of transport. Indeed, the three policies he announced in 1957 to help the industry--easy access to loan finance, tax incentives, and cargo support in respect of government goods--remained by and large the basic framework for shipping into the mid-1980s. On account of them, he is regarded as the architect of modern Indian shipping. The shipping industry has continued to place him at the top of the roll call of honour of those who fostered its growth. It admired him for his bold and fearless decisions to build Indian shipping, undeterred by the opposition of foreign shipping interests. In its estimation, Shastri was "a staunch supporter and champion of Indian shipping...burning with fervour and enthusiasm for the speedy, all round development, progress and expansion of Indian shipping". More importantly, the industry appreciated his taking "a very practical, wise and realistic view of the growth of shipping in the private and public sectors".[3] Shastri was less enamoured of pushing the public sector at the expense of the private sector. However, after his departure from the ministry in 1958, the consensus became consolidated in favour of the public sector, more in line with Nehru's ideological preferences. In this last respect, too, the overall framework of policy had been set by 1960.

Another political leader who proved to be a stout defender of the interests of Indian shipping was Raj Bahadur.[4] His apprenticeship in shipping came as a junior minister under Lal Bahadur Shastri, and he was apparently struck by the man's simplicity and dedication. Raj Bahadur went on to serve the ministry of transport for a long period of time though not continuously. Having joined the government as a junior minister in 1951, he became a minister of state in charge of shipping in the ministry of transport in 1957. He was elevated to the position of Minister of Shipping in 1962, and later worked as Minister of Transport from 1963 to 1965. In these positions, he was associated with all the major initiatives to help Indian shipping. After holding the civil aviation portfolio in 1965 and serving as India's ambassador in Nepal from 1968 to 1971, he returned to the ministry of transport, this time as a member of the cabinet. His long association with shipping had given him a deep and intimate knowledge of the industry, and he provided able and informed leadership as Minister of Shipping and Transport.

State capacity was reflected not only in the capabilities of the minsters but also of the civil servants in charge of shipping. The most eminent among the civil servants at the time was Dr. Nagendra Singh, whose contribution to the growth of Indian shipping has often been placed next only to that of Lal Bahadur Shastri. It is a testimony to the capacity of the state at the time that political and administrative leaders, though generalists to begin with, occupied their positions of responsibility for long stretches of time. Nagendra Singh served Indian shipping directly for a period of ten years.[5] From 1956 to 1966, he held the strategically important and powerful position of Director General of Shipping, while he simultaneously worked as Joint Secretary (1956-1962) in the ministry of transport and communications and rose to become Additional Secretary (1962-1964), Special Secretary (1964), and Secretary (1965-1966) in that ministry.

Nagendra Singh was the key civil servant in the formulation and implementation of decisions and in the establishment and growth of institutions that came to constitute the basic policy and institutional framework for shipping in the 1960s and 1970s. Those intimately connected with shipping were in awe of "his learning, dynamism, administrative abilities and above all his dedication and zeal for development of Indian shipping".[6] They admired him for his "single-minded, unstinted and devoted services to Indian shipping", and affirmed that all this "certainly entitled him to be placed among the front-rank of the leaders and builders of modern Indian shipping. Next to the late Lal Bahadur Shastri from the Union Government side he stands out prominently as the staunch and sturdy champion for the development and expansion of Indian shipping".[7] Similarly, they maintained that "it was during Nagendra Singh's tenure that a firm foundation for the future growth of shipping was laid".[8]

Dr. Nagendra Singh was of royal blood, coming from the ruling family of the princely state of Dungarpur in Rajasthan, a dynasty that had ruled the small state since the twelfth century.[9] His eldest brother succeeded to the throne in 1918, and Singh later sought to make his mark elsewhere outside the state. He studied at Cambridge University and entered the Indian Civil Service in 1938. In 1942, he was called to the bar at Grays Inn, London, after having distinguished himself in several of the law examinations. A fiend for amassing degrees, he earned some half-dozen doctorates between 1954 and 1965 from universities in India and abroad, including Cambridge, Dublin and Moscow. An indefatigable man with seemingly boundless energy, he literally carried two careers at once, serving both as a superb administrator and a prodigious, erudite scholar. At the ministry of transport, a major contribution of his, among others, was the drafting of the Merchant Shipping Act of 1958. He headed India's delegation to many international conferences and was elected president of the International Maritime Organization (1963-1965). He went on to become the Secretary to the President of India, and later Chief Election Commissioner. In 1973, his legal acumen led to his election as judge of the International Court of Justice, where he served as vice-president from 1976 to 1979 and as president from 1985 to 1988. When he died in 1988 at the age of 74, the next day, in an uncommon move, the Lok Sabha applauded his contributions and then adjourned in honour of his memory. Singh was the author of some twenty books on various subjects, particularly international law. The subject closest to his heart was the law of merchant shipping. Two compilations for which he is well known are *International Conventions of Merchant Shipping* (volume 8) and *Shipowners* (volume 13) in the British Shipping Law Series. He also functioned as a visiting professor at Geneva and several universities in India.

Indian shipping was thus truly served in this formative period by political and civil service stalwarts. They were the equivalent in post-independence shipping, albeit in the official realm, of what Walchand Hirachand and Narottam Morarjee had been in pre-independence shipping. The expansion of Indian shipping in this period was thus no accident. No doubt, there were other favourable factors at work, but the expansion was in substantial measure the result of the vision, acumen and dedication of very able leaders of the time. It is true that the overall framework was one of a highly interventionist state that imposed a rigid system of licensing and controls, but it was a positive state rather than a negative one, aiming to encourage growth rather than block it. The leaders of the time realized that there was a tremendous amount of work that needed to be done to advance development in a backward country, and they saw as their task the removal of obstacles to development rather than the placing of restrictions. And this task they performed with dedication.

Two anecdotes attest to this dedication, both related by S.N. Sanklecha, a former senior manager in one of the leading private sector enterprises, Great Eastern Shipping Company.[10] India's regulatory system, put in place with the Merchant Shipping Act 1958, required government approval of any acquisition of ships as a condition of release of foreign exchange. Such approval from the government came after clearance from a number of ministries (transport, finance, company affairs) and the planning commission. In one particular case, in the 1960s, Great Eastern was pledged to purchase a ship from a foreign party, subject to the condition of government approval. Meanwhile, prices of ships began to rise and the sellers were therefore eager to cancel the deal. On the other hand, as the deadline for closing the sale neared there was no approval forthcoming from the government. In desperation, the firm's head, Vasant Sheth, made his way to New Delhi and met with Nagendra Singh. It was discovered that the approval of the planning commission had not been obtained, and that it would take another week or ten days to get it, by which time the deadline for closing the deal would have passed. However, Nagendra Singh did not stand on form and let the usual bureaucratic procedures take their course; instead, he called the Secretary of the Planning Commission, asked for a personal appointment with him for that very day, and visited him along with the head of the firm. Apologizing "profusely" for the oversight, he obtained the approval of the planning commission and thus saved the deal from collapsing.

On another occasion in the early 1960s, Great Eastern was short of cash to pay its instalment of Rs. 20 million to a shipyard in Japan. The firm deputed Sanklecha to go to New Delhi and meet with Nagendra Singh to get a loan from the government for that amount, a hefty sum in those days. The reason for entrusting the task to Sanklecha was that "he had free access to Nagendra Singh in view of his academic pursuits". When Sanklecha met him and underlined the urgency of the situation, Nagendra Singh laughed and declared "Sanklecha, you do not seem to know how the Government departments work and that is why you are expecting the cheque in a matter of days". Still, he promised to do his best. Instead of waiting for the regularly scheduled meeting of the designated committee or calling a special meeting, he immediately circulated a memorandum to the committee members to approve the loan. When Sanklecha called on him again a few days later, he smiled and observed: "You do not seem to have the realization of what I am doing to assist you. In the government, one works on the principle that involve as many necks as possible so that your neck will not go". Great Eastern got the cheque and paid its instalment to the Japanese shipyard on schedule.

Nagendra Singh was not the only one in the bureaucracy to serve India's interests in shipping. Another stalwart was C.P. Srivastava, who fostered the growth of the public sector in shipping. Still another was L.M.S. Rajwar, who also served directly in the public sector in a subsequent period.

In retrospect, it would seem that the period was also characterized by a high regard for public norms of probity. Rules could still be bent in particular cases to do favours for those who had personal influence with the leadership, but by and large administration was rule-governed and exceptions were usually made in the larger public interest. Corruption had not made deep inroads as yet, and the top leadership was largely incorruptible and dedicated, and this had an impact throughout the administration. Apart from the nature of the leadership, which was held in high regard, a further factor that facilitated state autonomy and state capacity in this period was the low level of social mobilization.

THE DETERIORATION IN STATE POWER

The decline in state capacity became visible in the late 1960s though its roots lay in earlier years. By mid-1962, the legitimacy of the system was at its peak. Soon, however, social forces began to be unleashed that led to a serious deterioration in state power. First, there was the war with China in 1962 that undermined Nehru's authority and diminished his charisma.

Second, the escalation in defence expenditures that followed that war, as well as the one with Pakistan in 1965, fuelled inflation. Third, Nehru's death in 1964 removed the only unchallenged and neutral arbiter who was above the fray in the system. That made resolution of factional conflict within the ruling Congress party difficult. Fourth, an economic crisis in the mid-1960s emerging out of two consecutive droughts of serious proportions led to food shortages and rising prices, which triggered mass agitations. Besides, devaluation in 1966 added to the economic turmoil. The economic deprivation and the consequent higher level of social mobilization resulted in the erosion of political support for the Congress party. There thus occurred also the loss of institutional charisma. In the 1967 national elections, the Congress party lost power in about half of the states, while its majority at the centre was drastically reduced. Factional struggles broke out within the Congress party, and soon assumed an ideological form, with the group following Mrs. Indira Gandhi lurching to radicalism. Finally, the Congress party split in 1969, and India entered a different world than that in the Nehru era.

Mrs. Gandhi stayed on in power at the centre with the support of the Communist Party of India. She went on to enact a radical programme of nationalization of large parts of the modern economy, especially the entire banking sector, imposed an even more stringent regulatory framework on the private sector, particularly big business, and increasingly resorted to populist appeals and measures to rally political support, which served to heighten social mobilization. In the short term, all this made for a massive electoral victory for Mrs. Gandhi in 1971. The state seemed autonomous, but the apparent autonomy was based on the personalization and centralization of power rather than one undergirded by a strong party organization. Besides, through the adoption of increasingly radical programmes, the state now took on tasks for which it had little capacity. Growing state interventionism made the functioning of the economy hostage to favours by the government, widening the net for corruption.

Meanwhile, with the passage of a quarter century after independence, the values of the freedom struggle in terms of sacrifice for the national interest had receded in memory. Further instalments of nationalization and stringent controls over the private sector made for economic stagnation and inflation. The resulting mass suffering, combined with the revulsion against the rising corruption, fed into a political movement for the purification of the system. The opposition movement, in turn, reactively led to entrenching authoritarian tendencies in the state, which culminated in the declaration of a state of emergency in 1975. The emergency made for arbitrary and capricious rule, and the electorate in reaction rejected the Congress party under Mrs. Gandhi in 1977, and voted into power an alliance of several opposition parties. However, the high hopes held of the alliance collapsed as it soon dissolved, in the absence of a larger consensus, into factions driven by the quest for personal power. The lack of cohesion at the top led to a decay of the institutional framework, a decline in the effectiveness of the state, and the institutionalization of corruption.

The period after the mid-1960s thus saw enormous political turmoil and deterioration of state autonomy and state capacity. While shipping continued to grow during the period on the strength of the earlier momentum, the frequent changes in leadership, the divided nature of that leadership, and the consequent decline in state power were evidently soon to hamper the mounting of an adequate attack on the crisis that beset shipping from the mid-1970s.

NATIONAL SELF-RELIANCE AND THE COMMAND ECONOMY IN SHIPPING

The nature of the Indian shipping industry that began to take shape around 1960 did not stand apart from the overall new design for the reconstruction of the economy that was already under way at the time. Rather, it partook of its general aims and mechanisms. At the core of the design for economic reconstruction that had been launched with the Second Five Year Plan in the mid-1950s lay the aim of national self-reliance. Under it, given the continental nature of its territory and economy, India was sought to be transformed into an industrial power like the advanced nations, producing its requirements of industrial goods with its own resources, natural and human, and not dependent on others.

This core aim had a long ancestry, and over the sustained period of its development it had acquired legitimacy as a sacred object. Dadabhai Naoroji, in the manner of the latter-day dependency theorists in the postwar period, had argued in the second half of the nineteenth century that India's backwardness stemmed from the drain of economic surplus from India to Great Britain. Subsequently, to overcome this backwardness, the nationalist movement through its historic organizational instrument, the Indian National Congress, made India's industrialization the central plank of its economic programme. "Swadeshi" became the economic slogan for India's nationalist movement from the early years of the twentieth century, with a clarion call to Indians to patronise only local goods as against foreign manufactures. Mahatma Gandhi reinforced the message of Swadeshi by organising the public burning across India of mounds of foreign cloth and clothing, voluntarily surrendered by Indians. He further apotheosized self-sufficiency by his advocacy of an India economically organised around self-sufficient villages. Even though self-sufficiency at the village level evoked little enthusiasm among the middle classes that led the freedom struggle, its resonance with national self-sufficiency was nonetheless appropriated by the nationalists.

Finally, Nehru, with his conversion to socialism as an ideology and his admiration for the Soviet model of autarkic economic development, transformed the vision of self-reliance into a concrete economic programme. With him, political independence, economic nationalism, concern over national security, and opposition to imperialism, all combined to spur the formulation of an economic programme to replicate in India the industrial structure of the developed countries. The objective was not to seek comparative advantage, but to develop heavy and large-scale industry, capable of producing capital goods and consumer goods, both durable and non-durable. This objective was to be accomplished through a gigantic and rapid programme of import-substituting industrialization (ISI), to be carried out under the aegis of a state-directed command economy, with a central planning body establishing targets in various sectors and coordinating them in a series of five year plans. A dominant role in the achievement of such industrialization was accorded to the public sector encompassing state-owned enterprises. However, no liquidation or wholesale nationalization of the private sector was intended. Nonetheless, the private sector's fate was projected to be only that of a subordinate player in the future scheme of things, inevitably destined to be reduced to a minor appendage in the economy; in the meantime, it was allowed to grow within a comprehensive and tight regulatory framework of licensing and controls.

Some of these powerful ideas were not unique to India. They were also current in Latin America and elsewhere in the developing world, and had been given intellectual respectability by Raul Prebisch and the Economic Commission for Latin America. However, they had been independently arrived at in India and, indeed, far earlier, before and during World War II, especially in the thinking of its eminent leader, Jawaharlal Nehru. At base, the foundation with Nehru was ideological, for he abhorred capitalism and private profit even as he held the establishment of a socialist society to be a moral and sacred goal. Of course, the economic planners in independent India also advanced more instrumental reasons, such as export pessimism, in defence of the ISI strategy. It is important nonetheless to understand the ideological foundation of India's economic regime in order to adequately comprehend the subsequent difficulties in attempts to break away from it. It is noteworthy that the state which undertook the ISI strategy had substantial autonomy at the time; it also had considerable capacity for administrative implementation of the strategy and was relatively free of corruption at its higher levels.

The larger aim of national self-reliance, the ISI strategy, and the dominant role accorded to the public sector, all had their counterparts in the shipping industry. Most critically, corresponding to the aim of national self-reliance, the vision of India's participation in world shipping was by design confined strictly to its own national trades. This was to be assured through a comprehensive and stringent system of licensing and controls. The role envisaged for Indian shipping was thus different from the practice prevailing among the major maritime powers. Shipping is often described as a global industry, and nations such as Great Britain and, especially, Norway and Greece, among others, have thrived commercially on participation in cross-trades, rather than solely depending on their national trades. No such participation--which would have been equivalent to export promotion as against import substitution--was envisaged for India, however. The underlying rationale was that India had such a small share in its own trades that there was little point in going in for cross-trades when there was so much to be done at home. Moreover, it would have given rise to the question as to what criteria, given the limited resources of the country, to employ for rationing investment by the state if Indian shipowners were to engage in cross-trades. The objective of this inward-oriented policy thus was not to endeavour to build a shipping industry qua industry which provided a source of income, profit and employment for its nationals, even as it may participate in the carriage of India's trades, but one strictly meant to service only its national trades.

One implication of this approach to fleet building is that, since shipping is a global industry, then restricting it to the national trades ran counter to the requirements of competition in such an industry. Perhaps this aspect was largely mitigated during the period by the operation of several factors. One, despite the proclaimed global nature of the industry, most states followed cargo support policies for their own merchant fleets. Two, the operation of cartelistic arrangements in any case modified drastically the operation of so-called free markets, at least in liner shipping. Three, despite the claim, the shipping industry was not truly global at the time; rather, it was fragmented, again at least in liner shipping. Shipping services were largely organized under the conference system on a point-to-point basis between countries. Even the bulk trades were vertically integrated with the other activities of the multinationals. Four, the industry was based on a technology that was, apart from increasing size, largely stable during the time. That reduced to some extent the handicaps of being isolated from competition. However, these were contingent factors and change in them could confront the Indian shipping industry with difficult problems.

In contrast to shipping, the concentration on the national market had more serious consequences for the shipbuilding industry. Addressed to the small local market, the local shipyards could hardly compare in efficiency and pricing with yards elsewhere, which were founded on the idea of catering to both the domestic and foreign markets. In this, they reflected the larger inefficiencies of import-substituting industrialisation, regardless of sector. However, while there were no such immediate consequences for shipping, concentrating on national trades alone served to confine the vision of managements to the home front, with relatively little attention given to world developments, and prevented them from learning from competition in foreign markets.

The counterpart in shipping to import-substituting industrialisation was the aim of reducing the share of foreign lines in India's trades, with shipping firms under Indian management and control increasingly substituting themselves for foreign firms in the carriage of Indian cargo. The intent was, as in the case of all import-substitution, to benefit from entering a market that had already been made manifest by others and that was potentially susceptible to national appropriation and state protection. Towards this end, the state pressured the conferences to admit Indian lines and to provide them an adequate share of the trade. Significantly, in 1961, a pooling arrangement came into effect among the most important of the conferences in India's trades, the India-UK/Continent conference, which provided a substantial share to Indian shipping. The state also encouraged and supported during the period the diversification of the merchant fleet in respect of bulk carriers and oil tankers. Particularly noteworthy here is the dramatic launching in 1961 of the Jayanti Shipping Company in the private sector, with enthusiastic personal support from the highest level of the government, that of the prime minister, for the carriage of oil and bulk cargo.

Finally, here as elsewhere in the economy, the public sector was privileged by the state to assume the dominant role in the expansion of India's merchant fleet. The Industrial Policy Resolution of 1956 had already settled the issue of the role of the public sector in shipping, but the execution of its mandate in shipping had been delayed by leaders like Lal Bahadur Shastri and S.K. Patil, who were genuinely appreciative of the achievements of the private sector. By the end of the 1950s, however, the new leadership at the helm of the shipping portfolio reversed this posture and made an open declaration of its commitment to make the public sector dominant. Significantly, again, in 1961, the two largely somnolent public sector shipping corporations--Eastern Shipping Corporation and Western Shipping Corporation--were merged into the single Shipping Corporation of India (SCI), which eventually came to control half of India's tonnage.

The year 1961, at the beginning of the period of rapid expansion of the fleet, was thus an important watershed in the development of the Indian fleet. For, it marked the initiation of a long-term arrangement for cargo support through the mechanism of pooling arrangements with important conferences, the start of diversification of the merchant fleet through a dramatic entry in the oil and bulk trades, and the merger of the two public sector firms into SCI as the dedicated instrument for accelerated tonnage acquisition. With these elements in place, fleet expansion could then advance. The state further sustained the endeavour and set the pace for expansion through periodic goal-setting, not inconsiderable allocation of public funds, and a complex of promotional policies. A central role in all this was accorded to the public sector, and its expansion as well as that of the private sector was sought to be coordinated through the planning process.

Finance for Shipping Under Planning

That the tonnage expanded rapidly in the period from 1960 to 1980 is undeniable. That it did so ought not to be surprising in view of the considerable assistance that the government provided, especially financially. To be sure, the government did not recognize shipping to be a part of the core sector in its five year plans. However, in actual fact the government was forthcoming in manifold ways to help the industry in fleet expansion. Indeed, it would seem that the notion that shipping had low priority with the government, because of the higher value placed on steel and heavy industry, is more applicable to the subsequent period and may well be a rationalization for the later deterioration in state capacity. In the period under consideration, notwithstanding a stringent regulatory system of licensing and controls, the state acted as a positive force with an active and dynamic policy, facilitating, indeed pushing, fleet expansion. There were four elements in this dynamic policy: (1) direct budgetary support for fleet expansion in the public sector; (2) state finance for loans to shipping in the public and private sectors; (3) tax incentives for the internal generation of resources by shipping enterprises; and (4) facilitating acquisition of loan finance from foreign sources for both the public and private sectors.

THE BIG PUSH FOR THE PUBLIC SECTOR

After the initiation of the planning process in 1951, support for expansion of the fleet in the public sector was extended on the basis of overall forward planning for the economy as a whole. The various five year plans established the overall objectives for the shipping sector for each period, laid down the physical targets for tonnage acquisition of various kinds, and allocated the financial outlays for the public sector and private sector. The private sector often complained of the favoured and preferential treatment given by the government to the public sector and its crowding out effect on investment in the private sector. Valid as the complaint was, the favoured treatment was a function of high policy. The Industrial Policy Resolution of 1956 had assigned sea transport to the list of industries which were to be "progressively state-owned" and where the state was expected largely to "take the initiative" in starting new undertakings, even as private enterprise was allowed "to supplement" such state effort. There had not been much movement in this direction during the Second Five Year Plan (1956-1961), but with the change in leadership in charge of the shipping portfolio in the government near the end of that plan, and the emphatic support of the Estimates Committee, a reversal of the earlier state policy of a more evenhanded approach towards the two sectors was initiated and this was reflected in subsequent plans.

The Third Five Year Plan (1961-1966), which came at the beginning of the period of rapid expansion, was formulated amid considerable controversy over what its targets ought to be. Initially, the National Shipping Board, under the chairmanship of the highly respected business leader and former ambassador to the United States, G.L. Mehta, had recommended a target of 1.6M grt compared to the Second Plan's target of 0.9M grt. This target would have required an outlay of Rs. 1,430 million, with as much as 93 per cent of it in foreign exchange.[11] Subsequently, the Board reduced its ambitions to a more modest target of 1.4M grt. The Board's rationale for the target was that 100,000 grt had been added annually in the last two years of the Second Plan, and that momentum needed to be sustained.[12]

However, the Third Plan as finalized incorporated a target of a mere 1.08M grt,[13] which was only marginally higher than the achievement of 0.86M grt at the end of the Second Plan.

The financial outlay was not very much higher than the revised expenditure figures under the Second Plan (see Table 4.1). There was consequently deep disappointment in the shipping industry, and the National Shipping Board protested but only in vain. Mehta felt that the decision, "if left unaltered, would lead to a serious retardation in the pace of expansion of Indian shipping".[14] Observers wondered about the imbalance between the demand for transport capacity that planners were creating through planned development and the allocations that they made for transport. They termed the planners' action as "a great betrayal", and concluded that "India is slipping badly in her sense of independence, so far as promotion of her own shipping is concerned".[15] Of course, the planning commission itself "recognized that the expansion of shipping has a high priority" since it would make possible the saving of foreign exchange on the carriage of foreign trade. On the other hand, the foreign exchange constraint served to prevent it from pursuing any ambitious path. Indeed, it acknowledged its helplessness by noting that "the development programme for shipping, however, depends largely on the availability of foreign aid for this purpose, and of necessity has to be modest".[16]

What is more noteworthy than the overall target is the emphatic shift in the balance between the public and private sectors in plan outlays. The Third Plan made a provision of Rs. 550 million for ship acquisitions, and assumed that another Rs. 40 million would be forthcoming from the Shipping Development Fund, while the shipping companies would themselves generate Rs. 70 million for investment. The share of the two sectors in the total outlay was set at half and half. The shift between the two sectors is especially apparent in the actual tonnage to be acquired for overseas shipping either by way of replacement or addition. As against the figure of 91,200 grt for the private sector, that for the public sector was placed at 150,800. Astutely, refraining from a more active participation from the less lucrative coastal shipping, the public sector planned to acquire a mere 7,500 grt there compared with the expectation of the acquisition of 125,000 grt by the private sector.[17]

While the Third Plan made apparent the government's decisive tilt towards the public sector, it was not clear as to precisely what share for that sector in the country's tonnage was the ultimate goal. The government as such had not given serious consideration to the matter, but omens were already available of the general direction of its thinking. A planning group established by the planning commission had recommended that the public sector should have a share of 50 per cent of the total tonnage by 1975-76, a recommendation which had the endorsement of the planning commission as also of the parliamentary Committee on Public Undertakings.[18]

At first blush, the modest scope of the overall targets and outlays in the Third Plan seems inconsistent with the broader assessment of the period from 1960 to 1980 as one of rapid expansion. However, advance planning seems to have borne little relationship to the actual expansion as far as the merchant fleet was concerned. Take the Third Plan itself. Rather than setting the pace for the shipping sector, the planners had to keep catching up with developments there. After the plan was under way, the target was first revised to 1.25M grt and then again to 1.33M grt.[19] Indeed, the Minister for Transport announced that the tonnage was likely to be 1.8M grt by the time the plan would conclude on March 31, 1966. Meanwhile, he claimed that he had other proposals under consideration which were likely to take the total tonnage to 2.5M grt by that date--which would have been more than twice the figure that was originally planned.[20] The eventual achievement was over 1.5M grt compared to the original target of 1.08M. That this feat was accomplished without increasing the outlay--indeed, expenditures fell far short of the planned outlay, and were one-fourth lower than even those of the Second Plan (see Table 4.1)--underlines the poor relationship between planning and actual tonnage growth.

Subsequent events rendered planning even more problematic for shipping. Initially, the economic planners envisaged doubling the tonnage to 3.0M grt during the Fourth Five Year Plan (1966-1971),[21] while some public figures demanded a higher target at 3.5M, or even 4 to 5M grt.[22] However, unfortunately for them, after the conclusion of the Third Plan, planning entered a period of suspension as a result of the economic crisis in the mid-1960s and the political crisis that followed on the heels of it. In these circumstances, the originally drafted Fourth Five Year Plan could not be finalized and was jettisoned. There followed a planning interregnum which lasted for three years. Ironically, India achieved its long sought after goal of a tonnage of 2M grt in 1969 during this interregnum.

TABLE 4.1: OUTLAYS AND EXPENDITURES IN FIVE YEAR PLANS (RS. MILLION)

Plan	*Period*	*Outlay*	*Expenditure*
First	1951-1956	260	190
Second	1956-1961	480	530
Third	1961-1966	570	400
Annual	1966-1969	230	320
Fourth	1969-1974	1,410	1,550
Fifth	1974-1979	4,500	4,690
Annual	1979-80	1,650	1,470
Sixth	1980-1985	7,550	4,440
Seventh	1985-1990	8,270	9,810
Annual	1990-91	7,760	6,660

Source: India, Ministry of Surface Transport, cited in N.C. Jain, "Indian Shipping and Future Development" (project paper in typescript; Cardiff: Department of Maritime Studies and International Transport, University of Wales, 1993), Annexure III. Mr. Jain is an official in the Ministry of Surface Transport.

Despite the adverse circumstances, a new Fourth Five Year Plan (1969-1974) was finally adopted. The target set for shipping was a total tonnage of 4.0M grt, with 3.5M grt of it to be in actual operation by 1974 and another 0.5M grt to be on order. The expectation was that with this tonnage India would be able to carry 40 per cent of its overseas trades by the end of the plan.[23] At the end of the plan, India had in operation 3.0M grt while another 2.0M grt was under construction. Even though the actual achievement was not precisely congruent with what had been planned, it was a considerable accomplishment given the disturbed economic and political situation of the period.

After the end of the Fourth Plan, Indian shipping, along with world shipping, entered into a period of severe crisis, which rendered planning altogether meaningless. The Fifth Five Year

Plan (1974-1979) set a target of 8.6M grt for tonnage in operation and 1.0M grt on order. The target for the operational tonnage was later drastically reduced to 6.5M grt, while the actual achievement turned out to be 5.5M grt. Essentially, it seems that it was policy--along with the business environment--not planning, that was important in the expansion of shipping. However, planning provided a significant indicator of the importance that the public sector had in the estimation of the government. In the final analysis, what stands out is that the share of the public sector, either through state-sponsored investment or through nationalization of private enterprises, underwent a dramatic expansion in a matter of a decade and a half (see Table 4.2).

At the end of World War II, Indian tonnage was slightly less than 100,000 grt, which was entirely in the private sector, and four-fifths of it was owned by Scindia Steam Navigation. Little wonder that Scindia's shipping was taken to be equivalent to Indian shipping. About a decade later in 1956, over 90 per cent of the tonnage was still in the private sector, with the public sector's share at less than 10 per cent. Scindia owned over 60 per cent of the tonnage at that time. The next two largest enterprises, though with small tonnages, were India Steamship (16.9 per cent) and Great Eastern (8.2 per cent). Even by 1959, the public sector's share did not loom large, for it had increased to only 15 per cent; as late as 1964, it was still less than 20 per cent.

In 1960, the government had bought 80 per cent of the shares of Mogul Line, thus bringing it under Indian control as also within the public sector. Meanwhile, Jayanti Shipping, which had been established in the private sector in 1961, saw a meteoric rise. With its tonnage in 1964 at 311,161 grt, it stood out as the largest among the private sector companies, eclipsing Scindia. Its tonnage alone was larger than the total for the entire public sector. However, its existence in the private sector was short lived. Because of Jayanti's financial problems, the government took it over and placed it under SCI management in 1966, quickly boosting the share of the public sector. Meanwhile,SCI itself made a "great leap forward", expanding by three and a half times from 0.23M grt in 1964 to 0.82M grt in 1970. As a result, the public sector's share ballooned to nearly 50 per cent by 1970, literally achieving a half-decade

TABLE 4.2: EXPANSION OF THE PUBLIC SECTOR, 1956-1980

	1956		*1959*		*1964*	
Firm	*Grt*	*%*	*Grt*	*%*	*Grt*	*%*
Public Sector	44,237	8.8	111,504	15.0	267,518	18.9
SCI	42,297	8.4	101,002	13.6	231,117	16.3
Mogul Line	-	-	-	-	25,899	1.8
Jayanti	-	-	-	-	-	-
Private Sector	458,666	91.2	631,778	85.0	1,147,251	81.1
Scindia	308,064	61.3	278,307	37.4	305,679	21.6
India SS	85,192	16.9	132,796	17.9	133,229	9.4
Great Eastern	41,071	8.2	92,491	12.4	127,924	9.0
Jayanti	-	-	-	-	311,161	22.0
South India	-	-	-	-	-	-
Total	502,903		743,282		1,414,769	

earlier what the parliamentary Committee on Public Undertakings had envisaged for 1975-76. This dramatic increase is all the more impressive in the light of the fact that the country's total tonnage had, in the meantime, expanded by about three-and-a-half times from 0.74M grt in 1959 to 2.39M grt in 1970.

By 1975, the share of the public sector had gone up even higher to over 55 per cent, even as the country's tonnage increased to 4.46M grt. It stayed above 55 per cent in 1980 even while India's tonnage had gone up by more than a million grt to 5.68M grt. SCI alone owned more than 50 per cent of the country's total tonnage in 1975 and 1980. On the other hand, compared to SCI, the private sector companies were just pygmies. The largest of them, Scindia, had less than 10 per cent of the total tonnage and was less than one-fifth the size of the public sector giant, as were the next two largest companies put together--Great Eastern and India Steamship. Little wonder that an SCI chairman exclaimed: "To a large extent the saga of mo-

TABLE 4.2A: EXPANSION OF THE PUBLIC SECTOR, 1956-1980

	1970		*1975*		*1980*	
Firm	*Grt*	*%*	*Grt*	*%*	*Grt*	*%*
Public Sector	1,152,705	48.1	2,491,292	55.8	3,144,669	55.4
SCI	817,613	34.1	2,275,594	51.0	2,936,034	51.7
Mogul Line	29,680	1.2	194,153	4.4	191,640	3.4
Jayanti	295,298	12.3	-	-	-	-
Private Sector	1,244,743	51.9	1,972,341	44.2	2,534,767	44.6
Scindia	349,962	14.6	531,954	11.9	553,878	9.8
India SS	152,745	6.4	205,820	4.6	203,773	3.6
Great Eastern	171,689	7.2	318,756	7.1	371,201	6.5
Jayanti	-	-	-	-	-	-
South India	121,813	5.1	151,142	3.4	151,144	2.7
Total	2,397,448		4,463,633		5,679,436	

Source: (1) 1956 (figures for March 31): M.A. Master, *So I Rest On My Oars: Collection of Writings and Speeches, 1947-1970,* ed. by K.V. Hariharan (Bombay: M.A. Master Memorial Trust, 1977), I, p. 585, II, pp. 714-717; (2) 1959 (November 30): *ibid.,* I, pp. 647-51; (3) 1964 (December 31): T.S. Sanjeeva Rao, *A Short History of Modern Indian Shipping* (Bombay: Popular Prakashan, 1965), pp. 242-49; (4) 1970, 1975 and 1980 (December 31): India, Director General of Shipping, Bombay.

N.B.: (1) Mogul Line came under Indian control and into the public sector in 1960 when the Government of India purchased 80 per cent of its shares. (2) Jayanti came under the management of the Shipping Corporation of India (SCI) in 1966, and was merged into SCI in 1973.

dern Indian shipping is the story of the Shipping Corporation of India".[24] At the same time, by raising a shipping behemoth in the form of SCI, the state precluded the development of shipping giants in the private sector with the capacity and strength to compete with carriers in the international arena (see also Table 4.4).

Significantly, an even larger role was contemplated for the public sector in the future. A working group for shipping appointed by the planning commission for the Seventh Five Year Plan (1985-1990) regarded SCI as "the company with the best potential for growth in the 7th Plan period". It acknowledged that policy under the Sixth Plan (1980-1985) aimed at maintaining the public-private ratio in tonnage at 55:45 but found that the actual ratio at the end of that Plan would be 65:35. It then went on to recommend that "in view of the greater potential for growth in the public sector as compared to the private sector... the ratio between the public sector and the private sector may be kept at 65:35 in the 7th Plan".[25] Later, another committee of the planning commission to review transport needs to the end of the century also thought that this ratio "could be expected to continue in future". However, it felt that, in view of the large resources required for tonnage acquisition, the figure for the private sector may actually be lower, varying "between 30 and 40 per cent".[26]

Thus, for three decades after 1960 the public sector was seen by the planners as the engine for tonnage expansion to the end of the century. In comparing or planning for the tonnage shares of the public sector--essentially SCI--and private sector, there were "implied as well as explicit claims made by spokesmen of Shipping Corporation that private sector companies did not have the same level of enterprise and dynamism as SCI".[27] There is no doubt that SCI proved to be a successful organization during this period of expansion. Its efficiency was attested to by the World Bank when, prior to sanctioning a loan of US$83 million in 1972 for the purchase of six tankers, it made a thorough appraisal of the agency and concluded: "SCI is well managed and compares favourably in operation with many shipping companies in developed countries. New methods and techniques are gradually being introduced which should improve managerial and technical efficiency still further".[28]

Founded in 1961 during the heyday of planning and state power, with the positive state at its peak, the organization had the benefit of extraordinary leadership over its first decade when it saw such dramatic growth. Indeed, a SCI chief in the 1980s gave expression to a sentiment universally shared in the shipping community: "Much of the credit for the rapid expansion in the right direction must go to one man--Mr. C.P.

Srivastava, for ten years the Chairman and Managing Director of the SCI".[29] In a private interview in 1982, the then SCI Director (Planning), L.M.S. Rajwar, who himself later headed SCI, confirmed this assessment when he emphasized the factor of leadership in explaining the success of SCI:

> We had one person, Mr. Srivastava, who was associated with the company from the very beginning. He was the first MD and stayed on till about 1972 for about 10 years. He was a very dynamic person and his word carried a lot of weight in Delhi. He was a bureaucrat but spent almost all his entire career in shipping. He was a professional shipping manager. But, because of his stature and because of his having been with one of the prime ministers of the country, he was known. A man of ideas, impeccable integrity, and he is even today a very big name in shipping.[30]

It was not only the upper management that shared this opinion. Srivastava commanded respect and admiration at lower levels as well. A junior manager in 1992 asserted in private that "the most outstanding of the managing directors of SCI had been C.P. Srivastava. He was an IAS officer but had been D.G. Shipping and knew more about shipping than even the technical people. No captain could say this is the situation technically, because Srivastava would know 10 per cent more than the officer. His contribution was the greatest".[31]

Chandrika Prasad Srivastava joined the Indian Foreign Service in 1948 and the Indian Administrative Service (IAS) a year later. During the late 1950s, he worked as private secretary to the then Minister of Commerce Lal Bahadur Shastri.[32] This was an important event in his career. Indeed, his career reveals the inspiration talented civil servants drew from the dedication and patriotism of the political leaders of the time in pushing forward national projects. He came to devoutly admire Shastri: "Just look at the humility of the man.... His great genius was for man management. Whether he was speaking to a cabinet colleague, or to an orderly opening a door for him, he would speak in the same unhurried fashion. He was also very honest. Very practical, even though he had a great deal of idealism". Shastri had a tremendous impact on Srivastava's outlook and values. Srivastava himself became known as "one of nature's gentlemen", imbued by "his own special brand of pragmatic idealism".[33] Many years later, he wrote what is likely to be the definitive political biography of Shastri.[34]

For some three years, from 1959 to 1961, Srivastava worked as Senior Deputy Director General of Shipping. This prepared him technically in matters of shipping. When the SCI was established in 1961 through the merger of the Eastern Shipping Corporation and Western Shipping Corporation, he was appointed to head it as managing director. His tenure at SCI was interrupted when in mid-1964, on becoming prime minister, Shastri invited him to join his secretariat. When Shastri died in January 1966, Srivastava returned to SCI as both chairman and managing director, and provided it leadership of a high order for another half-dozen years. SCI saw rapid expansion, and its increasing clout and Srivastava's talents were reflected in his election to the presidentship of INSA three times. Meanwhile, his talents also received increasing recognition in international diplomacy, where unanimity in his election to important offices became the order of the day. In 1972, he was elected chairman of UNCTAD's committee on shipping at its Santiago session, and played a key role in developing recommendations on liner conferences. This was followed by his election to the chairmanship of the 48-nation preparatory committee to draft a code of conduct for liner conferences, where he endeavoured to find common ground between the developed and developing countries. As if in a natural progression, these positions led to his election as president of the UN Conference of Plenipotentiaries, which in 1974 adopted the UN Code of Conduct for Liner Conferences. Earlier, in June 1973, he had been elected Secretary General of the International Maritime Organization, an office that he held for an unprecedented tenure of four terms of four years each. From 1983 to 1991 he also served as the Founder Chancellor of the World Maritime University at Malmo in Sweden. Honours and decorations came to him in abundance, not only from India but also from the UK, France and Germany and several other countries. After his retirement, he headed the important Committee on Maritime Education and Training (COMET), which recommended the establishment of a maritime university in India.

While at the SCI, Srivastava in turn brought other younger talented managers to the enterprise and inspired them. One of them was L.M.S. Rajwar, who came to shipping from the railways in 1966. He later served as the leader of the Group of 77 at the UNCTAD conference on the liner code; "indeed, he can lay claim to having played a significant role in the conception and birth of that organization's Code of Conduct for Liner Conferences--acting, if not in a paternal capacity, then certainly as a midwife".[35] In 1985, he became chairman and managing director of SCI, and served in that position until 1989. Rajwar presided over the international review conference on the liner code in 1988 and, while the conference proved futile from the perspective of the developing world, he was respected as "one of that select group of individuals who can move with apparent ease between the diplomatic-political area and commerce".[36]

Leadership was, no doubt, important in the dynamic growth of the public sector during the 1960s and 1970s, but there were other factors that worked to its advantage as well, chief among them that SCI was favoured by the government since it belonged to the public sector; indeed, it was part of the government. The private sector often protested about the special treatment accorded to the public sector, but there was nothing underhanded about this since it was state policy to rely on the public sector for growth and expansion in sea transport. The special treatment towards the public sector was evident in several areas. First and foremost, it was apparent in the budgetary support that was made available to SCI in line with the priorities set in the five year plans. It is significant that by 1966 SCI, with a paid-up capital of Rs. 230 million, all subscribed by the state, was "the highest capitalized shipping company in India".[37] Second, SCI had privileged access to loans compared to the private sector, again because of the priority it commanded as an agency designated by the state for spearheading growth in shipping. Third, in spite of having grown by 1970 to be larger than the four largest private sector shipping companies put together, and by 1975 to be larger than the entire private sector, it was as a state enterprise exempt from the scrutiny and delaying process of the Monopolies and Restrictive Trade Practices (MRTP) Act. On the other hand, the private sector enterprises, which were puny in comparison to it, could not expand without being scrutinized in respect of the MRTP Act provisions, which put them at a disadvantage. Says Sanklecha: "Many times the applications for expansion were rejected. Even when they were eventually approved, it involved a time factor of six months. By then the opportunities of acquisition of ships were lost in some of these cases".[38]

Fourth, certain measures of cargo support were made available to SCI which were largely denied to the private sector. The government pressured the India-UK/Continent conference to admit SCI to its membership whereas it stood aside when Great Eastern was denied entry in this and other trades. Moreover, the allocation of routes and the distribution of cargo shares to Indian shipowners by the conferences was, at the behest of government, arranged to favour SCI. Scindia chairman Dharamsey M. Khatau called attention to the government's differential treatment in 1966:

> Private companies have not been permitted to enter trades in which the Shipping Corporation of India happened to offer service first. In the routes which were already adequately served by private sector companies, it was arranged that the Shipping Corporation should have a substantial share. In the trades in which the Corporation claims to coexist with private companies, executive patronage has been employed to conduct an unequal race. I cannot help feeling that Government does not hold the scales even between the Public and Private Sectors in the field of shipping.

The next year, he returned to the theme:

> It was because of the Private Sector's efforts that India was successful in securing participation for Indian shipping in the UK-Continental Liner Services. When, however, the Shipping Corporation of India came into existence, Government intervened to secure for it a share in that trade according to a formula under which, while our share remains the same, that of the Shipping Corporation goes on increasing.[39]

Again, in respect of the Japan-India trade, in the building of which Great Eastern had played a major role, "the government and the Shipping Corporation arranged matters in such a way that not only did Great Eastern not get membership of the Conference but was ousted from the Japan-India trade".[40] An even more interesting illustration of the government's stance was its action in the mid-1960s to place restrictions on Scindia's resumption of participation in the India-US trade, which it had pioneered in 1948. Only when Scindia threatened to go to court did the government relent.[41]

Even in regard to coastal trades, preferential treatment is said to have been accorded to SCI and, in the eyes of some, "the government was guilty of double standards in regard to the shipment of government cargoes by Indian ships".[42] Indeed, the discrimination in favour of SCI proved so glaring to Great Eastern that its chairman, A.H. Bhiwandiwalla, warned in a prescient statement in December 1961:

> All Government cargoes are offered first to the Shipping Corporation of India, and, if there is any overflow, it is offered to the Great Eastern Shipping Co. or any other line. Frequently, this policy is inconvenient to the consignees of cargo.... Besides the Government today is perhaps the largest single importer in this country. If, therefore, they follow a policy of preferring the Shipping Corporation of India to other Indian Companies...there will come a stage when the only company that can expand with any degree of confidence will be the Shipping Corporation of India.[43]

Fifth, and finally, the government benefited SCI immensely by reserving the import of crude oil exclusively for it. This trade was especially lucrative for SCI since the government contracted with it to pay for the freight on a cost-plus basis. The private sector had a strong grievance against the government on this count even as the government made an exception now and then at its discretion for one or another private company to acquire a tanker or two. In the product tanker trade also, the government gave preferential treatment to SCI.

However, these advantages for SCI need to be set against the fact that SCI had to bear the burden of social obligations expected of the public sector. The most important of these was the running of loss-making passenger and cargo services to the offshore Andaman and Lakshadweep islands. Over the period from 1970-71 to 1986-87, SCI incurred a total loss of Rs. 430 million on account of running these services;[44] in the 1980s, the annual loss from these operations was to the tune of Rs. 140 million. SCI was expected to absorb the total loss if it had an overall profit and only 20 per cent of it in case of an overall loss, a requirement which affected its ability to accumulate reserves.[45] Not until 1988 did the government rescind the obligation.[46]

Regardless of the notion that the private sector was discriminated against, what is significant is that the state bet on the public sector as the engine of growth in shipping and it was remarkably successful in achieving this aim. This growth was advanced by the same state through the additional mechanism of providing loan finance. Such finance was available to shipping in general, including both the public and private sectors, although the public sector may have been privileged because it owned such a large part of the total tonnage and also because it was part of the state that dispensed the funds.

LOAN FINANCE FOR SHIPPING

The Shipping Development Fund--or, more popularly SDFC, after the Shipping Development Fund Committee which administered it--was a key financial mechanism in the expansion of the merchant fleet. Although loans had been extended to the shipping sector on an ad hoc basis since the inauguration of economic planning in 1951, Lal Bahadur Shastri promised in 1957 to provide loan finance on a more systematic and sustained basis through establishing a permanent, non-lapsable fund. Later, the intent was given a statutory form under the Merchant Shipping Act of 1958, and as a result the SDFC came into operation in 1959. For its funds, the SDFC drew on grants and loans made available to it by the state plus repayments on loans given to shipping companies.

SDFC extended loans on easy terms, and for that reason they were limited to strictly shipping companies so that the funds were not diverted to other business activities. Companies receiving loans were required to have one or more directors on behalf of SDFC on their boards as a sort of watchdog. This was over and above the stringent controls that government had over shipping companies under its regulatory framework. The terms of SDFC loans were easy in four decisive respects. One, low interest rates were charged, which were in effect negative rates of interest. These varied over the period of the Fund's existence, being set at 3 per cent during 1959-1971, 4.5 per cent during 1971-1982, and 7.5 per cent during 1982-1987. Two, a significant period of initial moratorium on repayments was provided, generally of one to two years in duration. Three, a long period for repayment was allowed, varying from 14 to 17 years. Fourth, and importantly, the entrepreneur was required to contribute very little by way of funds for the purchase of vessels, since the loan could cover up to 90 per cent of the cost of new tankers or ships from foreign shipyards, and even up to 95 per cent of the cost in the case of new ships built at Indian shipyards.[47] In addition, SDFC provided guarantees and counter-guarantees to shipyards and banks for financing acquisition of ships abroad by Indian firms. While shipping companies in India justifiably claim credit for rapidly expanding tonnage in the 1960s and 1970s, it can be seen that it was no spectacular feat in enterprise, given the availability of loan finance on such easy terms.

By April 3, 1987, when it was abolished, SDFC had provided loans in the amount of Rs. 14.52 billion and paid another Rs. 567 million under guarantees and counter-guarantees. Most of the expenditure by way of loans, as much as 85 per cent, took place by 1982-83 (see Table 4.3). Over the period of its existence, SDFC issued guarantees and counter-guarantees for another Rs. 18.40 billion.[48] The contribution of SDFC to the build-up of Indian tonnage was thus enormous. On March 31, 1986 (by which time SDFC had loaned Rs. 13.37 billion), the net tonnage in operation purchased with its assistance stood at 5.21M grt, which was 90.5 per cent of India's total operative tonnage at the time.[49] Despite the large tonnage acquired, the real burden on the state was not excessive, amounting over a period of 27 years to some Rs. 1.75 billion by way of subsidy on interest.[50] That works out to about Rs. 65 million a year on the average. The state was thus able to help build a merchant fleet of over 5 million grt on the cheap. However, notwithstanding its readiness to extend loan finance for acquisition of ships, the Indian state never relented on its opposition to providing any operating subsidies despite pressure from time to time by Indian shipowners and members of parliament.

Despite the claim about its permanent and non-lapsable status, SDFC was not endowed adequately with funds. Consequently, it remained perpetually dependent on annual budgetary allocations from the state. To that extent, there was

TABLE 4.3: CUMULATIVE LOANS BY SDFC (RS. MILLION)

Year	*Loans Disbursed*	*Guarantees and Counter-Guarantees*	*Tonnage Acquired ('000 GRT)*
1959-60	28.7	-	66.9
1960-61	31.3	-	192.4
1970-71	1,420.9	308.7	2,503.0
1974-75	3,920.1	2,960.1	4,354.1
1978-79	7,638.1	8,068.9	5,272.2
1980-81	9,586.9	8,409.7	-
1981-82	10,639.6	8,971.7	-
1982-83	11,479.3	9,562.9	-
1983-84	11,882.2	11,162.1	-
1984-85	12,525.9	14,303.4	-
1985-86	13,374.3	16,561.0	-

Source: Dev Raj, *Shipping and Shipbuilding Industry in India* (Delhi: H.K. Publishers, 1990), pp. 48-49, where the figures are compiled from the annual reports of the Shipping Development Fund Committee for the years 1977-78 and 1987-88. The figures for tonnage acquired are cumulative.

always uncertainty for shipping companies about obtaining loans and therefore to plan expansion confidently. Even when loans were sanctioned, SDFC was at times not forthcoming with funds. Decisions on loans were made by SDFC on a case by case basis, and that left room for the operation of influence and pressure. One spectacular case that aroused a great deal of controversy was the very large loan given to Jayanti Shipping Company quite early in the history of SDFC on terms that were regarded as suggestive of favouritism. Indeed, the loan to Jayanti has been seen as the start of subverting the observation of proper norms in the disbursal of funds to Indian shipping.

A conjuncture of circumstances arose in the late 1950s and early 1960s to momentarily propel Jayanti into the forefront of Indian shipping. At the centre of this conjuncture was the dynamic and rather flamboyant personality of Dr. Jayanti Dharma Teja, who had acquired his business experience in the United States. Equally, there was the anxiety on the part of the planners to quickly expand the merchant fleet but without much state investment because of the constraint on resources.

The Indian fleet in 1960, towards the end of the Second Plan, consisted primarily of liner cargo vessels of modest size, invariably below 10,000 grt. While some beginning had been made in tramp shipping and also a token entry into oil tankers, the fleet was strikingly deficient in bulk carriers and tankers. On the other hand, there were taking place at the time huge imports of foodgrains from the United States and, in view of the inadequacy and deficiencies of the Indian fleet, these were being brought in by foreign vessels. Nehru himself had expressed alarm in 1959 at the large outflow of foreign exchange in freight payments to foreign carriers. Accordingly, "since the beginning of the Third Plan period the programme of expansion of tonnage has been weighted in favour of bulk carriers, ore-bulk-oil carriers and overseas tankers. This had necessarily to be so because about two-thirds of our overseas trade is composed of bulk commodities like iron ore, foodgrains and petroleum products".[51]

In May 1960, India entered into a long-term agreement with the United States for the import of 17 million tons of PL-480 foodgrains over the subsequent four years.[52] The state was anxious for expansion of the merchant fleet to carry its share of up to 50 per cent of the foodgrains that was not reserved for US carriers. At the same time, refineries in India were importing several million tons of crude oil annually, which was brought in by foreign tankers. India's anxiety to build its fleet tonnage rapidly, even if with foreign participation, had become evident in 1958 in the controversy over the Merchant Shipping Act. At that time, Indian shipowners were able to get the government to back down on its planned liberal welcome to foreign investors in the shipping sector and to limit foreign investment in shipping companies to 25 per cent. However, the government continued to discuss the issue with American shipping companies. One of these was the Kulkundis group.[53]

At this point, initially with the backing and equity participation of Kulkundis, Dharma Teja burst on the scene like a meteor. Shortly after the company's registration in February 1961, he brought on to the Indian register the country's first supertanker, marking India's entry into the overseas tanker trade. This acquisition represented an exemption for Jayanti by the government from the reservation of the oil trade for the public sector. Teja met with Nehru and impressed him immensely with his daring and dynamism. He convinced Indian decision-makers that there was a quick way to expand the Indian fleet exponentially through credit financing, rather than incrementally as was being done hitherto. He proposed to the government a bold programme for the acquisition on deferred payment of 13 bulk carriers, which would add 185,000 grt to the country's tonnage within three years. The ships were to be designed to carry foodgrain imports from the US and Indian exports of ore and sugar. The plan envisaged placing orders on a Japanese shipyard, with 10 per cent of the price to be paid only on delivery while the remaining 90 per cent would be paid later in seven equal annual instalments. Since the annual payments would come out of the ship's earnings, the only real demand on resources for investment was the initial payment of 10 per cent. A variation on the scheme was to acquire tankers and place them on long-term time charter with oil companies and pay the annual instalments out of the charter hire earnings.[54]

Deferred credits were not unknown to Indian shipowners, but the large scale on which Teja planned and the intent--that of quickly creating huge assets for a new shipping company with little initial investment--were novel for India. He himself explained the distinctiveness of his mode of financing and why it was particularly suited for underdeveloped countries anxious to build merchant fleets:

> There are three ways of building shipping tonnage that I know of--One by abundant capitalization like our public shipping corporation, the second is to build tonnage slowly but surely over a long period of time while increasing share capital and accumulating reserves and the third way--our way of adequate if modest share capital acquisition of very large tonnage in a short period on deferred payment terms and carrying the burden of paying for the vessels as a challenge which is to be met from the employment and earnings of the vessels. I somehow feel that the third way is most suitable for a poor country like ours, where capital formation is almost non-existent.[55]

With his personal access to Nehru, many doors opened for Teja in the government, and rules and regulations were bent to assist him in accomplishing his aims. The government gave him a loan of more than Rs. 200 million, relaxing its requirements on the extent of security needed and the duration of repayments, and, in addition, provided him bank guarantees, a measure that was unprecedented until then. This special treatment aroused a storm of controversy in the press and parliament. The Public Accounts Committee objected to the exceptional treatment given to Jayanti and the consequent deviations made from existing rules.[56] There were also suspicions over Teja being a mere front for foreign interests. However, everyone was enthralled by Teja's resourcefulness and drive as well as his actual accomplishments. By the end of 1964, his firm had emerged as the largest company with the biggest ships, which had added 311,161 grt to the country's tonnage (see Table 4.2). Its tonnage was larger than that of the entire public sector even as it put Scindia in the shade. Teja's ambition was to have his company alone acquire a fleet of 1 million grt by 1965. Meanwhile, Jayanti came under complete Indian control after the representative of the Kulkundis group withdrew from the board of directors.

Teja's mode of financing was unorthodox for Indian shipowners, but he showed them the way and soon other shipping companies began to follow his path. It is this path shown by a daring entrepreneur in the private sector which explains what would otherwise remain a mystery--the expansion of the Indian merchant fleet far beyond what was originally envisaged in the Third Five Year Plan, even as eventually less money was spent than planned. Teja's was thus a remarkable contribution; as a veteran observer of the shipping scene put it:

> The formation of Jayanti Shipping Co Pvt Ltd in February 1961 can be considered as an important landmark in the development of Indian shipping.... In the initial stages there was a lot of opposition and prejudice against the expansion undertaken by Jayanti Shipping, but as it emerged, Jayanti Shipping acquired ships which were very suitable for India's participation in the bulk cargo trades at favourable prices and credit terms. The big expansion undertaken by Jayanti Shipping not only added a sizeable tonnage on the Indian

Register but also spurred other Indian shipping companies to undertake expansion schemes. The mood of gloom and pessimism among Indian shipping companies was dispelled.[57]

A footnote to Teja's achievement is called for. Because of mismanagement, which was not related to the particular mode of financing, his company fell on difficult days. In exercise of its mortgage rights, the state took over the company in 1966 and placed it under the management of SCI, which act immediately boosted the public sector's tonnage. In 1971, Jayanti was made a subsidiary of SCI's, and finally in 1973 it was merged into SCI. The ships that SCI thus acquired proved especially profitable for it in the bulk and oil trades.

In the late 1960s, Indian politics had become fractious and had taken a more radical turn. Big business came under attack, with the Congress Party increasingly resorting to populist measures and appeals. One consequence was the further tightening of controls over big business through the passing of the MRTP Act while the other was large-scale nationalization of private enterprise in certain economic sectors. These larger trends were not without repercussions in the shipping sector. A form of "shipping populism" took hold in the SDFC, where a "need-based" approach was now adopted in granting loans. Under this approach, which emerged in 1969, loans were extended to companies, not necessarily on the basis of their financial creditworthiness, and thus their capacity to repay. Rather, contrary to principles of sound banking, SDFC as a state institution provided loan assistance to companies that were in need of funds because of their financially weak position and, consequently, lacking access to other commercial sources of funding. The policy's rationale lay in the possible diffusion of entrepreneurship and was in line with the reign of ideology prevalent at the time. However, its consequences were perverse.

One result of the need-based approach was that the shipping scene became populated with companies owning a mere one or two ships, with little strength to withstand the first whiff of recession in an industry which is so cyclical in nature. In the process, SDFC itself was potentially put at financial risk. By 1980, there were 62 shipping companies in India. Of these, 22 were one-ship companies, while another 12 were two-ship com-

TABLE 4.4: SDFC LOANS UP TO MARCH 31, 1977 (RS. MILLION)

Sector/Company	*Loans Sanctioned: Amount*	*Loans Disbursed Amount*	*%*	*GRT Addition Facilitated (Million)*
Public Sector	5,768.71	3,298.45	58.02	2.92
SCI	5,201.88	3,029.36	53.29	2.65
Mogul Line	487.84	256.56	4.51	0.24
Private Sector	4,016.52	2,386.29	41.98	2.14
Scindia	964.43	490.14	8.62	0.51
Great Eastern	641.14	609.64	10.72	0.53
India SS	437.05	246.97	4.34	0.07
Ratnakar	432.76	129.69	2.28	0.16
Chowgule	415.65	112.36	1.98	0.18
Damodar Bulk	346.92	215.69	3.79	0.14
Dempo	202.70	150.50	2.65	0.12
South India	189.18	189.18	3.33	0.15
Sagar	126.90	41.40	0.73	0.03
Total: All Companies	9,785.24	5,684.74	100.0	5.06

Source: Hardev Singh, "Tricolour on the High Seas", *Eastern Economist,* Annual Number 1979, December 29, 1978, pp. 1371-87. Only companies with loans sanctioned of more than Rs. 100 million are included.

panies. In all, 55 companies had six or less ships. There is thus evident a severe fragmentation of the industry, polarized between the massive behemoth of SCI in the public sector and a proliferation of minor companies in the private sector except for two or three medium-size companies. These last were, however, quite small in the international context. India was thus not preparing domestic giants, except for the one in the public sector, to be ready for international competition. Rather, it was dissipating resources among a large number of players who would have little chance of survival under recessionary conditions.

A second consequence was that the superior performance of financially sound companies was held against them and they were either denied loans or were provided only limited amounts for their expansion programmes. Such companies had then either to give up or reduce their expansion programmes or go to other commercial sources for finance at higher cost, which reduced their competitive position internationally. More generally, in line with the radical mood of the time, "the public sector Shipping Corporation of India received preferential treatment in getting loans from SDFC".[58] For example, by March 31, 1977, SDFC had advanced loans in the amount of Rs. 5684.74 million to shipping companies; of this, over 58 per cent was to the public sector, with SCI alone getting 53.29 per cent (see Table 4.4). Notwithstanding the distortions and the perennial scarcity of funds, SDFC played an extremely vital role in the spectacular expansion of tonnage during the 1960s and 1970s. It was a powerful mechanism in the hands of the state to accomplish its objective of building a large merchant fleet, and points to the utility of such an instrument in achieving similar objectives in the future.

OTHER FACILITIES FOR RESOURCE GENERATION

SDFC was not the only measure that the state employed to assist the shipping industry financially. The state also provided tax incentives to the industry to generate internal resources. The shipping industry could already avail of the 100 per cent depreciation over 20 years and the 25 per cent development rebate, instituted in 1955. Following the promise of Lal Bahadur Shastri in 1957, the rebate was increased in 1959 to 40 per cent specifically and only for the shipping industry.[59] The simple mechanism of the development rebate proved to be a powerful boost to the mobilization of savings for investment in shipping. It was, indeed, central to the expansion of tonnage during the golden era. It enabled shipowners to reduce their taxable income by setting aside for reinvestment from current earnings 40 per cent of the cost of new purchases of ships. This rebate was over and above the 100 per cent depreciation by instalments of 5 per cent a year. Thus, a combination of the rebate and depreciation allowed a shipowner to build a tax-exempt fund adequate to replace a ship at the original cost in as short a period as 12 years (40 plus 5 times 12 = 100). The rebate was especially attractive to shipowners since it was not dependent on case by case decisions of the government, but was available to all without conditions. When it was withdrawn in 1975, the shipping community universally protested against what it considered a retrograde move, and asked for its reinstatement. In addition to the development rebate, the shipping industry was able to avail of another tax privilege. When the 1957 budget imposed a wealth tax on companies, the shipping industry mounted a noisy campaign and obtained an exemption for itself.[60]

Beyond the measures of financial assistance provided by the state, the shipping industry was able to exploit with the help of the state the opportunities provided by foreign shipyards by way of deferred credits. As the shipbuilding industry revived in Europe and Japan after the war, vigorous competition ensued among foreign shipyards. To push sales, the shipyards extended deferred credits, with the active support of their states in the cause of export promotion.[61] The international environment was thus quite propitious for fleet expansion. Having been shown the way by Jayanti, Indian shipping companies seized the opportunity with guarantees and counter-guarantees offered by the state through SDFC, thus fuelling the Indian expansion during the 1960s. Subsequently, in 1969, to avoid cutthroat competition, the OECD countries agreed to stiffen the terms of export credits for sales of ships. As a result, a minimum of 20 per cent of the price was required as down payment at the time of delivery of the ship, with the remainder 80 per cent to be paid within a maximum period of eight years, at a minimum interest rate of 6 per cent.[62] These terms were hardened further in 1974, when a minimum down payment of 30 per cent was made obligatory, while the maximum period for payment of the remainder 70 per cent was reduced to seven years, and the minimum interest raised to 8 per cent.[63]

Getting the capital and the ships was only one requirement for the functioning of the shipping industry. It was equally necessary to assure adequate cargo for the ships so acquired. Here, too, the positive state was eager to help the industry.

CARGO SUPPORT FOR THE SHIPPING INDUSTRY

The state assured cargo for the shipping companies through several mechanisms, the principal one being facilitating the entry of Indian lines into the shipping conferences. The mechanisms also included bilateral shipping agreements with several countries, and coordination of shipment of government cargo.

THE USES OF CARTELS

At India's independence, its foreign trade consisted almost entirely of liner cargo while the prevailing model for organizing the shipping of such cargo was by way of conferences. From the very beginning, the Indian government favoured the operation of overseas trades through conferences in the belief that, without them, anarchy would prevail in the shipping arena. The major advantage of conferences for the government was that, once agreement on the entry of Indian lines and the tonnage allowed to them was reached, the monitoring and policing of affairs would be managed by the conferences themselves. Accordingly, the government supported the entry of Indian lines into conferences, notwithstanding the country's past experience when such conferences had crushed the rise of Indian shipping lines that dared to enter the overseas trade or even the domestic trades.

After a long history of having been forbidden to enter India's overseas trades, Scindia--along with India Steamship--was admitted in April 1948, soon after independence, to the most important and most lucrative conference in the country's trades, the India-UK/Continent conference, which was dominated by British shipping interests. The two lines were at the time allowed to enter only as "associate members", and could not run more than eight ships each on the route. When the Dutch freight war broke out in 1949, the conference allocated 45 per cent of the trade to the Dutch lines and only 8 per cent to India. The two lines protested at the humiliation, only to be told that they were merely associate members without voting rights. In 1950, both Scindia and India Steamship were admitted as full members but were restricted to running only 12 ships each, whereas they wanted the right to ply 17 ships each.

Subsequently, the number of ships allowed was increased to 18.[64] In all these negotiations, the Indian lines had the strong support of the Indian government; as Master noted: "They have stood solidly behind us in the negotiations that have been carried on for securing an entry for Indian lines in the various conferences that govern the carriage of overseas trades".[65] As if in agreement, SCI Director L.M.S. Rajwar observed nearly a quarter century later: "Through persuasion and helpful pressure exerted by the government Indian shipping lines were able to secure membership of all the Liner Conferences serving Indian trades".[66] Director General of Shipping R. Doraiswamy was more forthright: "Wherever there has been resistance from established foreign lines, Government have brought pressure on them through diplomatic channels to assist Indian lines".[67]

However, the trading rights of Indian lines remained restricted; the British interests in the conferences en route prevented Indian lines from being allowed to join as members, which barred them from engaging in the carriage of trade from wayports. Matters deteriorated to such an extent that eventually the Indian lines, with the backing of the Indian government, threatened defiance by vowing to pick up cargo at Colombo and other ports of Ceylon. Scindia chairman Dharamsey M. Khatau warned: "The Indian lines have made up their minds to stand firmly together and face the difficult future with determination to find their proper place in the trade of this country with the other countries of the world". And he added in good measure: "In coming to this decision, I am happy to say that we have the sympathy of our Government, because the Government of India not only wants to see the Indian merchant shipping grow to its full stature but also because unless Indian shipping can make its voice felt in the various Conferences that govern the different trade routes of the world and thus influence the various freight rates, India's trade with the world is bound to suffer".[68] Earlier, in 1957, the government demonstrated its readiness to intervene by pressuring the overseas conferences to forego their plans to impose a surcharge on cargoes headed for Indian ports.[69] Two years later, the government set up the Freight Investigation Bureau with the mandate to inquire into complaints about high and discriminatory freight rates.[70]

In 1959, when for the first time the India-UK/Continent conference met in New Delhi, negotiations over shares in the trades began between Indian and British lines. They were continued in London and Hamburg in early 1960. However, the two sides were unable to agree on arrangements that would satisfy the Indian lines. Eventually, in November 1960, an agreement was hammered out at New Delhi,[71] the central element of which was a pooling arrangement among the lines. Interestingly, this pooling was not only for cargo but also for freight earnings, thus consolidating the conference into a monopoly. Under the agreement, which came into effect on January 1, 1961, the Indian lines were allocated a share of about 30 per cent of the India-UK trade, which was to rise by 1 per cent every year in order to reach 39 per cent by 1971. This share was, in turn, divided equally between Scindia and India Steamship. Apparently, India's share was determined on the basis of past performance of its lines, plus a marginal and gradual increase in the future to allow British lines time to adjust. However, the government was not satisfied with the agreement "because it does not satisfy the legitimate demands or requirements of Indian shipping and Indian economy".[72] The criterion of past performance was soon undercut, however. In their arrangements with Pakistan, which did not have much of a share in the past, the British lines agreed to suddenly increase that country's share from 12.5 per cent to 25 per cent in 1962 as also to an annual escalation so as to have the share reach 39 per cent in 1971. India then wanted its agreement to be suitably amended to accommodate its interests.

Meanwhile, the public sector's Western Shipping Corporation had been admitted to the conference, and the Shipping Corporation of India succeeded to that membership when it was formed in 1961 out of the merger of the Western and Eastern corporations. This put greater pressure on the conferences since SCI also demanded a share. New negotiations followed, the end result of which was to increase the share of the Indian lines in the India-UK trade from 30.25 per cent to 39.48 per cent in 1962, which would rise by 1 per cent a year to reach 48.48 per cent in 1971. Correspondingly, the share of the British lines was reduced to 57.04 per cent and was scheduled to decrease to 48.48 per cent in 1971, thus putting the lines of the two countries on a basis of parity.[73] Similar concessions followed on other routes. While these concessions may seem largely commercial decisions made by shipping firms, the role of government was key. As Rajwar put it, "aware of the government policy that Indian ships should carry a fair share of the national trade, the Liner Conferences were wise enough to concede this share, though with some understandable reluctance, rather than confront the Indian Government".[74]

The question of distribution of shares among the Indian lines was settled by largely freezing the initial shares of Scindia and India Steamship, and allotting the sudden increase and future escalations to SCI so that the three lines would have equal shares by 1971. The entry of SCI into these trades caused a lot of heart-burning among the private lines since they felt that they had built up the trade over the preceding dozen years and that the muscling in by SCI went against the earlier understanding that the public sector would not compete in trades where the private sector was already present. They held the policy to be discriminatory since, on the other hand, the government disallowed private shipping companies from entering trades where SCI had opened services first.[75]

The pooling arrangements were of momentous significance in the expansion of Indian shipping, at least in the liner trade, even though little publicity was given to them. They assured Indian lines a substantial volume of liner cargo for the next decade and a half, and thus made it possible for them to expand tonnage with confidence. Since the arrangements covered not just sharing of cargo, but also of freight earnings, they obviated marketing even as they guaranteed revenues. In later years, shippers protested against the inefficiency of the shipping operators and the deterioration in service in the absence of competition. The only uncertain element in the arrangement for the shipowners was the economic adequacy of freight rates, where increases in rates by conferences to cover increases in costs often encountered resistance from the government, often at the insistence of shippers. By 1976-77, the share of the Indian lines in India's overseas liner cargo trade stood at 40 per cent, a not inconsiderable achievement, which was no doubt related to the conference system.[76] Contrast this figure with the share in liner cargo of 6.5 per cent in 1955-56, 9.0 per cent in 1960-61 and 19.8 per cent in 1970-71.[77] India had thus achieved what was set out as a goal by UNCTAD in the UN Liner Code. Perhaps 1976-77 was an exceptional year but it demonstrated the overall capacity of the Indian lines and also their ability to make use of the conference system.

It is ironic that the system of conferences or, more accurately, cartels--which in the past had been attacked by India and other developing countries for their monopoly power and erection of barriers to entry--proved highly beneficial to the building of merchant fleets in the developing world, once the political power of newly independent states was able to obtain entry for their lines. Indeed, developing countries attempted to make the privileges of monopoly permanent and universal through the UN Code of Conduct for Liner Conferences. Political independence was thus of momentous importance to provide the countervailing power for negotiations at the national and international levels.

Interestingly, the subsequent decline of India's liner shipping is related precisely to the decay of the conference system from the mid-1970s onwards. It is noteworthy nonetheless that the period of rapid expansion in India's tonnage corresponds closely with the presence of the pooling arrangements, which began on January 1, 1961 and formally ended on April 1, 1981.

THE BENEFITS OF BILATERALISM

The uses of monopoly for Indian lines were conferred not only by the conference system, but also by the bilateral trade and shipping agreements reached between India and other countries, especially those in the Soviet bloc. The important ones by the mid-1960s pertained to the Soviet Union, Poland, the German Democratic Republic, and the United Arab Republic (Egypt). The one with the Soviet Union had come as early as 1956 in the wake of the visit to India by Bulganin and Khrushchev in 1955 and had been revised and renewed subsequently. Since the public sector corporations at the time had little tonnage, the private sector companies took on most of the initial task of entering the trade on behalf of India.

Bilateral shipping agreements were the economic counterpart of the foreign policy of non-alignment. India conducted its shipping affairs with the OECD countries on the basis of membership in conferences and those with the Soviet bloc and some of the developing countries on a bilateral basis. The key feature of the bilateral agreements was parity in sailings and cargo allocation. Indian lines thus came to have a share of 50 per cent in the bilateral trades. Since the agreements tended to exclude third parties from participation, they were initially condemned by western business organizations. Later, however, even western countries joined in the practice in their shipping relations with the Soviet bloc.

Unlike the India-UK/Continent conference, these agreements concerned the creation of new trades, and therefore were regarded "as the first achievements of the independent Government of India".[78] As the Soviet Union developed into an important trading partner of the country, the bilateral arrangements were an immense boost to Indian shipping. There was accordingly satisfaction with bilateralism in shipping, which was seen as an essential building block in the expansion of the Indian merchant fleet. By the early 1970s, however, there was some concern at a new aggressiveness on the part of Soviet shipping in encroaching on India's trade with third countries in Europe, Africa and south America, while not allowing India a similar privilege.[79] Such Soviet activity compounded the problems of Indian shipping stemming from the decay of the conferences. Still, bilateralism sustained the Indian fleet to a certain extent while it reeled under the crisis that struck it in the mid-1970s. But the collapse of the Soviet bloc and its subsequent turn to market-oriented policies further added to the difficulties of Indian shipping.

COORDINATION OF GOVERNMENT CARGO

Entry into conferences and bilateral agreements took adequate care of the liner trades, but oil imports and the bulk trades lay outside that sphere. Most countries consider oil a strategic commodity and reserve its import for their own merchant fleets. For example, as early as 1928, France had enacted legislation that required two-thirds of its crude oil imports to be carried in French vessels.[80] Countries such as the US and UK have less need for such legislation since their oil majors own substantial tanker tonnage. Nonetheless, the US requires oil imports for the Strategic Petroleum Reserve to be shipped in American bottoms. As a result of its weak bargaining power India had allowed three foreign oil multinationals, when it signed agreements with them to build refineries in India in the early 1950s, to bring in crude oil under their own tanker arrangements. Even in the coastal tanker trade, the oil majors handled the bulk of the traffic, notwithstanding the reservation of coastal trade for Indian shipping.

The major break for the SCI, in relation to oil imports which were nominally reserved for it, came with the formation in 1964 of the Indian Oil Corporation (IOC) in the public sector. IOC was soon given responsibility for marketing petroleum products imported from the Soviet bloc. As public sector refineries came on stream under IOC with Soviet help, SCI was entrusted the task of handling imports of crude oil for them from the Soviet Union. Meanwhile, the bargaining position between the oil majors and the government underwent change. Recognizing that change, two of the oil multinationals approached the government in 1972, with a view to converting their Indian subsidiaries into joint ventures, with the government having majority equity. Events moved rapidly, and in 1976 all three foreign oil companies--Burmah-Shell, Esso and Caltex--stood nationalized by mutual agreement. In this fashion, the sole responsibility for the bulk of oil imports passed to Indian lines, primarily SCI. By the late 1970s, Indian ships carried around 60 per cent of POL (petroleum, oil and lubricants) and petroleum products; in 1976-77, their share was unusually high at 70 per cent.

With the thrust for industrialization in the Second Five Year Plan and the large role entrusted to the public sector, along with huge imports of foodgrains, the state emerged as the single largest importer and exporter. Shipping interests in India demanded cargo reservation of government-owned and government-controlled cargo for Indian shipping in order to build up the country's merchant fleet. In his important address to the shipowners in December 1957, where he had promised a permanent fund to provide loans on easy terms to the shipping industry, Lal Bahadur Shastri also pledged the setting up of a Shipping Coordination Committee to ensure that government cargo would, in the exercise of the government's choice as the shipper, be available to Indian ships. This committee was established in 1958.[81] This action was followed by the appointment in 1960 of a Chief Controller of Chartering, whose office soon came to be known as Transchart after its telegraphic code name. Government agencies were obligated to channel their shipping arrangements through Transchart, which in due course emerged as the largest chartering organization in the world. The government further required, after the principle first established by Great Britain, that all its agencies should buy FOB ("free on board") and sell CIF ("cost, insurance, freight") so that India would retain control over the making of shipping arrangements.

It is significant that, while Indian shipowners thus obtained cargo preference and right of first refusal, they were not given price preference. Some sources, however, maintain that a slight price preference of around 2 per cent was at one time, though no longer, allowed. Generally, Indian shipowners were required to compete with foreign operators, and decisions by Transchart were made on the basis of competitive bids. Transchart, however, did not have any coercive powers and some of the government's stronger agencies violated its own requirements on FOB and CIF with impunity. At best, Transchart handled about 20 per cent of India's trade, and of this about half was carried by foreign ships. As elsewhere, bargaining power was a factor; for example, Japan as an importer of iron ore from India insisted on shipping the bulk of it in its own vessels.[82] Still, India was able to assure a considerable amount of cargo for its own shipping.

The complex of arrangements under conference memberships, bilateral agreements, reservation of oil imports, and coordination of government cargo, provided sufficient assurance on cargo availability for Indian shipowners to plan on expanding tonnage. It is noteworthy nonetheless that India attempted to assure cargo for its merchant fleet through normal commercial mechanisms, rather than as a statutory requirement through legislation or executive decree. That has been held to be a distinctive feature of the Indian model of fleet development.[83] It is remarkable that India remained a free shipping zone, where any ship operator from anywhere could come to pick up cargo. Indeed, while there were multifarious restrictions on Indian operators as to whether and where they could operate, there were none on foreign operators.

MANPOWER

Persistent pressure from nationalist legislators and public opinion had forced even the colonial state to set aside, as early as 1927, the training ship *Dufferin* for the purpose of preparing officers for the merchant fleet. After independence, the state assumed complete responsibility for assuring adequate manpower for the operation of its merchant fleet through the training of officers, both navigators and engineers, and ratings. A complex of training institutions was established for the purpose. Chief among them were the Nautical and Engineering College, established in 1948 at Bombay, and the Directorate of Marine Engineering Training (DMET) at Calcutta. The name of the former institution was later prefaced by the words "Lal Bahadur Shastri" in dedication to the man who is regarded as the maker of modern Indian shipping. In 1950, three schools were established for the training of ratings. In 1972, the old t.s. *Dufferin* was replaced by the larger facility of t.s. *Rajendra.* As a result of all these arrangements installed by the state, shipowners were not handicapped by manpower shortages in a rapidly expanding merchant fleet; indeed, India provided some surplus for employment elsewhere in the fleets of other countries. In 1969, the state and the shipping industry joined together to found the Shri Narottam Morarjee Institute of Shipping to train onshore commercial staff.

Summary and Conclusions

The period from 1960 to 1975 represents a tremendous achievement on the part of India in building a substantial merchant fleet; it constitutes a genuine success story. Not only did the merchant fleet undergo a vast expansion physically in tonnage, but equally enormous capabilities were built in entrepreneurship, management and technical operations.

This achievement coincided with a quite favourable international environment, which certainly facilitated it. From the demand side for shipping services, the chief feature of this international environment was expanding trade, which grew at the rate of about 9 per cent a year between 1960 and 1973.[84] Trade expansion allowed entrenched cartels to accommodate new claimants to a share of the market. The conference system was strong, as a result of which shipping companies could count on assured cargo. In addition, a growing international economy provided new avenues of expansion for shipping, such as the oil trade and bulk commodities. On the supply side, ships could be purchased on easy credit terms because of vigorous competition among shipyards. Besides, except for the increasing size of ships, ship technology was largely stable, thus precluding demands for acquisition of new skills on the part of manpower and for restructuring of operations on the part of management. Apart from fuelling economic growth, and therefore international trade and the consequent demand for shipping services, cheap oil kept bunker costs low. In all, the international environment proved hospitable for the expansion of the Indian fleet.

Notwithstanding the favourable environment, the key explanatory factor for the rapid expansion of the Indian merchant fleet was state policy, which creatively seized the opportunities provided by the international environment. Growth was essentially state-driven, with the state exploiting every possible avenue to increase tonnage, provide the manpower to operate it, and assure the cargo for it. Whether it was to offer cheap loans to shipowners to buy ships, to provide budgetary support to the public sector for adding to the tonnage, to extend guarantees and counter-guarantees to utilize foreign credits or commercial loans, to pressure the conferences for the entry of Indian shipping lines, to open new opportunities through bilateral agreements, to coordinate shipment of government cargo, or to provide training institutions for officers and ratings to man the ships--in all these respects, the state seemed always ready to extend its cooperation and support. Key to the achievement was the nature of the state, which had both substantial autonomy and capacity over much of this period.[85] While the international environment was helpful, the priority factor in the growth of the merchant fleet was effective state policy. Particularly important was a farsighted leadership and a dedicated civil service. They apparently erred in imposing, on ideological grounds, an excessively rigid regulatory framework of licensing and controls, but this element was overshadowed by their positive role in expansion.

The genuine achievement in building extensive maritime power had spin-offs for India at the international level. India was not only considered a model worthy of emulation, its representatives also played a leadership role at UNCTAD in focusing the world's attention on the aspirations of the developing world for a share in "ruling the waves" and on the obstacles to obtaining it, and proposed constructive solutions towards that end.

The spectacular achievement did not mean that India had resolved all its problems in shipping. Its share in the trades, while respectable overall, fell seriously short of its objectives. In the bulk trade, the share was relatively small, standing at around 25 per cent on the average in the 1970s. In liner trades, the protection of cartels hid the vulnerabilities of the Indian industry. Besides these shortcomings, Indian shipowners felt increasingly frustrated by the straitjacket of the stringent regulatory framework, more particularly by the long and frequent bureaucratic delays in getting government approval for the purchase of ships. Foreign exchange remained a perennial constraint, even as foreign shipyards tightened credit terms while ship prices constantly escalated. Over and above these impediments, the poor infrastructure and the inefficiency of the overmanned ports were serious handicaps. It remained for the crisis of the mid-1970s to expose these weaknesses of Indian shipping to full view.

NOTES

1. "Nehru on Shipping", *Indian Shipping,* vol. 16, no. 5 (1964), pp. 10-14.

2. M.A. Master, *So I Rest on My Oars: Collection of Writings and Speeches 1947-1970,* ed. by K.V. Hariharan (2 volumes; Bombay: M.A. Master Memorial Trust, 1977), I, p. 163.

3. A.H. Maru, *Indian Shipping Since Independence August 1947* (Bombay: A.H. Maru, 1969), p. 250.

4. *The Times of India Directory and Yearbook 1977,* p. 860.

5. This section draws on his curriculum vitae in Nagendra Singh, *The Legal Regime of Merchant Shipping* (Bombay: University of Bombay, 1969), pp. 299-307; S.N. Sanklecha, *Tramping to Success: Story of the Great Eastern Shipping Company Limited* (Bombay: Popular Prakashan, 1994), pp. 64-68; Maru,

pp. 252-54; and "Obituary: Dr. Nagendra Singh", *Indian Shipping,* vol. 40, no. 10 (1988), p. 42.

6. Sanklecha, *Tramping to Success,* p. 64.

7. Maru, p. 253.

8. Sanklecha, *Tramping to Success,* p. 65.

9. Nagendra Singh, "Preface", in Brian Masters, *Maharana: The Story of the Rulers of Udaipur* (Ahmedabad, Gujarat: Mapin Publishing Pvt. Ltd., 1990), p. 17; and *ibid.,* pp. 43 and 133.

10. Sanklecha, *Tramping to Success,* pp. 66-68.

11. *Eastern Economist,* August 14, 1959, p. 246.

12. *Indian Shipping,* vol. 13, no. 7 (1961), p. 11.

13. *Eastern Economist,* April 15, 1960, p. 859.

14. Cited in Master, I, p. 661.

15. "Indian Shipping: A Great Betrayal", *Eastern Economist,* April 15, 1960, p. 859.

16. India, Planning Commission, *Third Five Year Plan* (New Delhi: 1961), p. 558.

17. *Third Five Year Plan,* p. 557.

18. India, Lok Sabha, Committee on Public Undertakings (1964-65), *Third Report: Shipping Corporation of India Ltd., Bombay* (New Delhi: Lok Sabha Secretariat, 1965), pp. 4-6. See also Committee on Public Undertakings (1971-72), *Twentieth Report: Shipping Corporation of India Limited* (New Delhi: Lok Sabha Secretariat, 1972), pp. 12-13.

19. India, Planning Commission, *Fourth Five Year Plan: A Draft Outline* (New Delhi: 1966), p. 303.

20. Master, I, p. 415.

21. *Fourth Five Year Plan: A Draft Outline,* p. 303.

22. Master, II, pp. 350-51.

23. India, Planning Commission, *Fourth Five Year Plan 1969-74* (New Delhi: 1969), p. 347.

24. L.M.S. Rajwar, "Trends in Indian Shipping", *Indian Shipping,* vol. 38, no. 5 (1986), pp. 15-21.

25. Cited in Sanklecha, *Tramping to Success,* p. 210.

26. India, Planning Commission, *Report of the Steering Committee: Perspective Planning for Transport Development* (New Delhi: Planning Commission, 1988), p. 198.

27. Sanklecha, p. 213, who refers to the articles by Vice Admiral R.K.S. Ghandhi, "Role of Public Sector in Development of Indian Shipping", *Indian Shipping,* vol. 36, nos. 4-5 (1984), pp. 11-15, and L.M.S. Rajwar, "Trends in Indian Shipping", *ibid.,* vol. 38, no. 5 (1986), pp. 15-21; and the booklet by SCI, *The SCI Story* (Bombay: SCI, [1986]).

28. Cited in Ghandhi, p. 13.

29. Ghandhi, p. 15.

30. Interview with Mr. L.M.S. Rajwar, Director (Planning), SCI, Bombay, September 23, 1982.

31. The quotation is not precise since it represents a later reconstruction of a conversation with Mr. C.C. Mehta, Manager (Coordination), SCI, Bombay, June 22, 1992.

32. See "Shri C.P. Srivastava", *Indian Shipping,* vol. 16, no. 9 (1964), p. 8; "Award of International Maritime Prize to Dr. C.P. Srivastava", *ibid.,* vol. 44, nos. 4-5 (1992), p. 27; and Maru, pp. 257-58.

33. "Man With a Mission: A Profile of C.P. Srivastava", *100A1,* July 1979, pp. 9-11.

34. C.P. Srivastava, *Lal Bahadur Shastri, Prime Minister of India, 9 June 1964 - 11 January 1966: A Life of Truth in Politics* (Delhi: Oxford University Press, 1995). Unfortunately, the volume has little to say on Shastri's role in respect of shipping beyond a mere five matter-of-fact sentences at p. 60.

35. "SCI: From Quantity to Quality", *Lloyd's Shipping Economist,* December 1986, pp. 28-32.

36. *Ibid.*

37. *Indian Shipping,* vol. 18, no. 7 (1966), p. 20.

38. Sanklecha, *Tramping to Success,* p. 215.

39. N.G. Jog, *The Saga of Scindia: Struggle for the Revival of Indian Shipping* (Bombay: Scindia Steam Navigation Co., 1969), p. 184.

40. Sanklecha, *Tramping to Success,* pp. 216-217.

41. *Indian Shipping,* vol. 18, no. 12 (1966), pp. 5-6.

42. Sanklecha, *Tramping to Success,* p. 50.

43. Cited in Sanklecha, *Tramping to Success,* pp. 50-51.

44. India, Lok Sabha, Committee on Public Undertakings (1987-88), *Forty-Fourth Report: Shipping Corporation of India Limited* (New Delhi: Lok Sabha Secretariat, 1988), pp. 48-50.

45. *Report of the Steering Committee,* p. 200.

46. India, Lok Sabha, Committee on Public Undertakings (1990-91), *Fifth Report: Shipping Corporation of India Ltd.* (New Delhi: Lok Sabha Secretariat, 1990), pp. 46-47.

47. N.C. Jain, "Indian Shipping and Future Development" (project paper in typescript; Cardiff: Department of Maritime Studies and International Transport, University of Wales, 1993), p. 3; and Indian Institute of Foreign Trade, *Role of Shipping Policy in the Export Strategy of India* (mimeographed; New Delhi: IIFT, 1977), pp. 8-10.

48. India, Ministry of Surface Transport, cited in Jain, Annexure VII.

49. Sanklecha, *Tramping to Success,* p. 119.

50. Sanklecha, *Tramping to Success,* p. 119.

51. *Merchant Marine Directory 1976,* cited in IIFT, *Role of Shipping Policy in the Export Strategy of India,* p. 34.

52. Master, I, p. 379.

53. Master, I, p. 347.

54. Sanklecha, *Tramping to Success,* pp. 56-57.

55. "Dr. Jayanti Dharma Teja's Review of Jayanti Shipping Company's Record of Expansion and Progress", *Eastern Economist,* January 22, 1965, pp. 187-88.

56. India, Lok Sabha, Public Accounts Committee (Third Lok Sabha), *Seventh Report* (New Delhi: Lok Sabha Secretariat, 1963), pp. 60-64.

57. Sanklecha, *Tramping to Success,* pp. 56-57.

58. Sanklecha, *Tramping to Success,* p. 120.

59. Jain, p. 4.

60. Rao, p. 155.

61. On the subject, see Jossleyn Hennessy, "OECD Shipbuilding Industries", *Eastern Economist,* August 26, 1966, pp. 389-92.

62. A.D. Couper, *The Geography of Sea Transport* (London: Hutchinson University Library, 1972), p. 185.

63. *Indian Shipping,* vol. 26, no. 7 (1974), p. 3.

64. Jog, p. 178.

65. Master, I, p. 191; see also *ibid.,* pp. 18, 162, 167, and 351-53, and Master, II, p. 327.

66. L.M.S. Rajwar, "Indian Shipping--Need for New Policy", *Indian Shipping,* vol. 35, no. 7 (1983), pp. 11-21 at p. 13.

67. R. Doraiswamy, "Main Elements of National Shipping Policy in India--Their Effect on Indian Shipping and Its Infrastructure", in Indo-American Chamber of Commerce, *The Role of Shipping in Indo-American Trade: Issues and Challenges--Report of the Seminar held on January 16-17, 1971* (Bombay: 1971), pp. 42-28.

68. *Economic Weekly,* February 27, 1960, p. 389.

69. Rao, p. 175.

70. India, Ministry of Transport and Shipping, National Conference on Shipping, Shipbuilding and Ports, December 1967, *Recommendations, Agenda Notes and Contributed Papers* (New Delhi: 1967), p. 123.

71. Address of India Steamship chairman Sir A. Ramaswami Mudaliar to the Annual General Meeting, *Eastern Economist,* October 6, 1961, pp. 660-61.

72. Statement by Raj Bahadur, Minister for Shipping, in *Indian Shipping,* vol. 14, no. 6 (1962), p. 14.

73. *Eastern Economist,* October 5, 1962, p. 643.

74. Rajwar, "Indian Shipping", p. 14.

75. Jog, pp. 183-84.

76. INSA, "Share of Indian Lines in India's Overseas Trade, 1975-76 to 1983-84" (typescript; made available by Mr. T.R. Nair of INSA). The precise figure is 39.98 per cent.

77. *Indian Shipping,* vol. 40, no. 12 (1988), p. 17.

78. Master, II, pp. 381-82

79. H.M. Trivedi, *Indian Shipping in Perspective* (New Delhi: Vikas, 1980), p. 24. See also India, Planning Commission, *Indian Shipping in the Time Perspective of 2000 AD: Report of the Planning Group on Shipping, September 1987* (chairman: L.M.S. Rajwar; Bombay: 1987), p. 202.

80. Planning Commission, *Indian Shipping in the Time Perspective of 2000 AD,* p. 208.

81. For an account of the early history and development of the Shipping Coordination Committee, see S.N. Sanklecha, *Tramp Shipping in India* (Bombay: University of Bombay, 1966), ch. IV.

82. India, Ministry of International Trade, *Report of the Sub-Committee Appointed by the Board of Trade to Study the Problems of Transportation of Bulk Cargoes by Indian Vessels* (New Delhi: 1963), p. 6.

83. Rajwar, "Indian Shipping", pp. 11-21.

84. Note also that the share of internationally traded goods and services in the world output doubled from 11 per cent in 1950 to 21 per cent in 1980. See Canada, Transport Canada, *Task Force on Deep-Sea Shipping: Report to the Minister of Transport* (Ottawa: 1985), p. 19.

85. For a parallel experience, employing similar policies but even more effectively, see Tae-Woo Lee, "Korean Shipping Policy: The Role of Government", *Marine Policy,* vol. 14, no. 5 (1990), pp. 421-37, and his larger study, *The Growth of Korean Shipping, 1962-1981: The Advantages of Combining a "Backward" Start with Imported Ideas* (Ph.D. dissertation;

Cardiff: Department of Maritime Studies, University of Wales, 1989). The state employed a whole array of measures in support of Korean shipping: operating subsidies; tax allowances; liberal loans for construction and purchase of ships; and cargo reservation under the "waiver system".

CHAPTER V

DECLINE AND STAGNATION, 1975-1990: SYSTEMIC CRISIS AND THE REVENGE OF THE MARKET

In the mid-1970s, the international system of shipping was struck by a severe depression of long duration, which in effect lasted until 1987. That depression had a serious impact on existing firms, leading to the liquidation of many. However, its consequences for the industry in the developing world were devastating. Ironically, this blow to shipping in the developing world came precisely at a time when it had been able to obtain international agreement at UNCTAD for some semblance of a fair and equitable share in world shipping. In 1974, UNCTAD endorsed, among other things, the formula of 40:40:20 to apportion cargo under liner conferences between one trading country, its other trade partner and third parties, in that order. Indeed, the hopes of the developing world extended beyond this formula, for more advances in meeting its aspirations were expected in other areas of shipping, such as bulk carriage. However, all these hopes were crushed under the weight of the crisis.

Although the depression lasted for a long period of time, it was initially taken to be part of the cyclical nature of the shipping industry, with the modal cycle consisting of some six or seven good years and three or four bad years. However, for the developing world the importance of the depression lay in its weakening the shipping industry, indeed incapacitating it, making it difficult for it to cope with the additional grave challenge that was thrown up by the technological revolution of containerization. As the container revolution accelerated the pace of globalization in the liner shipping industry, it increasingly meant the marginalization of much of the developing world in liner shipping, thus deepening the crisis for it.

Despite its much-vaunted strategy of national self-reliance, India reflected the larger trends that were manifest in the developing world during the course of the crisis. The immediate consequence of the crisis was to overwhelm the country's shipping industry and, in the process, to undo a large part of the beneficial impact of the earlier set of policies put in place by the state. The result was the marginalization of the nation's shipping, particularly liner shipping. The longer term consequence was to force a retreat on the part of the state as an actor in shipping and to widen the sphere of the market. In examining the various dimensions of the crisis, this chapter looks at: (1) the nature of the crisis in world shipping; and (2) the impact of the crisis on Indian shipping. The chapter that follows analyzes the factors that made for the particular pattern of impact on Indian shipping and, to that end, discusses (3) path dependency theory and the constraints on adaptability; and (4) the state's response to the crisis, especially in liner shipping. The two chapters together form an organic whole in that they look at the systemic crisis in shipping, its impact on national shipping, and the country's adaptation to it.

The Crisis in World Shipping

The crisis that affected world shipping from 1974 to 1987, with a short interruption between mid-1979 and mid-1981, consisted of two elements: one element constituted a structural break in the cyclical pattern of booms and recessions in shipping, both in terms of the causation of the crisis and its long duration. The other element represented a structural change in liner shipping in the world, originating in the technological revolution of containerization.

THE STRUCTURAL BREAK IN WORLD SHIPPING

After the long expansionary phase in international trade in the postwar period, the international economy entered a stage of uncertainty at the beginning of the decade of the 1970s. The cumulative pattern of chronic deficits in the US balance of payments, aggravated by the heavy expenditures on the war in Vietnam, put severe pressure on the US dollar. In response, the US in a dramatic move in August 1971 rescinded the convertibility of the dollar to gold, thus destroying a central pillar of the Bretton Woods system that had governed postwar international monetary relations.[1] Besides, the US levied a surcharge on imports and also imposed wage and price controls to check inflation. These American actions on currency and trade sent shock waves through the world markets, creating economic turmoil. The consequent economic disruption depressed shipping markets while costs escalated. Thus at the beginning of the 1970s there were already omens of trouble for shipping.

What, however, dealt a massive blow to world shipping was the quadrupling of oil prices in 1973 by OPEC, the Organization of Petroleum Exporting Countries. This action on the part of the new cartel of oil surplus states could be considered a political act. However, through it, OPEC displayed its understanding that the earlier price of oil did not really reflect the balance of forces of demand and supply, because of the arrangements fostered by the western states and their cartel of the oil majors. In its view, the political act simply overthrew earlier cartelistic arrangements to establish a price that more truly mirrored the forces of demand and supply in oil. Regardless, the first oil price shock in 1973 led to the disruption of international trade, marking a break in the postwar pattern of expansion. It also, relatedly, triggered a massive depression in world shipping.

The sequence in which the oil price shock affected international trade, and therefore shipping, proceeded in the following manner. The stupendous price increase reduced the consumption of oil and therefore the oil trade and, as a consequence, the demand for shipping. Indeed, the oil tanker trade was the first sector to be affected by the price hike. The surplus tanker tonnage, in turn, upset the balance between demand and supply in shipping more generally as tankers were diverted to the carriage of dry bulk cargo. Meanwhile, the oil price hike generated an economic recession, which then led to the slowing down of the production of goods, hitherto based on cheap oil. There followed a reduction of trade in consumer and producer goods as also in bulk commodities. The resulting surplus tonnage brought freight rates crashing down for shipping, while the continual entry of new ships, ordered earlier in a more confident era, compounded the problem. In the ensuing economic losses, many firms were forced to go under.

TABLE 5.1: WORLD SEABORNE TRADE (GOODS LOADED)

	Total Cargo			*Total Cargo*	
Year	*Million Tons*	*Change %*	*Year*	*Million Tons*	*Change %*
1960	1080	8.0	1980	3704	-2.0
1961	1150	6.5	1981	3559	-3.9
1962	1250	8.7	1982	3273	-8.0
1963	1350	8.0	1983	3231	-1.3
1964	1510	11.9	1984	3410	5.5
1965	1674	10.9	1985	3382	-0.8
1966	1770	5.7	1986	3459	2.3
1967	1910	7.9	1987	3505	1.3
1968	2107	10.3	1988	3692	5.3
1969	2312	9.7	1989	3891	5.4
1970	2605	12.7	1990	4008	3.0
1971	2699	3.6	1991	4120	2.8
1972	2901	7.5	1992	4220	2.4
1973	3274	12.9	1993	4312	2.2
1974	3304	0.9			
1975	3072	-7.0	*Average Annual Change*		
1976	3366	9.6			
1977	3468	3.0	1960-1973 = 8.9%		
1978	3550	2.4	1974-1978 = 1.8%		
1979	3828	7.8	1974-1987 = 0.7%		
			1980-1987 = -0.9%		
			1988-1993 = 3.5%		
			1960-1993 = 4.6%		

Source: UNCTAD, *Review of Maritime Transport* (various issues).

Slowly, however, over the following six years world trade began to expand again, albeit at a much slower pace, while a balance developed between demand and supply in tonnage as part of the old tonnage was scrapped. Freight rates then picked up again in mid-1979. It seemed that the boom turn in the cycle had arrived. However, the boom was short-lived, lasting only until mid-1981, for in 1979 OPEC delivered the second oil price shock, which doubled oil prices over the earlier increase. The second shock was an even more brutal blow to shipping markets, and the renewed depression lasted for another six years until 1987.

TABLE 5.2: WORLD SEABORNE TRADE BY BILLIONS OF TON-MILES

Year	*Total Trade*	*Change %*	*Year*	*Total Trade*	*Change %*
1965	5 849		1980	16 777	-5.1
			1981	15 840	-5.6
1970	10 654		1982	13 499	-14.8
1971	11 729	10.1	1983	12 580	-6.8
1972	13 103	11.7	1984	13 426	6.7
1973	15 403	17.6			
1974	16 386	6.4	1985	13 065	-2.7
			1986	13 856	6.1
1975	15 363	-6.2	1987	14 273	3.0
1976	17 053	11.0	1988	15 305	7.2
1977	17 517	2.7	1989	16 402	7.2
1978	17 034	-2.8			
1979	17 675	3.8	1990	17 161	4.6
			1991	17 873	4.2
			1992	18 228	1.9
			1993	18 800	3.1

Source: UNCTAD, *Review of Maritime Transport* (various issues).

The depression thus occurred in two phases, one from 1974 to 1979 and the other from 1981 to 1987, with a short interlude of recovery in between. Although there was much alarm and distress occasioned by the first phase, in retrospect it is obvious that the second phase was much more severe than the first one. Nonetheless, the period as a whole from 1974 to 1987 marks a dramatic contrast with the preceding years. While world seaborne trade expanded at the rate of 8.9 per cent between

1960 and 1973, it grew by only 0.7 per cent a year between 1974 and 1987. During the first phase of the depression, between 1974 and 1978, the growth rate had slowed down drastically to 1.8 per cent, while during the second phase from 1980 to 1987 it was a negative 0.9 per cent (see Table 5.1). The recovery in the years that followed the depression, however, did not match the growth rate of the postwar expansionary period, with the rate of growth between 1988 and 1993 being only 3.5 per cent. These trends based on the volume of seaborne trade are confirmed when distance travelled by cargo is also taken into account (see Table 5.2).

TABLE 5.3: TONNAGE OVERSUPPLY (SURPLUS TONNAGE AS PERCENTAGE OF ACTIVE WORLD MERCHANT FLEET)

Year	*%*	*Year*	*%*
1970	0.2	1986	20.3
		1987	19.0
1975	9.3	1988	15.3
1976	6.3	1989	10.8
1977	7.2		
1978	4.7	1990	10.7
1979	14.6	1991	10.4
		1992	11.5
1980	16.6	1993	11.3
1981	27.6	1994	9.7
1982	36.1		
1983	39.9		
1984	34.0		
1985	32.2		

Source: UNCTAD, *Review of Maritime Transport* (various issues) and UNCTAD/SDD/SHIP/3 of May 8, 1995.

Even after the depression struck in 1974, however, tonnage kept on being added to the world fleet on the basis of earlier orders in a more buoyant era. World tonnage stood at 289.93M grt in 1973, and expanded consistently year after year during the depression until it peaked at 424.74M grt in 1982. Thereafter, it declined gradually to 403.41M grt in 1988, with expansion resuming once again in 1989.

Tonnage that is laid up is an important indicator of the depth of a depression. Table 5.3 shows that in 1970 the laid-up tonnage was only 0.2 per cent of the world's active merchant fleet. By 1975, it had climbed to 9.3 per cent but declined somewhat in the subsequent three years. In 1979, it jumped to double digit figures and amounted to one-third or more of the active fleet from 1982 to 1985. Not until 1989 did it decline to around 10 per cent. The laid-up tonnage figures underline the severity of the crisis during the second phase, wreaking havoc on the shipping industry. For the industry, the depression was an unprecedented experience in the postwar period, matching the experience of the 1930s.

STRUCTURAL CHANGE IN WORLD SHIPPING

The containerization of shipping has been the most significant technological breakthrough since the invention of the steamship in the nineteenth century. It has made for a quantum leap in carrying capacity for a given ship tonnage, simply by facilitating rapid loading and unloading of liner or general cargo. Where earlier only some 60 tons could be loaded or unloaded per hour in break-bulk operations, containerization allowed 1000 tons to be so handled in the same time.[2] Containerization advanced the efficiency of liner cargo vessels by enabling them to spend more time in the actual carriage of cargo at sea than in loading and unloading operations at ports. While earlier the normal ratio for ship time spent at sea to that at port for liner cargo was 1:1, containerization is said to have changed it to 4:1.

Container shipping began in the US, where the origins of this highly efficient but most capital-intensive technology lay in the attempt by American carriers to overcome the serious comparative disadvantage of high labour costs. That it spread quickly to cover the entire globe in less than a quarter century is a tribute to its greater efficiency. But it also testifies to the capacity of the advanced economic powers to impose economic arrangements, corresponding essentially to their resource endowment, on others with an entirely different resource configuration, and at tremendous cost for the latter by way of re-equipping their ports and domestic transport systems. To that extent, the advance of containerization underlines the continued relevance of power and domination in an asymmetrically interdependent world economy. Once the developed countries shifted to containerization, the developing world had no alternative but to submit to the structural compulsions of participation in a world trading system, and to move to containerization even if only as shipper or consignee and not as shipowner. Meanwhile, the reduced crew costs as a result of technological change seemed to undercut the postwar rationale proffered by developing countries that they had a comparative advantage in conventional shipping because of its labour-intensive practices,[3] and that consequently the developed world ought to concede a wider role for them.

The march of containerization has been rapid, and has resulted in the restructuring of the world's liner shipping industry, in the concentration of ownership, and in the reorganization of its institutional arrangements. Little of this could have been suspected from its small beginnings in the mid-1950s. Malcolm McLean, the founder of Sea-Land Service, heralded the new age of container shipping in 1956 by starting container operations between New York and Houston (Texas), and singlehandedly compelled the shipping industry, first in the US and then in the world, to accept his innovative concept. A decade later, having developed and expanded container services in the protected trades of the US, Sea-Land began container services across the Atlantic to Europe in 1966. The following year, another American shipping company, Matson Navigation, started container services across the Pacific. Thereafter, container shipping spread rapidly. Its subsequent progress can be examined in terms of five successive phases.[4]

Phase 1, from 1966 to 1970, represents the birth of trans-oceanic container services on the three arterial east-west routes (transatlantic, transpacific and Asia-Europe). The challenge for the traditional carriers was enormous and immediately set them on a course of restructuring: "The substantial investment needed in containerships, containers and terminals demanded that the old established, conventional operators involve themselves in joint ventures, consortia and outright mergers in order to achieve the scale economies demanded by the new order". In the UK, nine important liner companies transformed themselves into consortia, elsewhere in Europe new groups such as Hapag-Lloyd and CGM arose, and in Japan its "big six" lines hastened to set up joint services both among themselves and with foreign lines.[5]

Phase 2, from 1971 to 1975, features the continuous growth of container capacity in the trades among the OECD countries (North America, Europe, and Japan), replacing the conventional mode of break-bulk shipping. It demonstrates the arrival of container shipping as the settled mode of carriage of liner cargo, not a passing fad of American inspiration. One indicator of this change was the launching of container shipping on a course of building vessels of larger and larger capacity and higher and higher speed. The earliest containerships were simply conventional ships that had been converted to carry containers. Later, cellular vessels dedicated solely to the carriage of containers were purposively built. McLean in 1969 figured that size and speed were, in the words of one observer, "the twin keys to enhanced productivity". The "first generation" of containerships had a capacity of less than 1000 teu (twenty foot equivalent units) while the "second generation" vessels were of 1300-1400 teu capacity. But in 1969 some carriers ordered "third generation" vessels of 2500-3000 teu capacity; often referred to as "motherships", these large "main haul" ships visited only a few mainline ports that were, in turn, served by feeder vessels in a given region. Later, "fourth generation" containerships of 3000-4000 teu capacity entered service. Depending on requirements, ships were built with fast speeds of 20, 25, 30 or more knots.[6] The higher speeds further enhanced the efficiency of container shipping by facilitating quicker turn-around of vessels.

Phase 3, from 1976 to 1985, marks the drive to, and achievement of, maturity by container shipping, with container penetration reaching levels of 75 per cent on the average in liner cargo trades. Indeed, on the main arterial (east-west) routes, along which flowed some 60 per cent of liner cargo, penetration was at the possible maximum of 95 per cent.[7] The world of liner shipping thus stood profoundly revolutionized. It was, however, transformed in other respects as well. The first wave of expansion of container shipping during Phase 2 had been led by OECD partners (US, Europe, and Japan), with the US as the leader. Now, during Phase 3, carriers from Hong

Kong, Singapore, South Korea and Taiwan joined in with fervour. Unexpectedly, several of them expanded rapidly and rose fast up the ladder of top carriers. The resulting explosion of capacity eroded the US position. In 1985 US Lines and Evergreen Line (Taiwan) started round-the-world (RTW) services along the main arterial routes.[8] They were soon joined by others, while around the same time still others launched pendulum services swinging between US, Europe and Asia, or even further to the US west coast. Such through services on fixed-day schedules along the east-west axis served to drain away the cargoes of the traditional end-to-end services between the different regions.

Phase 4, from 1985 to 1989, represents a period of great turmoil in the liner shipping industry. This was the inevitable consequence of the colossal expansion in container capacity during the preceding phase, and the unrestrained competition that followed it, as containerization reached saturation levels and capacity grew faster than trade expansion, particularly with the downturn in world trade following the second OPEC oil price hikes. The earlier discipline over competition in the market disappeared as the conference system weakened under the pressure of the rise of independent carriers, outside the discipline of conferences. For, with the achievement of maturity of container shipping the independent carriers, who may have traditionally managed to get less than 10 per cent of the trades, came to take control of huge shares of the trades, at times close to half,[9] and perhaps more than half in the north-south trades. Without the moderating influence of the conferences, competition was unusually severe. In the ensuing struggle over survival of the fittest, freight rates fell, carriers suffered heavy losses, and many shipping companies with well-known old names were driven to the wall. Particularly striking was the bankruptcy of US Lines. It was a traumatic period for liner shipping.

Phase 5, which began around 1990, marks the turn to consolidation and rationalization. Chastened by the turbulence of the earlier period, the liner industry moved from competition and confrontation over market shares to cooperation (read: cartelization). This was accomplished through the mechanism of stabilization agreements, which sought to place restraints on capacity, indeed to reduce capacity, so as to firm up and increase freight rates and thus avoid losses and possible liquidation. The Transpacific Stabilization Agreement (TSA) for the largest deep-sea container market in the world was reached in early 1989, and was followed in 1992 by the Trans-Atlantic Agreement (TAA)--which succeeded the earlier failed Euro-corde agreement--and the Europe Asian Trades Agreement (EATA). "1992 will go down as a watershed in the areas of both industry concentration and organization", noted the *BIMCO Bulletin.* It continued: "The traditional order of conferences has now ceded ground and authority to stabilization agreements on each of the volume axial routes, but the replacement of confrontational market share strategies by cooperative capacity management programmes has come too late for some second rank lines".[10] The stabilization agreements, incorporating both conference carriers and independent operators, were in reality cartels which looked suspiciously like the closed conferences of old, covering as they did close to 80 or 90 per cent of the trades of their respective areas.

The drive towards oligopoly in the liner shipping industry, as a result of its transformation and restructuring under the impact of containerization, is manifest in the increasing concentration of container capacity. Whereas in 1982 the top 20 carriers controlled 31 per cent of containerized shipping,[11] their share climbed to 38.8 per cent in 1990, to 41.9 per cent in 1992, and then again to 43.7 per cent in 1993.[12] Given the fact that the top carriers continue to order "fifth generation" containerships of 4000-5000 teu capacity (see Table 5.5), that share is likely to increase further. On the basis of their 1993 order position, the share was expected to rise to 44.8 per cent by 1995, but by 1994 it had already risen to 46.2 per cent.[13] The entrenchment of these powerful carriers is going to make future entry of new container shipping services by developing countries extremely difficult, as the established firms are likely to treat them as intruders.

Table 5.4 lists the top 20 container carriers in 1993. Four among them, each with a capacity of over 100,000 teu or more, constitute the "megacarriers"[14] of the trade: (1) Maersk Line (Denmark), with the largest and relentlessly-expanding container service empire in the world--referred to as the "Big Blue" of shipping--is respected for its culture of high-speed service and reliability; (2) Sea-Land Service (United States), which transformed the world of liner shipping with its innovation of container service, earlier occupied the top rank for many years; (3) Evergreen Line (Taiwan), which entered container service only in 1975, expanded with breakneck speed, and dominated container shipping during the 1980s; and (4) NYK Line/TSK Line (Japan). Other major carriers with 75,000 teu capacity and over include: (5) Mitsui OSK Line (Japan); (6) P&O Containers (UK); (7) K Line (Japan); (8) Hanjin Shipping Company (South Korea); and (9) Nedlloyd Lines (the Netherlands). Although some changes may take place in the ranking of the individual players, the group of 20 as a whole is likely to remain stable in the next few years, given the existing order position for new capacity (see Table 5.5). In the meantime, the list demonstrates the tremendous diffusion of container shipping outside the preserve of OECD countries, and testifies to the weakness of dependency theory, which could not have posited the rise of new powers in the shipping arena from the traditional periphery. As Table 5.6 well illustrates, Asia now controls almost half of the world's container carrying capacity, compared to 29.7 per cent with Europe and 13.6 per cent with the US.

The concentration in the industry is not only manifest in the capacities accumulated by the major players, but beyond that it is evident in the consortia arrangements that exist among them. An example of such consortia is the agreement in 1993 between Maersk Line, Sea-Land and P&O Containers--which, as "the strongest combined group in container shipping", were already cooperating to varying degrees in transatlantic, transpacific and Europe-Far East trades--to cooperatively provide a weekly service in the US-Middle East-India trade via the Suez.[15] Another example is the agreement among Nippon Yusen Kaisha (NYK), Hapag-Lloyd and Neptune Orient Lines to provide joint service on the East Asia-North America-North Europe route via Panama.[16] Still another example is the announced intention in 1994 to form an alliance among American President Lines (APL), Mitsui OSK Lines, Nedlloyd Lines, and Orient Overseas Container Line (OOCL); similar is the plan of K Line (Japan) and Hyundai Merchant Marine (South Korea) to form a global alliance.[17]

TABLE 5.4: TOP TWENTY CONTAINER CARRIERS 1993

		Total Capacity		*Ships by TEU Size*		
Operator	*Country/ Region*	*Ships Nos.*	*Capacity in TEUs*	*3500 plus*	*3000-3499*	*2500-2999*
Maersk	Denmark	92	174,088	14	13	8
Sea-Land	USA	81	147,765	12	-	12
Evergreen	Taiwan	73	144,140	2	11	20
NYK/TSK	Japan	75	122,130	5	5	9
Mitsui OSK	Japan	63	91,015	4	-	12
P&O Containers	UK	41	80,984	6	4	2
K Line	Japan	46	80,168	-	8	8
Hanjin	Korea (S)	33	77,398	4	-	18
Nedlloyd	Netherlands	47	75,938	5	-	6
Zim Israel	Israel	53	71,397	-	7	3
APL	USA	39	69,527	6	7	2
Hapag-Lloyd	Germany	29	63,222	6	1	1
Neptune Orient	Singapore	34	59,208	3	3	3
COSCO Shanghai	China	58	58,576	-	-	6
Yangming	Taiwan	23	56,330	3	8	-
OOCL	Hong Kong	22	53,074	-	8	7
United Arab	Gulf	51	50,371	-	-	-
Mediterranean	Switzerland	43	43,991	-	-	-
Hyundai	Korea (S)	12	40,359	5	-	6
DSR Lines	Germany	34	37,388	-	-	8
World Total		5,199	3,663,749			
Total Top 20		960	1,600,261 (43.7%)			

Source: John Fossey, "Top 20 Boost Share", *Containerization International,* November 1993, pp. 32-39. Data is as of September 1, 1993.

In summary, containerization escalated the globalization of the shipping industry. Globalization had begun soon after World War II--on American initiative in the carriage of oil and dry bulk commodities--through the establishment of flags of convenience (FOCs) arrangements in Panama, Liberia and Honduras. In this fashion, vertically-integrated American multinationals were able to combine western capital with cheap foreign labour, even as they paid few taxes, to defeat international competition. With the containerization of shipping, globalization became extended to the carriage of liner or general cargo. Its pace accelerated in the wake of the OPEC oil price shocks, as many traditional maritime nations opened second or international registries.

Table 5.5: TOP 20 CARRIERS BY CONTRACTED ORDERS 1993

	Total Capacity		
Operator	*Ships Nos.*	*Tonnage in TEUs*	*Orders by Ship Size (in TEUs)*
COSCO Shanghai	14	51,860	6x3800; 4x3765; 4x3500
Maersk	6	34,700	5x4800; 1x3424; 3x1542; 2x1325
Evergreen	8	33,832	8x4229
APL	6	28,800	6x4800
Neptune Orient	6	26,306	4x4392; 2x4369
Mitsui OSK	5	24,000	5x4800
CMA [France]	7	23,250	2x3400; 4x3300; 1x3250
NYK Line	4	18,208	3x4800; 1x3808
Sinotrans	8	15,920	4x2480; 2x2200; 2x800
Norasia Line	5	14,136	1x3000; 4x2784
Hanjin Shipping	3	12,072	3x4024
TMM [Mexico]	5	11,980	5x2396
Wan Hai Line	7	9,303	7x1329
Senator Linie	3	9,075	3x3025
Hapag-Lloyd	2	8,844	2x4400
P&O Containers	2	8,076	2x4038
Nedlloyd Lines	2	7,900	2x3950
Ivaran Lines	4	6,678	2x1827; 2x1512
Scaran-Delmas Vieljeux	3	6,600	3x2200
Contship	4	6,396	4x1599
World Total		436,890	
Total Top 20		333,936 (76.4%)	

Source: John Fossey, "Top 20 Boost Share", *Containerization International,* November 1993, pp. 32-39. Data is as of September 1, 1993.

TABLE 5.6: TOP 20 CARRIERS BY FLEET AND ORDERS: REGIONAL SHARES

Region	*Current Fleet*	*Capacity on Order*
Asia	49.1%	72.6%
Europe	29.7%	15.1%
USA	13.6%	12.3%
Others	7.6%	

Source: John Fossey, "Top 20 Boost Share", *Containerization International,* November 1993, pp. 32-39. Data is as of September 1, 1993.

Containerization resulted in the restructuring of the world shipping industry on a global basis in two respects. First, it made for the displacement of point-to-point individual services, which were replaced by "hub and feeder" systems focused on a few hubs or load centres served by mainline services, in turn, fed by feeder services from the regional ports. Second, it brought about the displacement of national lines organized under conferences, which were now replaced by multinational consortia of megacarriers. The disintegration of the conferences would perhaps have taken place in any case. An inkling of that was provided by the resistance of the western nations at the UNCTAD meetings to any attempt to extend the 40:40:20 formula to all liner cargo rather than limiting it only to that which was handled under conference arrangements. There was a strong suspicion among the developing world countries at the time that the western states intended to defeat the intent of the UNCTAD formula through having their lines switch to independent operations outside the conferences. In their eyes, the subsequent rapid disintegration of the conference system was not an accident of a change in technology but a consequence of western design. If this is correct, then what containerization did was both to accelerate the process and to provide legitimacy for it on grounds of technological change.

For much of the developing world, combined with the depression, the structural change was ruinous for its shipping industry. As one UNCTAD document said of the container revolution as also of Electronic Data Interchange (EDI), both pushed under the auspices of mega multimodal transport operators (MMTOs), "since virtually all MMTOs come from developed countries, their success may prove to be the traditional developing-country transport providers' ruin". At the same time, the longer-term prospect is a new international division of labour in shipping--for some, a "new dependency"--in which the megacarriers or MMTOs would continue to be from the developed countries while liner shipping companies from the developing world may hope only for a subordinate role "as feeder service operators and subcontractors for the mega-carriers and MMTOs".[18]

THE DIMENSIONS OF THE CRISIS IN INDIAN SHIPPING

The crisis in world shipping in both its aspects--structural break and structural change--inflicted great havoc on Indian shipping. The depression caused by the OPEC oil price hike in 1973 did not strike India immediately. There was some time lag, for some Indian shipping companies were reporting record profits even in 1976-77. This outcome may have been the result of several factors: the industry being sustained by the conference system that was still strong though under increasing pressure, the bilateral shipping arrangements with Soviet bloc countries, and the channelling of government cargo by Transchart. However, when the crisis finally struck, it proved to be a nightmare for most shipping companies.

THE INDUSTRY IN FINANCIAL DISTRESS

The first phase of the depression was not that disastrous, though the industry complained a lot, pleading to the government for help in its severe liquidity problems. The ability of the Indian companies to survive in this first phase largely intact has often been interpreted to be a reflection of the resilience of the Indian industry. However, it has already been seen that the depression during the first phase was not as severe when compared to its second phase. Since oil imports were reserved for the public sector on a cost-plus basis, India's tanker trade was largely insulated from the crisis. This was not the case with dry bulk cargo, where the crisis affected the viability of shipping comp-

TABLE 5.7: FINANCIAL PERFORMANCE IN 1984-85 OF SDFC-AIDED INDIAN SHIPPING COMPANIES (RS. MILLION)

Company	*Date of Balance Sheet*	*Net Worth*	*Debt*	*Debt-Equity Ratio*
Public Sector				
1. Mogul Line	3-31-85	-607.1	1225.7	
2. SCI	3-31-85	1025.9	9649.8	9.41:1
Private Sector				
3. Chowgule	3-31-85	117.1	979.2	8.36:1
4. Damodar	3-31-85	-167.4	319.4	-
5. Darabshaw	6-30-85	3.3	8.5	2.59:1
6. Dempo	6-30-85	-227.5	758.3	-
7. Essar Shipping	12-31-84	419.3	1327.1	3.16:1
8. Garware	9-30-84	2.5	303.7	116.86:1
9. Great Eastern	6-30-85	498.4	1272.5	2.55:1
10. Hede	8-31-84	-45.1	75.9	-
11. Hinengo	3-31-85	-0.9	2.6	-
12. India SS	3-31-85	-331.9	910.7	-
13. Indoceanic	12-31-84	-39.2	124.2	-
14. Mangala	12-31-84	6.0	30.3	5:1
15. Mercator	9-30-85	4.5	5.7	1.26:1
16. Nirvan	7-31-85	-12.2	29.3	-
17. Ratnakar	3-31-85	-199.3	742.4	-
18. Scindia	6-30-85	-161.2	1091.4	-
19. Seven Seas	12-31-84	-42.7	122.8	-
20. South India	9-30-85	93.0	625.5	6.72:1
21. Streamline	6-30-85	-10.9	19.1	-
22. Surrendra	12-31-84	-56.4	730.7	-
23. Thakur	3-31-85	-5.7	99.5	-
24. Tolani	6-30-85	21.8	341.5	15.63:1
25. Varun	11-30-85	26.8	170.1	6.34:1
Total Private Sector		-108.0	10091.2	
Total Both Sectors		310.8	20966.8	

Source: India, Planning Commission, *Indian Shipping in the Time Perspective of 2000 AD: Report of Planning Group on Shipping, September 1987* (New Delhi: 1987), p. 244.

anies on account of the inadequacy of cargo, the drastic fall in freight rates, the escalation in costs, the lay-up of vessels, and the consequent inability to make debt repayments. A little later, the crisis hit liner cargo shipping companies as well, not only on account of inadequate cargo and cost-price distortions but also because the diversion of the world's surplus tonnage from bulk carriers offered predatory competition as it poached on liner cargo.

The entire industry in its enfeebled state was then hit by the second phase of the depression, which devastated it. In the meantime, the pooling arrangements in the India-UK/Continent trades had been terminated, the conference system was already in decay under the impact of the growing power of independent operators, and the challenge from containerization had grown in intensity while India was largely defenceless against it. The consequence was the growing insolvency of shipping companies, and the rapid march towards the marginalization of India in liner shipping.

Some shipping companies were driven to bankruptcy.[19] Many defaulted on their loan repayments to SDFC, especially those that had been funded on the basis of need. As Sanklecha points out, "the losses sustained by most of the shipping companies from the year 1981-82 onwards wiped out their reserves and eroded their equity".[20] The depth of the financial adversity in the industry is reflected in the fact that in 1985, 25 companies owning over 90 per cent of the country's tonnage owed more than Rs. 20 billion in debt while their aggregate net worth (equity plus reserves minus losses) amounted to only Rs. 310 million (see Table 5.7). The situation of the companies in the private sector was worse; their net worth was minus Rs. 108 million while their debt was Rs. 10 billion; thirteen of them had a net worth in the negative. Particularly noteworthy is the negative net worth status of both of the liner companies in the private sector. Where it saw little hope of recovery or rehabilitation for companies, SDFC moved in to foreclose their mortgages. In brief, the depression brought extreme financial distress to the industry, even to some of the largest of the companies.

STAGNATION AND DECLINE IN TONNAGE

The financial distress of Indian shipping enfeebled the industry, calling a halt to its earlier thrust for tonnage expansion, even as it prevented it from responding adequately to the challenge of containerization with its demand for lumpy investments. In the 1980s, Indian shipping thus entered a period of stagnation. After several years of halting growth, the tonnage peaked in 1987, after which there occurred a decline.

TABLE 5.8: SHIPPING TONNAGE IN THE FIVE YEAR PLANS (MILLION GRT)

	Total		*Overseas*	
	Planned	*Achieved*	*Planned*	*Achieved*
First (1951-1956)	0.60	0.48	0.28	0.24
Second (1956-1961)	0.90	0.86	0.49	0.55
Third (1961-1966)	1.10	1.54	0.76	1.22
Fourth (1969-1974)	3.50	3.09	3.10	2.83
Fifth (1974-1979)	6.50	5.54	5.90	5.29
Sixth (1980-1985)	7.50	6.36	7.00	6.01
Seventh (1985-1990)	7.50	5.96	NA	5.44
Eighth (1992-1997)	7.00		NA	

Source: India, Planning Commission, *Five Year Plans* (First to Eighth).

Economic planning proved unavailing for the expansion of Indian tonnage during the period. The Fourth Five Year Plan (1969-1974), which came after several years of a planning interregnum, had set a target of 3.50M grt, but the achievement at 3.09M grt fell considerably short of it. The Fifth Plan (1974-1979) started out with high ambition, aiming for 8.6M grt, but reality forced a drastic reduction of the target to 6.5M grt; in the event, the actual achievement of 5.54M grt was short of even the reduced target by one million grt. The Sixth Plan (1980-1985) set more modest goals at 7.50M grt, but then the accomplishment at 6.36M grt did not even match the revised target of the previous plan. The Seventh Plan (1985-1990) perforce repeated its predecessor's target, but in actuality saw a decline to 5.96M grt. Thus the revised target set for the Fifth Plan (6.50M grt) remained unachieved even over the course of three five year plans. It was left to the Eighth Plan to lower its sights, establishing a target of 7M grt, a target lower than that of the previous two plans (see Table 5.8). If a depression is usually a time to go in for purchase of ships because of their low prices at the time, India (unlike China) failed to do it because of the financial straits in which its industry was placed. The most damaging aspect was its failure to purchase cellular containerships that could compete with foreign vessels, the result of which was to marginalize India in liner shipping.

The marginalization in liner shipping is made evident in the drastic reduction of liner tonnage, not only relative to other sectors but also in absolute terms. Table 5.9 provides data from 1970 onwards for India's tonnage by major categories of ships. It is clear that up to around 1980, tonnage in respect of oil tankers, bulk carriers and liner cargo ships was increasing absolutely. At the same time, the relative proportions among these categories changed over the years so as to provide India with a fairly diversified fleet.

After 1980, however, the pattern of absolute increases in all three categories of vessels began to change significantly. The tonnage for oil tankers and bulk carriers continued to display an overall rising trend even after 1980, although the trend did not remain unaffected by the depression in world shipping in the second half of the 1980s. Bulk carrier tonnage reached an all-time high in 1990, while tanker tonnage was at its peak in 1993. In strong contrast, the tonnage for liner cargo vessels began a consistent, consecutive and uninterrupted decline after 1980, when from its peak of 2.03M grt it fell to its lowest point of 0.82M grt in 1993. The story of stagnation and decline of Indian shipping after 1980, then, is really the story of the rapid decline of liner tonnage, which fell to less than half its size in a dozen years. It is patent that India's liner tonnage was decimated in the 1980s.

Ship tonnage does not count for everything in terms of utility in the carriage of cargo, however. A change in ship technology can transform the efficiency of ships in carrying

TABLE 5.9: INDIA'S TONNAGE BY VESSEL TYPES (GRT MILLION)

Year	Total Fleet	Oil Tankers	Bulk Carriers	General Cargo	Container Ships	Other Types
1970	2.40	0.29	0.79	1.22	-	0.10
1971	2.48	0.29	0.87	1.21	-	0.11
1972	2.65	0.29	0.94	1.31	-	0.12
1973	2.89	0.31	1.12	1.32	-	0.14
1974	3.49	0.53	1.49	1.31	0.01	0.14
1975	3.87	0.66	1.64	1.43	-	0.15
1976	5.09	1.13	2.05	1.74	-	0.17
1977	5.48	1.15	2.34	1.83	-	0.16
1978	5.76	1.13	2.55	1.90	-	0.18
1979	5.85	1.12	2.59	1.95	-	0.19
1980	5.91	1.14	2.56	2.03	-	0.19
1981	6.02	1.17	2.67	2.02	-	0.17
1982	6.21	1.26	2.79	1.99	-	0.17
1983	6.23	1.29	2.86	1.88	-	0.21
1984	6.42	1.32	3.05	1.80	0.001	0.24
1985	6.61	1.70	2.95	1.64	0.001	0.31
1986	6.54	1.78	2.94	1.45	0.001	0.36
1987	6.73	1.79	3.15	1.38	0.001	0.40
1988	6.16	1.71	2.73	1.28	-	0.44
1989	6.32	1.67	3.02	1.13	-	0.49
1990	6.48	1.66	3.18	1.11	-	0.52
1991	6.43	1.74	3.06	1.03	-	0.60
1992	6.56	2.02	2.91	0.98	-	0.65
1993	6.62	2.15	2.94	0.82	0.04	0.67

Source: UNCTAD, *Review of Maritime Transport* (various years). Figures for 1991 and after are as at December 31; all the rest are as at July 1. Tonnage is on the basis of flag of registration.

cargo as is abundantly evident with the development of containerships. A decreasing tonnage therefore need not signify decline in carrying capacity, but may indeed point to increased efficiency as a result of technological modernization. This has not been, however, the case in respect of India. For, the outstanding feature of the data in Table 5.9 is the literal absence until 1992 of containerships in the Indian fleet. Until then India's fleet strangely remained immune to containerization. Some tepid effort at acquiring a token tonnage is apparent in 1974 and the mid-1980s, but even this attempt petered out quickly. It was not until the container revolution was way into the stage of consolidation and rationalization during Phase 5 that India's public sector acquired in 1993 three cellular containerships of 1870 teu capacity each for the India-Europe trade. Throughout the period of the container revolution, India thus remained a bystander and an object, rather than a subject, of container services.

The marginalization of India in liner shipping is even more vividly demonstrated by the steeply declining share of Indian shipping in its liner trade. But liner shipping was not the only sector of shipping in which India thus stood marginalized. To appreciate this proposition, one needs to look at the data on India's share in its various national trades.

THE MARGINALIZATION OF INDIA: THE FALL IN MARKET SHARES

Indian shipping at the end of World War II had literally no participation in the country's foreign trade. As independence neared, it ventured overseas, and after independence the pace of its participation increased. As a result, its share in Indian cargoes grew. By the early 1960s, the share of Indian shipping in total cargo traded (imports and exports) by weight had reached the level of around 10 per cent (see Table 5.10). There was slow but consistent improvement during the remainder of the 1960s, with the average share for the decade as a whole being 13.2 per cent. The share improved further during the 1970s, with the average for the first half of the decade standing at 21.1 per cent, and for the second half at 36.5 per cent. Since then, however, stagnation has been the hallmark of Indian performance. The average for the 1980s was 36.4 per cent, while during the first four years of the 1990s the share declined to an average of 35.2 per cent. For almost two decades following 1975-76, India's share has thus hovered around 35 per cent.

TABLE 5.10: SHARE OF INDIAN CARRIERS IN INDIA'S TOTAL OVERSEAS TRADE (MILLION TONNES)

	Exports		*Imports*		*Total Trade*	
Year	*Total Cargo Actual*	*Indian Share %*	*Total Cargo Actual*	*Indian Share %*	*Total Cargo Actual*	*Indian Share %*
1960-61	6.63	13.7	17.86	7.3	24.49	9.0
1965-66	19.34	10.8	23.70	14.7	43.04	12.9
1970-71	30.09	19.3	22.45	20.5	52.54	19.8
1975-76	31.84	20.1	30.11	51.0	61.95	35.1
1976-77	35.39	21.7	28.90	64.9	64.29	41.1
1977-78	31.89	24.4	26.32	54.9	58.21	38.2
1978-79	30.92	19.8	32.00	52.2	62.92	36.3
1979-80	34.72	17.7	36.49	45.0	71.21	31.7
1980-81	32.93	15.7	42.00	45.3	74.93	32.3
1981-82	35.00	18.1	42.08	41.8	77.08	31.0
1982-83	31.67	20.5	43.14	55.5	74.81	40.7
1983-84	33.02	21.6	41.77	55.2	74.79	40.3
1984-85	37.06	20.8	43.72	48.7	80.78	35.9
1985-86	39.59	18.9	46.83	48.4	86.42	34.9
1986-87	41.61	19.7	45.52	54.4	87.13	37.8
1987-88	39.68	19.9	50.25	57.1	89.93	40.7
1988-89	45.48	16.6	56.47	48.4	101.95	34.2
1989-90	49.01	19.5	57.75	49.6	106.76	35.8
1990-91	48.78	18.8	60.57	48.9	109.35	35.5
1991-92	51.26	21.6	60.54	49.5	111.80	36.7
1992-93	47.11	16.3	75.19	46.5	122.30	34.9
1993-94	60.34	14.9	76.63	48.4	136.97	33.6

Source: Figures up to 1970-71 are from National Council of Applied Economic Research (NCAER), *Indian Shipping Industry: Retrospect and Prospect* (New Delhi: NCAER, 1993), p. 122; the figures after that are from two information sheets for 1975-76 to 1983-84 and 1984-85 to 1992-93 (in typescript), provided by Indian National Shipowners Association (INSA).

This level of share in total trade falls far short of Indian aspirations expressed at the dawn of independence, and maintained since then, even as it has been extremely slow in coming. More importantly, the share in the total trade is itself misleading since it masks serious weaknesses in the structure of Indian shipping.

A disaggregation of the data reveals an enormous imbalance among the shares for the different types of cargoes. There can be no doubt that Indian shipping has a substantial share in POL (petroleum, oil and lubricants) and POL products, which form about a quarter to a third of the country's total foreign trade and about one-half or more of its imports (see Table 5.11). During the second half of the 1980s, that share in the total trade for this type of cargo was on the average 71.8 per cent. Since this cargo type consists essentially of imports, the figure corresponds closely to the share in imports: 76.9 per cent. This is an impressive figure, but it is significant that the share in imports has been on a declining trend since its peak of 84.5 per cent in 1986-87, dropping to an average of 62.9 per cent in the first four years of the 1990s.

Even at its lowest point in the declining trend, the share of Indian shipping in total POL cargo stands in sharp contrast to that for dry bulk cargo, being far more than twice the size of the latter. Dry bulk cargo constitutes from one-half to three-fifths of the total foreign trade, with exports being about twice the level of imports. In the second half of the 1980s, the average share of Indian shipping in the total trade for this cargo type was 24.5 per cent (imports 35.4 per cent, exports 19.3 per cent). The data for the early 1990s basically repeats the pattern, the average for the period being 24.9 per cent (imports 37.8 per cent, exports 17.7 per cent). What is noteworthy is the falling trend made visible in 1992-93 and 1993-94, with the share at 23.3 per cent and 20.0 per cent, respectively. The figure for 1993-94 is the lowest in the table except for the two years of 1979-80 and 1980-81. Often, the focus on liner shipping limits the characterization of marginalization to it alone. However, it is evident that India, never too high to begin with in dry bulk shipping, has also become marginalized in respect of that sector as well.

TABLE 5.11: SHARE OF INDIAN CARRIERS IN POL, POL PRODUCTS AND OTHER LIQUIDS (MILLION TONNES)

	Exports		*Imports*		*Total Trade*	
Year	*Total Cargo Actual*	*Indian Share %*	*Total Cargo Actual*	*Indian Share %*	*Total Cargo Actual*	*Indian Share %*
1975-76	0.34	20.6	16.22	59.6	16.56	58.8
1976-77	0.04	75.0	17.22	70.1	17.26	70.1
1977-78	0.04	50.0	17.57	59.8	17.61	59.7
1978-79	0.04	50.0	19.09	63.4	19.13	63.4
1979-80	0.19	5.3	20.78	58.8	20.97	58.3
1980-81	0.02	-	23.53	57.8	23.55	57.8
1981-82	0.19	-	22.12	52.4	22.31	51.9
1982-83	0.51	41.2	23.51	68.9	24.02	68.4
1983-84	0.94	11.7	20.98	68.9	21.92	66.4
1984-85	1.57	55.4	20.20	71.6	21.77	70.5
1985-86	1.71	9.9	18.77	81.2	20.48	75.2
1986-87	2.08	21.6	19.32	84.5	21.40	78.4
1987-88	2.47	22.7	28.45	75.7	30.92	71.4
1988-89	1.93	10.9	28.50	69.9	30.43	66.1
1989-90	2.41	4.9	28.17	73.2	30.58	67.8
1990-91	2.98	15.8	30.83	66.3	33.81	61.9
1991-92	6.18	54.4	34.00	58.9	40.18	58.2
1992-93	3.05	7.5	42.99	60.9	46.04	57.3
1993-94	7.89	30.2	45.35	65.8	53.24	60.6

Source: Same as in Table 5.10.

It is understandable that India would have a low share in exports of dry bulk cargo, which consist primarily of iron ore, because of its weak bargaining power. Japan, which is the major importer of iron ore, insists on FOB terms for the bulk of the commodity, as does Korea. What is intriguing, however, is the absence of a strong showing by India in respect of imports, which are not insubstantial, where India's preferences ought to have prevailed. India's share in the imports during the 1990s has been less than 38 per cent whereas foreign lines took over 80 per cent of its exports. There is thus a profound imbalance in the shares of India and foreign countries in respect of their imports. Again, noteworthy is the declining trend manifest in the 1990s. It is obvious that India's policy on FOB terms for imports and CIF terms for exports on government account has not been working effectively. Critics maintain that foreign commodity cartels manipulate price quotations on Indian bulk commodity imports so as to retain control of shipping under their own auspices. A few harbour even more sinister beliefs, holding that some government agencies are in collusion with foreign suppliers, deliberately avoiding the routing of cargo through Transchart with the purpose of obtaining financial gratification from foreign sources.

If the position in respect of dry bulk cargo makes a poor contrast to that for POL cargo, the situation with regards to general or liner cargo is abysmal. Liner shipping, as is already apparent, has become the Achilles' heel of Indian shipping. Liner cargo is generally about 15 per cent of India's foreign trade, but this is high-value cargo compared to POL and dry bulk cargo.[21] While in the second half of the 1980s exports were about one-half to two-thirds of imports, a greater directional balance has evidently been developing in the 1990s; in 1991-92 and 1993-94, exports were larger than imports--a reflection of the new outward orientation in economic policy. The share of Indian shipping in the total trade in liner cargo during the second half of the 1980s was miserably low, standing at 17.9 per cent (imports 17.7 per cent, exports 18.0 per cent). Note that this performance represented a drastic fall, for in 1976-77 India's share in liner cargo was 39.9 per cent which, by 1979-80, had dropped to 28.8 per cent. More significantly, even at this low level of performance the share has been declining, a trend related to the failure to adapt to the container revolution. The early 1990s evidence a further decline from the very low figure of the 1980s, the average being 12.2 per cent (imports 12.7 per cent, exports 12.1 per cent). Especially noteworthy is the single digit figure of 8.8 per cent for 1993-94. Set against even the less than equitable norms of the UN Liner Code, such performance would seem egregious, especially for a country that has been the standard-bearer of maritime nationalism in the postwar period. It points to the vast chasm between rhetoric and achievement. Instead of import substitution, India has been increasingly engaged in the import of shipping services.

Table 5.11: SHARE OF INDIAN CARRIERS IN DRY BULK CARGO (MILLION TONNES)

	Exports		*Imports*		*Total Trade*	
Year	*Total Cargo Actual*	*Indian Share %*	*Total Cargo Actual*	*Indian Share %*	*Total Cargo Actual*	*Indian Share %*
1975-76	25.51	17.9	11.01	40.8	36.52	24.9
1976-77	28.64	19.3	8.76	56.3	37.40	27.9
1977-78	25.26	22.3	6.30	42.2	31.56	26.2
1978-79	25.31	18.3	8.48	33.0	33.79	21.9
1979-80	28.55	15.7	10.11	25.0	38.66	18.2
1980-81	27.90	13.5	12.56	25.0	40.46	17.1
1981-82	29.96	16.4	12.77	31.8	42.73	20.9
1982-83	26.88	18.7	13.48	41.3	40.36	26.2
1983-84	26.28	21.4	15.08	44.1	41.36	29.7
1984-85	30.53	19.0	16.52	30.3	47.05	22.9
1985-86	33.49	19.4	18.72	28.8	52.21	22.8
1986-87	34.70	19.5	16.69	37.4	51.39	25.4
1987-88	32.33	20.1	13.10	45.0	45.43	27.3
1988-89	37.89	16.9	18.68	32.5	56.57	22.1
1989-90	39.64	20.6	19.66	33.3	59.30	24.8
1990-91	38.30	20.0	19.28	41.6	57.58	27.2
1991-92	33.85	18.7	18.47	47.6	52.32	28.9
1992-93	35.96	17.3	23.16	32.7	59.12	23.3
1993-94	37.27	14.9	20.39	29.2	57.66	20.0

Source: Same as in Table 5.10.

TABLE 5.12: SHARE OF INDIAN CARRIERS IN GENERAL CARGO (MILLION TONNES)

	Exports		*Imports*		*Total Trade*	
Year	*Total Cargo Actual*	*Indian Share %*	*Total Cargo Actual*	*Indian Share %*	*Total Cargo Actual*	*Indian Share %*
1975-76	5.99	29.0	2.88	42.0	8.87	33.3
1976-77	6.71	31.3	2.92	59.9	9.63	39.9
1977-78	6.59	32.5	2.45	52.2	9.04	37.8
1978-79	5.57	26.6	4.43	40.6	10.00	32.8
1979-80	5.98	27.6	5.60	30.0	11.58	28.8
1980-81	5.01	28.1	5.91	38.8	10.92	33.9
1981-82	4.85	29.7	7.19	26.6	12.04	27.8
1982-83	4.28	29.7	6.15	35.3	10.43	32.9
1983-84	5.80	23.9	5.71	34.0	11.51	28.9
1984-85	4.96	20.9	7.00	26.1	11.96	23.9
1985-86	4.39	18.5	9.34	21.7	13.73	20.7
1986-87	4.83	20.1	9.51	22.8	14.34	21.9
1987-88	4.88	17.2	8.70	14.7	13.58	15.6
1988-89	5.66	15.9	9.29	14.5	14.95	15.1
1989-90	6.96	18.4	9.92	15.0	16.88	16.4
1990-91	7.50	14.1	10.46	11.6	17.96	12.6
1991-92	11.23	12.1	8.07	14.0	19.30	12.9
1992-93	8.10	15.3	9.04	13.6	17.14	14.4
1993-94	15.18	6.8	10.89	11.6	26.07	8.8

Source: Same as in Table 5.10.

What stands out then from the analysis of cargo shares is that the apparent achievement of Indian shipping in total trade, modest as it is, is rather deceptive. For, India has done poorly in dry bulk cargo and, especially, in the high-value category of liner cargo. These are the trades where Indian shipping has had to compete with foreign carriers which have the advantage of more modern equipment and globally organized services. India's superior performance in respect of POL, which upgrades its overall record, stands in a less favourable light when viewed against the fact that the state has had, by fiat, a monopoly over both oil imports and tanker tonnage. That fact is not in itself objectionable since many states reserve POL imports, or the bulk of them, for their own shipping in view of the strategic nature of the commodity. However, what it underlines is that the real test, then, of the country's performance in shipping lies in its market shares in dry bulk cargo and liner cargo. Here, notwithstanding the tendency of public relations officials to pat themselves on the back for India's achievements in shipping, the dominant conclusion that the statistical evidence dictates is that India has become marginalized in world shipping.

India's poor performance has important implications for the country's revenues and foreign exchange earnings besides employment and capital accumulation. Adequate data is not available on India's freight bill for seaborne trade, and the respective earnings of foreign and Indian carriers. However, a serious study by the National Council of Applied Economic Research (NCAER) attempts an analysis of the trade and financial data for 1991-92, and comes to the conclusion that the total freight bill of Rs. 62.6 billion was shared by Indian and foreign carriers in the ratio of 30:70.[22] The outflow of foreign exchange on account of the import of shipping services was Rs. 25.2 billion (the difference between the freight bill of foreign carriers for Rs. 43.9 billion and that of Indian carriers for Rs. 18.7 billion). While the precise percentages may be disputed, the financial figures are not inconsistent with what has been documented above in respect of tonnage capacity and share in trade and with what is known about the freight value of different types of cargoes. If anything, there has been a deterioration in India's share since 1991-92. A later estimate published by the American firm, Oppenheimer & Co., states: "There is an outflow of foreign exchange of approximately Rs. 40 billion ($1.27 billion) annually through freight payments to foreign shipping companies. This annual outgo is the result of the declining share of Indian ships in the country's overall overseas trade in the last decade".[23]

The sharp disproportion and imbalance in the shares of Indian and foreign carriers stands out as a severe indictment of the national shipping industry and, relatedly, of state policy. The failure to invest adequate resources, and on time, into national shipping displays a narrow book-keeping approach to planning and does not demonstrate a full comprehension of the annual drain--which some term as "bleeding" or "haemorrhaging"--of foreign exchange and economic surplus. It reflects the loss of a larger integrated vision about shipping and its role in national development, and is indicative of the lack of seriousness of purpose on the part of the political leadership.

An important question arises as to whether the stagnation and decline in India's tonnage and the decline in its market shares of national trades is all a consequence of the depression and structural change in world shipping. No doubt, the origins of the crisis lay in the external environment, but the consequences were not necessarily inevitable. Much depended on the behaviour of the industry and the state. In order to appreciate this proposition, it is necessary to examine the Indian case in a comparative context, which takes account of the performance of the shipping industry in other countries.

INDIA AND WORLD SHIPPING

How does India's performance in terms of tonnage acquisition compare with the performance of the world shipping industry? To answer that question, India's performance is here examined comparatively, relative to that of the world shipping industry as a whole and also to that of some major maritime powers. The first aspect is analyzed by looking at changes in India's share of world tonnage.

India's changing share in world tonnage (see Table 5.13) largely follows the pattern of the three-period demarcation that emerges in respect of the growth in the country's absolute tonnage. There is not a complete correspondence between the two patterns, however, because world tonnage has its own dynamic of expansion and contraction, which then has an impact on fluctuations in national shares. Since independence, India's share has increased by three and a half times. Within this long stretch of time, three periods can be distinguished. The first period from 1948 to around 1960 corresponds closely to that for India's absolute tonnage. It saw a slow but steady rise in India's share, which increased from 0.39 per cent in 1948 to

TABLE 5.13: INDIA'S SHARE IN WORLD TONNAGE (100 GRT AND OVER)(AS AT JULY 1)

	World Tonnage				*World Tonnage*		
Year	*Number Ships (000s)*	*Mill. GRT*	*Indian Share (%)*	*Year*	*Number Ships (000s)*	*Mill. GRT*	*Indian Share (%)*
1948	29.34	80.29	0.39	1970	52.44	227.49	1.06
1949	30.28	82.57	0.47	1971	55.04	247.20	1.00
				1972	57.39	268.34	0.99
1950	30.85	84.58	0.49	1973	59.61	289.93	0.99
1951	31.23	87.25	0.52	1974	61.19	311.32	1.12
1952	31.46	90.18	0.53	1975	63.72	342.16	1.13
1953	31.79	93.35	0.53	1976	65.89	371.99	1.37
1954	32.36	97.42	0.52	1977	67.95	393.68	1.39
1955	32.49	100.57	0.56	1978	69.02	406.00	1.42
1956	33.05	105.20	0.55	1979	71.13	413.02	1.42
1957	33.80	110.25	0.57				
1958	35.20	118.03	0.57	1980	73.83	419.91	1.41
1959	36.22	124.94	0.60	1981	73.86	420.83	1.43
				1982	75.15	424.74	1.46
1960	36.31	129.77	0.66	1983	76.11	422.59	1.47
1961	37.79	135.92	0.71	1984	76.07	418.68	1.53
1962	38.66	139.98	0.72	1985	76.39	416.27	1.59
1963	39.57	145.86	0.83	1986	75.27	404.91	1.62
1964	40.86	152.99	0.95	1987	75.24	403.49	1.67
1965	41.87	160.39	0.95	1988	75.68	403.41	1.53
1966	43.01	171.13	1.05	1989	76.10	410.48	1.54
1967	44.38	182.09	1.04				
1968	47.44	194.15	1.00	1990	78.34	423.63	1.53
1969	50.28	211.66	1.06	1991	80.03	436.03	1.49
				1992	79.73	445.17	1.47
				1993	80.66	457.92	1.44

Source: Lloyd's Register, *Statistical Tables 1991,* p. 35, and *World Fleet Statistics: December 1993,* p. 43. Figures for 1992 and 1993 are as at December 31.

0.60 per cent in 1959. The second period of accelerated growth in share extends from around 1960 to 1987, by which time the share had increased to 1.67 per cent--the high point in the data. Over this period, India's tonnage was expanding at a rate faster than that of world tonnage. Within this long period there is a trough from 1967 to 1973 but, as if in compensation, also a big jump in the share over the years from 1974 to 1978. These years of the mid-1970s are followed by meagre growth for about the next decade. The final period starts with a steep decline in 1988, with the years up to 1993 marked by a slow but consistent drift downwards. Over the years of this final period, India's capacity was largely static while that of the rest of the world was expanding.

While India's share of world tonnage increased rather substantially in the post-independence era, interestingly this expansion flowed rhythmically with the fortunes of world shipping. The entire postwar period right down to 1982 was one of tremendous expansion for the world industry. The three decades of the 1950s, 1960s and 1970s saw world tonnage expand five-fold from 82.57M (1949) to 413.02M grt (1979). In a way, this expansionary stage allowed the world shipping industry to accommodate an expanding Indian tonnage. On the other hand, the 1980s experienced stagnation and decline in the world industry, which had its repercussions for Indian shipping. Only in 1991 was world tonnage able to advance over its earlier high point of 1982. It is obvious that the fortunes of Indian shipping have been, to a great extent, tied up with the fortunes of the world industry. This is not surprising, for shipping is an international industry, integrally linked in turn with the fate of international trade.

However, the rhythmic correspondence between Indian and world tonnages is not perfect, and India's behaviour is not an exact replica of international trends. Whereas world tonnage started on a path of recovery and expansion after 1988, India's share in it began a downward descent for a half-dozen years after its peak in 1987. India thus did not benefit from the recovery and expansion in the world shipping industry in the early 1990s, for its share continued to decline. Since this last period of Indian stagnation and decline is not simply a reflection of international trends, it highlights precisely the importance of internal factors at work in its performance.

World averages, however, can hide important aspects of a situation. It is therefore necessary to further examine Indian performance in comparison with that of other specific maritime powers. Of course, a genuine comparison of this nature runs into a serious problem in that many countries, especially the developed market economies, resort to registering their ships under flags of convenience (FOCs) rather than under their own national flags. Comparisons based on tonnage figures under national flags can therefore be misleading inasmuch as they are not based on tonnage under a country's genuine ownership or control. For example, in 1993, 70 per cent of the fleet owned by the US and over 75 per cent of that owned by the UK and Sweden were registered under foreign flags (see Table 5.14). The corresponding figure for Germany was over 60 per cent and that for Greece and France over 50 per cent. Nor are FOCs limited to tankers and bulk carriers; as of November 1, 1994, more than 35 per cent of the shipboard container slots in service were in vessels flying FOCs, and the trend has been accelerating.[24] Repeated laments about the decline in shipping capacity of one or another western power have therefore to be treated with some scepticism.[25] For, the essential reality is that effective ownership and control remain with the traditional maritime powers even though their vessels fly the flag of some minor power in the periphery. The FOC phenomenon itself nonetheless underlines the tenacity of the powerful economic centres to hold on to their dominant position in the hierarchy of maritime power and also points up their capacity to change the operational norms of the international regime towards that end when comparative advantage shifts elsewhere.

The problem of comparison has been more recently alleviated by the publication by UNCTAD of data for the top 35 maritime powers based on their total tonnage, incorporating figures on the size of their fleets regardless of whether the vessels were registered under the national flag or foreign flags. Table 5.14 provides data for 1993 on total tonnage in DWT (deadweight tonnes) for 23 of the top 35 maritime powers as well as for a few other countries in India's neighbourhood. The percentage of the total tonnage that is registered under foreign flags is indicated within parentheses.[26] For purposes of comparison, the table provides data for 1990 as well. The table also

TABLE 5.14: SHIPPING TONNAGES OF SELECTED COUNTRIES (DWT MILLION)[27]

Year	*1970*	*1975*	*1980*	*1985*	*1990*	*1993*
Greece	16.99	37.54	67.05	55.36	81.98 (57)	115.15 (54)
Japan	40.28	64.48	67.32	63.45	80.31 (56)	84.78 (65)
USA	16.11	15.61	22.19	23.04	55.11 (66)	54.12 (70)
Norway	31.39	45.59	38.89	25.72	55.08 (33)	51.08 (36)
UK	38.69	53.42	43.81	21.79	25.65 (69)	22.72 (77)
USSR/Russia	15.26	20.11	25.89	28.15	29.27 (3)	21.07 (24)
Germany	12.28	13.61	13.33	9.24	12.75 (63)	16.60 (66)
Denmark	5.07	7.15	8.70	7.42	11.53 (40)	11.96 (44)
Italy	10.33	15.60	17.95	14.37	11.69 (7)	11.91 (23)
Sweden	7.25	12.24	6.63	4.23	5.53 (51)	11.57 (81)
France	9.45	18.14	20.86	13.71	6.13 (50)	7.01 (52)
Hong Kong	0.99	0.59	2.65	11.33	29.79 (89)	33.30 (84)
Korea (South)	1.29	2.39	6.84	11.77	15.72 (27)	18.56 (47)
Taiwan	1.69	NA	NA	NA	10.54 (36)	11.90 (38)
Singapore	0.55	6.22	12.55	11.19	7.52 (38)	9.00 (29)
Iran	0.17	0.74	1.93	3.86	8.62 (0)	8.00 (0)
Kuwait	0.99	1.67	4.22	3.51	4.65 (39)	4.31 (23)
Saudi Arabia	0.05	0.28	2.65	5.25	2.72	4.18 (78)
China	1.19	4.25	10.22	15.92	25.09 (20)	30.11 (29)
India	3.78	6.28	9.45	10.76	10.78 (4)	11.15 (7)
Brazil	2.42	4.29	7.55	10.04	9.87 (4)	10.15 (15)
Philippines	1.29	1.21	2.91	7.57	3.47 (5)	4.01 (7)
Indonesia	0.75	1.06	1.86	2.67	2.39 (35)	4.01 (36)
Malaysia	0.04	0.49	1.01	2.58	2.46	3.16
Pakistan	0.76	0.65	0.63	0.65	2.52 (80)	0.52
Sri Lanka	0.004	0.11	0.13	0.97	0.53	0.45
World	326.1	546.3	682.8	664.8	595.7 (43)	654.9 (50)

Source: UNCTAD, *Review of Maritime Transport* (various years). Figures within parentheses are for the percentage of the tonnage registered under foreign flags.

includes information on tonnage by five-year intervals from 1970 to 1985 for the same set of countries. This information is not comparable with that for 1993 or 1990, since it is based only on tonnage under national flag and does not cover FOC tonnage. Its inclusion is, however, pertinent to comparing India's performance with a number of selected countries over the period of the depression.

India's performance emerges as weak when seen in comparative perspective. Perhaps it would be unfair to compare India with developed market economies with their advantages of intensive industrialization, high levels of trade, long maritime tradition, and established position in world shipping. However, it is noteworthy that quite a few small countries from among them rank high in the world's list of top 35 maritime powers in 1993: Greece (1), Norway (4), Denmark (11), and Sweden (14). Similarly, several medium and small but economically dynamic countries outside Europe are ahead of India in total tonnage--Hong Kong (5), South Korea (9), and Taiwan (13). Their superior performance demonstrates the centrality of overall economic strength and dynamism of a country, especially in international trade, to maritime power. It is noteworthy, too, that they have functioned under the American or western political and military umbrella.

Interestingly, these three countries were nowhere near India's tonnage in 1970 and 1975, or even in 1980, but by 1985 Hong Kong and South Korea had pulled ahead of India and certainly by 1990 they had left it far behind. Taiwan in 1990 had come almost abreast of India. The advance of these three countries underlines the serious setback to India's maritime position after 1980. A similar finding emerges from a comparison with China (6), which in 1970 had only one-third of India's tonnage. Even in 1975, China's fleet was only two-thirds the size of India's. But by 1980, China was slightly ahead of India, and by 1985 its tonnage was half as much larger than India's while by 1990 it was almost two and a half times larger. Note also that several other countries made substantial advance in their tonnage between 1980 and 1985: Iran (100 per cent); Saudi Arabia (98 per cent); Indonesia (44 per cent); and Malaysia (155 per cent). By contrast, India expanded its tonnage by a mere 14 per cent.

The comparative data yields a significant proposition: the condition of the shipping industry of any particular country or set of countries does not necessarily follow the business cycles of world shipping. For, it is apparent that Hong Kong, South Korea, Taiwan and China--as also several other countries in Asia--advanced rapidly in their absolute tonnage and their share of world tonnage during the 1980s, precisely the decade of stagnation and decline in world tonnage. A country's tonnage thus need not be simply a reflection of trends in world shipping. The fact that India did not expand tonnage during the 1980s therefore had to do with factors internal to the country rather than merely and inevitably because of international forces.

CONTAINERIZATION IN COMPARATIVE CONTEXT

The picture of India that emerges from the examination of the status of its tonnage in the 1980s and the assessment of its performance in a comparative context is reinforced by taking a comparative look specifically at its performance in respect of acquisition of cellular containerships. Table 5.15 provides data by five-year intervals from 1975 to 1990 (plus 1993) on containership tonnage in the fleets of several Asian countries (plus Brazil). The table shows India literally bereft of any containership tonnage over a long period. Not until 1993 did India acquire some presence in container shipping. While Iran, Pakistan and Sri Lanka continue to repeat India's past performance, the experience of several other countries displays an instructive contrast. In 1970, except for Japan, no country in Asia had any containership tonnage. By 1975, South Korea and Singapore had made a significant entry and by 1980 Hong Kong, Malaysia and Kuwait had joined them with substantial capacity while China had made a token appearance. By 1985, the group had expanded to include Indonesia, the Philippines and Brazil. India was the last to join the group in 1993. By then, Singapore, South Korea, China and undoubtedly Taiwan (although it does not appear in the table) had assumed a commanding position among Asian fleets, with each possessing a million or more grt in containerships. Indeed, China's national line COSCO had not only joined the major league (Tables 5.4 and 5.5) but by September 1, 1994 it had risen to the fourth place among the top twenty carriers.[28] It remains to be seen how India will be able to overcome the handicap of having to succeed with such a late start in the face of the entrenched domination of world shipping by foreign operators. Strangely, the entry by the Shipping Corporation of India (SCI) into its own national trades was viewed with resentment, in some eyes insolence, by foreign carriers: "there are unstated hints of irritation at SCI having injected around 40,000 teu each way annual capacity".[29]

TABLE 5.15: COMPARATIVE STATEMENT ON CONTAINER SHIPS UNDER NATIONAL REGISTRY AS AT JULY 1 ('000 GRT)

	1975 Tonnage	*1980 Tonnage*	*1985 Tonnage*	*1990 Tonnage*	*1993 Tonnage*
Hong Kong	-	259	311	559	603
Korea (South)	18	278	325	668	1163
Singapore	55	449	603	951	1483
Iran	-	-	-	-	-
Kuwait	-	83	265	139	86
Saudi Arabia	-	-	83	67	67
China	-	4	327	846	1027
India	-	-	1	-	44
Brazil	-	-	44	87	147
Philippines	-	-	28	61	97
Indonesia	-	-	59	77	71
Malaysia	-	106	189	198	292
Pakistan	-	-	-	-	-
Sri Lanka	-	-	-	-	-
World	6226	11274	18364	23799	31271

Source: UNCTAD, *Review of Maritime Transport* (various years). Regrettably, comparable information on Taiwan is not available. The figures for 1993 are as at December 31.

The marginalization of India in respect of container carrying capacity is, no doubt, damaging for national shipping and the national economy in that container cargo is high-value cargo.

However, India's marginalization went beyond the mere absence of such capacity, for the container revolution had a profound impact in other respects as well. During Phase 4, the restructuring of the industry proceeded further so as to transform the organization of liner cargo shipping on the main arterial routes, with the "motherships" of a select few major players touching at a few mainline ports and relying on "feedering" with smaller vessels through a "hub and spoke" system for the regional trades. One area particularly affected was that of much of the southern rim of Asia; as the *Lloyd's Shipping Economist* (LSE) remarked in 1990: "There are few regions of the globe where the hub-feeder container transport system does not feature to any significant degree, but it is in South and South East Asia, extending from Suez to the China Sea, where the modern concept of feedering has really come into its own".[30] The change took place with astonishing speed; as the same journal had noted a year earlier: "in the space of four years, these trade routes have been totally transformed by shipping lines which have redefined their service operating strategies to the extent that they are fast becoming interlinked with each other and with the busy Europe-Far East mainstream container trades".[31]

Two consequences followed from the change. The first one was that India did not escape the container revolution but, in the absence of a vigorous and watchful state policy, the revolution was carried out by foreign rather than Indian lines. As LSE pointed out in 1986, because of the "relatively unrestricted markets" of India, unlike those of South America, "the big European carriers and US operators have containerized their services independently of indigenous companies".[32] In "the aggressive expansion of their services" that followed, the foreign lines came to "dominat[e] the Indian maritime sector".[33] It is sometimes averred that India could not go in for container shipping because of the lack of adequate cargo generated by the country. However, it was not so much a question of inadequate cargo than that a multitude of foreign lines simply grabbed the available cargo through a preemptive strategy. The impact on Indian liner shipping was simply devastating.

The subcontinent became saturated with foreign carriers. As many as 25 carriers on the average were present in its major

TABLE 5.16: NUMBER OF LINES OPERATING ON DIFFERENT LINER TRADE ROUTES OF INDIAN SUBCONTINENT (IS), 1990-1994

Trade Route	*1990*	*1991*	*1992*	*1993*	*1994*
Europe-IS	25	29	27	25	24
Far East-IS	28	14	24	25	32
IS-Mediterranean	19	16	23	20	15
IS-Middle East	14	21	27	23	31
IS-North America	12	9	12	13	18

Source: UNCTAD/SDD/SHIP/5 of April 18, 1995, p. 14.

trade routes in 1994 (see Table 5.16). At the same time, India's liner shipping had only a minuscule share in its own container trades. For example, in the India-US container trade in 1994, India's share was only 1.05 per cent in sharp contrast with the large figures of the top four carriers: American President Lines (APL) 25.53 per cent; Sea-Land 12.18 per cent; Maersk 10.25 per cent; and NOL 10.13 per cent (see Table 5.17).

The second consequence was that, because of the inadequacy and inefficiency of the logistics infrastructure under state administration, India was also marginalized on the main shipping lanes as it came to be avoided by mainline ships. A huge subcontinent thus came to be served through feeder services from transhipment ports at Singapore and Colombo and others in the Gulf (for some examples, see Table 5.18). With the massive shift to feeder operations, end-to-end services to the subcontinent were drastically reduced; in the words of LSE, "the general trend on East-West liner routes has been to view Southern Asia as a glorified wayport".[34] Nothing could have been a bigger blow to India's national psyche--as often acknowledged by members of the shipping community in private--that not Bombay or Calcutta, nor Cochin or Madras, with their vast hinterlands, but Colombo in small Sri Lanka, was a hub for feedering to the subcontinent.

TABLE 5.17: MARKET SHARES OF MAJOR CARRIERS IN INDIA-US TRADES

Carrier	*Total Trade 1994*	
	Number TEUs	*Share (%)*
American President Lines	61,443	25.53
Sea-Land Service	29,301	12.18
Maersk	24,657	10.25
NOL	24,371	10.13
Hoegh Line	14,671	6.10
Evergreen	14,656	6.09
P&O Containers	14,370	5.97
NYK	11,561	4.80
Mitsui-OSK	10,893	4.53
United Arab	6,967	2.90
K-Line	4,181	1.74
OOCL	3,848	1.60
Croatia	3,748	1.56
Hanjin	3,214	1.34
National Shipping (S. Arabia)	2,747	1.14
Shipping Corporation of India	2,532	1.05
Yangming	1,376	0.57
DSR-Senator	927	0.39
Zim	746	0.31
Others	718	0.30
Hyundai	516	0.21
Pakistan National Shipping	372	0.15
Cho Yang	313	0.13
Hapag-Lloyd	259	0.11
Nedlloyd Lines	250	0.10
Total	240,631	

Source: Adrian Bascombe, "A Sexy Trade", *Containerization International,* April 1995, pp. 55-59.

Table 5.18: SERVICES OF MAIN US-INDIA CARRIERS, MARCH 1, 1995

Carrier	*Sailing Frequency*	*Indian Ports or Feeder Arrangements*	*Tran-shipment Hub*
APL			
--US West Coast	Fixed day weekly	Feeder services to all major ports	Singapore or Colombo
Sea-Land			
--US East Coast	Fixed day weekly	Direct calls at J.L. Nehru. Uses common feeders. VSA between Maersk, P&O, and Sea-Land	Direct
--US West Coast	Fixed day weekly	J.L. Nehru in joint service with Maersk and P&O	Singapore
Maersk			
--US East Coast	Fixed day weekly	Direct calls at J.L. Nehru. Uses common feeders	Direct
--US West Coast	Fixed day weekly	J.L. Nehru in joint service with P&O and Sea-Land	Singapore
NOL			
--US East Coast	Fixed day weekly	Uses dedicated feeder services	Colombo
--US West Coast	Fixed day weekly	Dedicated service to Bombay	Singapore

Source: Adrian Bascombe, "A Sexy Trade", *Containerization International,* April 1995, pp. 55-59. VSA = Vessel Sharing Agreement.

SUMMARY

After the early 1970s, the international system of shipping was hit by an unprecedented crisis, which flowed from a structural break triggered by the OPEC oil price hike and from structural change represented by the container revolution. That systemic crisis had repercussions in India as well. Neither the command economy nor the policy of self-reliance was able to stem its impact. India's shipping industry was severely mauled and damaged; several shipping companies became insolvent; both liner companies in the private sector were, in effect, eliminated from liner shipping; the country's tonnage saw stagnation and decline as did its share in the national trades. In sum, India became marginalized in dry bulk and, particularly, liner shipping.

Whilc India undoubtedly suffered as a result of the worldwide depression in shipping, its poor performance over the long period of two decades after the initial oil price shock in 1973 was not all inevitably related to that international phenomenon. This is made evident by the subsequent different trajectories followed by world shipping and Indian shipping. The recovery and expansion in world shipping after 1988 did not seem to have much effect on India, for little new addition to its tonnage took place. More importantly, India's performance stood in sharp contrast to that of many countries in Asia. In particular, unlike them, India failed until very late to adapt itself to the container revolution. The specific pattern of India's performance points up therefore the importance of looking at internal factors, especially state policy, in any analysis of the experience during the crisis and after.

NOTES

1. Robert Gilpin, *The Political Economy of International Relations* (Princeton: Princeton University Press, 1987), pp.134-42.

2. John G. Kilgour, *The U.S. Merchant Marine: National Maritime Policy and Industrial Relations* (New York: Praeger, 1975), p. 57.

3. See UNCTAD document TD/B/CN.4/5 of July 29, 1992.

4. See the article by the senior vice-president of Nippon Yusen Kaisha (NYK Line), Hiroshi Takahashi, "Facing the Future", *Containerization International*, June 1992, pp. 48-49. I follow the chronological demarcation by Takahashi, but provide my own descriptive content.

5. Jon Webb, "Rationalization--But Where to Now?", *Lloyd's Shipping Economist,* June 1987, pp. 18-20.

6. Richard Gibney, "Jumbo Misconceptions and the Big 13", *Lloyd's Shipping Economist,* June 1987, pp. 22-23.

7. Webb, p. 18.

8. See C.K. Kim, *An Innovation in Liner Shipping: The Round-the-World Service as a Global Strategy* (Bremen: Institute of Shipping Economics and Logistics, 1987).

9. Peter Gaskell, "Little Profit From More Volume", *Seatrade Business Review,* May-June 1990, pp. 133-37. The rapid change in this respect is conveyed by the example of the trade between India (West Coast) and the UK; in 1975, the share of independent operators was 6 per cent, but by 1982 it had become 55 per cent. See Lalit M.S. Rajwar, "The Liner Code: Its Philosophy and Approach", *Indian Shipping,* vol. 36, no. 6 (1984), pp. 29-31.

10. "Container Lines Stake Their Future on Trade Stabilization", *BIMCO Bulletin,* January-February 1993, p. 49, based on a Drewry report.

11. Fred Winkler, "The Present and Future of Liner Shipping", *BIMCO Bulletin,* July-August 1993, pp. 17-18.

12. John Fossey, "Top 20 Boost Share", *Containerization International,* November 1993, pp. 32-39.

13. John Fossey, "Asian Delight", *Containerization International,* November 1994, pp. 52-54.

14. Although no agreed definition of a megacarrier exists, one UNCTAD document lays down three criteria: (1) over one billion US$ in assets or annual revenues; (2) significant presence as a "global carrier" in the world's major trade routes; and (3) a minimum teu capacity, such as 80,000 or 100,000 teus. See UNCTAD/SDD/MT/4 of February 25, 1994.

15. Fred Winkler, "Liner Shipping", *BIMCO Bulletin,* March-April 1992, pp. 56-57.

16. Fred Winkler, "Major Tendencies in Container Shipping in 1993", *BIMCO Bulletin,* January 1994, pp. 77-78.

17. *Bimco Bulletin,* vol. 89, no. 3 (June 1994), pp. 45-46, and *Containerization International,* August 1994, p. 46.

18. UNCTAD/SDD/MT/4 of February 25, 1994, p. 16.

19. Among the companies, where SDFC foreclosed mortgages in order to sell the mortgaged ships, were: Nilhat Shipping, R.A.J. Lines, and Sujwala Shipping. The companies that were taken into liquidation included: Thakur Shipping, Damodar Bulk Carriers, Seven Seas Transportation, Indo Oceanic Shipping, and Dempo Steamships. See S.N. Sanklecha, *Tramping to Success: Story of the Great Eastern Shipping Company Limited* (Bombay: Popular Prakashan, 1994), p. 115.

20. Sanklecha, p. 115.

21. One government document noted in 1967 that while liner cargo constituted 25 per cent of India's foreign trade in weight, it was estimated to be 75 per cent in value. See India, Ministry of Transport and Shipping, National Conference on Shipping, Shipbuilding and Ports, December 1967, *Recommendations, Agenda Notes and Contributed Papers* (New Delhi: 1967), p. 34.

22. The shares of Indian carriers and foreign carriers in the import bill of Rs. 38.5 billion and in the export bill of Rs. 24.1 billion were in the ratio of 36:64 and 20:80, respectively. National

Council of Applied Economic Research, *Indian Shipping Industry: Retrospect and Prospect* (New Delhi: NCAER, 1993), pp. 61-62. At first sight, the ratios seem to differ somewhat from those in the tables on India's trades. The difference stems from the fact that the figures in the tables refer to weight while the present ratios refer to value even as the freight carried by Indian flag ships is of lower value. Note the comment: "The share of Indian shipping in the freight earnings is far less than its share in the sea-borne cargo. For example, in the case of imports, in 1991-92, the share in import earnings was only 36 per cent as against 50 per cent share in the cargo.... The relatively lower level of freight earnings of Indian flag vessels is largely on account of their low share in the general cargo trade for which freight rates are high as compared to other cargoes". Asian Institute of Transport Development, *Indian Shipping Industry: Critical Issues in Global Context* (New Delhi: 1993), p. 13.

23. Oppenheimer & Co., Inc., *International Research: Indian Shipping Industry* (April 10, 1995), p. 5.

24. John Fossey, "A Matter of Convenience", *Containerization International,* March 1995, pp. 53-55.

25. See Helen A. Thanopoulou, "The Growth of Fleets Registered in the Newly-Emerging Maritime Countries and Maritime Crises", *Maritime Policy and Management,* vol. 22, no. 1 (1995), pp. 51-62, which attributes the prolonging and deepening of the maritime crisis of 1973-1987 as well as the alleged loss of OECD hegemony to the rise of newly-emerging maritime countries.

26. Note that "foreign flag" is not the same thing as FOC or "open registry" flag. The figure for the share of the latter in the world tonnage in 1993 was 37.1 per cent. The breakdown by type of vessel is: oil tankers, 43 per cent; bulk carriers, 37 per cent; general cargo ships, 31 per cent; and container ships, 28 per cent. See UNCTAD, *Review of Maritime Transport 1993*, pp. 20-22.

27. The figures are based on flag of registration (vessels of 100 grt and over) except when followed by parentheses, in which case they are for the total fleet (vessels of 1000 grt and over), including parts that are under national flag as well as foreign flags.

28. John Fossey, "Asian Delight", *Containerization International,* November 1994, pp. 52-54.

29. David Eller, "Europe-Gulf-India Reaches Saturation", *Containerization International,* June 1994, pp. 44-49.

30. "Feedering Comes Into Its Own", *Lloyd's Shipping Economist,* July 1990, pp. 14-16.

31. "Changing Strategies for Changing Markets", *Lloyd's Shipping Economist,* September 1989, pp. 14-16.

32. "Different Routes to Containerization", *Lloyd's Shipping Economist,* October 1986, pp. 16-20.

33. K. Balasubramanian, "India Misses the Boat", *Containerization International,* October 1993, pp. 55-57.

34. "Different Routes to Containerization", *Lloyd's Shipping Economist,* October 1986, pp. 16-20.

CHAPTER VI

SYSTEMIC CRISIS AND THE STATE: PATH DEPENDENCY, STATE POWER AND PERFORMANCE

The systemic crisis had enormously serious consequences for the shipping industry in India. It resulted in the marginalization of India in dry bulk and, particularly, liner shipping. The course and extent of this outcome has been dealt with in some detail in the preceding chapter. The purpose of the present chapter is to assess the role of state policy in the outcome. That role is examined in reference to state policy before the onset of the systemic crisis as well as during the crisis.

THE PARADOX OF PAST SUCCESS: PATH DEPENDENCY THEORY AND THE CONSTRAINTS ON ADAPTABILITY

In the late 1950s, the Indian state had evolved a set of policies which proved to be highly successful in assuring the rapid growth of the country's shipping tonnage. From 0.67M grt in 1958, the tonnage expanded to 5.76M grt in 1978, that is, it grew more than eight and a half times over a 20-year period. Although the growth fell short of expectations in terms of obtaining an adequate share of the national trades, Indian tonnage had expanded at a rate faster than that of the world's shipping industry; its share of world tonnage grew two and a half times from 0.57 per cent to 1.42 per cent. By 1975, India had emerged as the largest maritime power in the developing world and, corresponding to this level of accomplishment, it was playing a leadership role in that world's diplomacy in shipping during the 1970s. Little wonder that the set of policies which had made for such success became entrenched in the state even as the industry increasingly found them irksome. Paradoxically, however, the same set of policies which had made for such success over the 1960s proved to be a constraint on the industry's adaptability to the challenge that emerged from adversity when the depression struck in the mid-1970s and when the container revolution gathered speed during the late 1970s and 1980s.

The influence that past decisions and developments concerning technology and institutions exert on future outcomes is technically termed as "path dependence" in the social sciences.[1] The concept underlines the relevance of history to economic performance in so far as past decisions and developments structure future constraints and opportunities. What may have been thought of as efficient or effective institutional solutions to societal problems at one time may no longer remain so when the environment undergoes change. Indeed, institutions developed earlier may create problems in terms of adaptation to change in the environment. Previous institutional solutions may "lock in" or "fence in" actors on given paths or trajectories, rendering adaptation to new circumstances difficult. It is the argument here that past decisions by the state in the shipping arena, which were at one time helpful to the shipping industry or were marginal in their effect, created severe problems for the industry in its possible adaptation to the new environment of world shipping marked by the structural rupture and structural change. This is not to say that earlier policies were necessarily wrong, but that under changed circumstances their consequences for the industry turned out to be perverse. This argument is developed in respect of four areas: state aid, state controls, lack of adequate cargo reservation, and the public sector.

THE PITFALLS OF STATE BENEVOLENCE

Indian shipping companies suffered grievously as a result of the depression that struck the industry in the mid-1970s. Part of the reason for this fate was the very generous financial treatment extended to them earlier by the state. The state provided funding on very liberal conditions; SDFC loans covered up to 90 per cent of the price of vessels, at very low rates of interest (which were 4.5 per cent in the 1970s and 7.5 per cent in the 1980s), and long amortization periods of up to 18 years. Of considerable significance was the state's liberal, or in some eyes imprudent, stance on high capital gearing or leveraging. SDFC norms allowed for debt equity ratios of 6:1 in cases where it provided loans and 10:1 where it extended only guarantees for foreign exchange loans. However, in actual practice these norms were not followed strictly. One study found that the average debt equity ratio for 20 of 25 companies funded by SDFC was "around 70:1 by 1985, a level of gearing that would have frightened many a landlubber".[2]

The high debt equity ratios arose apparently from the policy shift in the late 1960s, in line with the radical populism of the time, to provide loans on the basis of "need" rather than on commercial considerations. This pattern of financing led to the mushrooming of shipping companies. However, it provided little cushion when the depression struck. The lack of cushion was further aggravated by state policy to restrict loans to strictly shipping companies and not to provide them to companies that diversified into other areas, for fear that the cheap loans would get diverted elsewhere. The lack of diversification meant, however, that there were no other internal sources of funds to fall back on in the event of a downturn in the business cycle in shipping. Such an eventuality occasioned little concern earlier because Indian shipping, along with world shipping, functioned from 1960 to 1975 in a buoyant international trade environment. However, when the depression struck, the short-term consequence was that, with few exceptions, the shipping companies began to default on their debt repayments from 1982 onwards. SDFC had too much at stake; by then, it had disbursed loans worth Rs. 10.6 billion while Rs. 7.4 billion of the principal was outstanding.[3] By March 31, 1986, payments of Rs. 2.31 billion towards principal and Rs. 1.34 billion in interest were overdue. Also due by then were Rs. 490 million on account of payments made by SDFC on its guarantees.[4] Because of the vast public funds involved, SDFC reacted to the defaults by foreclosing mortgages and taking companies into receivership. The paradoxical consequence of earlier state generosity was that "the shake-out of the recession was, therefore, bloodier than may have been necessary".[5]

The hammer blows to the financial position of the shipping companies had several severe consequences. First, the companies were so crippled financially as to be unable to go in for tonnage expansion at a time when bargain purchases could be made. This was especially so for companies in liner shipping, which needed to go into containerized shipping if they were to survive. Second, the state's dismay at the financial debacle that the shipping companies, and as a consequence SDFC, had met with led the state to beat a retreat from directly disbursing loan capital to shipping companies. The state abolished SDFC in April 1987, and the function of providing concessional finance to the private sector for tonnage acquisition on sound commercial principles was then handed over to a new financial agency, specifically set up for the purpose--Shipping Credit and Investment Company of India (SCICI). The funding of purchases in the public sector continued to be the responsibility of the state. The two initial tasks required of SCICI were to implement a rehabilitation package for those sick companies which could be restored to health, and to recover the loans that were due to SDFC.

Third, the state's experience with the provision of concessional finance to shipping companies had longer-term implications for state assistance in the future. It made the Ministry of Finance unsympathetic to the industry's demands for assistance, even as it reduced the influence of the ministry in charge of shipping. As Sanklecha points out:

> The government was faced with the prospect of losing a large part of the funds it had lent for the development of shipping. There was disillusionment in government circles about the role of Indian shipping in the development of the Indian economy. The Shipping and Transport Ministry lost its credibility and clout with other ministries and especially with the Finance Ministry, because large government funds lent to shipping companies were in danger of being lost.... The acquisition proposals etc. referred by the Shipping and Transport Ministry to other Ministries would not be cleared for a long time.[6]

In general, in contrast to the situation in the 1960s when shipping had in actual fact been treated favourably and generously, henceforth shipping became downgraded in the eyes of the state. Even when its demands were justified, they failed to receive genuine sympathy, at least on time.

CONTROLS, INWARD ORIENTATION, AND PLANNING

The competitiveness and adaptability of Indian shipping, and therefore its commercial success and survival, were seriously compromised by the regulatory system of controls and licensing that was adopted by the Indian state. The origins of the system lay with the colonial state during the time of World War II. The colonial state then exercised control on the movement and employment of ships through the mechanism of licensing. After the war, the wartime regulatory system was incorporated into the Control of Shipping Act 1947. That Act was taken over, through an amendment, by the Indian state after independence. The Directorate General of Shipping issued licences to shipowners, which entitled them to ply ships in the coastal trade or on designated routes in overseas liner trades; in the case of tramping trades, at one time each voyage required a specific licence.

The licensing system was subsequently consolidated, refined and expanded under the Merchant Shipping Act of 1958. One of the early voices to attack the excessive powers reserved for the state was that of the late M.A. Master. In his opinion, expressed before the legislation was enacted into law, the draft bill tremendously expanded state control over shipping, conferring upon the state "extraordinary and far-reaching powers for controlling, regulating and directing the movements and the daily working of ships". He believed that "the Director General thus becomes the dictator of the shipping industry. Shipowners are reduced to the position of a cipher".[7] The criticism had little impact, and the shipowners learnt to live with the system even as they fretted over having to operate under its constraints.

The regulatory system installed under the Merchant Shipping Act covered the shipping industry in a most comprehensive way, including the purchase and sale, the chartering in and out, the repair, and the employment of ships. In respect of all these aspects, specific approval of the state was necessary. This entailed involved and time-consuming procedures, the net result of which was to increase the capital cost of ships for Indian shipowners, and make their operations commercially less competitive compared to their foreign rivals. On the other hand, competitiveness was key to survival, for the shipping industry was global in scope and fiercely competitive. Unlike other domestic industries, national shipping met international competition in greater force with few elements of state protection. Indeed, some 37 per cent of the world's tonnage operated under flags of convenience, which suffered little taxation and no bureaucratic restrictions. Where speed was of the essence, India's regulatory system imposed excruciatingly long delays, requiring approval by layers upon layers of authorities. Take, for instance, the purchase of ships. In the words of the late Vasant Sheth, then chairman of India's largest shipping company in the private sector:

> When we wish to buy a ship, we have to apply to the DG [Director General] Shipping, with 29 extra copies of the application, who makes his recommendations to the Ministry of Shipping and Transport; the Executive Director-SDFC also makes his recommendations to the Ministry; the application along with the recommendations are considered by an Acquisition Committee of the SDFC who then make their recommendations; the matter is then referred to the Finance Ministry. In addition, of course, MRTP [Monopolies and Restrictive Trade Practices] approval is required. Eventually the Ministry of Shipping & Transport directs the DG Shipping in Bombay to issue the necessary permission.
>
> When one wants to arrange any sort of foreign exchange finance, once again we have to make an application to DG Shipping who makes his recommendations to the Ministry of Shipping & Transport, who in turn refer the matter to the Finance Ministry; who then, after consulting the Reserve Bank of India return the papers back through the same channel through which they were received.[8]

Sheth had commented only on the formal aspects of the requirements; one of his deputies, Dr. S.N. Sanklecha, called attention to the informal aspects of the process:

> SDFC also acted as the Acquisition Committee on the basis of whose recommendations the government approved or disapproved the purchase of ships by shipping companies. The SDFC Executive Director's office in Bombay, which examined and processed shipping companies' applications

for purchase of ships, held up the applications for many months by asking for irrelevant information and data, and often for frivolous reasons did not send their recommendations to the Acquisition Committee. Even when recommendations for some of the acquisition proposals were made after much delay, the Acquisition Committee itself further delayed their decision on these applications. The provisions of Monopolies and Restrictive Trade Practices Act, which made it incumbent on the major shipping companies in the private sector to seek approvals to building or purchase of ships, added another delaying dimension since clearance under the MRTP Act required six months in the normal course.[9]

Shipowners felt the MRTP requirement to be particularly irritating in an industry which was so capital intensive that it brought many transactions within the purview of the Act's provisions and therefore resulted in delays. Such delays compelled the state in the early 1980s to exempt shipping from the MRTP regime.

Sheth estimated that it took eight to nine months to obtain approval for purchase of a ship.[10] If only in retrospect, one Director General of Shipping, Praveen Singh, acknowledged in 1991: "There was a time when ship acquisition requests used to take anything from 12 to 18 months".[11] The financial consequence of expected delays in state approval was that foreign brokers in their quotations always included a premium on sales to Indian shipowners and a discount on purchases from them. That had the effect of increasing the capital cost of ships for the Indian shipping industry, thus reducing its competitiveness. What intrigued the industry was that approval for the purchase of specific ships was almost always granted, perhaps with the original request marginally modified, but it often took months to get it. There were, of course, exceptions, for "at times we are able to get decisions very quickly from the Government of India, even if it involves inter-ministerial liaison or consultation, but more often than not, it is very time consuming".[12]

The private sector was not alone in being subjected to delays because of controls. The procedures for the public sector were no less, if not more, onerous. The proposals for investment by the public sector required scrutiny and approval at several levels. As one SCI chairman explained to parliament's Committee on Public Undertakings (COPU):

> After our proposal is formulated, we go to our Ministry. It has to be approved by the Public Investment Board (PIB). Before that a meeting is held in which again all agencies of the Government, including the Planning Commission, the Ministry of Finance, the Economic Affairs Department, the Project Appraisal Division, everyone is present and one of the issues which is considered every time is whether this order can go to an Indian Shipyard. Only if everyone is satisfied that this ship should go abroad and not to an Indian Shipyard, is the approval given. After that, the Public Investment Board's meeting is held where again all these agencies are represented and where the SCI is asked to give a presentation of their project. After the Public Investment Board have their approval, we submit another formal request to the Government saying that here is our project which has been approved by the PIB. Then, of course, it goes to the Government and is approved by the Cabinet. So, there are a number of stages....[13]

Formally, the process of approval was expected to be completed in six months, but the actual time taken was often "inordinately long". For example, one proposal to acquire two tankers was initiated in July 1977; the SCI board approved it in December 1978, while the government sanctioned it in July 1980. COPU admitted that "the delay and long procedures involved in clearance of proposals have proved major hurdles in the acquisition of vessels".[14]

The sale of ships by shipping companies also required state approval. Here, too, the state barred companies from simply exercising their commercial judgement in what were private business transactions. Instead, it insisted that sale could take place only after the completion of what it regarded as the normal life of the vessel. Furthermore, where SDFC had provided loans, the state would not allow sale if the price offered did not cover the outstanding loan payments.[15] Approvals of sales could take two to three months.[16] In essence, state policy precluded asset turnover by way of buying and selling ships by Indian companies, a practice which companies elsewhere regarded as essential to their profitability and financial viability.

The requirement of state sanction extended beyond purchase and sale of ships. If a company wanted ship repairs to be done abroad, it had to obtain prior permission of the state. It was state policy that, in the first instance, repairs ought to be done at Indian repair yards. On the other hand, Indian companies found this to be a more expensive, time-consuming, and technically unsatisfactory proposition. Similarly, state permission was necessary for the import of spare parts.

An even more demanding and unrealistic requirement was that known as the *pari passu* obligation, under which Indian companies were required to order an equivalent tonnage from an Indian shipyard when they bought ships abroad. Indian shipowners found themselves at a severe disadvantage compared to their foreign competitors as a result of this requirement, because of: the inevitable price escalations, with the state finally determining the price at the time of delivery; the long delays on delivery, extending into years; and the relatively poor quality of the products from the local yards. For example, Great Eastern had to pay an extra Rs. 90 million for four ships ordered from Indian shipyards. Its chairman pointed out in the mid-1980s that it cost about twice the price of Rs. 160 million to have a panamax bulk carrier built locally than it would to order it from a Japanese or Korean shipyard.[17] The resulting increase in capital costs and the consequent higher debt repayments made the blow from the depression all the more severe for the local shipping industry. It is obvious that there was a heavy price paid by the local industry for the benefits it received from the state by way of concessional finance. Even a state-appointed committee acknowledged the burdens placed by the *pari passu* obligations:

> the prices of ships built at Indian shipyards are 40 per cent to 50 per cent or even more higher than the prices of comparable ships available in the international market. Moreover, Indian shipyards take a long time to deliver these ships; the time lag between placing the order and delivery could be about 4 to 5 years or more whereas foreign shipyards deliver ships in 18 to 30 months. It is possible that

> by the time indigenously built ships are delivered the market requirements may change and the available market opportunities missed. This is more so in a cyclical and highly volatile industry like shipping where timing of acquisition is an important ingredient in a successful shipowner's strategy. Moreover, shipping being a capital intensive industry, high cost ships per se pose a tremendous burden on the shipowner and adversely affect his profitability and cash flows.[18]

The deployment of ships was also subject to state approval. Indian shipping companies had to obtain a licence to operate on given routes. Only three companies were allowed to enter the overseas liner trade--Shipping Corporation of India, Scindia Steam Navigation Company, and India Steamship Company--but even they were limited to routes for which a specific licence had been obtained. Other companies were barred from entering the liner trade on the ground that it would result in overtonnaging. Chartering in and chartering out of vessels also required approval of the state. In short, as one senior manager at Scindia put it in 1969, the law states "you can own a ship but you shall not use it unless the Director General of Shipping permits you to do so".[19] Earlier, in 1963, Master had warned "Indian shipping companies can do nothing today with their ships without the permission and the sanction of the Government of India".[20] The authorities frowned on chartering in of foreign vessels because it meant outflow of foreign exchange. On the other hand, they opposed chartering out of vessels, because the purpose of the Indian merchant fleet was to serve the national trades, not to engage in cross trading. In contrast, shipping companies around the world let out ships on long-term time charters as a hedge against any fall in freight rates in a cyclical industry. The fact that Indian shipping companies were largely prevented from doing that meant increased vulnerability for them; more particularly, they "were exposed to the full force of the shipping depression and sustained heavy losses".[21]

Although the regulatory system owed its origins to wartime controls to provide support for the war effort, its underlying aim under the regime of economic planning was to assure the rational and optimal utilization of resources. This latter aim, in the state's view, required the far-flung system of controls to see that the industry functioned according to the overall goals of the planners. The state saw capital and foreign exchange as particularly scarce resources, and controls were directed towards their conservation. This objective was also accompanied by a profound distrust and terrible fear of business and industry indulging in cheating and capital flight. As Director General of Shipping Praveen Singh revealed in 1991:

> When it is a matter of foreign exchange involvement to the tune of a couple of hundred million dollars, I do not think the industry can be given a completely free hand, without the government assuring itself that the investment is necessary and shall be of benefit to the economy.... It does not make good economics to advance money and then have the returns undermined by cutthroat competition....
>
> Give me a procedure against a malady that afflicts a whole lot of foreign exchange transactions in the country: over and under-invoicing. After all, when a party is likely to profit in terms of 10,000 dollars a day, there has to be some basis to judge whether this figure should have been 12,000 or 8,000. A reasonable assurance about this certainly will be required by the ministry of finance. In absence of any scrutiny what is the safeguard against juggling, when the amounts involved are so high? .... the counter-argument is, how would you then safeguard against over and under-invoicing, particularly when the amounts involved are so high?[22]

Even though the shipping industry claimed that it was a net earner of foreign exchange and could earn vastly more if it had the freedom to buy and sell ships, the state would not exempt the industry from the controls or give it any special consideration. The state would not allow it direct access to the foreign exchange it earned and avoid the controls. As Transport Secretary P.M. Abraham stated in 1991:

> Purchase of ships very much depends upon the foreign exchange available. We cannot freely permit buying as the country does not have that much money going around. But, where sale is concerned all the foreign exchange earned has to come to the national kitty, from where it gets divided between various claimants, on the basis of their need and

priority.... Thus, it is just not possible to have one to one relationship between the export capability and import entitlement. The revenues of exports come to the national kitty, but where imports are concerned, plea for finance has to be considered on priority basis.... When we permit a company to buy, we are releasing scarce foreign exchange, denying it at the same time to somebody else.[23]

Regardless of the justification for it, the restrictive regulatory framework, with its rigid procedures, placed serious constraints on the flexibility and adaptability of the Indian shipping industry. It rendered it uncompetitive in relation to the world industry, and reduced its capacity to face the full brunt of cutthroat competition to which it was exposed in the wake of the depression and structural change. In a note of dissent to the report of a planning group, Vasant Sheth underlined that the controls had "wiped out all our competitive advantages and have placed Indian shipping companies at a great competitive handicap as compared with their international competitors". He acknowledged that the government had been generous in providing financial assistance but reiterated that "this assistance has been neutralized to a large extent by the regulatory regime imposed by the Government in respect of shipping". He added that the controls had "put fetters on freedom and flexibility of shipping operations".[24]

The impact of the regulatory framework went beyond the constraints it placed on the flexibility of management in the industry. In a subtle but crucial way, it focused the management's energies at New Delhi, where it had to go for approval for everything. Economic planning reinforced this dependence on the state, for it determined how much tonnage and what kind of tonnage was to be acquired. The corporate plans of the companies had to fit in with the aims of the planners on the number, type and size of vessels to be acquired for the merchant fleet. Indeed, it would not be farfetched to say that the planning process and the regulatory system shifted the locus of managerial decision-making from the shipping companies to the state, which in effect became their upper management. In this manner, some of the key functions of management withered or were lost because of the excessive dependence on the state. N. Vaghul, chairman of SCICI, the agency entrusted with the rehabilitation of shipping companies affected by the depression, underlined this aspect of the industry in 1989:

> the Indian shipping tonnage composition is largely dictated by the cargo requirements assessed by the Transchart and other user Ministries. To the extent the shipowners are required to follow this policy reference in acquiring tonnage, there gets established a basis of dependence. In the process, the shipowners tend to take investment decisions with less than healthy thoroughness and rigour. When such decisions run aground, there is naturally a tendency to shift the logical corporate accountability to Government.[25]

If, on the one hand, economic planning and controls thus fostered dependence on the state, on the other hand they made Indian shipping insular in relation to the outside world in an industry where awareness of the international business environment and interaction with it was of the essence. This insular outlook was poor preparation for grappling with the depression. As Vaghul pointed out:

> in a paradoxical way, the Indian shipping industry's overdependence on the extremely accommodative and liberal financial assistance and other supports from Government of India may have detracted from its strength and resilience.... Owing to the lack of a systematic build-up of global financial information on shipping, we tend to introvert and localize the industry's problems and their solutions. This is obviously quite erroneous as the Indian shipping industry cannot survive, in an atmosphere alienated from overseas market conditions such as what the indigenous industry has trained itself to be....
>
> One could therefore conclude that there has been some lack of a macroperspective and long-term strategies. Apart from the plan targets and the industry's own short-term assessment, there was perhaps no systematic planning of the market horizon and drawing up of a reasonably long-term perspective.[26]

The dependence on state--and correspondingly the relative insulation from the international environment--was structurally built into the planning process and the system of licensing and controls. An unusually competent management could, of course, struggle to overcome what was structurally induced, but it was likely to be an exception. That such an exception could arise is illustrated by the Great Eastern Shipping Company (GES), and its performance can be appreciated by a comparison with Scindia Steam Navigation. There can be a valid objection against such a comparison in that the two companies operated in two entirely different types of commercial shipping, Scindia in liner shipping and GES in tramp or bulk shipping. However, that difference in itself is potentially an important element in orienting managements differently in regard to their international environment, at least in the context of the time. The closest analogy to liner shipping is that of the bus that, as a common carrier, plies on set routes on fixed time schedules at fixed rates for traffic that is available at the point of departure and en route. On the other hand, bulk shipping is like the taxi which goes from one point to another on the basis of a contract negotiated beforehand, usually at prevailing market rates.

Scindia Steam Navigation: Scindia had developed as an economic counterpart in shipping to the political nationalism that dominated the Indian scene during the 1920s and 1930s. It had grown through a dogged struggle against British shipping hegemony, and by independence Scindia shipping was synonymous with Indian-owned shipping. By 1950, however, the pioneers who built the company had either retired or passed away. Scindia's de facto leadership passed to Mrs. Sumati Morarjee, the daughter-in-law of one of the founders who had been the company's financial bulwark in its early years.[27] She remained at the helm until the state ordered the handing over of the management of the company to SCICI in 1987. What had brought Scindia to this fate of being taken in receivership by SCICI?

After passing through a long struggle spread over some four decades against British domination of the Indian trades, Scindia finally found itself from 1961 onwards in a situation where it was assured of a substantial share in the India-UK/Continent trade. This happy circumstance was the result of the pooling arrangements worked out under the auspices of that trade's conference. The share did not match its ambitions but, when supplemented by its participation in the bilateral shipping arrangements as well as the expanding trade of the country, it provided Scindia with adequate room for growth in its specialization of liner shipping. Following the British model of the time, Scindia was overly attached to liner shipping and did not attempt diversification until the late 1960s and even then not on a large scale. Indeed, during the 1950s it was hostile to tramp shipping, declaring publicly that its days were finished.

A number of circumstances combined to induce complacency in the management. The 1960s and early 1970s were boom years in international trade, the conferences were strong, pooling arrangements prevailed in the country's important trades which obviated exertion in marketing, ship technology was relatively stable, and profits flowed in regularly. The company's orientation was necessarily turned inward, focused largely on the acquisition of ships, where its accumulated political capital from the past was helpful with the decision-makers in New Delhi though it did not always prevail. By contrast, marketing and the international environment were not as salient.

Its halcyon days were, however, rudely interrupted by the depression of the mid-1970s. That was an unusual experience for it after the long spell of prosperity. Meanwhile, as the container revolution gathered momentum and the independent operators became more aggressive, the pooling arrangements came to an end in 1981. In its financially debilitated state, resulting from the first phase of the depression, Scindia made a feeble attempt to meet the container challenge with the uncompetitive equipment of "combi" ships, which combined carriage of containers and break-bulk cargo. As a consequence, the company found itself being eased out of the market in liner shipping, almost its sole business. More serious grief lay ahead, however.

When the second phase of the depression hit, Scindia headed straight for financial collapse.[28] For six years in a row it made huge losses (see Table 6.1). In 1982, it began defaulting on its debt repayments. When Scindia failed to meet its commitments to foreign creditors, SDFC had to assume the burden of payments under its guarantees. With no cash, the company was unable to pay its floating and shore staff even as the maintenance of the ships suffered. Worried over the recovery of their dues, foreign creditors had three of the company's ships arrested abroad. By the beginning of 1987, the company had practically ceased operations. That year, failing to make its debt repayments, the company was taken under receivership by SCICI on behalf of the state.

TABLE 6.1: SCINDIA'S LOSSES IN THE 1980S

Year	*Loss During the Year (Rs. Million)*	*Cash Loss (Rs. Million)*
1981-82	160.3	34.0
1982-83	172.1	46.8
1983-84	259.4	139.4
1984-85	94.4	-26.7
1985-86	294.5	171.8
1986-87	292.9	187.8
Total	1,273.6	553.1

Source: Scindia Steam Navigation Company, *Annual Reports* (various years).

Once a nationalist icon, Scindia now received rather shabby treatment from SCICI, with the latter apparently more interested in recovering the SDFC loans rather than saving the company. The new management failed to rescue the company from slow death, with the state simply proving unresponsive to any of its four successive proposals for restructuring. By the mid-1990s, the company seemed inevitably destined for the corporate graveyard.

The other liner shipping company in the private sector, India Steamship, also received heavy blows from the depression and the container revolution. Although it avoided a fate comparable to that of Scindia's, it was nonetheless severely wounded and saw a long period of decline. From a peak of 26 ships of 249,053 grt in 1978, its fleet had been downsized to 12 ships of 192,838 grt by 1995; even the latter set of figures was an exaggeration, for four of the ships were laid up since they could not be sold because of labour problems. Its fleet had grown very old, containing no ship acquired after 1983. In 1993, the company formally withdrew from the liner trades, traditionally the backbone of its business.[29]

Great Eastern Shipping: When Vasant Sheth, who had managed GES from its very founding in 1948, died in 1992, the eminent British shipping journal *Fairplay* wrote: "Just once in every generation there is a formative character. Indian shipping has just lost that man, Vasant Sheth.... he was the first Indian to realize the potential for bulk cargoes there. He bought the first Indian tanker, the first Indian OBO [ore-bulk-oil] and the first clear vision that India could have a private sector shipping fleet, despite all the restrictions that a single minded socialist government could put in his way".[30]

Sheth built GES to become India's largest shipping company in the private sector and its most profitable shipping enterprise, with a reputation around the world as one of the best managed shipping firms internationally. He guided it through the depression--without ever occasioning a single default on its loan repayments--to emerge even stronger with an expanded tonnage and higher efficiency and greater profitability. To the extent that GES was run by an entrepreneurial genius who provided vision and dynamic leadership, perhaps it is unfair to compare its performance with other companies. But what is of concern here is the particular orientation of his approach to management, central to which was the international market. While the nature of its core business, bulk shipping, partly contributed to that orientation, it was not sufficient for success, for other companies in bulk shipping did not perform as well and many were seriously damaged by the depression.

Given the remarkable performance of GES, it is difficult to imagine that it owes its origins to the endeavours of a young man still in his teens. At age 19, Vasant Sheth, after completing a four-month course in business in England, went to the US in 1947 and applied to the US Maritime Commission for the purchase of a liberty ship. A year later, when the ship was released, it became the occasion to launch the new company GES with Sheth at the head of its management. The purchase was no accident. Sheth was the youngest son of a Gujarati trading family that specialized in the sugar trade and was adept at chartering vessels for importing sugar from Java. Unlike Scindia, where nationalism was a strong motive in taking to shipping, for the Sheths shipping was a profit opportunity, though the father was an ardent nationalist. From that small beginning of a single ship, GES expanded to become the largest shipping firm in the private sector. Its experience well confirms Adam Smith's adage that those who endeavour to serve their private interest end up indirectly serving the public interest. As Sanklecha puts it: "It has been stated that credit for the birth of Indian shipping in India goes to Scindia Company and for giganticism of development to government-owned Shipping Corporation of India. To Great Eastern however goes the undisputed prize in that crucial area of business: Profits".[31]

TABLE 6.2: COMPARATIVE PROFITABILITY OF SELECTED SHIPPING COMPANIES (GROSS PROFIT AS % OF CAPITAL EMPLOYED)

Company	*1988-89*	*1989-90*	*1990-91*	*1991-92*	*Average*
SCI	8.9	12.9	7.3	9.4	9.6
Great Eastern	13.0	19.6	15.6	29.7	19.5
Essar	14.6	16.2	11.5	8.6	12.7
India Steamship	11.9	7.5	-2.0	3.5	5.2
Scindia	4.2	4.0	-3.2	3.0	1.9
Varun	15.7	18.8	15.7	14.1	16.7
Chowgule	8.3	11.8	5.0	13.3	9.6

Source: S.N. Sanklecha, *Tramping to Success: Story of the Great Eastern Shipping Company Limited* (Bombay: Popular Prakashan, 1994), p. 233.

In the management of the company, Sheth was ably assisted by his cousin, K.M. Sheth, reputed for his superb organizational and administrative abilities. In 1960, another relative, Sudhir Mulji--with a degree in economics from Cambridge, and a talent for negotiations and cultivating high-level contacts in New Delhi and abroad--joined the team. This formidable troika made for the success of GES as a business enterprise, which had few problems in establishing a strong equity base because of the loyalty it commanded with investors since it provided them with robust and reliable dividends.

As the pioneer of bulk shipping in India, GES encountered a lack of understanding and sympathy from the state, perhaps under the influence of Scindia and India Steamship which were then dominant in the liner trades. It found particularly irksome the requirement of obtaining a licence for each voyage, a potent barrier to effective participation in bulk trades. Moreover, as it sought entry into the oil trade, GES met with resistance from the state and was allowed to purchase India's first tanker only on the condition that in the future the oil trade would be reserved for the public sector. It is not that GES did not endeavour to enter the liner trades, but the existing liner companies, with the tacit approval of the state, barred it from membership in the conferences, and it was perforce left to make its mark in the bulk trades. By 1960, partly because of the heavy food imports and the appearance of Jayanti on the scene, the state had become more receptive to tramping. It readily issued global licences for tramping even though other procedures and restrictions of the regulatory framework continued to remain in place.

The very nature of bulk shipping imposes on management the requirement to be competitive in world shipping, but the GES management additionally brought to the business its own eagerness and zest to compete, and accordingly it was very attentive to the international environment in which it had to function. Of course, its enthusiasm for competition made it chafe at India's regulatory framework which was putting it at a disadvantage with its foreign rivals. GES was therefore from the very beginning in the forefront of advocating the removal of controls; after Vasant Sheth's death, the role of critic of the regulatory framework was taken over by his successor, K.M. Sheth. During the 1980s, GES was so angered by interference at the hands of SDFC that it actually contemplated paying off the loans in advance in order to put an end to it.[32] Indeed, it advocated that Indian-owned ships be allowed to register under flags of convenience and that India itself open a second, international register.

The management's sensitivity to the international environment is made obvious by the unusual move, for an Indian shipping company, to open an office in London under Sudhir Mulji during the depression so as to have "a window on the international developments in shipping". That move aided the company immensely in its business:

> It enabled the company to fix the employment of its OBO carriers which were heavy loss making units in the depression, at better rates because of the company's presence in the London market. The company also was well-informed on the ship sale and purchase market, shipping finance availability, charter markets etc. because of the valuable information provided by the London office.

Subsequently, in 1985, GES established a subsidiary in London, and this again was of tremendous benefit to the company in avoiding the constraints of the regulatory framework:

> Unfettered by the cumbersome government restrictions and procedures the London company was able to raise loans and buy ships promptly at the low prices prevailing at that time when the shipping industry was about to come out of the depression. Great Eastern, the Indian company also, when it did not get or did not expect to get the government approval in time for the ships purchased, arranged the purchases through the London company and bought the ships from the London company when the government approvals were at long last available.[33]

The management's keen awareness of the international environment led GES, with the onset of the depression, to the conclusion that the expansionary era in postwar shipping was at an end and that henceforth financial survival precluded reliance on loan finance. Accordingly, it moved to strengthen its equity base, which enabled it to emerge largely unscathed, indeed strengthened, from the depression. Whereas its debt equity ratio in 1985 was 2.55:1, relatively low among Indian companies, it had brought it down to 1.32:1 in 1988-89 and then to an amazingly low 0.45:1 in 1991-92.[34] Again, it was about the first Indian shipping company to develop expertise in foreign currency management to hedge against losses from changes in exchange rates following the collapse of the Bretton Woods system.

GES also emphasized the sale and purchase of vessels for the purpose of making profits--not necessarily for the carriage of cargo--and diversification into non-shipping activities, such as real estate, in preparation for the inevitable downturn in shipping as a cyclical industry. Its instinct for profit also made for serious attention to tax management, so that "the company in its 44 years of existence therefore paid taxes in a few years only".[35] All this was sought to be done "within the four corners and fetters of Government regulations and controls",[36] but that did not prevent an occasional raid on the firm's premises by the revenue authorities.

GES provides an illustration of the kind of performance in a world setting that was largely precluded by the regulatory system but was achieved only by conscious and deliberate effort, aided by a touch of genius. If competitiveness was key to survival in world shipping, India's regulatory framework--regardless of its intentions or its necessity in the context of underdevelopment--constrained Indian shipping from being prepared for it. GES, however, endeavoured to enhance its competitive edge by pushing against the constraints of the regulatory framework to the limit through adoption of business practices associated with efficiency and success in international shipping markets.

THE FALLACY OF RELIANCE ON COMMERCIAL MECHANISMS

The Indian shipping scene in the post-independence period was dominated by a strange paradox: while the country's regulatory framework constrained its own shipowners in multifarious ways, foreign shipowners were free from any controls by the Indian state. Indeed, India was literally a free trade zone where any foreign shipowner, whether flying a national flag or a flag of convenience, could pick up cargo without let or hindrance at the hands of the state.

If competitiveness has been one key to survival and success in shipping, protection is another--a practice that has often been, and continues to be, resorted to by both developing and developed countries in open and hidden forms. In the post-independence period, the state in India has not been averse to protection, but its preferred mode of operation has been reliance on commercial mechanisms. Thus, the state encouraged shipping companies in the liner trade to enter the privately-managed conferences in order to obtain a share of the national trades. Again, it arranged for a share for Indian lines through bilateral shipping agreements with Soviet bloc countries. Similarly, it exercised its right as a shipper to channel government cargo to Indian shipowners through Transchart.

However, the state resolutely resisted compulsory cargo reservation for Indian shipowners. It failed to enact legislation to reserve liner cargo for its national fleet even when the UNCTAD Code for the Conduct of Liner Conferences had in 1974 legitimized the reservation of a share of 40 per cent of such cargo for the national lines, or again even after 1983 when the code came into effect. On the contrary, Indian shipowners were expected to secure their cargo through normal commercial arrangements in competition with foreign shipowners. Even in respect of obtaining cargo through Transchart, there was no automatic right to cargo for Indian shipowners; they had to compete in price with foreign companies. The irony, however, is that in this competition while Indian shipowners operated under the constraints of the country's regulatory framework, foreign shipowners did not. The playing field was thus structured in favour of foreign shipowners.

Reliance on commercial mechanisms during the 1960s and early 1970s was no handicap; indeed, it was helpful in the expansion of India's tonnage. The conferences were strong; the pooling arrangements in the most important of the conferences were extremely useful; the bilateral agreements served the interests of the Indian lines; and the command economy channelled government cargo through Transchart. However, the utility of all these commercial mechanisms to Indian shipping was premised on their continued viability and availability. Gradually, however, after the early 1970s these mechanisms either collapsed or were eroded, with the result that Indian shipping was left defenceless against the onslaught of foreign competition.

In the wake of the depression, independent foreign operators became extremely aggressive in their invasion of the Indian market and weakened the conferences; the pooling arrangements ended in 1981 and the Indian lines were left to desperately, but only vainly, struggle on their own for a share of their national market; the container revolution enabled the foreign lines to supplant, and eventually decimate, Indian shipping in the liner cargo trades; the disintegration of the Soviet bloc and the Soviet Union finally put an end to the bilateral shipping arrangements;

and the liberalization of the Indian economy reduced the cargo that could be channelled through Transchart. Yet, in the face of all this change which removed the protection earlier provided by reliance on commercial mechanisms, the Indian state failed to provide cargo support in compensation.

The inaction of the Indian state at the domestic level stands in dramatic contrast to the assertive leadership given by it in international diplomacy relating to shipping. On the international scene, India was forceful and outspoken about the aspirations and rights of developing countries. It was a moving force behind the adoption of the UNCTAD code which, with its 40:40:20 formula, gave the merchant fleet of any developing country the right to 40 per cent of its liner trade. Yet, India failed to enact any legislation to allow its fleet to benefit from this right. In discussing the drastic disparity between India's rhetoric and practice, one of Scindia's top managers, P.T. Dalal, commented:

> The main reason of the Government's inactivity in this sphere is its timidity. The Government is afraid that shipping being international any attempt on its part to control or direct any of the activities of the Conferences or foreign shipping lines legislatively would invite instant retaliation from other governments.

If it is timidity that is the explanation on account of the fear of retaliation, it is of long standing. But Dalal went on to maintain that the fear was groundless:

> There are instances of other countries having introduced a certain type of discipline in ship operating in the interest of their own trade and commerce to which Shipping Conferences have acquiesced and which have provoked no retaliation from other countries. The American example is the most outstanding in this respect. Even an ex-Colonial country like Sri Lanka and a new country like Bangladesh have used their sovereignty to regulate international shipping in relation to their own trade and commerce with beneficial effects for themselves and without creating any confrontation with other nations.[37]

He then referred to another factor at work with the state: "It is also afraid that though India possesses a sizeable mercantile marine of its own particularly in the liner field and even though the Public Sector in this sphere has been occupying 'the commanding heights' in this field, Indian liner shipowners will not rise to the occasion to support the Government in such measures".

At the heart of the issue lay a profound dilemma that had set the state in conflict with itself. On the one hand, from the beginning India as an independent state has been eager to build a merchant fleet appropriate to the country's size and cargo generation. On the other hand, as a developing country it has been as vitally keen that its exports are not hurt by uneconomic measures. These two interests have been lodged in two different ministries, of which the stronger and more eminent, with the greater clout and the backing of powerful economic interests, has been the Ministry of Commerce as against the Ministry of Shipping in its various incarnations. In any case of conflict between the two, Commerce has always won over Shipping. Thus, the state has been divided within itself, and that has precluded the enactment of any statutory scheme of cargo reservation. What is more, the split between the ministries reflects a deeper division within society--that between shippers and shipowners.

The entry of Indian shipping companies into the conferences after independence did not occasion any conflict between shippers and shipowners. That was so because the conference system was the dominant private mode of business in handling liner cargo, and it was recognized as having merit in organizing regular service for shippers in what otherwise would be an anarchic situation, with the resulting unreliable service and volatile freight rates. Having encouraged the Indian lines to join the conferences, the state was also aware of the potential impact on its exports of high freight rates, secretly and arbitrarily fixed by such cartels. In order to develop some check against the monopoly power of the conferences, the state encouraged the formation of shippers councils. The first one to be formed was the Western India Shippers Association; established in Bombay in 1962, it is the most active and the most powerful among the councils. Subsequently, two other councils were organized--Eastern India Shippers Association at Calcutta in 1964 and the

Southern India Shippers Council at Madras in 1966. Out of these developed a federal association, the All India Shippers Council, which started functioning in 1967 at New Delhi, with a secretariat provided by the Federation of Indian Chambers of Commerce and Industry. Besides the zonal councils, it had as its members many chambers of commerce and export organizations.

With the patronage of the Ministry of Commerce, this shippers lobby grew very powerful. The shippers tasted blood as the conference system crumbled under the impact of the depression and as the fierce competition among container carriers brought down freight rates and provided other lucrative incentives to them. In due course, a sort of tacit cross-border alliance or collusion developed between the foreign shipping companies and Indian shippers to the detriment of Indian shipowners. Meanwhile, the dominant foreign carriers began to directly penetrate the shipping community within the country by terminating their agreements with Indian agents and setting up their own agency networks. The trend was inaugurated by Maersk in 1990, which was subsequently followed by P&O Containers and American President Lines.[38]

With their greater economic muscle, the shippers thwarted any attempt by the state to provide cargo support for the Indian lines on the plea that they would get neither competitive freight rates nor comparable service. Thus, a commercial mechanism which the state had encouraged over the years came to block it later in its endeavour to aid Indian shipowners. The consequence was that Indian shipowners were squeezed between a free trade regime internationally and state controls domestically.

THE HEGEMONY OF THE PUBLIC SECTOR

By design, the public sector had been the dynamo of growth in tonnage acquisition during the 1960s and 1970s. By 1975, through its own thrust for growth and the takeover of other companies, SCI as the designated public sector carrier owned over half of the country's tonnage. It literally possessed the "commanding heights" in shipping, with other firms simply overshadowed by its hegemonic presence. Its fleet was the most diversified of the shipping companies in India, reigning as the leader in every branch of shipping: liner, dry bulk and, particularly, tanker. SCI was not simply the dominant actor in shipping in India, it also ranked among the largest companies in the world. At the same time, it took pride in being the most professionalized in its management, unlike other shipping companies in India which were run by the owners and their families. In addition, SCI contradicted the usual image of public sector firms as loss-making enterprises, for through much of its history it has made profits. Its level of profitability may not match that of Great Eastern--one of the strong themes in Sanklecha's study of GES--but its profits have been considerable, especially in recent years (see Tables 6.2 and 6.3).

TABLE 6.3: PROFITABILITY PROFILE OF SCI: NET PROFITS

Year	*Rs. (Mill.)*	*Year*	*Rs. (Mill.)*
1960-61 to 1976-77	1116.6	1985-86	75.0
1977-78	-147.4	1986-87	64.4
1978-79	-370.1	1987-88	358.7
1979-80	-18.5	1988-89	545.3
		1989-90	1011.0
1980-81	183.6		
1981-82	47.4	1990-91	545.0
1982-83	-244.4	1991-92	1089.0
1983-84	-516.4	1992-93	1431.0
1984-85	22.7	1993-94	1676.0

Source: Shipping Corporation of India Ltd., *History and Growth* (Bombay: [1991]), p. 37, and *Annual Reports* (various years). Figures until 1985-86 are for net profits after deduction of depreciation and interest, while those for later years are after deduction additionally of tax.

Several factors explain SCI's record of relative success among the public sector enterprises. First, there was the extraordinary leadership provided by C.P. Srivastava during SCI's formative years. Second, because of that, the firm had developed a tradition of substantial autonomy from the bureaucracy in New Delhi. The fact that the firm was located in Bombay was helpful, too, for not only was it thus far from the national capital but it also functioned in that city's overall commercial and entrepreneurial culture in contrast to the capital's bureaucratic culture. Third, importantly, the very nature of the business SCI was engaged in compelled a certain level of efficiency, for shipping involved a considerable measure of international competition. Fourth, the state was helpful to SCI in so far as it was state policy to have the public sector secure the commanding heights. Membership in conferences, large financial resources, and government cargo were easier for it to obtain because of its being a part of the state. It had a major advantage over all other shipping companies to the extent that it had a monopoly over imports of crude oil. On the other hand, it had to bear the burden of being directed by the government to carry out the social obligation of running some loss-making services to offshore islands as well as often being forced to order the more costly vessels from Indian shipyards.

Notwithstanding its dominant position, SCI, too, was not immune to the impact of the shipping depression or the container revolution. It made losses in five out of the seven years from 1977-78 to 1983-84 (see Table 6.3). It also defaulted on its loans from SDFC. More crucially, it suffered as well from the general decimation that struck India's liner shipping. Of course, SCI did not go under like Scindia, because it was a diversified company and in addition it had the benefit of its large earnings from the cost-plus arrangements on oil imports not being seriously affected by the depression. Further, the state helped SCI in its capital restructuring. In 1989-90, the state increased SCI's share capital from Rs. 702 million to Rs. 2612 million and then again to Rs. 2823 million in 1990-91 by conversion of outstanding loans into equity. The state also waived the penal interest on unpaid interest in the amount of Rs. 87.5 million.[39] Ironically, either by accident or by design, SCI emerged from the crisis in actual fact as the only Indian liner shipping company, for the crisis effectively removed Scindia and India Steamship from participation in liner shipping. Henceforth, though pronouncements may formally be made in the name of Indian liner shipping companies, in reality they were understood to mean only SCI.

Particularly striking was SCI's failure to make a dent in container shipping. Since SCI loomed so large on India's shipping horizon, the country's failure on containerization was really SCI's failure. It was not until the end of 1993 that SCI bought its first three cellular ships. The causes for its failure to respond adequately and on time were, to a considerable extent, related to its being part of the public sector. First and foremost, it was limited in its capacity to operate as an autonomous commercial organization, since all important investment decisions required the approval of the state bureaucracy, which meant inordinate delays. SCI's managers spent a lot of their time commuting to New Delhi to educate decision-makers and to persuade and cajole them on various issues. This was part of the general framework of the public sector and not something specific to SCI, but it bore heavily on it since it had to compete with foreign companies unlike other domestic industries which operated under the protection of a controlled economy.

Second, notwithstanding SCI being more efficient than many public enterprises, as a public sector undertaking impregnated with the bureaucratic ethos it could not compete in service and efficiency with foreign megacarriers, once the protection extended by the pooling arrangements and strong conferences was removed. Its representatives may claim that as a state enterprise they could not deal in unethical practices--such as furnishing bills of lading to exporters before goods were actually loaded or providing under the counter monetary or foreign exchange gratification[40]--but it meant the diversion of business to others. Its procedures were too inflexible to compete in service with foreign rivals, who had all the freedom to operate in India through their agents.

Third, foreign rivals were helped indirectly by the personnel policies of SCI. After Srivastava's departure from SCI, just as the shipping depression had started and the container challenge was beginning to be mounted, the state began making appointments to the top positions from outside SCI. This was the prerogative of the state as the sole shareholder of the company. However, it affected prospects of promotion for those already in the organization. Besides, salaries were poor at SCI in comparison to those offered by foreign companies. A senior UNCTAD official, who had served in India for many years and knew well the situation, commented privately in 1995:

> Indian shippers were looking for new markets and the new markets required also the new transport technology. Many of the original shippers who were devoted to the national fleet

at that time turned away. From the management point of view of SCI, many people left at that time and tried to find new kinds of employment with agencies which were at the time beginning existence or were left over from the British. Since those companies were representing foreign interests, they made available their knowledge and skills and their relationships to the foreign companies. Forbes is one of the examples. Their skills and capabilities and relationships to the traders, they took them away from SCI and made them available to the companies which were coming on behalf of foreign interests.

(They left because of the opportunities?) My pay-went-up kind of arguments. But there are many other arguments. The other argument has equal validity because of the Indian Civil Service system. The top people came from the civil service, because of the rotating service, naval people. Those people are not commercially minded. I had the feeling that there was some dissatisfaction--many of the younger ones who had the capability and did not come on top and did not have an opportunity because people from outside came. The motivation was not there. By leaving the company they kept the position and pleased the foreign counterparts.[41]

Whatever its other strengths, SCI as a public sector enterprise, subordinate to the state bureaucracy in the making of key decisions, was constrained in its capacity to adapt to fast-moving market forces. It is in this fashion that the market took its revenge on the liner sector of a state enterprise which had risen to the commanding heights under the wings of the state.

Path dependency theory enables us to understand how precisely the institutions and practices that had once been helpful in the rapid expansion of the merchant fleet--state aid, state controls, reliance on prevailing commercial mechanisms, and the public sector--attenuated, if not undermined, the capacity of the industry to adapt as the environmental conditions changed. However, one needs to go further and analyze how state power itself had, in the meantime, suffered deterioration, which affected adversely the task of coping with the challenge.

THE STATE AND THE CRISIS IN SHIPPING

It requires no strenuous effort to discern that the deterioration in state power in India was coeval with the period in office of Mrs. Indira Gandhi. Further, her own actions in splitting the Congress party, pushing populist programmes, centralizing and personalizing power, and finally declaring a state of emergency --all these underline her role in the destruction of the country's political institutions. An important question remains, however. Was she principal or agent of larger structural forces in the change? After all, her splitting the Congress party and her populist measures, such as bank nationalization, were heartily endorsed by the electorate in national elections. Such popular approval cannot be easily ascribed to political manipulation or demagogic appeals, for when the populace did not approve her actions, such as the emergency, it also rejected her at the polls. Still later, notwithstanding the past experience of the emergency, it voted her back to office. Consequently, without in any way understating the role of individual leaders, it is important to look at the larger political and social context in which they must perforce operate.

THE DECLINE IN STATE AUTONOMY AND CAPACITY

In several theoretical contributions to comparative politics during the 1960s, long before the deterioration in state power in India was evident, David Apter delineated four different types of political systems with variant performance capabilities.[42] This four-fold typology was based on combining the poles of two analytical dimensions: authority (hierarchical and pyramidal) and values (consummatory and instrumental). The political system that is of interest here is the reconciliation system which combines pyramidal authority (as in federal systems) and instrumental values (non-ideological). In this system there is a dispersion of authority, with the constituent units differentiated, in good measure, culturally and ethnically. Multiple loyalties are an important facet of the system. The system's values are predominantly of an instrumental nature. Unlike the mobilization system, which is its polar opposite, the reconciliation system more or less accepts society as it is and provides a framework for the processing of only moderate change. The system's goals emerge, in the fashion of the market place, out of conflict among many groups with different aims, rather than imposed from above by a determined leadership with a comprehensive ideology. The very structure of the reconciliation system militates against the use of coercive techniques.

While several consequences flow from the inherent structure of the reconciliation system, what is of interest here is the system's tendency towards immobilisme and stagnation. A chief characteristic of the system is, not some fervent overall vision for society but conflict among groups, even as there is great diversity in society and polity. As a consequence, it is difficult to reach political consensus on policy. The principal problem in the system is not knowledge or awareness of demands and of the environment, but action. As more groups are mobilized into politics and expectations rise, the government may also become politically stalemated, overwhelmed by massive and contradictory demands. The government may become the prisoner of particular powerful groups. In this condition of decisional immobilisme, crises seem essential for making decisive breakthroughs in policy. In the meantime, as the system fails to adequately meet popular demands, the result is likely to be, apart from political corruption, social frustration. In turn, frustration may lead to frequent changes in government, indeed pressures may build up for change to a different type of political system.

Models do not necessarily predict, they only delineate tendencies. However, the reconciliation system as one of the ideal types abstractly, but presciently, maps out the consequences that flow from its inherent structure. Interestingly, such consequences became concretely manifest in post-Nehru India, especially in respect of decisional immobilisme. It would, of course, be a valid objection against this ideal type that it does not fully correspond to the regime under Nehru. For, that regime had the attributes of a larger political vision, a national design for development, and a broad set of policy innovations, even though the overall system was of the reconciliation type.

In justification, however, several features can be said to set apart the social and political context under which the system functioned during the Nehru period. First, the government that came into power in the post-colonial state was a legacy of a successful national liberation movement, albeit non-violent, not the instrument of an ordinary political party. Second, it was headed by a charismatic leader with broad, genuine nationwide appeal. Third, economic complexity and social mobilization were at a much lower level at the time, which consequently attenuated political conflict to a certain extent. These conditions underwent change by the time Nehru passed away. It is precisely then that the inherent implications of the reconciliation system began to work themselves out more fully, and the system's key characteristics became manifest: political instability, frequent changes of government and therefore of its personnel, and decisional immobilisme. These developments evidence the overall decline in state autonomy and state capacity, the two elements of state power.

Shipping affairs in the government did not remain unaffected by these larger changes in the polity. Ministers in charge of the shipping portfolio changed more frequently, commitment to the national project in shipping weakened, and the level of knowledge declined, with adverse consequences for national shipping. A veteran analyst of the scene has given vivid, perhaps harsh, expression to these trends:

> So far as the ministries directly concerned with the transport sector are concerned, the ministerial incumbents change quite often. They hardly have time to develop a professional grip of the subject. The members of the bureaucratic machinery in the ministries also keep on changing due to the exigencies of administration. The prevailing situation hardly leaves any scope for indepth understanding of the subjects they handle, much less dedication. Consequently, the process of policy formulation and decision-making keeps on drifting and *ad hocism* sets in.... the Ministry of Shipping and Transport did not enjoy the continuity of the Ministers and Secretaries. They are frequently transferred. Even the office of the Director General is understaffed because the vacancies remain unfilled for a number of months and in some cases, years.[43]

Again, he commented on the decline in knowledge:

> The interest and awareness on the subject has become diffused. The standard and level of comprehension of the subject is now touching almost the bottom line with gradual disappearance of the old timers and stalwarts like Dr. Nagendra Singh, in official as well as nonofficial circles. Inter-ministerial wrangles have increased disproportionately in the absence of officers commanding respect and credibility at a senior level. Consequently, the decision-making process has become highly dilatory and sterile.... The overall deterioration in the decision-making system and the casualness as well as callousness in implemental actions seem to have reached an intolerable level. This is in sharp contrast to the situation prevailing in sixties. This is highly unfortunate when the tasks before Government demand a much higher degree of proficiency and professionalism.[44]

There was thus no longer a leadership at the helm with a long-term vision. This was sorely missed because of the fragmented or "balkanized" nature of decision-making, where several ministries were involved with shipping and associated subjects: Commerce, Finance, Labour, Planning, Railways, and Surface Transport.[45] The system lacked the capacity to plan for integrated long-range strategies. There was a premium on the short term, where ministries often worked at cross-purposes. What has been said of Canada seemed to be true of India: "there is lacking the cohesiveness and unity of purpose that characterizes the shipping policies of most other nations, quite apart from any questions of the actual merits of such policies".[46] Symptomatic of the decline in the capacity for long-range planning was the neglect into which the National Shipping Board had fallen, with the consequent erosion of its functioning. As Desai once pointed out: "We are living in an era, wherein institutions established for laudable objectives are neither active nor fully dead but only formally existing. One such institution is the National Shipping Board".[47] It is in this changed environment, marked by a deterioration in state power, that shipping was enveloped by the worldwide depression and structural change.

THE SOURING OF THE STATE-INDUSTRY RELATIONSHIP

Even before Indian shipping was touched by the crisis following in the wake of the OPEC oil price shocks, it was faced with problems at the hands of the state. Part of the souring of the relationship between shipping and the state stemmed from the general radicalization of politics under Mrs. Gandhi in the late 1960s. Certain measures aimed at private business in general affected shipping as well. These included the Monopolies and Restrictive Trade Practices Act--which required review by the MRTP Commission of proposals for expansion of business--and the inclusion of a clause in loan agreements to convert loans into equity at the discretion of the state, thus holding the Damocles sword of backdoor nationalization over the private sector.

The 1971 war over Pakistan's military crackdown in East Bengal, which had resulted in the exodus of some 10 million refugees to India, made for cooperation between the shipping industry and the navy in military operations. For the moment, the industry felt that the state would draw the right conclusion from the event about the strategic importance of the industry and treat it sympathetically. However, the war had other less favourable consequences. The suspension of aid by the United States--which had sided with Pakistan in the war to the extent of engaging in gunboat diplomacy against India--as also the achievement of food self-sufficiency by the country reduced imports and therefore the demand for shipping.[48]

Meanwhile, other decisions by the state had a more direct effect on the industry. Finance Minister Y.B. Chavan announced withdrawal from 1974 onwards--subsequently changed to 1975--of the generous development rebate, which had been of momentous importance in the expansion of tonnage since its introduction in 1959. Further, there were changes in regard to SDFC loans which reduced the moratorium period from two years to one, and increased interest rates from 3 per cent to 4.5 per cent. Again, the *pari passu* obligations were imposed on the industry in 1977, under which Indian companies acquiring ships from abroad had to place orders for equivalent tonnage on an Indian shipyard, even though it was more costly and of poorer quality and its delivery unreliable. This requirement compounded the problems of shipowners as they were already facing difficulties in acquiring ships because order books at foreign shipyards were full.

One measure that ostensibly ought to have led to a higher priority for the shipping industry was the government resolution on export policy which was placed before parliament in July 1970, underlining the importance of exports to the national economy. Among other things, the resolution explicitly acknowledged the need for intensifying efforts for the expansion of the merchant fleet, the strengthening of existing services, and the launching of new ones.[49] Ironically, by underlining the importance of exports the resolution only served to strengthen the hands of the shippers lobby and the Ministry of Commerce in opposing cargo support for Indian shipping on the ground that it would hurt exports. While it thus faced a tougher posture at the hands of the state, the shipping industry was struck by the crisis in international shipping.

Not used to shipping's periodic adversity, instead having been accustomed only to a long period of expansion in its recent history, the industry in India understandably screamed for help as it incurred losses and encountered difficulties in meeting its debt repayment obligations as a result of the crisis. In retrospect, the appeals for help may seem exaggerated during the first phase of the depression, for far worse was yet ahead in the second phase. After much pleading by the industry, the state responded at the end of 1978 with a decision to provide financial relief by way of a three-year moratorium on payments of instalments that were due for the year ending March 1979.[50] It also set up a high-powered committee under Dr. R.M. Honavar, chief economic advisor in the ministry of finance, to study the issue of further assistance. The relief, however, took a long time to reach the affected companies while stringent conditions were imposed on companies before assistance could be given. The industry insisted on more liberal help.

As the government under the Janata Party, which had succeeded the Congress party, itself faced instability because of divisions within, there was difficulty in arriving at a quick decision. The Minister for Shipping and Transport reportedly informed a delegation from the Indian National Shipowners Association (INSA) that "in the prevailing critical political situation, it may not be possible for the Government to apply its mind to the problem".[51] Disappointed, INSA had to wait for a decision until after the elections. In 1980, the Congress party returned to power. To provide relief to the industry, the new government issued guidelines on the basis of the recommendations of the Honavar committee. However, these measures, which provided a moratorium on debt repayments on a short-term basis, were characterized by INSA as "totally inadequate".[52]

The shipping markets had revived in 1979 but the revival was short-lived. Within two years the second phase of the depression struck before the shipping companies had a chance to stabilize themselves after the effects of the first phase. The second phase of the depression confronted the industry and the state with problems of a much more serious nature. The state then extended further relief in 1983, but INSA found it "mostly inadequate to meet the continuing situation".[53] As losses mounted, most of the companies defaulted on their debt repayments.

Overwhelmed by the enormity of defaults, which reduced the influence of the Ministry of Surface Transport with the Ministry of Finance, the state decided on a more radical change in course and retreated from its direct role in funding tonnage acquisition. Indeed, its focus shifted from assistance for development of shipping to recovery of loans. The state abolished SDFC as its funding agency for shipping in 1987, and it entrusted the task of managing the recovery of past loans, the rehabilitation of sick companies, and the financing of future tonnage acquisition in the private sector, to a new public financial institution specifically created for the purpose, the Shipping Credit and Investment Company of India (SCICI). SDFC's function of deciding on proposals for new tonnage was given to a Ship Acquisition Licensing Committee (SALC). SCICI was to have some developmental role in financing tonnage acquisition by companies, but over a period of time this role has eroded to a considerable extent and SCICI has become more or less a regular banking institution, with its activities no longer limited to shipping. As a banking institution, however, SCICI was influential in advising shipping companies on management and the international environment and in having the state relax somewhat its restrictive policies and to streamline them.

As the shipping depression waned by 1987, it would have been time to resume the path of tonnage expansion. Unfortunately, however, India began to face severe foreign exchange problems and that put a severe constraint on fresh acquisitions. The Ministry of Surface Transport had to work within very limited amounts of foreign exchange allocated by the Ministry of Finance. Finally, as the decade of the 1990s opened, the foreign exchange problem ballooned into a full-blown crisis, which precipitated the adoption of an economic stabilization and structural adjustment programme. The crisis marked the launching of a completely new phase in economic policy which consciously sought to steer India from a command economy to a competitive market economy, and from national self-reliance to integration with the world economy. These changes would affect shipping policy as well. Meanwhile, apart from the general stagnation and decline in tonnage, the depression years left behind a legacy of India's marginalization in liner shipping as a result of its failure to adapt to the container revolution. That failure is, indeed, the most outstanding characteristic of the period.

THE FAILURE IN CONTAINER SHIPPING

A complex phenomenon such as the failure of India to develop a presence in container shipping over a period of some two decades cannot obviously be attributed to any single factor. There were evidently a number of factors at work. One factor that can be ruled out is that somehow the industry and the state were unaware of developments in regard to the new technology. If they were not already informed, two events in December 1967 must have provoked them to sit up and take notice of the coming challenge. First, in an important address in New Delhi on "India and the Technological Revolution in Shipping" before the 25th meeting of the National Shipping Board, the country's highest advisory body on shipping, Dr. Nagendra Singh called its attention to some matters of utmost urgency, particularly the fact that "the entire shipping industry is today in the throes of an unprecedented technological revolution... comparable only to that vast change which took place in the 19th century when the sail was replaced by the steam engine". While he discussed the increasing size of bulk carriers and oil tankers, his focus was on containerization. He reminded the Board not only of the inadequacies of Indian ports, but also of customs procedures and of rail and road transportation, for "containerization is not merely a new method of transportation. It is an entirely new concept--almost a new philosophy which brings shipping industry in line with other modern industries by applying the technique of mass production".

Singh held that India had no choice but to adopt this technology: "I do not think personally that we can keep away from the current technological changes. International maritime commerce is inter-connected and developments anywhere have an impact everywhere". He underlined as well that one consequence of the new mass technology and the related high capital costs would be the need to create large shipping companies. This development was already apparent abroad, where several leading companies had combined to launch container companies. He then warned: "This is a development which we cannot ignore. It is clear that in future only large companies will be able to hold the field in face of stiff competition and the requirements of large resources of capital". He underscored the urgent and important nature of what he was discussing, and urged expeditious study and action, for: "The economic stakes are high. The changes are taking place at a dizzy pace. And the pace is accelerating with every passing year".[54]

Second, the same month in New Delhi--at the National Conference on Shipping, Shipbuilding and Ports--the powerful Shipping and Transport Minister, Dr. V.K.R.V. Rao, devoted his forceful address largely to the "vast and unprecedented technological changes" in the maritime arena. He warned that "the entire concept of shipping is changing rapidly and we would be left far behind if we do not take necessary action fairly soon to meet the new challenge". Wistfully, he added: "What about India? We do not have a single container ship in our fleet". Like Nagendra Singh, he saw no choice: "we will have to do our best to find the requisite financial resources. We just cannot afford to be left behind".[55]

As if this were not enough, a year later in December 1968, a special three-day high-powered "seminar on containerization" was held in Bombay, with Rao's support, at which were present nearly all the key decision-makers in industry and state connected with shipping, numbering over 200.[56] That seminar endorsed the need to go in for containerization. At the same time, in recognition of the complex problems that the issue of full-fledged containerization raised--particularly, the massive financial investments required and the serious inadequacies of the ports and inland transportation--the seminar underlined the "need for reaching the objective through a phased programme in a reasonable period of time".[57] In 1969, as a follow-up to the seminar, the central government set up a working group to examine the modalities for implementing containerization in India. The group's overall recommendation was that the scope for containerization of India's potential cargo was "extremely impressive" and that containerization was essential for protecting the country's competitive position. It also made more concrete proposals for setting up the appropriate infrastructure, such as port facilities and inland container depots.[58] With these important events, containerization became a perennial subject for discussion in the industry's major journal.

Thus, early knowledge of the container revolution was not the problem. Still, perhaps the rapidity with which the revolution would gather speed was underestimated, and in this Indian decision-makers were not alone; that rapidity astonished the industry elsewhere as well. In India's particular case, what caught industry and state largely unawares was the ferocity with which the challenge occurred. For that the first OPEC oil price shock--an event which they could not have foreseen--and India's own geographic location were important factors. What the oil price shock did was to create a huge booming consumption centre in India's neighbourhood, especially the Persian Gulf area, between two massive production centres, one to its west around the Atlantic (US and Europe) and the other to the east (Japan and the newly industrialized countries). As container ships brought consumption goods to the Gulf area, they had little to take back in return and, rather than go back empty, they engaged in cutthroat competition for Indian cargo. With that started the weakening of the conferences and the decimation of Indian liner shipping. Thus, India's geographic location, next door to the Gulf and simultaneously close to the east-west arterial shipping routes, proved to be damaging for its liner shipping. The second OPEC oil price shock aggravated the challenge for India even further.

In coping with the challenge, India's liner shipping companies were also handicapped by their inadequate equipment. Rather than go in for acquisition of container ships, they acquired "combi" or semi-container ships. Perhaps the seeds for this choice of technology had been sown at the 1968 seminar, with its recommendation for a phased programme. More particularly, the seminar had recommended that "Indian Liner Shipping should urgently consider adapting its existing vessels not only for palletization and pre-slinging but also for the introduction of containerization in its existing ships pending acquisition of container ships".[59] While "appropriate technology" of less than the advanced level prevalent in developed countries is often recommended for developing countries, it is usually for domestic production of goods, often in protected markets. However, the combi equipment was a poor competitor for the cellular containerships with their low unit costs. Perhaps it could have worked in more normal times, but the dumping of shipping capacity by foreign lines in the 1970s and 1980s precluded that possibility.

As the foreign container lines confronted the Indian lines with a daunting and formidable challenge by their increasing inroads in the liner trades, Indian shipping companies belatedly mounted a weak and faltering response. They began offering container services in 1978 with combi vessels. The end of the pooling arrangements in 1981 came as a rude awakening for the liner shipping companies, already weakened by the depression. They hastily formed a local consortium called Indian Container Lines. India Steamship contributed its own secondhand cellular containership of 300 teu capacity, while Scindia brought in a chartered cellular vessel of 500 teu capacity.[60] Both had to withdraw the vessels soon after because of huge losses resulting from lack of adequate cargo when pitted against foreign competition.[61] India's mini-consortium thus failed to take off as did other attempts at developing cooperation with foreign carriers. As both India Steamship and Scindia were meanwhile crippled financially, SCI was left alone to carry the responsibility for Indian liner shipping.

SCI had opened its first container service in 1978 with some two dozen combi or semi-container vessels, each with a capacity to carry about 300 teus apart from break-bulk cargo. These vessels had begun joining the fleet after 1971, but had been employed chiefly for break-bulk services.[62] In 1984, SCI began providing regular full container sailings on the India-UK/Continent route, but still employing only its combi ships. Finding that it could not compete with foreign carriers with such equipment, it began in 1985 fully containerized services by chartering cellular ships of 850 teu capacity. At the same time, SCI expanded its container operations to North America. Later, it upgraded these services by employing 1200 teu vessels on charter. In the subsequent five years, SCI lost Rs. 730 million on its container services, which were cross-subsidized from its other activities.[63] At work in these losses was, no doubt, the dumping of capacity by the foreign competition, but also economies of scale. One estimate in the mid-1980s placed the cost of operation of a 4000 teu capacity vessel at 7 cents per teu mile; in contrast, the cost in respect of a 1100-1400 teu vessel was 16 cents and that for a 600-800 teu vessel 22 cents, let alone 30-32 cents in the case of the combi vessels owned by Indian shipping lines.[64]

Regardless, SCI was determined to go ahead with acquiring its own cellular vessels, for--in the words of chairman L.M.S. Rajwar--"complete dependence on foreigners for serving our export trade would be suicidal for the country".[65] Keeping in view the draft availability at Indian ports and the requirements of India's trade, SCI settled on a scheme for the acquisition of cellular vessels of 1500 teu capacity for the next stage in its programme of phased development, with these vessels scheduled to replace the chartered ships in 1987-88. However, India's decision-making processes thwarted SCI's quest for cellular capacity. Serious efforts to obtain government approval for four secondhand cellular ships began in February 1984, but it is a commentary on the state's decision-making processes that the matter dragged on for years.[66] COPU was struck by the "lackadaisical approach" to the purchase.[67] There also developed a loss of enthusiasm in the SCI management after the failure of the state to provide cargo support.[68]

In the meantime, what occurred was not that which had been posited as part of a phased programme but something entirely different. As the world shipping industry pulled out of the depression, charter rates climbed precipitously from US$7,000 a day to $12,500-13,000 a day. SCI therefore decided in 1988 to discontinue its chartered arrangements, and reverted to employing its own combi vessels.[69] In June 1991, however, because of the heavy losses from the combi vessels, SCI terminated its container operations, and offered container services through slot charter arrangements with Contship for India-UK/Continent and with the Vessel Sharing Agreement consortium for India-US East Coast/Canada.[70] Only in January 1994 did SCI return to container operations on the India-UK/Continent sector with its own three new cellular vessels of 1870 capacity each. This was the result of a conscious "decision to enter the fray to establish its foothold in this vital sector of liner shipping which is otherwise monopolized by foreign lines".[71]

Over the long period until SCI inducted its own cellular vessels, Indian shipowners saw several serious deterrents to adding cellular containerships. One was the poor state of the country's infrastructure.[72] The ports were physically ill-equipped to handle large containerships. Besides that, there was the extremely poor productivity of port labour.[73] The delays at the ports would have rendered the capital-intensive vessels uneconomical. The fact that foreign vessels were able to operate through the inefficient Indian ports and take away the container business was not considered an adequate counter-argument. For foreign carriers India was merely one wayport in a much larger operation, primarily served by feeder vessels, whereas for Indian vessels it would be their home base and thus impinge on them more. Another deterrent was the assumed lack of adequate cargo. Certainly, in retrospect, Indian managers have underlined the point that India just did not have the cargo volume to justify acquisition of large cellular vessels, for India unlike Taiwan and Hong Kong was not a major trading nation in manufactures. True, the export of garments had started picking up in the 1970s, but not in large enough volume to justify acquisition of containerships. To the critics who are not convinced by the argument--because, after all, foreign carriers managed to collect enough cargo for their operations--the managers respond by pointing out that for such carriers Indian cargo is just a supplement at marginal cost whereas for Indian carriers it would be their central business. Again, the critics make the point that countries like Denmark, Greece or Norway do not have enough national cargo of their own but they do operate containerships.

The last point goes to the heart of the matter, though the issue has not been articulated as such, in that it would have required a fundamental reconceptualization about the functioning of national shipping in order to adapt to the requirements of the new order in liner shipping. Hitherto, Indian liner shipping had confined its sights to the carriage of national cargo, and it had found it easy to enter an ongoing system of end-to-end transportation on fixed routes under the protection of the conferences. Adaptation to a new hub and feeder system alongside round-the-world or pendulum transportation services, outside the confines of carrying merely national cargo, was beyond the Indian experience. It would have required, too, exploring possibilities of joint ventures or consortia with foreign shipping lines. Even if Indian shipowners had been creative or innovative in this regard, they would have most probably been thwarted by the state's rigid regulatory framework. Reconceptualization of the function of national shipping was therefore required at the level of the state. There is little evidence that it was ever seriously entertained. In the alternative, the state needed to have a policy of cargo reservation for Indian shipping lines. Significantly, countries like South Korea had built their shipping through cargo reservation.[74] This alternative was more in consonance with India's past experience, though it had been managed privately under the auspices of the conferences. In the end, the efforts for it came to nought but it is necessary to explore the reasons why.

THE CARGO RESERVATION SCHEME AND ITS FATE

In the situation of increasing competition from independent operators from the mid-1970s onwards--who progressively ate into the cargo of the conference system--a situation soon worsened by the termination of the pooling arrangements in 1981, the foremost and strongest exponent of cargo reservation was H.M. Trivedi. Truly a professional and a technocrat with vast experience stretching over some four decades in shipping management at Scindia and the India-UK/Continent conference, he was among the very few left on the shipping scene after a quarter century of independence who had creative ideas, held them with strong conviction, and had the courage to express them openly, though sometimes abrasively. He gave wide and frequent expression to his views through articles in journals and speeches; in addition to two books on capital and labour in India, he put together a collection of his writings and addresses on Indian shipping which, published in 1980, includes 113 items in nearly 550 large-size pages.[75] Trivedi was also the son-in-law of the doyen of Indian shipping, M.A. Master.

With that kind of background, it is not surprising that his core ideas sprang from a fervent nationalism. At the centre of them stood the imperative to protect national shipping against what he perceived to be the depredations of foreign shipping. His approach was protectionist, and stood at the other pole from that of his eminent contemporary, Vasant Sheth, who favoured removing all controls and letting Indian shipping stand on its own feet. Perhaps their opposed preferences stemmed from the fact that the influences that formed the two personalities professionally issued out of two different types of shipping--his in liner shipping against Sheth's in tramp shipping. While Trivedi's approach may seem old-fashioned, he was at the same time for the energetic adoption of the most modern technology by Indian shipowners.

In 1972, Trivedi was elected to the upper house of parliament from the state of Gujarat, and in 1974--some eight months before the declaration of emergency--Mrs. Indira Gandhi appointed him as the junior Minister of State for Shipping. In his position as minister, he attempted to meet head-on the problem of the declining share of Indian liner shipping in the national trade through a cargo reservation scheme. To understand that scheme, it is necessary to look at his rationale even though it was expressed more forcefully after his departure from office. Foremost in importance in his views, as in the case of those of his father-in-law's, was the national interest, not particular sectors or companies in shipping--and the proper and effective use of state power to serve it. For that national interest--say, in the promotion of exports--he was eager to discipline both shipowners and shippers, stating bluntly: "If Indian lines expect shippers to be disciplined... it is equally obligatory on them to be disciplined".[76] He consequently favoured a comprehensive national policy that covered all aspects of shipping in an integrated manner to replace the then fragmented treatment of tonnage, port infrastructure, shipyards and cargo in separate compartments. Writing in 1982, he was saddened by the spectacle of "Indian shippers avidly responding to inducements overt or covert by the same foreign lines at the expense of the share of Indian lines in India's own overseas trades".[77] Earlier, in 1978, he had warned, with some prescience, of the portents to come:

> The chips are down.... get ready, Gentlemen, for a mortgage of Indian exports to foreign lines.... Containerization has come to stay in the world's major trades. The time may not be too far when the inherent advantages of this system may well be exploited for operating on India's trades from neighbouring third countries in the Indian Ocean or Persian Gulf. This threat is not as imaginary as it may sound. It is, in fact, being planned. The Lash may encroach on our shares in the Bay of Bengal, West Coast/Europe trades, the Roll-on Roll-off and container on our trades to West Asia and with only the box touching the Indian ports (and not the vessel) our trades to Europe, USA and Japan. The whole structure of our national participation based on traditional ships, as members of conferences, may come crashing round our ears. It seems as if it has.
>
> ...the collusion of brokers and shipping agents with shippers in inviting "fly by night" operators.... These agents--the established ones--representing foreign lines wield considerable influence among shippers and have at their disposal sizeable resources. They play a major role in diverting cargo to non-conference, preferably non-Indian, ships.[78]

Nor was Trivedi impressed with the behaviour of state agencies "with their callous disregard of national interest": "Public sector undertakings like STC and MMTC are enjoined to buy f.o.b. and sell c.i.f. as far as possible. But what is the picture? These undertakings have acted in clear violation of the guidelines of Government".[79] He was disenchanted by the failure to discipline these agencies.[80] Trivedi was evidently also dismayed that: "We behave as if we were not a sovereign nation with any power to regulate the flow and shipment of our import and export trades." He did not have any reservations over India having a right to 40 per cent of its liner trades, a legitimate share in 20 per cent of the cross trades of every country with which India traded, and either an internationally agreed percentage or a percentage established by India "as a sovereign nation" in the bulk trades, along with "an overwhelming portion" of the trades in oil and petroleum products.[81]

Of particular concern to Trivedi was that: "Day by day, over the last five years, and more so with the predatory encroachment by international container consortia and inducements by foreign lines to which these agencies including shippers have fallen a prey, the share of Indian lines in India's own trades is steadily falling". For him, the UNCTAD Code was useless, it was dead. The important question for him was: "How do I put an end to the encroachment of foreign lines on my trades with share of Indian lines falling below legitimate entitlements?" He warned that: "We are now at a crucial stage in Indian shipping. To evolve a policy and execute it without fear or favour in the interests of Indian shippers and shipowners will call for a bold and innovative exercise of power as a sovereign nation".[82]

Given this set of views, it does not come as a surprise that, as a minister in Mrs. Gandhi's government, Trivedi in mid-1976 commissioned the Indian Institute of Foreign Trade to prepare a study on cargo management, chiefly with a view to developing institutional arrangements for the aggregation and allocation of cargo among shipping lines. The Institute quickly responded within two months with an 85-page document.[83] Its central recommendation was to set up a statutory autonomous corporation for centralized aggregating, booking and shipping of cargoes to assure an adequate share of the trades to Indian shipowners as also the desired service and satisfactory freight rates to Indian shippers.

The promptness of the response is surprising, but the report in its essentials was a replication of a scheme developed by Trivedi himself in 1971, not so much to protect the national shipping industry but rather to promote Indian exports.[84] The report provided additional justification for the new corporation by its review of the lack of professionalism among brokers and their indifferent service to shippers; the haphazard marketing process with its fake or fictitious bookings and overbookings; and the anarchy prevalent with the entry of large numbers of independent operators outside the conference arrangements. It did not seek to remove any of the existing structures, however. Rather, the new corporation was to sit as an overarching agency over them, with the purpose of monitoring their work and allocating cargo to shipping lines so as to best promote the interests of both shippers and shipowners by assuring fair and reasonable freight rates and services to various destinations. As Trivedi later put it, the corporation "will be the sole and exclusive shipping agent for all lines--both Indian and foreign--operating in India's trades. The nexus between the private shipping agent and the shipowners must be broken".[85]

The government did not release the report for public comment until about two years later in June 1978. In the meantime, however, the defeat of Mrs. Gandhi in the national elections in early 1977 called an end to Trivedi's tenure as minister. With that died any hope of enacting legislation for cargo reservation. Some believe that if anyone could have successfully pulled off such a scheme, which was essentially his brainchild, it would have been Trivedi. It is difficult to see how that is plausible, for Trivedi had no political base. The cargo reservation scheme was a matter of politics, not technical sophistication. For, it was bound to run into the full force of opposition of most of the country's trade and industry, far more powerful than the shipowners.

Even before the report was released, though Trivedi had meanwhile left the government, the shippers associations got wind of its broad intent and they mounted an orchestrated campaign to preemptively discredit the project. There followed seminars and protests against the report. A national seminar organized by the All India Shippers Council (AISC) at Calcutta in January 1978 rebuffed the move. Its chairman, V.D. Chowgule, subsequently warned that "if the Government finally decides to implement the proposal in whatever manner, I am afraid it will be a dangerous experiment".[86] A special meeting of the Association of Shipping Interests at Calcutta in September questioned the very premise of the rationale for the agency by alleging that Indian shipping lines already had an adequate share in cargo.[87] In taking this position, it neglected to take into account the cargo carried by independent operators outside the sphere of the conferences, which was precisely the motive for suggesting a centralized allocation agency in the first place. The counter-attack against the proposal continued. Nonetheless, to some extent the shippers were on the defensive because the declining share of Indian lines could not be ignored. However, at the AISC annual meeting in Cochin in 1981, Chowgule in his presidential address asserted that shippers were not to blame for the lack of patronage of the national lines, and laid bare the rationale for the opposition:

> there are many factors responsible for the present state of affairs. The quality and adequacy of shipping services provided by the national lines leaves much to be desired. Their marketing organizations and sales services are not satisfactory; the freight rates are on the higher side. It is therefore no wonder that in commercial transactions which are, by and large, governed by commercial considerations, the shippers are attracted by the services offered by outsiders, particularly non-conference container operators who are not only giving more satisfactory and faster services but also offering much lower freight rates.... even the public sector undertakings and Government Departments who are the major importers and exporters of our cargoes, particularly bulk cargoes, have also found it more economical to avail of the services by outsiders.[88]

At the base of the aversion of shippers to any centralized cargo allocating agency lay a fundamental distrust of the bureaucracy and the public sector, a distrust which had been generated out of their years of experience in interacting with them. As one broker explained in private: "In market, the consumer is supreme. In India it is the other way around. Here, you produce something and you say to the consumer: you bloody well take it; if you don't take it, I will have the government control".[89] The shippers wanted to avoid precisely this prospect of government dictation.

Chowgule then touched upon another aspect in arguing against any preferential treatment for national shipping lines: "A major factor behind [why] our cargoes go to non-conference operators is the inadequacy of container services provided by the Indian lines". This really goes to the heart of the dilemma that confronted shipowners and shippers. If shipowners were to go in for such costly vessels as cellular containerships they needed some assurance of their being utilized by shippers, hence the proposal for a centralized cargo agency. On the other hand, shippers could not commit themselves to any preferential arrangement for national shipping lines unless they had adequate container capacity, if then.

The most telling argument that the shippers employed and with the greatest effect with the state was that any such arrangement would have an adverse impact on exports. The president of the Eastern India Shippers Association reportedly declared, invoking the name of the relevant ministry for his cause: "The Commerce Ministry was not likely to tie up exports with any such monolithic organization.... Indian exports can survive without Indian shipping but Indian shipping cannot without Indian exports".[90] That takes us directly to the real block to any cargo reservation scheme. The Ministry of Commerce is a very powerful ministry since the balance of payments is critical for the Indian economy. Besides, it has been vested with important responsibilities in the matter of transportation and infrastructure. However, its approach to the question of shipping rests on a very different logic than that of the Ministry of Surface Transport. An official with responsibilities in the area of transportation explained in private, even though in the post-liberalization era but with cargo reservation still a subject of continuing concern:

> Even before liberalization, the Ministry of Commerce was the one ministry which was always in terms of its inputs, in terms of its stand, "liberal" or "global", for the same reason that we always dealt with the world market. This is one ministry in the Government of India whose mandate is to increase international trade. Because this is our mandate--it has always been--we will promote the interest of international trade and not necessarily of the Indian national carrier, and this will apply both to Air India and SCI. Our interest is to increase the facilities of infrastructure and bring in competition, because the Indian exporter, with increased competition, then gets a better price. Because he gets a better price, exports increase. Our logic has been: you globalize and increase trade, and automatically there will be enough place in it for more and more Indian players and more effective and more efficient service flowing. (This is an institutional position?) Yes.

The second point I would make is that traditionally both the shipping sector and air sector--the entire infrastructure sector--in India has always been public sector driven, so automatically that means that SCI will be the main player on the shipping side and on the air side Air India. It has also been the mandate of this Ministry to bring in competition and private sector involvement. Our mandate has been this. Now the times have shown us to be right. The entire Government of India's policy is this.

Whenever we take a policy stand in a particular matter, this has been the philosophy behind it. For example, cabotage law, it was us that demanded that exemptions be given on cabotage law for increased containerization. Because, again, it is our mandate; we are the nodal ministry on introducing containerization. Containerization is key to international trade. Tomorrow the key to international trade may be EDI [Electronic Data Interchange]; we are also the nodal ministry for EDI. So it is not an accident. We are in the frontline.

Exporters interests we also mind; reports that come to us from export councils; we get reports, complaints. It is our duty to put their views across. This becomes our philosophy, this is the origin of our philosophy. Exporters will come and complain. Another place where all these things are discussed is called SCOPE Shipping meetings.

We believe in voluntary approach, we believe in consensus. We believe that the Indian shipping industry must convince the users that it is in their interests. We believe in consensus, we do not believe in statutory compulsions. We opposed this mandatory reservation of cargo. We say, yes, we want to preserve Indian shipping and we want efficient and good Indian shipping which can work at a global level and be competitive. We believe in competition, globalization, private sector involvement.[91]

The institutional logic of the Ministry of Commerce does not answer the question as to how a developing country makes a breakthrough in the world of liner shipping dominated by consortia of megacarriers, but it nonetheless enables us to understand its diametrically opposed position to that of the Department of Shipping in the Ministry of Surface Transport.

It also enables us to comprehend why its view, with the muscle of trade and industry behind it, prevails within the state. It is no surprise then that the proposal for a centralized cargo agency simply met a slow death.

However, aside from the difference in philosophical approach, the Ministry of Commerce may not be innocent of attempting to protect its own power and interests. It, no doubt, conceives of its mandate as representing the interests of the shippers, and they include among their numbers the powerful export houses. But the Ministry of Commerce--with the public sector enterprises of Minerals and Metals Trading Corporation (MMTC) and State Trading Corporation (STC) under its own wings--is the biggest shipper of them all. Of course, through them, it has direct experience of the problems in working with whatever control mechanisms exist in cargo support, such as Transchart, and that also has some bearing on its position. But a cargo reservation programme would plausibly place the work of these organizations, to some extent, under the control of the Ministry of Surface Transport. Regardless, what is clear is that the Ministry of Commerce has been able to foil any attempt to provide effective cargo support to Indian shipping.

THE ENTITLEMENT VOUCHER SCHEME

As the share of Indian liner shipping in cargo continued to decline during the second phase of the depression in the face of competition from foreign carriers, threatening its very existence, the Ministry of Surface Transport cast about for a solution that would assure cargo for the national lines. It felt its hands strengthened by the coming into effect in 1983 of the UNCTAD Liner Code, providing for the right of the country's shipping to 40 per cent of its national cargo handled by conferences. Meanwhile, a new dynamic leader, Rajesh Pilot, had become the Minister of State for Surface Transport in the government of Rajiv Gandhi, who had received a massive electoral mandate after his accession to power. Pilot was eager to do something for the beleaguered liner industry, even as he was aware of the sensitivity of the business class to any suggestion of a cargo reservation scheme under the state bureaucracy. He promised parliament in 1986 to bring forward legislation to implement the UNCTAD Liner Code.

In the meantime, the press leaked the outlines of a new Entitlement Voucher Scheme, under which Indian shippers and foreign buyers would be required to acquire, through first employing an Indian ship, a voucher that would entitle them to employ a foreign ship. A shipper or buyer would by using an Indian ship obtain a voucher in the value of 150 per cent of the freight paid, which could then be used to employ a foreign ship to the extent of the voucher. In this fashion, the proportion between Indian and foreign ships would be kept at 40:60 as required by the guidelines of the Liner Code. The vouchers would be transferable and therefore marketable. The proposed system thus did not have the rigidity of the cargo reservation scheme, nor dependence on a large bureaucracy.

Despite its lesser reliance on a bureaucracy, the proposal met with the same fate as the cargo reservation scheme. Again, as with the earlier proposal, the shippers engaged in a preemptive attack to foil any such system from coming into effect. Chowgule warned that Indian lines were not likely to have the capacity to carry 40 per cent of the national trade for a long time. He believed the system would lead to serious delays and unhealthy practices, while foreign buyers will shift their orders to other sources; the consequence would be adverse for exports.[92] More broadly, he underlined that "the relentless laws of economics are no respecters of patriotic sentiments, even less of Government fiats".[93] He suggested, instead, reliance on a voluntary approach, which in reality meant no approach at all.

The Ministry of Commerce supported the shippers, agreeing that India was not in a position to carry "national cargo in national bottoms". There followed a cold war between the Ministry of Surface Transport and the Ministry of Commerce, with the former eager to push forward the legislation, while the latter stalled on discussing it. Cargo reservation was unacceptable to Commerce because of its belief that "if we are compelling the exporters to export through Indian vessels, it may act as a damper on exports". The Transport Secretary confessed, "unfortunately we have not been able to carry conviction to the Commerce Ministry".[94] Prime Minister Rajiv Gandhi himself was ambivalent; on the one hand, he promised cargo support for Indian shipping; on the other, he said it could not be done at the expense of trade and exports. More specifically, he warned SCI on its silver jubilee anniversary in 1986: "At the age of 25 years, one grows and becomes mature. Spoon feeding and mollycoddling should stop. You must stand on your own". With the state divided within itself, "neither the concerned Ministries nor the Cabinet secretariat have been able to find ways and means of resolving this dilemma. This also gives an impression that no further efforts are likely to be made in this direction and the situation is allowed to drift".[95] Like the earlier proposal on a centralized cargo agency, the Entitlement Voucher Scheme also fizzled out.

SUMMARY AND CONCLUSIONS

Indian shipping received severe body blows from the structural break in the world's shipping industry by way of the OPEC-generated depression during the 1970s and 1980s. To that extent, the international system has a powerful bearing on its performance. However, the decimation of the country's liner shipping and the continued marginalization of its bulk shipping, and relatedly the prolongation of the decline and stagnation in tonnage beyond the world depression, are strongly related to the nature of state policy. In the first place, past state policy established procedures and practices that, in line with path dependency theory, placed constraints on the adaptability of Indian shipping both to the structural break and the structural change in world shipping. These constraints are especially noteworthy in respect of four areas: provision of loans without commercial prudence; imposition of a rigid system of controls and licences; lack of statutory protection for cargo support; and the hegemony of the public sector. The consequence was that when the gales of depression hit Indian shipping, it was poorly equipped to cope with them.

Secondly, the structural change in world shipping by way of containerization presented a serious dilemma for Indian shipping. In the face of cutthroat competition--and that it was--Indian shipping required cargo support in order to risk making huge investments in capital-intensive equipment. Because of deep divisions within the state, and in turn within society, the state was unable to provide cargo support on a statutory basis. What was made strikingly clear by the episode was that the old policies had become irrelevant though they continued formally to prevail. On the other hand, with the deterioration in state power, the state was bereft of any new ideas about strategy to succour its national shipping in the face of foreign competition. The industry was left to fend for itself in what in an earlier era had been described as the battle between "the giant and the dwarf".[96] The state stood aside as the liner industry was ground and crushed and brought to the same condition as it was under colonialism. The malaise exposed the hollowness of the country's international diplomacy in which it provided assertive leadership, but failed to match it with appropriate action at home. In the event, the result was that, already made prostrate by the impact of international forces, Indian shipping was handicapped in its endeavour to adapt to a new environment, squeezed as it was between the requirements of a system of state controls on one side and the incapacity of an economically weak and politically divided state to provide support, on the other.

NOTES

1. Douglass C. North, *Institutions, Institutional Change and Economic Performance* (Cambridge: Cambridge University Press, 1990), pp. 92-104, 112-17. See also Geoffrey M. Hodgson, "Economic Evolution: Intervention Contra Pangloss", *Journal of Economic Issues,* XXV, no. 2 (June 1991), pp. 519-33.

2. The citation is from an authoritative source: N.C. Singhal (Managing Director, SCICI), "Indian Shipping: Past, Present and Future--Financial Aspects", *Indian Shipping,* vol. 40, nos. 3-4 (1988), pp. 13-17.

3. Dev Raj, *Shipping and Shipbuilding Industry in India* (Delhi: H.K. Publishers, 1990), pp. 48-49.

4. Singhal, p. 13.

5. S. Parthasarathy, "Financial Aid to Shipping Industry", *Indian Shipping,* vol. 41, nos. 6-7 (1989), pp. 9-14.

6. S.N. Sanklecha, *Tramping to Success: Story of the Great Eastern Shipping Company Limited* (Bombay: Popular Prakashan, 1994), pp. 149 and 201.

7. M.A. Master, *So I Rest On My Oars: Collection of Writings and Speeches 1947-1970,* ed. by K.V. Hariharan (2 volumes; M.A. Master Memorial Trust, 1977), I, pp. 274-79.

8. Vasant Sheth, "Chairman's statement to the shareholders for the year 1981-82", in Sanklecha, pp. 182-84.

9. Sanklecha, pp. 150-51.

10. Although GES often thought that it was a special object of discrimination by the state, other companies also complained. Here is an instance from Scindia: "I had referred last year to a second-hand bulk carrier of 57,000 DWT negotiated by us for $6.25 million but because of the delay of getting Government approval for our financial arrangements, this ship could not be purchased. In the meantime prices of ships have risen sharply and for your information I may say that when the same bulk carrier was again available in April this year, we had indicated a price of $9 million, but the shipowner was not prepared to sell the ship at this price. In July we placed an order for a bulk carrier of 54,000 DWT with Rheinstahl Shipyard and we immediately applied to the Government for approval. Unfortunately the approval was only received recently. In the meantime, the Yard withdrew the agreed price and is now asking for a higher price and offering delivery about a year later". Speech of Scindia Chairman Krishnaraj M.D. Thackersey to the 51st Annual General Meeting, *Eastern Economist,* December 30, 1970, pp. 37-38.

11. *Indian Shipping,* vol. 43, nos. 1-2 (1991), p. 4.

12. Sheth, in Sanklecha, p. 184.

13. India, Lok Sabha, Committee on Public Undertakings (1987-88), *Forty-Fourth Report: Shipping Corporation of India Limited* (New Delhi: Lok Sabha Secretariat, 1988), p. 8.

14. *Ibid.*, pp. 8-9 and 27.

15. Sanklecha, p. 151.

16. Sheth, in Sanklecha, p. 186.

17. Sanklecha, p. 186.

18. India, Planning Commission, *Indian Shipping in the Time Perspective of 2000 AD: Report of Planning Group on Shipping, September 1987* (chairman: L.M.S. Rajwar; Bombay: 1987), pp. 220-21; see also pp. 211-212.

19. P.T. Dalal, "Indian Shipping in Different Sectors of Foreign Trades", *Indian Shipping,* vol. 21, no. 5 (1969), pp. 15-19.

20. Master, I, p. 355.

21. Sanklecha, p. 151.

22. *Indian Shipping,* vol. 43, nos. 1-2 (1991), pp. 4-6.

23. *Indian Shipping,* vol. 43, no. 5 (1991), p. 31.

24. Planning Commission, *Indian Shipping in the Time Perspective of 2000 AD,* pp. 229-232.

25. *Indian Shipping,* vol. 41, no. 4 (1989), p. 26.

26. N. Vaghul, "Indian Shipping Industry--A Provocative Evaluation", *Indian Shipping,* vol. 39, no. 12 (1987), pp. 5-6, and 10.

27. See N.G. Jog (ed.), *Sumati Morarjee: Felicitation Volume--Service to Indian Shipping* (Bombay: Smt. Sumati Morarjee Shashti-Abdi-Poorti Celebrations Committee, 1970).

28. For the account after 1981, I have drawn on the following documents of Scindia Steam Navigation Company: *68th Annual Report; Chairman's Statement at the 71st Annual General Meeting of the Company on 5th September, 1990;* and

74th Annual Report and Statement of Accounts 1992-1993. See also Sucheta Dalal, "Who is Killing Scindia Steamship?", *Times of India* (Bombay), May 29, 1995.

29. India Steamship Company Limited, *52nd Annual Report 1980,* p. 3, *66th Annual Report 1994,* pp. 5-6, and *67th Annual Report 1995,* p. 3.

30. Cited in Sanklecha, p. 238. This section draws on Sanklecha's justifiably admiring and proud as well as highly informative biography of Vasant Sheth and his company, *Tramping to Success.* Sanklecha served GES for 42 years from its origins in 1948 to his retirement in 1990. He became company secretary in 1951 and senior vice president (corporate) in 1987. During the course of his service, he completed his Ph.D. at the University of Bombay, which published his dissertation *Tramp Shipping in India* (Bombay: University of Bombay, 1966). His other major work is *Economics of Shipping and Other Papers* (Bombay: Bhandarkar Publications, 1982). As the foremost authority on Indian shipping, he has published over 70 articles.

31. Sanklecha, *Tramping to Success,* p. 10.

32. Sanklecha, *Tramping to Success,* p. 118.

33. Sanklecha, *Tramping to Success,* pp. 201-202.

34. Sanklecha, *Tramping to Success,* pp. 116 and 235.

35. Sanklecha, *Tramping to Success,* p. 199.

36. Sanklecha, *Tramping to Success,* p. 198.

37. P.T. Dalal, "Indian Shipping in Relation to Long-Term Export Strategy", *Indian Shipping,* vol. 26, no. 3 (1974), pp. 11-17.

38. See K. Balasubramanian, "India Misses the Boat", *Containerization International,* October 1993, pp. 55-57.

39. SCI, *40th Annual Report 1989-90,* p. 11, and *43rd Annual Report 1992-93,* p. 5.

40. Planning Commission, *Indian Shipping in the Time Perspective of 2000 AD,* pp. 204-205.

41. From an interview at UNCTAD, Geneva, May 4, 1995.

42. See David E. Apter, *The Politics of Modernization* (Chicago: University of Chicago Press, 1966). For a summary view, see Baldev Raj Nayar, *The Modernization Imperative and Indian Planning* (New Delhi: Vikas, 1972), ch. I.

43. H.B. Desai, *Indian Shipping Perspectives (Critical Reflections)* (New Delhi: Anupama Publications, 1988), pp. 93 and 146. The author served for many years as Professor at the Indian Institute of Foreign Trade, New Delhi, and is a regular writer on shipping affairs in Indian journals.

44. H.B. Desai, *Current Issues in Indian Shipping* (New Delhi: Commonwealth Publishers, 1989), pp. 64-65. Nor was this perception confined to academicians; a veteran labour leader states: "Similarly, our shipping once upon a time could boast of persons within our administration who had deep knowledge of shipping and its various nuances. Such persons could chart their way within the limitations of the policies laid down by the government to ensure progress and development of our shipping. For instance, Dr. Nagendra Singh and Dr. C.P. Srivastava dominated and guided our shipping for long years". Leo Barnes, "Human Resource Development", *Indian Shipping,* vol. 43, no. 4 (1991), pp. 28-32.

It may have been an unusual occurrence, but nonetheless significant that, when COPU asked the Transport Secretary in the early 1980s to explain the decline in the share of Indian shipping in the country's trade, he responded: "I do admit that I had not done that much study". It is difficult to imagine a more important issue to be informed about, and the committee expressed surprise at the official's lack of preparation. See India, Lok Sabha, Committee on Public Undertakings (1981-82), *Forty-Third Report on the Shipping Corporation of India Ltd.* (New Delhi: Lok Sabha Secretariat, 1982), pp. 5 and 57.

45 See Hans Jurgen Peters, *India's Growing Conflict Between Trade and Transport: Issues and Options* (Working Paper 345; Washington, D.C.: World Bank, 1990), pp. 37 and 43.

46. Canada, Transport Canada, *Task Force on Deep-Sea Shipping: Report to the Minister of Transport* (Ottawa: 1985), p. 41.

47. Desai, *Indian Shipping Perspectives,* pp. 113-117.

48. *Eastern Economist,* October 18, 1971.

49. *Indian Shipping,* vol. 20, no. 7 (1970), p. 3.

50. *Eastern Economist,* January 11, 1980, p. 79.

51. *Indian Shipping,* vol. 31, no. 11 (1979), pp. 5-6.

52. *Indian Shipping,* vol. 35, no. 8 (1983), p. 3.

53. *Indian Shipping,* vol. 35, no. 8 (1983), p. 3.

54. Nagendra Singh, "India and the Technological Revolution in Shipping", *Indian Shipping,* vol. 19, no. 12 (1967), pp. 17-20.

55. India, Ministry of Transport and Shipping, National Conference on Shipping, Shipbuilding and Ports, December 1967, *Recommendations, Agenda Notes and Contributed Papers* (New Delhi: 1967), pp. 1-8.

56. See India, Director General of Shipping, *Seminar on Containerization: Bombay, December 1968* (Bombay: 1968). Twenty-five papers on different aspects of containerization were presented.

57. *Indian Shipping,* vol. 20, no. 12 (1968), pp. 9-23.

58. India, Ministry of Shipping and Transport, *Report of the Working Group on Containerization* (New Delhi: 1971).

59. The text of the seminar's conclusions appear in *Indian Shipping,* vol. 20, no. 12 (1968), pp. 18-19.

60. *Indian Shipping,* vol. 33, no. 4 (1981), pp. 3 and 7; *ibid.,* no.6 (1981), p. 3; and *ibid.,* no. 12 (1981), p. 16.

61. AISC chairman Chowgule pointed out in 1983 that the charge for carrying one container (teu) by foreign carriers from Hong Kong and Singapore to Europe and USA for door-to-door service was $1000-1200 whereas it was $1600-1800 by Indian lines for service between India and Europe from pier to pier. V.D. Chowgule, "Problems of Indian Shippers", *Indian Shipping,* vol. 35, no. 1 (1983), pp. 11-14.

62. *Indian Shipping,* vol. 32, no. 11 (1980), pp. 7-11.

63. L.M.S. Rajwar, "Paper Presented by Shri L.M.S. Rajwar on Role of National Lines", *Indian Shipping,* vol. 41, no. 9 (1989), pp. 9-11.

64. N.M. Trivedi, "Address of Shri N.M. Trivedi", *Indian Shipping,* vol. 37, no. 4 (1985), pp. 18-19.

65. *Indian Shipping,* vol. 39, nos. 1-2 (1987), pp. 11-12.

66. Committee on Public Undertakings (1987-88), *Forty-Fourth Report,* pp. 61-64.

67. India, Lok Sabha, Committee on Public Undertakings (1990-91), *Fifth Report: Shipping Corporation of India Ltd.* (New Delhi: Lok Sabha Secretariat, 1990), p. 8.

68. Desai, *Current Issues in Indian Shipping,* p. 18.

69. SCI, *39th Annual Report 1980-81,* p. 8.

70. SCI, *43rd Annual Report 1992-93,* p. 9.

71. SCI, *44th Annual Report 1993-94,* pp. 9-10.

72. One chairman of SCI perceptively notes the relationship between the infrastructure of developing countries and the performance of their shipping: "The productivity of ships of the developing nations is virtually half that of developed

nations.. Interestingly, when ships of developing nations are trading between developed countries they seem to produce the same level of cargo turnaround. Otherwise, obviously developed nations would not charter vessels of developing nations. Therefore, it can be derived that ships per se of developed and developing nations are equal in their productivity: it is the environment in which they operate which is unequal. By environment, it means ports, roads, railways and other infrastructural facilities". P.P. Radhakrishnan, "Paper by Capt. P.P. Radhakrishnan", *Indian Shipping,* vol. 44, nos. 11-12 (1992), pp. 29-33.

73. For an authoritative assessment of India's poor infrastructure and low labour productivity, see the study by Hans Jurgen Peters, *India's Growing Conflict Between Trade and Transport.* Peters notes: "Poor productivity is a sad hallmark of most entities involved in serving the container trades.... Despite the low wages in India, the costs of handling containers and their cargo in ports is about 80 percent higher (on a per unit basis) than in more costly Japan or the USA. The explanation lies in the fact that in India on average 25 workers are assigned to a job for which in the other two countries five workers accomplish about three times the daily output of their 25 Indian counterparts". More striking is the comparison with Singapore, where the cost of handling one teu container is US$100 as against $218 in Bombay and $170 at the relatively more efficient port in Madras. See Peters, pp. 11-12.

An earlier comparison was made by SCI chief P.C. Shukla in 1981 for handling a container from the ship to its stuffing or destuffing: Calcutta $450; Haldia $250; Bombay $250; Madras $300; and Cochin $187. On the other hand, the cost in New York or Montreal was $150; Sydney $170; and Japanese ports $100. *Indian Shipping,* vol. 33, no. 1 (1981), pp. 21-22. Lower efficiency at Indian ports was reflected in differential freight rates: Bombay-UK $1300 as against Singapore-UK $600. H.N. Fotedar, "Containerization in Ports: Problems and Perspectives in India", *Indian Shipping,* vol. 36, no. 7 (1984), pp. 11-12.

74. See Tae-Woo Lee, "Korean Shipping Policy: The Role of Government", *Marine Policy,* vol. 14, no. 5 (1990), pp. 421-37, and *The Growth of Korean Shipping, 1962-1981: The Advantages of Combining a "Backward" Start With Imported Ideas* (Ph.D. dissertation; Cardiff: Department of Maritime Studies, University of Wales, 1989). Particularly noteworthy is the "waiver system", under which cargoes were reserved for Korean ships unless a "waiver" had been obtained. Besides, 50 per cent of inbound cargo purchased with government aid, loan or other funds had to be carried in Korean flag ships.

75. H.M. Trivedi, *Indian Shipping in Perspective* (New Delhi: Vikas, 1980).

76. H.M. Trivedi, *Indian Shipping in Perspective,* p. 136.

77. H.M. Trivedi, "Integrated Policy for National Shipping", *Indian Shipping,* vol. 34, no. 5 (1982), pp. 7-12. See also H.M. Trivedi, "Indian Shipping--Some Basic Issues", *ibid.,* vol. 33, no. 5 (1981), pp. 19-21, and Trivedi, *Indian Shipping in Perspective,* especially pp. 128-55.

78. H.M. Trivedi, *Indian Shipping in Perspective,* pp. 129, 136-37, and 149-50.

79. H.M. Trivedi, "INDSHIP, the Centralized Cargo Shipping Agency", in Trivedi, *Indian Shipping in Perspective,* p. 133.

80. H.M. Trivedi, "Indian Shipping--Some Basic Issues", *Indian Shipping,* vol. 33, no. 5 (1981), p. 19.

81. H.M. Trivedi, "Integrated Policy for National Shipping", pp.7-12.

82. H.M. Trivedi, "Integrated Policy for National Shipping", pp.7-12.

83. Indian Institute of Foreign Trade, *System Approach to Shipment and Carriage of Export Cargo* (typescript; New Delhi: IIFT, 1976). The study was prepared by Dr. H.B. Desai; I am grateful to him for supplying me a copy of this document as

also of the one on the "entitlement voucher scheme", discussed below.

84. H.M. Trivedi, "Shipping Strategy for Exports to New Markets", in Trivedi, *Indian Shipping in Perspective,* pp. 196-212.

85. H.M. Trivedi, *Indian Shipping in Perspective,* p. 150

86. H.M. Trivedi, "INDSHIP", p. 129.

87. "Central Cargo Booking Agency: Comments of Association of Calcutta Shipping Interests", *Indian Shipping,* vol. 30, no. 12 (1978), pp. 17-19.

88. "Shippers and Shipping Trade: Deliberations at AISC Annual Meeting", *Indian Shipping,* vol. 33, no. 6 (1981), pp. 11-17. Indian shippers are not unique in this regard. Compare: "Shippers insist on the necessity to be able to select freely ocean carriers and are strongly opposed to any Canadian flag proposals that could result in increased freight rates, subsidies or cargo reservation programmes". Transport Canada, *Task Force on Deep-Sea Shipping,* p. v.

89. Interview Notebook II, p. 126.

90. Cited in H.M. Trivedi, "INDSHIP", p. 129.

91. Interview Notebook II, pp. 142-43.

92. See Indian Institute of Foreign Trade, *Entitlement Voucher Scheme: A Case Study of Cargo Support to National Ships* (typescript; New Delhi: IIFT, 1986), p. 16.

93. "Cargo Support to the Fore: AISC Annual Meeting", *Indian Shipping,* vol. 39, nos. 1-2 (1987), p. 7; see also *ibid.,* vol. 38, no. 5 (1986), p. 5.

94. Committee on Public Undertakings (1987-88), *Forty-Fourth Report,* p. 41.

95. Desai, *Indian Shipping Perspectives,* pp. 224-38.

96. "The Giant and the Dwarf" is the title of an article which Mahatma Gandhi wrote in *Young India* (March 26, 1931), commenting on the unfairness of competition between British shipping and Indian shipping. See N.G. Jog, *Saga of Scindia: Struggle for the Revival of Indian Shipping and Shipbuilding* (Bombay: Scindia Steam Navigation Co., 1969), p. 84.

CHAPTER VII

RESTRUCTURING THE STATE-MARKET RELATIONSHIP, 1990-1995: LIBERALIZATION AND THE CONTINUING CONSTRAINTS

Propelled by economic crisis, a large part of the developing world has since the early 1980s witnessed the implementation of programmes of stabilization and structural adjustment, often under the auspices, indeed duress, of the international financial institutions. These programmes have largely had economic liberalization as their central thrust, focusing on the shrinking of the role of the state in the economic sphere and a corresponding widening of the sphere of the market. This trend coincided with, and was in considerable measure inspired by, the ideological resurgence of market-oriented policies in some of the key advanced industrial states, such as the UK and the US. Meanwhile, the rapid globalization of the world economy placed increasing pressures on controlled economies to relax or break down barriers to international economic exchange and the entry of external economic actors. The collapse of communism in the former Soviet bloc and the adoption of market and outward oriented policies by the successor states sacralized liberalization into the regnant economic ideology. With much of the world increasingly converging on political democracy and economic liberalism as the preferred frameworks for the conduct of politics and economics, some even posited the end of history in the sense of the exclusion of any alternative frameworks in the future.[1]

The wider forced-draft economic liberalization in the developing world has often spilled over into the arena of shipping as well. True, shipping is an international industry and it has seen increasing globalization in the postwar world, beginning with the resort to flags of convenience (FOCs) and accelerating with the container revolution. At the international level, rapid globalization has affected most dramatically the regime in liner shipping, which has seen a shift from the "fair competition" envisaged by the UNCTAD Liner Code to "free competition", resulting in a tremendous concentration of economic power, primarily in the megacarriers of the developed economies. At the national level, as countries have undertaken reform of economic policy, they have also brought shipping within its compass.[2]

India, too, has partaken of the larger global trend towards economic liberalization, and it launched a drastic programme of stabilization and structural adjustment in 1991 in the midst of a major economic crisis. The purpose of this chapter is, then, to examine the nature of the liberalization effort in shipping and to make a preliminary assessment of its impact. However, this recent liberalization episode had been preceded by an earlier endeavour in the mid-1980s, though not provoked by any crisis. Some liberalization took place in the shipping arena as well at the time. Accordingly, this chapter as a whole first takes a summary look at (1) the measures of economic liberalization during the 1980s. It then goes on (2) to examine in greater detail the record on liberalization in the 1990s as also (3) the constraints that continue to limit growth in shipping. Since three basic elements are essential to the operation of shipping--ships and, relatedly, finance for their acquisition; cargo; and man-power--the treatment of both liberalization and the continuing constraints revolves around that triple classification.

Economic Liberalization and Shipping in the 1980s

The late 1960s and the beginning of the 1970s had seen a massive trend towards economic radicalism in India. During the reign of socialist ideology in that period, the state nationalized large segments of the private sector, especially banking and coal. At the time, key business leaders had warned that such massive takeover of private business by the state would retard economic growth. When inflation and economic stagnation did occur in the early 1970s, Mrs. Indira Gandhi jettisoned her radicalism and called a halt to further large-scale nationaliz-ation, even though she did not reverse the outcomes of the earlier policy. When she was defeated in the 1977 elections, the Janata Party as a hastily-formed coalition of several political groups took over power. Following its professed commitment to the ideals of Mahatma Gandhi, the party's economic programme laid emphasis on agriculture and the rural areas as also on small scale industry. The Janata government was divided over the issue of the public sector, with some parts of it hostile to it. Its stay in office was, however, short-lived as it soon fell prey to factional conflict. In the meantime, both law and order and the economic situation deteriorated.

Mrs. Gandhi returned to power in 1980, not on any promise of advance towards socialism, but on the slogan of providing "a government that works". On the basis of her experience with the public sector and her assessment of the condition of the economy, Mrs. Gandhi stealthily initiated a process of liberalization--though she shrewdly refrained from calling it as such--through some relaxation of the system of controls and licences. Clearly, she no longer counted on the public sector for advancing economic growth. However, concerns over national unity came to the forefront during her last administration, sidetracking it from a serious attack on the economic front, indeed eventually leading to her assassination in 1984.

Her son, Rajiv Gandhi, who succeeded her as prime minister, immediately called for new elections, in which he received a massive mandate, largely due to sympathy for his mother. With his assumption of power, for the first time a prime minister in office openly and forthrightly favoured liberalization of the economy. Further, in reversal of the past policy of reserving the commanding heights of the economy for the state and of following the inward-oriented economic strategy, he pushed through a substantial package of reforms which further relaxed licensing and controls. This initiative was all the more astonishing since the country was not confronted by any imminent economic crisis. No doubt, liberalization was consonant with the young leader's personal modern and technology-oriented outlook. However, underneath the policy reversal lay a profound disappointment with the performance of the public sector and strong misgivings about the prospects of economic growth over the medium and long term under its auspices. The massive mandate in the elections helped give reform a push.

The key feature of the changes installed by Rajiv Gandhi was reliance on the private sector--instead of the public sector--as the mechanism for economic growth in the future and the provision of the required resources and appropriate environment to facilitate its performing that role. The public sector was expected to play a complementary but subsidiary role to the private sector, concentrating on the core sector, primarily infrastructure. More specifically, the MRTP requirements were relaxed while 25 broad categories of industries were delicensed; permission was made automatic for expansion of industrial capacity by 33 per cent a year. There was also a considerable relaxation of the trade regime.[3] The new prime minister sought to redefine national self-reliance so as to make it compatible with a shift from an inward orientation to an outward orientation and integration with the world economy. In the Seventh Five Year Plan (1985-1990), he declared: "Self-reliance does not mean autarchy. It means the development of a strong, independent national economy, dealing extensively with the world, but dealing with it on equal terms".[4] His economic advisor, L.K. Jha, explained the young leader's position: "Self-reliance for a country like India cannot have the limited meaning of the country not being influenced one way or another by external economic forces. It should instead be measured in terms of India's contribution to the shaping of the international economic forces".[5]

In retrospect, it is possible to play down the extent of liberalization launched by Rajiv Gandhi and also to criticize him for its halting and limited pace. However, he was the first person who as prime minister openly advocated liberalization and initiated a change in overall economic strategy. On account of that, he was subjected to bitter attack by his opponents, both within and outside the party, for his betrayal of the legacy of socialism inherited from his grandfather and mother. He himself confessed that liberalization as a slogan, unlike socialism, was not popular with the masses and wished there were some more acceptable term available instead. Indeed, his economic policy may have had some role in the defeat of his party in the 1989 elections. From a historical perspective, nonetheless, against heavy odds he legitimized debate on the performance of socialism and the public sector, where earlier they had been regarded as icons.

Besides, Rajiv Gandhi left behind a manifesto prepared for his party for the 1991 elections--in the midst of which he fell victim to an assassination--which came to be regarded as his last political will and testament, promising further liberalization.

This document from a fallen leader gave legitimacy to the more radical liberalization effort of the successor government. The manifesto pledged the establishment of "a sound policy framework: encouragement of entrepreneurship, development of capital markets, simplification of the regulatory system, bringing in new technology and increasing competitiveness for the benefit of the common man". It promised "a sustained effort, through R&D and otherwise, to improve the international competitiveness of Indian industry", and asserted that "foreign investment and technology collaboration will be permitted to obtain higher technology, to increase exports and to expand the production base". More significantly, it pointedly underlined that specific spheres could no longer be the assured preserve of the public sector, declaring that his party would "abolish the monopoly of any sector or any individual enterprise in any field of manufacture, except on strategic or military considerations, and open all manufacturing activity to competition".[6]

Along with the substantial instalment of economic liberalization in general, the Rajiv Gandhi administration introduced certain measures for relaxing and streamlining the regulatory framework for shipping. Among these measures was the liberalization, simplification and speeding up of the process of acquisition of vessels. The state now assured shipowners that applications for acquisition of ships would henceforth be cleared within six weeks. Besides, to add flexibility to the process, it was ready to allow purchase of tonnage in excess of the requirements assessed by the Tonnage Acquisition Committee (TAC) to the extent of 25 per cent. It scaled down the *pari passu* obligation to buying only one vessel from an Indian shipyard for every three ordered from foreign shipyards instead of the earlier ratio of 1:1. In addition, orders for vessels on Indian shipyards could be placed without any reference to the TAC-assessed requirements. The state further allowed shipping companies to diversify into non-shipping areas even as it allowed other companies to enter shipping. Again, it agreed to permit companies to acquire vessels for cross-trading provided they were limited solely to that purpose. The state was also willing to allow companies to enter into joint ventures.[7] The most significant policy decision during the Rajiv Gandhi administration concerned the withdrawal of the state from the responsibility for direct disbursal of funding to shipping companies, transferring it instead now to a public financial institution, the Shipping Credit and Investment Company of India (SCICI).

Although these measures were inspired by the aim to lift Indian shipping out of the depression and to get it back on the track of growth and expansion, unfortunately they failed to generate enthusiasm for tonnage acquisition. There were three main reasons for the failure: One, the measures came too late, when the shipping depression was over and prices of ships had increased, so that Indian companies could not avail of the benefit of the earlier lower prices. Two, the Indian companies had been mauled so badly by the depression that they were deterred from any large-scale acquisition of tonnage. Three, India was too strapped by the foreign exchange constraint to allow shipowners to buy much tonnage from abroad. Besides, any thrust for new acquisition, especially in liner shipping, required determined cargo support from the state and the shippers, whereas the most noteworthy feature of the administration's relationship with the shipping industry was its failure to provide cargo reservation, notwithstanding the coming into force in 1983 of the UNCTAD Liner Code. That simply made improbable the buying of cellular containerships, because of the heavy commercial risk involved.

In general, the liberalization of the regulatory framework was of little consequence for Indian shipping. It may have been useful in a different period when the shipping companies were financially healthy. But unfortunately, in the aftermath of the depression, they were not. The real need of Indian shipping was for generous financial assistance and cargo reservation to enable it to overcome the damage done by the depression. However, in its condition of financial stringency and bureaucratic conflict, the state was unable to provide either. The chief characteristic of the period therefore remained stagnation and decline in tonnage.

Fiscal Crisis of the State and Economic Liberalization

The 1980s had seen substantial economic growth, with the economy expanding at the respectable average annual rate of 5.3 per cent, a growth rate higher than that witnessed by any other decade since independence. However, this commendable performance, which contradicted the "Hindu rate of growth" label pinned on India by economists, nonetheless masked an emergent fiscal crisis of the state. The fiscal deficit had been climbing in the 1980s, and the problem was compounded by the populist policies of the minority National Front coalition which took over power after the 1989 elections. Chief among these policies was the waiving of repayments of loans that had been extended by public sector banks to farmers. Finally, a full-blown economic crisis erupted in 1990, featuring high inflation at a rate of nearly 15 per cent a year and a critical balance of payments situation where the country could hardly muster foreign exchange reserves for more than three weeks of imports.[8]

Meanwhile, faced with multiple crises, the coalition fell in late 1990, with a minority breakaway faction succeeding to power. Without much of a support base of its own, the resulting shaky government could ill afford to face parliament with tough decisions required under the circumstance; in the event, it even failed to present the annual budget. It readily obtained, however, an initial loan instalment from the IMF and mortgaged part of India's gold reserves abroad to avert defaulting on its debt repayments.

The severe foreign exchange crisis during 1990 and 1991 strangulated the shipping industry in respect of acquisition of new tonnage. The restrictions imposed by the Reserve Bank of India in March 1991 on access to foreign exchange called a virtual halt to new acquisitions over the remainder of the year;[9] little wonder that tonnage failed to expand. When the government resigned in early 1991, new elections were called, which were briefly interrupted by the assassination of the Congress party leader Rajiv Gandhi. As the largest party, even though without a majority, the Congress party then returned to power in mid-1991 under the leadership of P.V. Narasimha Rao.

The new government immediately adopted a set of drastic measures to put India's economic house in order and to restore investor confidence. The principal measures were devaluation of the rupee by some 20 per cent, the abolition of export subsidies, and an increase of 30 per cent in fertilizer prices in order to reduce subsidies. The longer term aim of the government was no less than the transformation of the state-driven economy into a market-driven one, integrated into the world economy. The key reform here was the bringing forward of a new industrial policy that abolished across a broad front the licensing system that for some four decades had required permission of the state for establishing and expanding industrial capacity. Henceforth, no administrative permission was necessary for entrepreneurs to enter, expand, and diversify in the industrial arena. Further, marking a reorientation of the national economic posture, the new industrial policy widened the sphere open to the private sector, making available to it several areas hitherto reserved exclusively for the public sector (such as steel, aircraft, and shipbuilding). In the future, only eight (later reduced further to six) core areas relating to strategic, infrastructure, and high technology industries were reserved for the public sector. Besides, the state also promised to bring about partial privatization of the public sector to the extent of 49 per cent of equity of particular firms. This was, however, less a genuine attempt at reducing or reforming the public sector and more an effort at resource mobilization in order to control the fiscal deficit. In any case, movement on privatization has been limited and halting.

Though trade reform for the moment remained modest, the government was intent on redirecting the economy on an outward-oriented course. Finance Minister Manmohan Singh openly declared that the aim of the new government was to integrate India into the world economy. Globalization and liberalization became the new watchwords. It was not clear, however, whether the government was carried away by a mindless rush to do the opposite of what had been done in the past, or it genuinely felt that policies in the name of the new slogans would actually serve India's interests. In the latter case, interests apparently would be taken to be determining and would lead to the modification of policies, if necessary for the sake of interests. It is noteworthy that, regardless of the assessment of the merits of the liberalization effort, this radical instalment of economic reform was made in the context of an economic crisis.

The shipping industry largely welcomed the new outward orientation, viewing the expected expansion in India's international trade in the future as beneficial for it. As a result, share prices of shipping stocks rose. Furthermore, the devaluation enabled the shipping companies to earn higher profits because of the lower value of the rupee. Meanwhile, as foreign exchange reserves improved because of loans from the IMF and World Bank and the inflow of funds, the government agreed to make available foreign exchange to cover 30 per cent of the cost of ships, provided the companies arranged for the remainder through their own sources or raised commercial loans abroad.[10] In addition to these spill-over effects from the general economic liberalization, the state also pursued liberalization specifically in reference to the shipping industry. Here, liberalization was energetically pressed forward by a young dynamic leader who was put in charge of the Ministry of Surface Transport, Jagdish Tytler. Some considered him to be the most committed to liberalization after Finance Minister Manmohan Singh and Commerce Minister P. Chidambaran.

Ships and Ship Finance

The Partial Dismantlement of Controls

As with the economy in general, there was a dismantlement of a large part of the regulatory framework for shipping; indeed, Transport Minister Tytler claimed in early 1995 that his ministry had "totally changed the direction in shipping from total control to total de-regulation and liberalization".[11] Key to the deregulation was the concept of automatic approval. The state agreed to automatically provide licences to applicants for purchase in respect of all categories of ships, except for crude oil tankers and offshore supply vessels (OSVs). Further, shipping companies were allowed to acquire vessels through cross-border leasing arrangements. Foreign investors were allowed to own shipping companies in India to the extent of 100 per cent of equity; however, foreign investment of over 51 per cent of equity required prior approval. To facilitate access to foreign financing by Indian shipowners, the Merchant Shipping Act was amended to allow foreign creditors to seize Indian ships mortgaged to them, in the event of failure to pay back the loans, without having to go through the Indian court system. When they sold ships to foreign buyers, Indian companies were now allowed to retain the sales proceeds abroad for limited periods to use towards making new purchases. Indian companies were also no longer required to obtain permission of the state to charter out their vessels abroad. Since it would affect their own business interests in the national trades, Indian shipowners have not pressed for similar freedom from approval of the state for chartering in foreign vessels. Permission for sale or scrapping of ships was promised to be forthcoming within two weeks of application.

Although the *pari passu* obligation in terms of compulsory purchase of ships from Indian shipyards has not been abolished, the state has not been too active in enforcing it in view of the difficulties of the local yards to meet the requirements of the shipowners and the delays in delivery.[12] Meanwhile, shipowners have been allowed to apply to the Reserve Bank of India for permission to use foreign exchange without any upper limit for repairs abroad. Consistent with the general guidelines on privatization in the public sector, privatization of SCI up to 49 per cent of equity was promised. In 1991-92, 18.5 per cent of SCI's equity was sold to public financial institutions, while sale of another 10 per cent was envisaged for 1995. The proceeds of these sales of equity, however, go to the general revenues of the central government, rather than the company, in order to reduce the fiscal deficit. Besides, as long as the state retains 51 per cent of the equity, that will enable the ministry to continue to exercise control over SCI at the cost of the latter's managerial autonomy.

As part of the delicensing thrust, the new regulations allowed any shipping company to enter liner routes where existing companies were not already licensed to operate vessels. With the virtual demise of Scindia and the decline of India Steamship, SCI is literally the sole liner company representing Indian shipping, but it has already preempted all the main liner routes. When it has been suggested that all liner routes be thrown open to all Indian companies, as they are to all foreign companies in any case, SCI has put up resistance on the ground that the idea is hypothetical since no Indian company is presently interested in liner shipping. It would seem nonetheless that the restrictive provision acts as a barrier to entry for any company eager to rise to the challenge in the future. As regards coastal shipping, the state withdrew controls over routes and rates for Indian companies. In a major break with the past, it also relaxed the cabotage laws to permit foreign container companies to aggregate cargo from coastal ports, provided the cargo was intended for mainline vessels visiting Indian ports.

With the adoption of the various liberalization measures, a sea change in the regulatory framework for shipping was apparent. Though not fully, Indian shipowners had been given the freedom to buy and sell ships seemingly comparable to shipowners elsewhere. However, the picture was not as liberal as it would appear at first glance. For one thing, tankers for crude oil lay outside the freedom granted. This had been done probably to protect the interests of SCI, which has had a near monopoly of the carriage of crude oil imports. Even though the private sector is not excluded from the oil trade, "the company's tankers are given preferential treatment in government chartering and only if the SCI cannot provide a suitable tanker are the private tankers hired".[13] However, private shipowners have been insistent that the oil trade should be opened to all *Indian* shipowners, for the country is paying the penalty of higher transport costs because of the cost-plus formula.[14]

Furthermore, some of the reforms have been enacted on a discretionary basis; for example, the policy allowing chartering out of ships is for one year at a time and is renewed annually. More importantly, the automatic licensing system has not been as automatic as has been suggested, because the ministry has continued to exercise control under the cover of new guidelines. Indeed, industry representatives have complained of the resurfacing of licensing by the backdoor through the imposition of "conditionalities" while providing automatic clearance. As INSA has pointed out:

> it is the experience of the shipping companies that instead of liberalizing the procedure for acquisition, a number of additional conditions are now being stipulated by the Ministry of Surface Transport in granting approvals even under what is termed as 'automatic clearance procedure'. It is a matter of concern that in the context of further liberalization of the Ex-Im policy, under the automatic clearance system, further restrictions should be sought to be imposed even placing the pre-condition of restricting the trading operation of ships proposed to be acquired. As is known, Sec[tion] 42 of the M.S. Act has been amended removing the requirement to obtain prior approval of the Government

> for acquiring ships except under emergencies. While the licensing for import of ships under the Ex-Im policy 1992-1997 has removed any licensing requirement for import of coastal ships, in the case of ocean going ships imports are permitted without a licence from the DGFT on the basis of approval or guidelines issued by MOST as per Clause 78 of the new Hand Book of Procedures. As the automatic approval system was specifically intended as a measure of liberalization and simplification of procedure, it is very necessary to ensure that such pre-conditions are not imposed in granting approvals for ship acquisition under this scheme.[15]

Besides, the bureaucracy's mind set is said to have not changed; its acceptance of the reforms has been grudging and it has continued to see its role as determining what should or should not be allowed to occur. There has been resistance to allowing the free operation of market forces on the part of decision-makers in the ministry, the Directorate General of Shipping, and SCI, who believe that there should be an overall determination of the types and number of vessels to be acquired and specific permission accorded as to who should be allowed to acquire them. The SCI, in particular, has been the home of shipping nationalism. Captain P.P. Radhakrishnan, its chairman and managing director from 1991 to 1995, often expressed scepticism about the virtues of what he regarded as reckless liberalization. In his opinion, the purpose of the merchant fleet is to serve the national interest, and he reminded his audiences that all nations exercise control over shipping to that end. He was particularly opposed to the mushrooming of shipping companies with one or two ships, which led to the fragmentation of the national fleet among a large number of small operators who did not have the capacity to meet the challenge from foreign carriers. Additionally, he strongly supported cargo reservation for the local industry.[16]

Notwithstanding the doubts and the hesitancy, the reforms have nonetheless meant loss of power for the bureaucracy to the extent that there has been a shift from the state-driven nature of the industry until 1990 to a market-driven industry since then. However, simply to enact measures of liberalization or to partially withdraw from a licensing role is not painful financially for the state, for they do not cost anything. The more important question is as to what responsibilities the state continues to shoulder to aid the industry more positively. Here, it would seem that the state has either shed its role as a provider of concessional finance or continues to be seriously constrained from helping the industry by the shortage of foreign exchange.

THE END OF CONCESSIONAL FINANCE

In the midst of the financial debacle that Indian shipping encountered during the second phase of the shipping depression in the 1980s, the state undertook a major review of financing for shipping. In 1986, it decided to abolish the Shipping Development Fund Committee (SDFC) under the Ministry of Surface Transport, until then the principal funding agency for shipping. Instead, a new agency with a more commercial orientation to lending, the Shipping Credit and Investment Company of India (SCICI), was created to take over SDFC's function of serving the financial needs specifically of shipping in the private sector. The state itself thus got out of the business of providing concessional finance to the industry in the private sector. The mandate of SCICI, which came into existence in 1986, was three-fold: to work out a rehabilitation programme for shipping companies that had turned sick during the depression; to recover the principal and interest that the companies owed the state; and to provide development financing for the shipping sector.[17]

After a review of the financial situation of the shipping companies, SCICI selected 17 companies which were sick but considered to be potentially viable, and developed a restructuring programme for them. The chief mechanisms for rehabilitation were the reduction of the debt of the companies to the market value of their fleets and the capitalization of their overdue interest payments. In this task, SCICI was remarkably successful. By 1991, most of the companies had been turned around and had begun making their loan repayments to the state regularly, some indeed on an accelerated basis. A notable exception was the Scindia Steam Navigation Company, which was taken to be a special case because of the gravity of its financial problems. While the rehabilitation package had no doubt been useful, the recovery of the companies was in considerable measure due to the revival of shipping markets around the world.

In view of the huge investment made by the state by way of loans and guarantee assistance to shipping companies, the task of recovery of the debt was a challenging one for SCICI. By March 31, 1987, such loans and assistance amounted to Rs. 8,160 million while a sum of Rs. 3,190 million was overdue in payments for principal and interest. By 1992, this task had largely been accomplished, either by the sale of assets of both viable and non-viable companies or by routinizing recoveries from the rehabilitated companies. A sum of Rs. 3,865 million had been recovered by March 31 of that year.

In its developmental role, SCICI initially adopted the formula of 20:40:40 for lending. Under the formula, shipping companies were required to contribute 20 per cent of the purchase price of a vessel from their own resources. Of the remainder, SCICI was to provide half of it as a rupee loan for up to 15 years at an interest rate of 7.5 per cent. This interest rate was below market rates because of a marginal subsidy from the state amounting to 5 per cent; even this small subsidy subsequently became a casualty of liberalization as the state withdrew most subsidies. SCICI was to arrange the other half as a commercial loan from foreign sources. On such foreign commercial loans, SCICI charged an extra spread of 1.5 per cent, which industry sources considered to be excessive. SCICI worked with a debt equity ratio of 4:1 but intended to bring it down to 3:1, and perhaps even lower to 2:1. The low debt equity ratio was perceived to be both a commercially prudent measure and also an incentive for the industry to rely on the capital market for raising resources.

The industry regarded the total package as a good mix of equity contribution, partially subsidized rupee loan, and commercial foreign loan. The large component of domestic finance (60 per cent) was considered a good protection against foreign exchange fluctuations.[18] Then, suddenly, on instructions from the Ministry of Finance, in order to reduce the draft on its foreign exchange resources, the formula was changed to 20:20:60, where the commercial foreign loan was to constitute 60 per cent of the cost of the vessel as against the earlier 40 per cent. In the words of an industry leader: "This has substantially increased the financing cost of vessels eroding seriously even the marginal benefit of low interest on rupee loans by exposing shipping companies to risk of higher currency fluctuations and thus higher rupee cost of debt servicing of foreign exchange loans".[19] Besides holding the drastic change to be counter-productive, he also objected to the provision incorporated in loan agreements that allowed SCICI to convert part of the loans into equity at far below market prices.

TABLE 7.1: SCICI LOANS (RS. MILLION)

	Sanctions			*Disbursals*		
		Share of Shipping			*Share of Shipping*	
Year	*Total*	*Amount*	*%*	*Total*	*Amount*	*%*
1988	1,438.4	978.3	68.0	605.0	536.0	88.6
1989	3,119.7	2,513.6	80.6	1,379.0	1,250.1	90.7
1990	3,211.7	2,880.5	89.7	2,257.2	2,182.4	96.7
1991	3,315.8	2,553.3	77.0	1,670.0	1,392.0	83.4
1992	4,090.0	2,985.1	72.9	1,709.1	1,288.4	75.4
1993	7,608.5	2,343.3	30.8	4,862.8	3,195.4	65.7
1994	16,983.3	5,718.1	33.7	10,066.3	5,179.1	51.5
1995	37,198.1	5,502.8	14.8	14,406.6	3,160.1	21.9
Total	76,965.5	25,475.0	33.1	36,955.9	18,183.3	49.2

Source: SCICI, *Annual Reports* (for the years 1988 to 1995). Figures are for fiscal year ending March 31.

More importantly, SCICI's self-definition of its role underwent a major change. Initially, SCICI was to be the nodal agency for providing development finance for Indian shipping. Shortly after its establishment, SCICI began to diversify its activities beyond shipping, partly to reduce its exposure because of the cyclical nature of the industry. But gradually, even as SCICI continued to proclaim shipping to be a priority, the industry was eclipsed in its profile of activities. By 1995, shipping's share in loans sanctioned had come down to less than 15 per cent, and in loans disbursed to about 22 per cent, from the high point in 1990 when it was 90 per cent or over (see Table 7.1). Indeed, chemicals as well as other services had higher shares in loans sanctioned than shipping in 1995. Significantly, there was also reconceptualization by SCICI of its main mission as it "consciously shifted its emphasis from providing loan finance for shipping projects to being an arranger of funds for shipping projects".[20] The developmental role of SCICI in shipping had thus become limited largely to an occasional seminar during a fiscal year. The Ministry of Surface Transport objected to the transformation of SCICI's role, but without much impact.[21]

The industry has, as a consequence, watched with dismay and concern the narrowing, indeed closure, of access to development finance. As the industry's mouthpiece maintained in 1994:

> gradually over the years, the developmental role of SCICI has been diluted with the consequence that shipping no longer has the support of a nodal developmental financing agency.... presently it has increasingly assumed the role of a commercial bank and the terms and conditions of its financing to shipping industry are less developmental and more market oriented with its shipping portfolio currently reduced to less than 40 per cent. The terms currently offered by SCICI are not more favourable than those provided by other Indian developmental institutions and commercial banks.
>
> .... The terms of the facilities offered however do not reflect a developmental role.... it is relevant to note that from its association with the shipping industry by converting a large portion of loans into equity on favourable terms, SCICI has also been substantially benefited.[22]

Even if its share has gone down in the total SCICI portfolio, shipping cannot be said to have suffered in absolute terms. On the contrary, in the three years from 1993 to 1995, loans to it increased substantially over the previous three years. Of course, the comparison may not be fair in that the earlier three years saw a severe foreign exchange constraint as a result of the balance of payments crisis. Indeed, that last fact points up what has been the single most critical factor influencing tonnage acquisition in India, apart from the condition of the market.

THE FOREIGN EXCHANGE CONUNDRUM

The lack of foreign exchange has been a perennial problem for Indian shipping, and has acted as a powerful constraint on the industry in its endeavour to expand the fleet. That it is a powerful constraint can be easily demonstrated. The capacity of the Indian shipyards to supply vessels of the quality and at the competitive prices that the shipping industry wants is limited. The industry has therefore perforce to purchase ships abroad. But, working under a controlled foreign exchange regime it cannot just go abroad and purchase them. Rather, it has had to obtain the permission of the state, in one form or another, to do so. Until 1991, the Ship Acquisition Licensing Committee granted permission to individual companies to acquire vessels but only within the limits of the amount of foreign exchange (FE) allocated to it by the Ministry of Finance. The allocation of foreign exchange, in turn, has depended on the situation in respect of the country's FE reserves. The impact of shortage of foreign exchange is thus immediate. Take, for example, the severe balance of payments crisis in 1990 and 1991. The two years saw gross (as against net) additions to the merchant fleet drop dramatically to 166,315 grt and 137,633 grt, respectively, from 407,521 grt in 1989, only to rise to 551,756 grt with the easing of the crisis in 1992 (see Table 7.4).

For the Indian shipping industry, foreign exchange is a critical bottleneck that determines the limits of its growth. On the other hand, the industry sees itself as part of the solution. It casts the state as an uncomprehending, wooden bureaucratic apparatus that refuses to exploit the industry's potential for contributing to the country's FE earnings. For years, the industry has maintained that it has been a net contributor annually to the FE pool. Not only that, its leaders have pointed out that "not many, outside our industry, are aware that shipping is the largest earner of net foreign currency revenue".[23] The industry has argued that on the average a new ship pays for itself in eight years from its own earnings whereas its normal life is about twenty years. That means that the ship could not

TABLE 7.2: FOREIGN EXCHANGE EARNINGS/SAVINGS BY INDIAN SHIPPING (RS. MILLION)

Year	*FE Earnings/ Savings*	*FE Expenses*	*Net Operating Surplus*	*Finan-cial Costs*	*Net Inflows*
1984-85	9,718.0	7,475.5	2,242.4		
1985-86	12,313.6	9,634.3	2,679.2		
1986-87	12,615.9	8,964.1	3,651.8		
1987-88	12,174.0	7,394.5	4,779.4		
1988-89	13,345.6	6,624.1	6,721.5		
1989-90	19,867.2	7,199.1	12,668.1	1,076.9	11,591.2
1990-91	21,864.4	9,201.4	12,663.0	955.3	11,707.7
1991-92	26,980.9	10,454.6	16,526.3	950.5	15,575.8
1992-93	31,760.7	12,378.9	19,381.8	1,296.1	18,085.7
1993-94	42,850.0	12,966.0	29,884.0	1,397.9	28,486.1
1994-95	42,060.6	13,233.2	28,827.4	2,296.6	26,530.8

Source: INSA, "Incentives to Indian Shipping: INSA Plea to Government", *Indian Shipping,* vol. 41, no. 12 (1989), pp. 7-14; INSA, *Annual Review 1993-94,* p. 47; and INSA, *Annual Review 1994-95,* p. 48.

Notes: (1) Net Operating Surplus = FE Earnings/Savings minus FE Expenses. (2) Net Inflows = Net Operating Surplus minus Financial Costs. (3) FE Earnings/Savings includes Sales Proceeds of Ships which for each of the years from 1990-91 to 1994-95 were 76.1, 518.4, 955.5, 8088.7, and 4208.5 million rupees. (4) The figures for 1989-90 to 1994-95 are based on statistics from varying numbers of companies, usually between 10 and 20, covering about 80 per cent or over of the fleet and pro-rated for the total fleet.

but add to the FE earnings of the country. Further, the industry has provided data documenting its point about the substantial contribution that shipping makes to the FE pool of the country (see Table 7.2). For instance, in each of the two years 1993-94 and 1994-95, the net FE inflows on account of shipping services are estimated to be about Rs. 27 billion. However, the state has usually downplayed the industry's claim, holding it to be exaggerated in its assessment of shipping's contribution in that it lumps together net earnings actually made in foreign currency and assumed savings in foreign exchange that would not have been possible were Indian tonnage not in existence. On the face of it, that is not a strong counterpoint, since the country would have to pay out in foreign exchange to foreign carriers if Indian tonnage were not available.

More recently, the state-established public financial institution, SCICI, has in a study based on computer models upheld the industry's position. It has estimated the number of years it takes for a vessel to pay for itself, and the multiples it earns in foreign exchange in the course of its lifetime over the costs in foreign exchange in acquiring it. A new product tanker of 30,000 dwt would pay for its FE costs in 6.6 years and earn 4.1 times the value of such costs, whereas the figures for a new bulk carrier of 60,000 dwt were 8.1 years and 4.0 times (see Table 7.3). There were substantial gains in foreign exchange no matter what the age of the vessel at the time of purchase. SCICI concluded:

> Contrary to the general impression the acquisition of ships from abroad comes through, on careful analysis, as one of the most liquid means of utilization of our external reserves. Given the country's external trade volume which need to be serviced by sea cargo service, the country has the compulsion of spending on ship freight which would be only in foreign exchange except to the extent Indian ships are used. The earnings of Indian ships by carriage of Indian cargo, even though it might be denominated in rupees, should, therefore, count as earning in foreign exchange, or at the very least, direct saving of foreign exchange. This goes for oceangoing merchant shipping, offshore oil support services and coastal shipping.[24]

Long before the findings of this study appeared, the industry had appealed to the state for the setting up of a special FE fund to which its FE earnings would be credited, and which it could then freely avail of in the acquisition of ships. The state has invariably dismissed such pleas. Industry sources have often cited Finance Minister Manmohan Singh using before them the analogy of the Punjabi farmer to dismiss any special consideration for shipping. He is said to have maintained that the Punjabi farmer also could claim special access to foreign exch-

TABLE 7.3: FOREIGN EXCHANGE SAVINGS IN SHIP ACQUISITION

	Age (Years)	*FE Capital Outflow (Cost of Acquisition) (Rs. Mill.)*	*Pay-back Period for FE Capital Outflow (Years)*	*Multiple of Foreign Currency Earnings Over FE Outflow*
Product Tanker 30000 DWT	New	323.8	6.64	4.15
Bulk Carrier 60000 DWT	New	423.4	8.12	4.02
Product Tanker	4	282.3	5.67	3.08
Bulk Carrier	4	332.1	5.93	3.83
Product Tanker	8	257.4	5.18	1.91
Bulk Carrier	8	282.3	5.04	2.76

Source: "Overview of Indian Shipping: SCICI's Survey", *Indian Shipping,* vol. 42, nos. 2-3 (1990), pp. 19-26.

ange on the ground that by creating food surpluses for the country he is saving foreign exchange. It would have been a legitimate question for the industry to have raised, however, whether the two cases were really equivalent. For, Indian shipping has to compete with foreign shipping at freight rates determined by the international market whereas the Indian farmer, with his agricultural inputs heavily subsidized by the state, produces for a protected market with high support prices set by the state. The analogy is patently mistaken.

The shipping industry has also asked that it be accorded the status of an export-oriented industry. Such a status would enable it to benefit from export promotion subsidies and also entitle it to claim part of its FE earnings for its import needs. However, the industry's pleas have met with a cold reception.

Regardless, the liberalization programme in the 1990s began in the context of a FE crisis and was meant to relieve it. Although for a couple of years, shipping benefited from the easing of the FE situation, there has been no end to the foreign exchange constraint. At one point, the state asked the industry to raise its FE requirements through commercial loans, but effective January 1995 it placed a "cap" (ceiling) for several months on external commercial borrowings (ECB) in view of the rising short-term foreign debt. Under this new action, the Ministry of Finance barred approval of applications from both public sector enterprises and private companies to borrow abroad; only financial institutions were permitted to borrow, but even for them there was a ceiling of $250 million. INSA noted: "it is understood that ECB clearance will not be given to any fresh proposals of shipping companies for external currency borrowings for acquisition of ships during the period. As such, it would appear that up to end March 1995, the acquisition programmes of Indian shipping companies would come to a halt and the position even thereafter remains uncertain".[25]

Subsequently, greater uncertainty was added to the acquisition programme of shipping companies. New ECB guidelines promulgated by the Ministry of Finance in February 1995, and then repeated in May 1995, limited access to loans of up to US$15 million only if their maturity period was a minimum of three years; loans of over $15 million were required to have a maturity period of at least seven years. They further specified priority for allocation of ECB to the power sector and export-oriented companies and projects.[26] Shipping was not recognized as an export-oriented industry. These actions are, again, an illustration of how the acquisition programme of the industry is fundamentally a hostage to the foreign exchange constraint. What the episode underlines is the fact that the state's newly-acquired expectation that the industry should in the age of globalization and liberalization compete with foreign carriers is not matched by its recognition of the disparity in constraints to which the industry is exposed in the competition and, better still, by its doing something about it.

THE ABSENCE OF A LEVEL PLAYING FIELD

The notion of liberalization has implied the reduction of state intervention in economic affairs, leaving the arena to market forces where economic actors would compete on the basis of their resource endowments. The argument put forward in behalf of liberalization is that it advances societal welfare because of the greater efficiency that competition fosters. Of course, in the competition presumably the more efficient enterprises would emerge as victors. Though made in the name of efficiency, however, the argument often comes from those who are already strong, economically and politically, and are not necessarily or inherently more efficient.

Such strength on the part of economic actors has at times been acquired through protectionist measures in the first place. Note that Great Britain as the country that pioneered liberalism in the industrial age--a liberalism that was then emulated by others or was forced on them--shifted to it only after a long period of mercantilist policy. That move, indeed, was based on "the confidence that British technological and industrial supremacy was so great that she need fear no rivals".[27] In view of the threat that British supremacy thus posed to their industry and industrial aspirations, lesser developed countries formulated the infant industry argument as a counter-proposition in order to provide protection to local industry until such time as it was strong enough to stand on its own feet and compete with British industry. This initiative represented an effort on the part of weaker economies to create an even playing field through the deliberate mechanism of state policy that sought to bolster local industry. In the specific case of Indian shipping under the colonial state, Mahatma Gandhi had underlined the farcical aspect of the British motivated penchant for laissez faire and competition by drawing a contrast between the British giant and the Indian dwarf.[28] He had thus emphasized the need for an even playing field and for a certain equivalence in strength among economic rivals if the competition was to be regarded as fair.

What is striking, however, is that protectionism among the industrially advanced states in regard to shipping is not a policy simply of the past but continues to prevail in the very present. Many OECD countries follow restrictive policies on cabotage and cargo reservation and provide many subsidies of different kinds to their shipping industries.[29] This is patently clear in the case of the United States.[30] However, the conception of protection for the national merchant fleet has to be extended to encompass the policy in respect of flags of convenience (FOCs) and international registries. For, the intent of such regime-transforming policy is to defeat the competition from those who would otherwise have a comparative advantage if shipping operated solely under an international regime where there was a genuine link between ownership and the national flag of vessels. The competitiveness of western shipping is enhanced through such mechanisms as open and international registries, making for the potent combination of western capital and technology with low-cost labour from the lesser developed countries. Over 37 per cent of the world's tonnage today is under FOCs.[31] Protectionist policies, subsidies and FOCs all powerfully underline the fundamental point that liberalism is not an end in itself but is a means to an end, which in a territorially divided world is defined by national power and welfare.

In line with that last point, the basic question to address therefore in any analysis of liberalization is whether it is being pursued mindlessly for its own sake or to subserve the national interest. It is a basic presumption here that--for a country of India's size and population, its strategic compulsions, and the serious drain of economic surplus because of import of shipping services--a merchant fleet is an essential national requirement. Consequently, the standard for assessing state policy cannot be simply whether the state has reduced its role in shipping affairs. That, no doubt, is important, especially if the role has been a negative one, even if in its origins it was positive. Rather, the standard ought to be whether, without excessive cost to the rest of the economy, the policy promotes the growth of the national fleet, adequate to assure for it a legitimate share in its own and world trades, or at least that it sees to it that there is an even playing field for its national carriers in competition with foreign operators.

Several aspects are relevant in regard to providing an even playing field, but in an industry which is as highly capital-intensive as shipping the primary one pertains to capital, for without capital there can be no ships to carry cargo. It is well known that a substantial part of the costs of shipping companies are capital costs. Here, shipping companies in India are clearly at a disadvantage compared to their foreign counterparts.

Perhaps because of the worldwide competitive nature of the shipping industry, the rate of profit is low in the industry as if in fulfilment of Marx's prediction of the falling rate of profit in competitive capitalism. There is a story well known in shipping circles in which an aspiring entrepreneur asks a veteran of the shipping industry a sharp question with a view to entering it: "Is it possible to make a small fortune in shipping?" The answer comes: "Yes--if you start with a big one". On account of the low profit rate in the industry, states that are eager to maintain a merchant fleet provide financial and cargo support through a wide repertoire of mechanisms, which are not always apparent, in order to lower the cost of capital and to make the industry attractive for investors.

In the matter of attracting capital, a capital-short country like India presents special problems for the industry. Capital costs are steeper for Indian companies, making competition tougher for them in world shipping. The higher incidence of capital costs is evident in several respects.[32] Interest rates in India are far higher than in OECD countries, perhaps twice as much if not higher. At the same time, it is difficult for shipping companies to mobilize funds from the market because of the high dividend expectations of Indian investors. Whereas western investors may be happy with dividends of 10 to 12 per cent, Indian investors want dividends of about 20 per cent net of taxes, not irrationally given the high interest rates. Further, Indian shipowners are at a relative disadvantage when they have to obtain loans abroad; as against the spread of 1.5 per cent for foreign shipowners, the spread for Indian shipowners is about 2.5 per cent. Thus, capital costs for Indian shipowners are higher and tend to make their operations less competitive. Moreover, since the Indian rupee has been progressively depreciating over the years (roughly, from Rs. 8 to one US dollar in 1980 to Rs. 35 in 1995 and to Rs. 38 in early 1996), it correspondingly erodes the reserves of Indian shipowners for purchase of foreign vessels. It is apparent, then, that the Indian shipowner faces a highly uneven playing field, especially in the context of liberalization. As a senior manager in the industry expressed it:

> With integration into the global economy an Indian shipping company has to contend with a situation where the foreign competitor appears to have all the cards stacked in his favour--the ability to raise equity resources in the international markets at lower costs than his Indian counterpart, the freedom to choose his flag and crew, the flexibility to opportunistically time his investment decisions to enjoy the freedom to independently decide the type and age of his ship and the ability to raise commercial loans on far more favourable terms.[33]

Earlier, before globalization and liberalization, certain practices existed that neutralized the comparative disadvantage of the Indian shipowner. Among these were the generous financial assistance provided by the state for tonnage acquisition, cargo support because of strong conferences, and lower-cost manpower. These have now either disappeared or become seriously attenuated (see below on cargo support and manpower). Especially noteworthy is the withdrawal of the state from the provision of financial assistance to the industry. As one study of the industry maintains, "concessional finance has almost disappeared and there is hardly any tax incentive". In addition, the state withdrew from providing guarantees and counter-guarantees, which added to the reluctance of foreign banks to lend to Indian shipowners. The latter had to depend on local banks for guarantees, which increased the capital cost because of the monopoly position of the banks. As a consequence, "while a mechanism, which had helped acquisition of ships in the past, has been dispensed with, there is no substitute mechanism in place".[34]

Not only that, the state has more recently enacted measures that, rather than providing incentives to badly needed investment in shipping, have tended to penalize Indian shipowners and thus deter investment. These have included, for example, the imposition of income tax effective April 1, 1995 on interest payments by Indian shipowners to foreign creditors for external commercial borrowings.[35] The imposition of the tax--or more correctly, the withdrawal of the earlier exemption from paying it--raised the cost of borrowings by 25 per cent, "making such borrowings unviable".[36] Since the payment of this tax would have to come out of the Indian company's funds, it would serve to reduce its profit margins, for shipping is an industry in which freight rates are determined by the international market, not the Indian company or the Indian industry.[37] Besides this tax, the state also levies a tax of 3 per cent on interest payments on loans from financial institutions, which increases the capital costs of Indian companies.

Again, in 1995 the state partially withdrew an incentive, which had been available to Indian shipping companies since 1990, to set aside an amount up to the equivalent of total income in a reserve account for purchase of ships over the subsequent eight years. After 1995, the incentive was restricted to shipping companies and then only for 50 per cent of the income solely from shipping operations, while multipurpose companies were altogether barred from availing of the incentive. If the purpose of the incentive is to build the merchant fleet, for which the state as such no longer provides concessional finance, then the rationale for the action lacks both plausibility and realism in its proffered explanation: "There is no justification for allowing deduction with reference to income from activities other than operation of ships. Further, the present 100 per cent deduction is excessive keeping in view *the improved situation in the shipping industry*".[38]

Still again, the rate of depreciation for ships has been placed at 20 per cent of the written down value of the assets while it is 25 per cent for plant and machinery in other industries, which are subject to less wear and tear compared to ships. Interestingly, for other types of carriers, such as aircraft and motor vehicles, the depreciation rate is 40 per cent.[39] The industry's demand for treatment similar to that for other carriers, or at least a depreciation of 33.33 per cent, would not seem to be unreasonable. It is noteworthy that in these various aspects the industry has had the support of the Ministry of Surface Transport, but it is a commentary on the relative lack of clout of that ministry that this support has often been ineffectual in the face of Finance Ministry's perception--largely mistaken in the eyes of observers of international shipping--that the industry has been mollycoddled. Not without cause, there has been dismay and disappointment in the industry at the stepmotherly treatment accorded to it by Finance.

It is manifest that the Indian industry is at a serious disadvantage compared to its foreign counterparts, especially FOC operators, in the matter of capital accumulation for the expansion of tonnage. Over and above all the other limitations, however, there is the powerful constraint of the lack of adequate foreign exchange, even in the best of times, which terribly handicaps the Indian industry. It is patently unfair therefore to expect Indian shipowners to compete effectively with foreign shipping, given the domestic environment in which they operate. There is consequently a strong case for the active participation of the state in assuring a level playing field, which not surprisingly has become the foremost demand of the industry in the liberalization period. For the state to refrain from assisting Indian industry in its handicapped situation under the notion of some imagined ideal of liberalism is to be more royal than the king, in view of the protectionist policies of the advanced industrial countries. It is mistaken to assume that market forces in and of themselves would serve the national interests of India when the international market itself is structured against them. Of course, from the perspective of the decision-makers it is far easier to let foreign operators carry an increasing share of India's trade, even if it is costlier for the country's interests over the longer term, than to engage in the more demanding task of actively devising and implementing policies to positively assist the local industry with real resources, institutional and financial.

However, an active policy posture in the age of liberalization does not necessarily mean a replication of policies of other states for construction and operating subsidies. The provision of such subsidies is, in any case, beyond the capacity of the Indian state without harming other desirable economic and social objectives. Nor is it necessary for the state to go into the business of directly providing loans on a case by case basis. Such bureaucratic involvement in the affairs of individual companies is not desirable either. However, far more preferable would be policies on the pattern of the earlier liberal development rebate, reflective of the vision of Lal Bahadur Shastri, which do not call for a direct draft on already collected state revenues. The Indian state need not be squeamish about providing such assistance, since states around the world do so widely. Nor would such policies be unprecedented on the Indian scene, for the state after all provides dispensation from taxation for selected sectors, such as small scale industries or backward districts or export-oriented industries. Such policies may need to be applied discriminatingly in areas of the industry where India is particularly deficient or where returns on investment are marginal, such as cellular containerships and dry bulk carriers. Additionally, it would appear more productive to avoid seemingly petty policies, such as imposing taxes on interest payments on loans. Further, since foreign exchange is a serious bottleneck that strangles the growth of the industry, a more sympathetic attitude is called for towards retention of foreign exchange earnings--even if only of future increments--by the industry for tonnage acquisition, without detailed involvement of the bureaucracy. Policy actions along the aforementioned lines would contribute towards generating movement towards a level playing field.

TONNAGE GROWTH BY REDEFINITION OF NORMATIVE STANDARDS

The economic planners had hoped to increase the national tonnage from 6.36M grt to 7.5M grt during the Seventh Five Year Plan (1985-1990), while transforming the fleet into a modern efficient one by discarding overage vessels and diversifying into specialized and container vessels. Unfortunately, the target of 7.5M grt was the same as that in the Sixth Five Year Plan (1980-1985) but, still, achievement fell far short of the target. Instead of increasing, the tonnage declined by 0.4M grt to 5.9M grt, while no container vessels were added to the fleet. There then followed two years of a planning interregnum as well as economic crisis; meanwhile, the Congress party was replaced by a minority government headed by the National Front coalition. There was little change in tonnage over these two years.

When the Congress party returned to power in mid-1991, it initiated the process of liberalization and also the formulation of the Eighth Five Year Plan (1992-1997). The planners basically followed the Seventh Plan in establishing as their chief objective the "acquisition of a modern, diversified fleet capable of fulfilling the national objective of export promotion and improved balance of payments of the country". They laid down as their target the achievement of a tonnage of 7M grt by the end of the Plan in 1997,[40] a target which was lower than that of the previous plan. Significantly, the tonnage target had remained the same or lower for over 15 years. The planners recognized that 1.9M grt of the existing tonnage--that is, about a third--needed to be replaced because of its being overaged, but they provided for the replacement of only about 1.5M grt during the Eighth Plan because of the resource constraint. They further proposed to add about 1M grt to the tonnage, which would take the total tonnage to 7M grt. They understood Indian ships to be carrying about 36 per cent of the Indian seaborne trade and thought that, while that share was reasonable in POL, "it is not so in bulk carriers (26 per cent as against target of 50 per cent) and liner (21 per cent as against 40 per cent target)". The planners had fixed the tonnage target apparently with a view to raising the Indian share to 45 per cent of the total trade.[41] In the area of containerships, the Tonnage Acquisition Committee recommended acquisition of 36 cellular vessels during the Eighth Plan, of which 26 were to be in the 1400-2000 teus range while the remainder would be feeder vessels of 600 teu each.

While the tonnage target chosen was, indeed, very modest, it still required immense amounts of capital for investment for its achievement. One authoritative source characterized the investment requirements of Rs. 250 billion or US$ 8 billion as simply "colossal".[42] The consensus in the industry was that the target was unachievable, given the huge capital outlays required. Even to meet the Finance Ministry's norms on raising 30 per cent of the investment internally was expected to place a heavy burden on shipping companies by way of domestic resource mobilization to the tune of Rs. 75 billion.[43] A study by the New York investment firm Oppenheimer & Co. concurred, holding that "despite the recent growth, we do not expect the Plan target of 7 million grt to be achieved". In its view, "the biggest problem facing shipping companies continues to be the mobilization of large capital requirements and high financing costs", while "the inability to raise the necessary capital in foreign exchange is the main reason for the anticipated shortfall" in tonnage targets.[44]

The important question remains as to what the achievement has been during the first three years or so of the Eighth Plan. It would seem that Indian shipping has, partly as a result of liberalization, resumed in some measure the path of growth, albeit gradual. In each of the calendar years from 1992 to 1995 there has been a *gross* addition of over half a million grt. The total tonnage had expanded from 5.9M grt on January 1, 1992 to 6.7M grt on July 1, 1995, which until then was the highest figure in the history of Indian shipping, finally passing the previous peak of 6.4M grt in 1985 (see Table 7.4).

The revival of growth has been accompanied by the formation of many new companies, facilitated no doubt by liberalization. There were 73 companies on December 31, 1994 compared to 59 on the same date in 1990.[45] Two of them--Shreyas Shipping, an Indian flag subsidiary of the Bombay-headquartered Transworld Group, and Shahi Shipping--with their serious plans for feeder services to the Gulf ports and Colombo with cellular containerships,[46] represent the new developing face of Indian shipping. Earlier, Indian lines had neglected feeder services. A noteworthy development has been the recent emergence of Madras as a new centre of shipowners, hitherto concentrated in Calcutta and, particularly, Bombay. There has been some inflow of foreign capital, but not much because India is not an attractive destination when compared with the FOC nations. The most important event in Indian shipping since liberalization has been the acquisition by SCI of three containerships of 1870 teu each and their induction into service in 1994 on the India-UK/Continent route. The aim of SCI is to develop a "niche" for itself on this lucrative route rather than a network of services to compete with the major container carriers. For the present, the service has been running at a loss, and there has been some questioning on commercial grounds whether the shareholders--especially with the partial privatization of SCI--should be asked to bear the burden of such losses. The shipping nationalists within SCI, however, maintain that there is no alternative for India but to participate in the container trades. To improve the viability of its container operations, SCI has entered into an agreement with Zim Lines of Israel to offer joint services.[47]

Even though the merchant fleet reached a new peak in 1995, it represented only a marginal improvement over the figure of a decade earlier. Besides, the marginal change affected the various segments of the fleet differently, least of all the overseas fleet. If the figures for 1985 are indexed at 100, then the indices for the total fleet and overseas fleet in 1995 are

TABLE 7.4: TONNAGE IN OPERATION AND GROSS ADDITIONS 1976-1995 (GRT ON JANUARY 1)

Year	*Overseas*	*Coastal*	*OSVs*	*Total*
		Tonnage in Operation		
1976	4,135,566	370,763	-	4,506,329
1980	5,373,863	255,615	-	5,629,478
1985	6,005,585	328,178	30,241	6,364,004
1986	5,672,845	246,399	56,921	5,976,165
1987	5,415,242	312,828	74,807	5,802,877
1988	5,231,819	342,709	100,652	5,675,180
1989	5,145,861	323,305	119,948	5,589,114
1990	5,432,806	321,756	157,412	5,911,974
1991	5,533,447	359,837	163,666	6,056,950
1992	5,378,703	397,077	163,765	5,939,545
1993	5,647,568	481,733	158,382	6,287,683
1994	5,611,425	466,561	175,870	6,253,856
1995	5,663,569	506,822	174,029	6,344,420
1995*	6,015,241	510,178	174,583	6,700,002

* Figures for July 1

105.28 and 100.16, respectively, while those for the coastal fleet and OSV [offshore supply vessel] fleet are 155.46 and 577.31. The expansion of the coastal and OSV fleets has been well deserved, especially in view of the long term decline of the coastal fleet in the past. However, the stagnation in the overseas fleet cannot be said to improve the chances of Indian shipping to enhance its share of foreign trade.

With the merchant fleet at 6.7M grt at mid-1995, the expectation was that the target of 7M grt was within reach of being achieved before the end of the Eighth Plan on March 31, 1997. There was then the further surprising announcement by the government that the target of 7 million grt had, in fact, been

TABLE 7.4A: TONNAGE IN OPERATION AND GROSS ADDITIONS 1976-1995 (GRT ON JANUARY 1)

Year	*Overseas*	*Coastal*	*OSVs*	*Total*
		Gross Additions During Year		
1976	619,050	51,688	-	670,738
1980	245,669	17,372	-	263,041
1985	409,032	4,626	26,680	440,338
1986	319,127	29,572	17,886	366,585
1987	280,722	31,295	25,845	337,862
1988	257,970	7,724	22,826	288,520
1989	368,611	1,446	37,464	407,521
1990	119,945	40,116	6,254	166,315
1991	96,200	41,334	99	137,633
1992	521,714	28,719	1,323	551,756
1993	561,090	9,474	17,488	588,052
1994	450,255	60,466	640	511,361
1995**	389,854	14,133	-	403,987

** Figures for January-June.

Source: INSA, *Annual Review 1994-1995,* p. 43. Figures are for ships of 150 grt and over.

achieved on December 1, 1995, far ahead of schedule.[48] This development raises the intriguing question as to how this feat was accomplished, given the initial scepticism about achieving the target in view of the huge investment required.

Part of the explanation for the ease in achieving the target, it would seem, lay in short-circuiting new investment through verbal redefinition of what needed replacement in the fleet. The state revised the age norms for replacement of ships in the fleet in 1995, so that they could now be employed for a longer duration than before. For example, the age norm for bulk carriers and liner vessels was increased from 20 years to 25 years, while that for OSVs from 16 years to 20 years.[49] The impact of this change in age norms was to instantly reduce the ship replacement requirements to a third of the planned target.[50] Whereas the Eighth Plan had set the target for replacement at 100 ships of 1.41M grt, the revision in the age norms reduced it to 44 ships of 0.52M grt. Thus, the plan targets, which were at one time considered beyond achievement, had been swiftly accomplished ahead of schedule simply by redefinition of norms. While the revision in age norms may not seriously affect the comparative age status of the Indian fleet, since it has been younger (15 years in 1994) relative to the world fleet (17 years), it does not correspond to the Eighth Plan's objective of building a "modern" fleet.[51] This ought to be a matter of some concern, especially since some of India's ships have in recent years been subjected to detention in European ports because of their poor condition--something unheard of in the past. Further, Indian ships have been targeted for priority inspection by E.U. Port State Control Committee and the U.S. Coast Guard.[52] Such actions are, no doubt, reflective of the growing unilateralism in shipping on the part of the developed countries,[53] but Indian policy is likely to make its ships more vulnerable targets for them.

Even if it were to be maintained that earlier age norms were excessive and that the tonnage increase represents real growth, it demonstrates something awry about the calculations of the planners. For, instead of India's share in its cargo trades moving from 36 per cent towards the target of 45 per cent, it has been going the other way. As against 35.5 per cent and 36.7 per cent in 1990-91 and 1991-92, respectively, the share was lower at 34.9 per cent in 1992-93 and still lower at 33.6 per cent in 1993-94. Particularly dismal in the latter two years was the performance in respect of general cargo (14.4 per cent and 8.8 per cent) and dry bulk cargo (23.3 per cent and 20.0 per cent) (see chapter V). Liberalization cannot therefore be said to have sparked any reversal of the decline of India's share in its trades. The industry is thus in need of an active state policy that mitigates its marginalization in shipping. Meanwhile, it seems that one factor in India's failure to improve its share in the various trades has been the progressive erosion of cargo support from the state.

THE DWINDLING CARGO SUPPORT

The acceleration of globalization evident in the rise of container shipping brought about the disintegration of the shipping conferences. The crumbling of the conference system removed the mainstay of cargo support for India's liner shipping and was the chief factor in its decline. The liberalization of the early 1990s further weakened cargo support for Indian shipping by, firstly, "decanalizing" several commodities which were earlier traded on a national aggregated basis through central state agencies and, secondly, by eroding the legitimacy of state-directed cargo support.

Under the command economy, the state "canalized" or arranged for the import and export of several bulk commodities, such as fertilizers or fertilizer raw materials, under its own auspices and then distributed them to intermediate or end users within the country. Trading in these commodities was expected to be conducted on FOB basis for imports and CIF basis for exports, so that India would retain control over their shipping. Such shipping arrangements were handled by the state chartering organization, Transchart, which was more generally responsible for the shipment of all cargo of state agencies and enterprises. Transchart accorded preference to Indian carriers provided their freight rates were competitive. In practice, the system had some serious weaknesses, with some state agencies flouting state policy and making their own direct arrangements for transport while Transchart lacked the power to penalize them for deviating from established norms. However, liberalization delivered a further blow. More than a half-dozen bulk commodities that were earlier canalized under state auspices, such as fertilizer, rock phosphate, newsprint and sulphur, were now thrown open to trading by individual firms, whether in the private sector or public sector. With that, the responsibility for arrangements for shipping them passed into the hands of these firms, and to that extent Transchart lost control over a considerable part of its business. Further, public sector firms took advantage of the new economic climate with its thrust for liberalization to brazenly violate established state policy on FOB and CIF terms in trading, thus shifting Indian cargo to foreign carriers.

The impact on Transchart of the removal of several commodities from the canalized regime is visible in the decline in its share of the cargo. Whereas the average share of Transchart in India's total cargo during the second half of the 1980s was 20.6 per cent. it fell drastically by a third to 13.9 per cent in the first four years of the 1990s; particularly noteworthy is the decline to 11.4 per cent in 1992 and still further to 9.4 per cent in 1993 (see Table 7.5). The decline in the last two years can be attributed to the rapid expansion in trade, but what is striking is the fall in actual tonnage from 21.3 million tons (MT) in 1989 or 18.1 MT in 1990 to 12.9 MT in 1993 and then to 12.5

TABLE 7.5: CARGO HANDLED BY TRANSCHART

		Share of Transchart		*% Share in Transchart Cargo*	
Year	*Total Trade (Mill. Tons)*	*Actual*	*%*	*Indian Vessels*	*Foreign Vessels*
1980	74.9	13.7	18.3	41.5	58.5
1985	86.4	19.9	23.0	57.0	43,0
1986	87.1	16.9	19.4	71.6	28.4
1987	89.9	15.9	17.7	74.5	25.5
1988	101.9	21.3	20.9	58.4	41.6
1989	106.8	23.4	21.9	58.5	41.5
1990	103.4	18.7	18.1	66.4	33.6
1991	103.9	17.4	16.8	61.5	38.5
1992	122.3	13.9	11.4	55.3	44.7
1993	136.9	12.9	9.4	58.8	41.2
1994	Data Missing	12.5	-	57.1	42.9

Source: Figures for 1980 to 1991 are from National Council of Applied Economic Research, *Indian Shipping Industry: Retrospect and Prospect* (New Delhi: NCAER, 1993), pp. 38 and 122. For 1992, see *Indian Shipping,* vol. 46, no. 6 (1994), p. 37; and for 1993 and 1994, see INSA, *Annual Review 1994-1995,* p. 47. Total trade in million tons refers to trade for fiscal year beginning April 1.

MT in 1994. It is quite evident that Transchart's role has quickly and quite dramatically diminished. While the industry also claims that there has been a decline in the share of Indian vessels in the cargo handled by Transchart, the contrast between the liberalization years since 1991--limited in number in any case--and the earlier period does not seem sharp enough.

"Decanalization" was not the only element to affect Transchart's role. The Ministry of Commerce also initiated a move to have the state repeal the directive on FOB and CIF terms in respect of government cargo,[54] instituted as far back as 1957, which it and its supporters now regarded as anachronistic in the new era of liberalization. The ministry went one step further and mooted the idea that, with the country taking to the path of liberalization, there was no longer the need for a central organization for coordinating shipping arrangements for government cargo, and called for the abolition of Transchart.[55] Moreover, it advocated that individual state agencies should have the freedom to decide on whether FOB or CIF terms were desirable rather than be bound by national guidelines. In this, it had the support of many ministries, which were anxious for their own public sector enterprises to assume control in the matter of shipment of their cargoes. The issue was framed in terms of acquiring administrative flexibility in shipping arrangements, but observers saw a grab for patronage in the plan to dismantle Transchart as a transparent and effective organization working in the national interest.

After several years of debate at the highest levels within the government, the cabinet decided in early 1996 to affirm existing policy and reject the move to abolish Transchart or to modify the guidelines on FOB and CIF terms.[56] The affirmation of policy represented a rearguard action to save some semblance of cargo support, which was otherwise rapidly eroding. It was a moment for the Ministry of Surface Transport to savour its first victory in a long time in its contention with the Ministry of Commerce, even if it was only to prevent the overthrow of established policies and institutions. The explanation for the victory lay, ironically, in the same phenomenon that has impeded tonnage expansion--the shortage of foreign exchange. With the rupee fast depreciating in the last months of 1995 and early months of 1996 and the balance of payments situation under pressure, the government was loath to endorse further drain of foreign exchange. It still remains to be seen how effectively the new instructions will be followed, for even in the past state agencies found ways to bypass policy on the issue. Even if fully implemented, it would only preserve an already-circumscribed area of cargo support, not widen it. Attempts in the direction of the latter have invariably been marked by failure.

In the 1970s and 1980s, the Ministry of Surface Transport had failed in its endeavours to establish cargo support for India's liner shipping on a statutory basis after the 40:40:20 formula of the UNCTAD Liner Code. With SCI bringing into service its three newly-acquired cellular container vessels in 1994--"Indira Gandhi", "Lal Bahadur Shastri", and "Rajiv Gandhi"--the issue of cargo reservation again came to the fore. The ministry put forward with considerable fanfare a plan--known as the "modified cargo support scheme"--to establish committees at each of the major ports to ensure that India's liner shipping was progressively allocated an increasing share. The aim was to quickly reach the UNCTAD norm of 40 per cent of the country's liner cargo in freight value terms. In the first stage, the plan was to be implemented in three important trades, hoping to increase India's share to 30 per cent (from the prevailing 18.3 per cent) in the India-UK/Continent trade, to 20 per cent (from 10.2 per cent) in the India-Japan/Far East trade, and to 25 per cent (from 16.2 per cent) in the India-US/Canada trade. The committees at the ports were to consist of representatives from INSA, Indian shipping lines, and regional shippers organizations.[57] The plan avoided the term "reservation", apparently since it was seen as inconsistent with the general zeal for liberalization, and was characterized as "cargo support through voluntary action by shippers".[58]

While the plan raised hopes at SCI, it met the same fate as earlier schemes that sought to establish cargo reservation. At one time, it was given out that the plan had the approval of the Ministry of Commerce. However, there was a howl of protest from shippers. Acting on behalf of their interests, Commerce quickly scuttled the whole plan by declaring that it was meant to be implemented on a voluntary basis, which is to say that there was to be no plan at all. For, where there is no teeth, there can be no bite. The shippers had a big laugh at the naivete of the Ministry of Surface Transport. The pleas of the shipping industry that all countries provided cargo support for their shipping through open and hidden ways fell on deaf ears.

THE LOSS OF COMPARATIVE ADVANTAGE IN MANPOWER

Up to the time of the OPEC price hikes, India had a comparative advantage in manpower because of its low-cost labour. That element compensated for the country's many other constraints and made its shipping competitive in the world. The breakdown of the conference system, the increased resort to FOCs, and the opening of second or international registries that followed in the wake of oil price hikes manifested the acceleration of globalization in shipping. The escalation in globalization had a significant impact on India's human resources in the shipping industry. However, this impact did not become manifest until the shipping depression had ended in 1987.

As late as 1987, a state-appointed committee had commented on the manpower surplus being generated by India's training institutions, stating:

> these training institutions have churned out officers in such large numbers that they cannot be absorbed by the Indian fleet. As a result, there is a surplus of trained officers despite the fact that a number of Indian officers are employed on foreign flag vessels. Similarly, India also has facilities for training crew and presently, despite the fact that a number of Indian ratings are employed in foreign flag ships, there is a large surplus.[59]

As the depression lifted in 1987, the revival of the world's shipping markets sparked an exodus of officers and crew from India to foreign flag fleets. Part of the reason for the exodus was not only the attraction of the higher salary levels abroad, but also the discriminatory tax treatment of personnel in India as against those Indians who worked abroad in foreign fleets, with the former having to pay higher taxes.

Around 1990, there were 14,000 active certified Indian officers, but 11,000 of these were employed in foreign fleets, with only 3000 available for some 400 Indian flag ships.[60] In the early 1990s, about 40 per cent of the Norwegian merchant fleet was manned by Indian officers and crew.[61] Such export of manpower has, no doubt, been of considerable benefit to the country, for besides providing employment it added to the country's foreign exchange earnings. One estimate put the foreign exchange remittances of Indian shipping personnel employed abroad at US$250 million, which amounted to some 40 per cent of the Indian shipping industry's net foreign exchange earnings of $620 million in 1992-93.[62] Indeed, another study more broadly noted that "the foreign exchange earnings of the country by way of remittances made by Indian officers and seamen manning foreign ships is now almost half of the net foreign exchange earnings of Indian flag ships through sea-borne trade".[63]

Notwithstanding its contribution to foreign exchange earnings, the exodus served to affect the Indian shipping industry adversely. In the short run, it made for an acute shortage of officers for Indian ships in the late 1980s, constraining and curtailing their operations. At that time, while 4500 officers were needed to run the fleet, only 3000 were available. Subsequently, fast-track training programmes helped to reduce the shortage to 26 per cent of requirements in 1992 and to about 12 per cent in 1995.[64] However, the industry has continued to face the problem of not having an adequate number of officers, particularly more experienced ones at the higher levels.

Over the longer term, the exodus resulted in eliminating India's comparative advantage in low-cost manpower. In the first place, it led to a steep rise in salary levels in India. Even though Indian salaries continued to fall far short of international levels, in combination with the higher manning levels on Indian vessels, they made total personnel costs largely equivalent between India and foreign fleets. One study of manning levels and personnel costs on comparable Indian vessels and Indian-manned foreign vessels found that an Indian vessel has a staff complement of 47 as against that of 26 on the foreign flag vessel (see Table 7.6). As for wage costs, the study concluded that "an Indian flag vessel is very marginally cheaper in direct manning costs for a bulk carrier, about 3 per cent and very marginally higher for a tanker, about 3 per cent. Thus, it can be said that presently the direct manning costs are about the same" (see Table 7.7). It added, however, that "manning of Indian flag

TABLE 7.6: COMPARATIVE MANNING LEVELS ON INDIAN AND FOREIGN FLAG VESSELS (MANNED BY INDIANS)

Category	*Indian Flag Vessel*	*Foreign Flag Vessel*
Officers	12*	10
Petty Officers	5	-
Crew	28+	14@
Total	45	24
Additional crew for Tankers	2	2

* Includes one cadet

\+ Includes deck (13), engine room (7) and catering crew (8)

@ General purpose crew

Source: S.P. Mohile, "Competitiveness of Manning of Indian Ships", *Indian Shipping*, vol. 45, nos. 1-2 (1993), pp. 13-19.

vessels is in fact, higher" if account is taken of their higher victualling and repatriation costs, higher medical expenses because of higher age profile of Indian crew, and higher capital costs of ships because of providing larger living accommodation, dining and recreation space. The study's final conclusion was that "presently manning costs of Indian flag vessels are no longer competitive and are definitely higher than those of foreign flag vessels".[65]

It is not only in the matter of the wage bill that the Indian ship industry has lost its competitive edge. The exodus of personnel has affected the industry's operational efficiency in other ways as well. For one thing, foreign flag fleets have attracted the more dynamic and experienced officers. Equally, they have benefited from the fact that it is the more energetic, younger ratings that have gone abroad, in the process raising the average age level of ratings in the Indian fleet (50 years). Furthermore, even though the personnel may be Indian on both the national and foreign vessels, there prevails a disparity in the work ethic among their respective crews. As Sanklecha has pointed out: "there are dual standards in regard to work and discipline for Indian crew who man the Indian ships and Indian crew who man the foreign ships and it works to the detriment of Indian ships".[66]

TABLE 7.7: COMPARATIVE ANNUAL WAGE BILL FOR INDIAN AND FOREIGN FLAG VESSELS (MANNED BY INDIANS) (IN US DOLLARS)

	Bulk Carrier 45000 DWT		*Tanker 68000 DWT*	
Category	*Indian*	*Foreign*	*Indian*	*Foreign*
		Gross Wages		
Officers	137,689	242,988	148,568	242,988
Petty Officers	28,758	-	43,295	-
Crew	107,810	158,856	131,137	191,544
		*Leave Reserve**		
Officers	96,383	-	103,998	-
Petty Officers	15,817	-	23,813	-
Total	386,457	401,844	450,811	434,532

*No provision for leave reserve on foreign vessels because of contractual employment

Source: Same as in Table 7.6.

Liberalization in the context of a situation of fiscal deficit has also meant that the state is no longer able or willing to continue shouldering the full burden of establishing and running the comprehensive and well-developed network of institutions for training of personnel. Earlier, such a burden was entirely borne by the state. Now, however, the industry has had to share some of the responsibility. Some shipping enterprises, such as the Shipping Corporation of India in the public sector and the Great Eastern Shipping Company in the private sector, have set up their own training institutes. Also, the shipping industry at home, as well as that abroad which benefits from employing Indian personnel, has begun to contribute monetarily a certain amount per Indian employee for the support of training institutions in India, as also to loan faculty members to them when needed.

Changes in the international environment have thus neutralized the earlier comparative advantage that the Indian shipping industry had in terms of low-cost manpower. Accordingly, it is incumbent upon the state in India now to assure through positive action that there is some compensation extended to the industry for the constraints under which it has to operate in the competition with foreign enterprises.

SUMMARY AND CONCLUSIONS

Liberalization has been valuable to the extent that it has led to the dismantlement of controls that served to place serious constraints on the functioning of the shipping industry. Liberalization has done the necessary task of substantially sweeping away the accumulated legacy of a rigid regulatory framework that may have been functional in a different era. In this respect, perhaps the dismantlement has not proceeded to its logical end in order to eliminate the intervention of the bureaucracy in the commercial functioning of the industry, half of which is owned by the state. Privatization of SCI to the extent of 28 per cent of equity is not likely to make any difference to the domination of it by the bureaucracy.

However, there has not been adequate recognition that globalization and liberalization do not mean simply the shrinking of the role of the state. More appropriately, they mean the redefinition of a continuing, but more positive, role for the state in the nurturing of the national merchant fleet. It is impressive that most nations, even those that are in the forefront of advocating liberalization, have programmes of cargo support and subsidies of various kinds, both open and hidden. In India's case, protection is especially warranted for the industry because of the absence of a level playing field in which it has to operate. First, the industry faces the constraints of underdevelopment, that is, the capital constraint and the foreign exchange constraint. Second, it confronts an international market in which the developed countries are already entrenched, based on the cumulative historical advantage of an earlier policy of protection. As a consequence, India has to adopt state policies that compensate for the industry's handicaps in the area of ship finance and cargo support. However, such policies need to be formulated with an eye towards avoiding the heavy hand of bureaucracy in relation to the industry.

NOTES

1. Francis Fukuyama, *The End of History and the Last Man* (New York: Free Press, 1992).

2. For comparative analyses of liberalization in shipping, see the following UNCTAD documents: (1) TD/B/CN.4/5 of July 29, 1992: "Industry and Policy Developments in World Shipping and Their Impact on Developing Countries"; (2) TD/B/CN.4/-34 of April 20, 1994: "Progressive Liberalization and the Development of Shipping Services in Developing Countries"; and (3) UNCTAD/SDD/SHIP/5 of April 18, 1995: "Progressive Liberalization and the Development of Shipping Services in Developing Countries: Country Experiences".

3. See Baldev Raj Nayar, *The Political Economy of India's Public Sector: Policy and Performance* (Bombay: Popular Prakashan, 1990), ch. 2.

4. India, Planning Commission, *Seventh Five Year Plan: 1985-1990* (New Delhi: 1985), p. v.

5. L.K. Jha, "Indian Economy in Eighties and Nineties", *Mainstream,* Republic Day 1987, p. 22.

6. Indian National Congress (I), *Election Manifesto: General Election 1991* (New Delhi: AICC, 1991), pp. 22 and 35-38.

7. *Indian Shipping,* vol. 40, nos. 8-9 (1988), pp. 3-5; *ibid.,* vol. 41, no. 9 (1989), pp. 7-9; and *ibid.,* vol. 42, no. 1 (1990), p. 13.

8. This section relies on Deena Khatkhate, "India on an Economic Reform Trajectory", and Baldev Raj Nayar, "The Public Sector", in Leonard A. Gordon and Philip Oldenburg (eds.), *India Briefing 1992* (Boulder, Colorado: Westview Press, 1992), chs. 2 and 3, respectively.

9. S.N. Sanklecha, *Tramping to Success: Story of the Great Eastern Shipping Company Limited* (Bombay: Popular Prakashan, 1995), pp.228-29.

10. Sanklecha, pp. 229.

11. Jagdish Tytler, "Development of Indian Shipping: From Total Control to Total De-Control", *Indian Shipping,* vol. 47, nos. 1-2 (1995), pp. 7-9, and Jagdish Tytler, "EC-Indian Maritime Cooperation", *ibid.,* vol. 46, nos. 2-3 (1994), pp. 11-13.

12. Indian National Shipowners Association (INSA), *Annual Review 1994-1995* (Bombay: INSA, 1995), p. 23.

13. *Maritime International,* June 1995, p. 13.

14. On the cost-plus formula and the controversy surrounding it, see "The Case of the Shipping Corporation of India: Synopsis" and "The Rejoinder by Great Eastern Shipping Co. Ltd.: Synopsis", in *Maritime International,* June 1995, pp. 13-17. One source in early 1995 stated in respect of India's oil transport that "the current rates are nearly double those in the rest of the world". See Oppenheimer & Co. Inc., *International Research: Indian Shipping Industry* (New York: April 10, 1995), p. 11. SCI, however, maintains that its cost-plus rates cannot be compared to market rates at their low point and that over the longer run the arrangement works out to the benefit of the state.

15. *Indian Shipping,* vol. 47, no. 6 (1995), pp. 3-4.

16. See, for example, P.P. Radhakrishnan, "Changing Scenario of Indian Shipping", *Indian Shipping,* vol. 47, nos. 4-5 (1995), pp. 17-18. Note his comment: "I shudder to think with the

liberalization and the Government of India removing all restrictions for foreigners to set up shipping companies in India what would happen to Indian shipowners if the mighty giants in international shipping decide to come to India, even on a trial basis. I would repeat the oft-said cliche that total market capitalization of India is smaller than one or two investment organizations in U.S. Same is true for shipping. Global shipping giants are there, waiting to swallow the shipping of developing countries".

See also P.P. Radhakrishnan, "Paper by Capt. P.P. Radhakrishnan", *Indian Shipping,* vol. 44, nos. 11-12 (1992), pp. 29-33: "The Government should find ways and means to provide concessional and copious finance for ship acquisition instead of getting deterred by the sabre rattling of developed nations.... It is indeed necessary to protect the domestic industry at all cost and in spite of the tendency to use fashionable words like liberalization etc., it cannot be gainsaid that there is merit in a certain amount of protectionism".

17. The discussion below on SCICI draws on the annual reports of the organization for the years 1988 to 1995.

18. K.M. Sheth, "Indian Shipping--Prospects and Challenge", *Indian Shipping,* vol. 42, no. 1 (1990), pp. 7-10, and K.M. Sheth, "Indian Shipping Review and Prospects", *ibid.,* vol. 42, no. 9 (1990), pp. 5-12.

19. Sheth, "Indian Shipping Review and Prospects", p. 8.

20. SCICI, *Annual Report 1993,* p. 6.

21. N.K. Kurup, "Ministry Unhappy Over SCICI for Non-Shipping Projects", *Financial Express* (New Delhi), November 9, 1993.

22. "From the Bridge", *Indian Shipping,* vol. 46, no. 6 (1994), pp. 3-5.

23. R.L. Pai, "From the President's Desk: Indian Shipping--The Opportunities Ahead", in INSA, *Annual Review 1993-94,* pp.3-5.

24. "Overview of Indian Shipping: SCICI's Survey", *Indian Shipping,* vol. 42, nos. 2-3 (1990), pp. 19-26

25. *Indian Shipping,* vol. 46, no. 12 (1994), pp. 3-5.

26. INSA, *Annual Review 1994-1995,* p. 10. The requirements were slightly relaxed in early 1996, but only for the large financial institutions, by reducing the maturity period to five years. *Economic Times* (Mumbai), February 17, 1996.

27. See Robert Gilpin, *U.S. Power and the Multinational Corporation: The Political Economy of Foreign Direct Investment* (New York: Basic Books, 1975), p. 75.

28. See N.G. Jog, *Saga of Scindia: Struggle for the Revival of Indian Shipping and Shipbuilding* (Bombay: Scindia Steam Navigation Co., 1969), p. 84.

29. For an elaborate chart on the subsidies provided by different countries, see U.S. Maritime Administration, *Maritime Subsidies 1993,* replicated in *Indian Shipping,* vol. 46, no. 1 (1994), pp. 12-13. See also the document UNCTAD/SDD/SH-IP/3 dated May 8, 1955 on "Ship Finance for Developing Countries: Report by the UNCTAD Secretariat", pp. 23-25.

30. Note the comments of an Indian authority on shipping: "Cargo support is extended by major maritime nations to their national flag shipping. According to a recent survey 37 maritime countries provide cargo support. About 40 per cent of all cargo carried by U.S. ships were preference cargoes made available under U.S. regulations. Japanese steel industry controls about 200 million tonnes of cargo per year and most of this cargo is made available for carriage to Japanese ships. Chinese and EEC steel industries also exercise control over shipment of large volumes of cargo through f.o.b. terms of purchase. The bulk of grain cargo are controlled by a few grain trading houses or by centralized buying agencies in China and Russia. In many developed countries the right to channelize cargoes to shipping lines of their choice is retained through control over terms of shipment--buying f.o.b. and selling c.i.f." S.N. Sanklecha, "Need to Strengthen Infrastruc-

ture in the Context of Globalization of Shipping", *Indian Shipping,* vol. 46, no. 4 (1994), pp. 11-15. See also India, Planning Commission, *Indian Shipping in the Time Perspective of 2000 AD: Report of Planning Group on Shipping, September 1987* (chairman: L.M.S. Rajwar; Bombay: 1987), ch.XVII.

31. UNCTAD, *Review of Maritime Transport 1993,* pp. 20-22.

32. This paragraph relies on R.L. Pai, "Paper by Mr. R.L. Pai", *Indian Shipping,* vol. 44, nos. 11-12 (1992), pp. 19-24.

33. Pai, p. 23.

34. Asian Institute of Transport Development, *Indian Shipping Industry--Critical Issues in Global Context* (New Delhi: 1993), pp. 28-29.

35. *Indian Shipping,* vol. 46, no. 12 (1994), p. 4.

36. INSA, *Annual Review 1994-1995,* p. 9.

37. The tax requirement was subsequently rescinded, but the episode indicated the thoughtless and haphazard nature of decision-making in regard to shipping. See *Indian Shipping,* vol. 47, no. 7 (1995), p. 3.

38. "Budget Proposals and Shipping", *Indian Shipping,* vol. 47, nos. 1-2 (1995), p. 3, and "Changing Scenario of Indian Shipping", *ibid.,* vol. 47, no. 3 (1995), pp. 3-6.

39. *Indian Shipping,* vol. 47, nos. 4-5 (1995), pp. 4-6.

40. India, Planning Commission, *Eighth Five Year Plan 1992-97* (New Delhi: 1992), pp. 237-41.

41. "Imperatives of National Fleet Expansion", *Indian Shipping,* vol. 44, no. 3 (1992), pp. 3-5.

42. N.C. Singhal, "Shipping Investments in India's Changing Shipping Scenario", *Indian Shipping,* vol. 47, nos. 4-5 (1995),

pp. 19-24. Mr. Singhal is vice-chairman and managing director of SCICI.

43. INSA, *Report of Directors 1992-93* (Bombay: 1993), p. 5.

44. Oppenheimer & Co., Inc., *International Research: Indian Shipping Industry* (New York: April 10, 1995), pp.3 and 9-10.

45. See Directorate General of Shipping, "Statement Showing Particulars of Indian Tonnage as on 31.12.1994" (Bombay: 1995), pp. 25-26. Note that more than half (38) of the companies on that date owned only one or two ships.

46. Adrian Bascombe, "Everybody's Doing It", *Containerization International,* May 1995, pp. 63-67. Shreyas Shipping has already purchased three 400 teu vessels but they have been chartered out to the Dubai-based operation of the Group--Orient Express Lines--until early 1997, when Shreyas will start its own feeder services. The one 350 teu vessel owned by India Steamship Company is also on charter to Orient Express Lines, which owns six 450 teu vessels for feeder services in the Middle East and Asia. Shahi Shipping plans to purchase one 250-350 teu vessel.

47. *Economic Times* (Mumbai), February 11, 1996.

48. *Indian Shipping,* vol. 47, no. 10 (1995), p. 3.

49. "Revision of Age Norms", *Indian Shipping,* vol. 47, no. 3 (1995), pp. 5-6.

50. "Address of Mr. Vasudevan, D.G. Shipping", *Indian Shipping,* vol. 47, nos. 4-5 (1995), pp. 13-15.

51. Note some of the other younger age figures for cargo carrying ships: Japan 9, Norway (NIS) 13, Singapore 14, Hong Kong 12, and Taiwan 13. "World Cargo Fleet Totals 451.06 Mln. grt", *Indian Shipping,* vol. 47, no. 6 (1995), pp. 7-10.

52. INSA, *Annual Review 1994-1995,* p. 28.

53. On this unilateralism, see Lawrence D. Barchue, Sr., "'International Shipping Policy': A Dilemma for Developing Countries" (Paper for the Maritime Policy Seminar, November 2-6, 1992; Malmo, Sweden: World Maritime University, 1992), pp.1-7.

54. *Indian Shipping,* vol. 45, nos. 1-2 (1993), p. 3, and no. 3 (1993), pp. 5-6.

55. See the following and other news stories around the same time in the press: (1) "Move to Wind Up Transchart Opposed", *Economic Times* (New Delhi), June 7, 1993; (2) "Transchart Fate Uncertain", *Financial Express* (New Delhi), December 16, 1993; (3) "PM Steps in to Resolve Row Over PSU Cargo Shipment", *Business Standard* (Calcutta), April 8, 1994; and (4) "Controversy: Transchart Continuance", *Economic Times* (New Delhi), May 9, 1994.

56. "Decision on Cargo Preference to Boost Shipping Industry", *Economic Times* (Mumbai), February 9, 1996, and "Govt. Launches Crackdown on PSUs Violating Cargo Norms", *ibid.,* February 10, 1996.

57. "New Scheme to Implement Liner Code", *Indian Shipping,* vol. 46, no. 5 (1994), pp. 3-4.

58. *Containerization International,* July 1994, p. 18.

59. Planning Commission, *Indian Shipping in the Time Perspective of 2000 AD,* p. 187.

60. Shashikant N. Ruia, "An Overview of National Shipping", *Indian Shipping,* vol. 42, no. 1 (1990), pp. 11-16.

61. "Modernization of Training Facilities for Merchant Navy Personnel", *Indian Shipping,* vol. 46, no. 5 (1994), pp. 5-6.

62. G. Raghuram, V. Venkata Rao, and Sidharth Sinha, "Training Programme on Shipping Management", *Indian Shipping,* vol. 46, no. 6 (1994), pp. 25-31.

63. "Indian Shipping: Critical Issues in Global Context" [excerpts from a study by the Asian Institute of Transport Development], *Indian Shipping,* vol. 46, no. 1 (1994), pp. 7-11.

64. S.P. Mohile, "Focus on Human Element in Shipping", *Indian Shipping,* vol. 47, no. 3 (1995), pp. 23-26.

65. S,P. Mohile, "Competitiveness of Manning of Indian Ships", *Indian Shipping,* vol. 45, nos. 1-2 (1993), pp. 13-19. INSA maintains that "the total wage liability on board an Indian ship is 12-15 per cent higher than on FOC ships". INSA, "Shipping and the National Economy", *Indian Shipping,* vol. 46, nos. 2-3 (1994), pp. 7-9.

66. S.N. Sanklecha, "Indian Shipping--Its Competitiveness in International Shipping Environment", *Indian Shipping,* vol. 44, nos. 11-12 (1992), pp. 7-18.

CHAPTER VIII

CONCLUSION: MARGINALIZATION AND THE LIMITS OF LIBERALIZATION

After a major thrust in expansion of tonnage during the 1960s and 1970s, India's shipping entered an extended period of stagnation and decline, at the end of which it stood basically marginalized in world shipping. Not only did India's tonnage capacity largely stand still for nearly a decade and a half after 1980, but there was a profound fall in the share of its shipping in some of the trades. Overall, during this period Indian shipping's share in the country's overseas cargo stayed around 35 per cent, rather than the expected norm of 50 per cent. However, while this modest but inequitable share may seem respectable, even it has seen some erosion in recent years.

More importantly, the figure for the share of Indian shipping in the country's overseas cargo is an overall composite result that masks major failures. For, this figure also covers the carriage of oil, which has formed about a quarter to a third--indeed, even a higher proportion more recently--of India's foreign trade. Oil is considered a strategic commodity, and many states adopt policies reserving a substantial part of oil imports for their own shipping. In similar fashion, India has also reserved the import of oil for its public sector carrier. That cargo reservation has tended to give an undeserved exaggerated notion of India's record of performance in the carriage of its trades. The exclusion of oil and oil products from the analysis, on the other hand, reveals severe imbalances in the participation of Indian shipping in the different trades and makes manifest the fact that in the carriage of dry bulk cargo and, especially, liner cargo India is effectively marginalized.

Take general cargo first. In 1976-77, India's share in this trade was about 40 per cent. There then followed a general descent where India's share progressively dipped until it reached the egregiously low level of less than 9 per cent in

1993-94. Behind this dramatic fall in market share lay the failure of Indian shipping to adapt to the container revolution. Until the beginning of 1994 India had practically no tonnage in cellular containerships. The decline is less dramatic in dry bulk cargo but no less damaging. In dry bulk cargo, India never achieved even the modest level of market share that it did in general cargo. The share of Indian shipping in dry bulk cargo has generally been less than 25 per cent. In other words, India never broke out of its marginalized state here.

Although Indian officialdom tends generally to proclaim the country's accomplishments in building shipping capacity, the achievement after a half-century of effort does not admit of much self-congratulation. Particularly in the case of general cargo, India is almost where it was at the time of independence. Interestingly, this poor performance cannot be attributed to liberalization, which, in effect, was not put in place until 1991. Rather, it took place largely under the auspices of a command economy, where the state owned half the country's tonnage, and points up the weaknesses in adaptation of a controlled economy, at least in the Indian context. What is noteworthy is that after the burst of expansion of tonnage during the 1960s and 1970s, India was unable to sustain the momentum to enable it to break out of its marginalized status in the dry bulk cargo trade or to prevent its fall to that status in the general cargo trade. Since the period following the early 1970s represents the acceleration of globalization in shipping, India can be said to have failed to adapt to the new international context in shipping. The more important question, however, is as to what have been the causes for this failure.

International System vs Domestic Structures

In an increasingly interdependent world, the search for explanation of any policy or process concerning the political economy raises the issue of the weight that ought to be accorded to the international system and to domestic structures.[1] Certainly, the very international nature of the overseas shipping industry would seem to suggest that the international system ought to be the starting point in any analysis of a country's performance in respect of its share in international traffic. The notion of the international system here relates to deeper structures and institutionalized practices, rather than short-term changes, such as business cycles, though the latter are, no doubt, important in terms of the challenges that they pose for individual countries.

The international system can be viewed as consisting of two basic elements: a structure of power and a set of values and norms. While the two can be analytically distinguished, they are, of course, dynamically related. Indeed, realism, as the dominant school of thought in the study of international politics, regards values and norms as essentially reflective of the structure of power. However, the institutionalist school treats values and norms--"international regimes" in academic short-hand--as having considerable independent potency of their own in international conduct, even if they may have initially originated in a given structure of power. Regardless of the resolution of the debate between the two approaches of realism and institutionalism,[2] it is noteworthy that different issue-areas vary in the nature of international regimes that prevail among them by way of principles, norms and practices governing conduct. The nature of the international regime in a given issue-area can, then, be of material significance in determining the scope allowed to the international structure of power or to domestic structures in affecting state behaviour and performance.

Krasner has made vivid the differential impact of international regimes by highlighting the different organizing principles in the operation of the two chief modes of international transportation--shipping and aviation.[3] The international regime for shipping, based as it is on the principle of the freedom of the seas, is in theory a market-based one in sharp contrast to that of the authority-based international regime in aviation, where state sovereignty prevails over the national airspace. Important as this distinction may be analytically, however, in actual practice, state behaviour reveals it to be overrated. For, state sovereignty, and therefore relative national power, are just as manifest in shipping as they are in aviation. They appear to have shaped and circumscribed the market in shipping as well.

Since state sovereignty and relative national capabilities matter in shipping, the structure of world power has been critical to the formation of international regimes. Powerful states have from time to time installed international regimes favourable to their own interests. This proposition is demonstrated historically in the shift from mercantilism to liberalism in the regime-determining policies of Great Britain. In the contemporary era, it is evident in the creation by the United States soon after World War II of an additional parallel regime of "flags of convenience", which undercut the requirement of a genuine link between ownership and national flag that prevailed under the traditional regime in shipping. This regime-construction was undertaken to protect the shipping interests in bulk trades of vertically integrated American multinationals when faced with competition from other maritime fleets with lower labour costs. Again, after the collapse of the Soviet bloc, the United States and the European Union have increasingly resorted to unilateralism in matters relating to international shipping. More generally, they have used their economic and political leverage to shape the international regime in accord with their policy preferences through the emasculation and dismantlement of institutions that had sought to aid the development of shipping capacity in the developing world, such as the Shipping Division of UNCTAD.

Historically, powerful states have protected particular institutions in the market that were beneficial to their interests. Thus, the shipping market in liner cargo was for a full century after 1875 dominated by cartels under the leadership of Great Britain. Though the cartels had emerged from the activities of private actors, they had the tacit or explicit endorsement of powerful states after legislative inquiries into their working. Furthermore, despite the vaunted claim about the market-based nature of its international regime, the shipping sector continues in practice to be riddled with protectionism, in which the advanced industrial states, most particularly the United States, have served as models for the underdeveloped countries. The supposedly market-based regime in shipping has thus not prevented states from intervening in the market to protect the interests of their maritime fleets. In the ultimate analysis, it is the world structure of power that has been determining in state behaviour rather than any norms of sovereignty-transcendent international regimes. Of course, this is not unique to shipping, but reflects what is part and parcel of the functioning of the larger international political economy. Even as they proclaim the virtues of liberalism, powerful states have erected strong tariff and non-tariff barriers in the protection of their domestic industry, and this profound modification of liberalism by powerful states to transfer adjustment costs to weaker states in the defence of national interests has been legitimized in western scholarship as "embedded liberalism".[4] Thus, it is apparent that the sharp contrast drawn between the aviation regime as authority-based and the shipping regime as market-based is highly exaggerated. Indeed, regrettably, the theoretical distinction itself, when divorced from reality in terms of the actual practices of the advanced industrial states, tends to become a handy tool in the polemic of these states against the quest of the developing world for an equitable international economic order.

State sovereignty and national power, because they make bargaining and outcomes a function of relative capabilities, have undoubtedly enabled western states to advance their interests in shipping as elsewhere. This is evident in the disparity between their share in the world's shipping tonnage and their share in world trade. For example, in 1980, the developed market economies (together with the flag of convenience countries) owned 82 per cent of the world tonnage while their share of the world's cargo turnover was 55 per cent; on the other hand, the developing countries owned 10 per cent of the tonnage while they handled 39 per cent of the cargo turnover.[5] Of course, the disparity was even sharper earlier. At the same time, however, the western states served to provide the countries of the developing world, as they emerged into statehood in the postwar period, with models of policy and policy instruments to foster and protect their own national merchant fleets. It is precisely the acquisition of sovereignty by India in 1947, and the supportive measures for development that it made possible, that explain the contrast in fleet expansion before and after independence. Indeed, the earlier attainment of a sort of proto-sovereignty even before independence, because of a radicalized nationalist movement after World War I, allowed the Scindia Steam Navigation Company to survive in sharp contrast with the sad experience of other entrepreneurial efforts at shipping before that war.

Of course, the different states in the developing world have varied in their performance in the area of shipping. The record of accomplishment of China, South Korea, Taiwan and Malaysia in the last two decades nonetheless demonstrates that states can foster and advance their shipping capacity within the structure of the existing international system, precisely because it is not so market-based as it is proffered to be. India itself during the 1960s and 1970s showed that it could make rapid and substantial advance in the development of a merchant fleet. Without understating the impact of the international system, especially with the acceleration of globalization, it is clear that domestic structures emerge as critical for performance in respect of shipping. The international environment, no doubt, continues to provide challenges for states, but meeting such challenges successfully requires creative adaptation on their part. Ultimately, therefore, it is the domestic structures of sovereign states that have priority in explaining performance in regard to shipping.

DOMESTIC STRUCTURES

The dominant feature of India's record of performance in shipping in about the decade and a half after 1980 has been stagnation and decline. Two possible hypotheses in relation to the internal setting can be advanced in the explanation of this record. First, the vulnerabilities of the developing countries that spring from the domestic structures of underdevelopment are so overwhelming and deep-rooted that they undermine their efforts to overcome underdevelopment, regardless of the formal endowment of state sovereignty. In other words, developing countries encounter such a potent "underdevelopment trap" that state sovereignty does not provide enough leverage to attenuate it in building an adequate national merchant fleet that has a fair share of participation in the international shipping industry. Two powerful constraints in this underdevelopment trap have been the capital constraint and the foreign exchange constraint, and India is an eloquent example of their influence in inhibiting the development of an adequate merchant fleet.

Second, as against the underdevelopment trap, there is the policy hypothesis, under which, while the vulnerabilities are recognized as having considerable significance and as largely recalcitrant to elimination, they can nonetheless within a certain range be mitigated by "getting the policies right". This line of argument has ample support in the success of several developing countries in building large merchant fleets, even in the technologically advanced and capital intensive container sector, and India's own performance in the rapid and substantial acquisition of tonnage during the 1960s and 1970s provides an apt illustration of it. While underdevelopment undeniably imposes constraints, effective and timely state policy can to a certain extent overcome them.

There is no doubt that the international environment changed during the 1970s in a manner that was adverse to the interests of much of the developing world. The structural break in world shipping by way of a long-term depression--induced by the OPEC oil price shocks--and the structural change by way of the container revolution generated an upheaval in world shipping of massive proportions. These developments also accelerated the pace of globalization in world shipping, and it would be foolhardy to deny that they thereby strengthened the market as against the state, a market largely dominated by the developed world. As the tonnage-surplus countries of the developed world dumped capacity in the developing world, which confronted a situation of a depression of long duration and rapid technological change, the merchant fleets of many of the developing countries were decimated. In India, quite a few shipping companies went into liquidation, and the country entered a period of almost a decade and a half during which its tonnage remained stagnant. While its overall share in the national trades hovered at a modest level, India was thoroughly marginalized in liner shipping.

Behind India's dismal performance during the period lay failure in timely policy adaptation. State policies that had proven to be productive in a less complex and more protective era during the 1960s and 1970s continued in place long after they were no longer functional in an age of greater complexity and ruthless competition, when the old supports of cartelistic cargo sharing and bilateral agreements were gone. In a sense, India became a victim of its past success by continuing with policies that had once been instrumental in that success. To a certain extent, "path dependency" theory sheds light on the failure of the industry to adapt to the new challenges because of the structures and practices created by past policy of the state.

Critical in the failure in policy adaptation by the state was the deterioration in state power that had meanwhile taken place.

This deterioration in state power was evident in both its constituent elements of (1) state autonomy to build policy consensus and (2) state capacity to implement policy effectively. Therefore, where timing was of crucial importance in an international industry such as shipping, India took an inordinately long time to come forward with change in policy until it was too late, at least for liner shipping.

It is true that, in contrast, the international environment in the 1960s and early 1970s had been propitious for tonnage expansion. But so it was largely during the 1950s, when India's tonnage saw only slow and gradual expansion. The fundamental reason for the slow growth in the 1950s was the policy stalemate within the state as a result of opposed value preferences within the leadership. However, once the consolidation of power occurred in the national leadership, the state decided on a determined line of action. No doubt, that line partly erred in installing a regulatory system of stringent licensing and controls and in excessively favouring the public sector because of ideological considerations. Nonetheless, tonnage expanded rapidly as a result of the creative use of policy instruments that exploited the favourable international environment. State autonomy was then also backed by effective state capacity. The state was guided by a stable political leadership with a national vision and a due recognition of the place of shipping in it. That leadership had an integrated understanding of economics and politics as well as of the interplay between national power and international politics. It also had at its disposal a knowledgeable, effective and largely incorruptible civil service for the implementation of policy.

Starting with the late 1960s, however, India's political system started on a path of deterioration in state power. Governments became less stable and more preoccupied with assuring their tenure in office. Meanwhile, both society and state administration had grown more complex with advancing development of the economy. State autonomy declined, and it became harder to develop policy consensus. State capacity also suffered. The bureaucracy was increasingly fragmented and lacked effective coordination. It is this changed nature of state power that would seem to largely explain the failure in timely policy adaptation to the new challenges thrown up by the structural break and structural change in shipping. Instead, the state's major policy action in response to the crisis was to retreat from directly providing concessional finance to the local shipping industry, at least in the private sector. Only a major balance of payments crisis in the early 1990s made for change in the state-market relationship in shipping as part of a larger economic liberalization.

Liberalization and its Unfinished Business

To a state increasingly strapped for funds because of its fiscal deficit, the economic liberalization adopted in 1991 in the midst of a balance of payments crisis has provided an easy way out in the shipping arena since it has been taken to mean a retreat of the state, allowing the market to take its autonomous course. The new expectation is that firms must fend for themselves in the market. To a considerable extent, liberalization seems the right prescription, for economic planning and the rigid regulatory framework of licensing and controls had come to impede efficient decision-making by firms. Where international experts advised that "long and short-term plans should be formulated in a general way, leaving sufficient room for the initiative and strategic planning of the shipping companies",[6] India had earlier adopted the opposite course by undertaking detailed planning. Even though economic planning rarely achieved the results that were envisaged for shipping, it proved to be constricting and confining for the industry. Liberalization therefore accomplished the necessary task of sweeping away the old system of excessive controls, which clearly had become dysfunctional for the health of the industry.

In one sense, liberalization has not been carried through to its logical conclusion. The state directly controls half the country's tonnage, placed formally in the hands of a single public sector firm, Shipping Corporation of India (SCI). That is not a prescription for an efficient local industry, especially in the cultural and political context of India, where ministers and bureaucrats invariably tend to assert control over the management of public sector enterprises. On the other hand, in the era of world megacarriers it would seem unwise to break up India's one large-sized company that has the potential to become a significant player in international shipping. What seems required therefore is that the firm have full commercial autonomy, without the control, direction and supervision of the state. Parenthetically, state involvement in the management of the corporation tends to result also in the distortion of policy-making, as the energies of policy-makers get more focused on the running of a single firm rather than developing effective policy for the country's industry as a whole. Meanwhile, it is unfair to SCI to have its investment programmes be a hostage to the restrictive and dilatory processes of the government when the private sector has been relieved of them. If SCI is to have commercial autonomy, however, it has to be rooted--in line with property rights theory--in the private ownership of equity which would provide the necessary incentive to perform. Divestment, then, has to be on a more radical scale than currently envisaged so as to remove control over SCI by government as a matter of right because of its overwhelming majority ownership.

Liberalization needs to be extended to other areas as well that have so far been excluded from its purview, often to protect SCI's interests. One area pertains to the liner trades, where new entrants are barred from routes where SCI already operates services. Even if there are no companies currently interested in liner shipping, that is no reason to restrict it formally to SCI alone. The other area, where shipping companies are undoubtedly eager to enter, is the oil trade. Again, there is no reason why they should be excluded from bidding in that trade. The country's strategic interests would be adequately protected through restricting the trade to *Indian* firms only. But among the Indian firms rivalry should be allowed, indeed encouraged, to have full play. If SCI presently uses the oil trade to cross-subsidize its container trade operations, then specific support to it for those operations should be provided on some other open and transparent basis. More generally, liberalization should fully embrace the principle of encouraging rivalry among domestic firms in order to advance efficiency.[7] It is only through such competition that viable players can emerge to enter the global market. By the same token, bigness needs to be fostered, rather than distrusted and blunted as had been the case earlier with India's economic planning in reference to the private sector, especially under the MRTP regime.

THE NEED FOR A STATE-INDUSTRY PARTNERSHIP

Given the increased complexity of the economy and the known dysfunctional implications of the old regulatory framework of rigid controls and licensing, the new reliance on the market seems to be the correct prescription for the shipping industry. However, what needs to be remembered is that the market involved in this context is essentially the international market. In that market, it is noteworthy that the Indian industry faces an uneven playing field, with foreign megacarriers already entrenched there. In an earlier era, Mahatma Gandhi had called attention to an analogous uneven playing field by characterizing the proffered competition between British shipping and Indian shipping as an unequal battle between "the giant and the dwarf".

Correspondingly, in the international market as presently constituted, it is unreasonable to expect the current dwarfs of Indian shipping to compete with the world's contemporary giants. Consequently, what liberalization requires in the particular context of shipping in India, as more generally of shipping in the developing world, is not the mindless retreat of the state in favour of the market in shipping but a redefinition of the role of the state that takes account of the industry's specific context. Commitment to liberalization does not bar all state support to domestic industry. Most states raise barriers to free trade in order to protect local industry, with the advanced industrial states having turned the erection of non-tariff barriers into a fine art. The latter states do not apparently see any contradiction between their advocacy of liberalization and their practice of protectionism. To withdraw state support altogether from the local industry in developing countries in the name of liberalization is, then, to be more royal than the king.

Liberalization in the developing world therefore calls for the continued involvement of the state in the protection of industry but not in the manner as of old when the state acted as commander and administrator. Rather, it demands a redefinition of the role of the state so that it acts as a facilitator and sympathetic supporter of local enterprise, fully accepting the legitimacy of such enterprise. Indeed, liberalization calls for a "new partnership" between the state and industry in the defence of national interests.

Radical sceptics are likely to look askance at any such notion of partnership, for it is evocative of their *bete noire* of the state conceived as "a committee of the bourgeoisie". But all successful examples of economic development point to an essential cooperation between state and economy as a prerequisite to their success. And, indeed, there is a fundamental truth in the oft-ridiculed declaration that "the interest of General Motors is the interest of the United States". For, when General Motors suffers, so does the American economy as a whole, workers included. It is hard to imagine any example of successful development based on an adversarial relationship between state and economy. The existence of socialist regimes, if there are still any genuine ones left, does not contradict this proposition, for such regimes do not represent antagonism but integration between the two branches of the political economy.

In the Indian case, the idea of an authentic partnership, however, calls for a sea-change in the attitudes of elite and mass, for it runs counter to the political culture of the last half-century, where business, especially big business, has been considered an adversary, rather than a partner, in nation-building. That political culture, in turn, has deep roots in the societal traditions of caste and lack of mutual trust. Therefore, the construction of a genuine partnership is likely to prove to be a demanding task.

Assuring an Even Playing Field

The idea of a state-industry partnership is not meant to suggest that the state should be mindless in extending support to the industry. The foremost aim of the partnership should be to build a merchant fleet that is globally competitive, and not one that relies on the state as a permanent crutch. From one perspective, Indian shipping is not without certain competitive advantages. First, India is a generator of a not inconsiderable volume of cargo. In 1993-94, its seaborne trade amounted to 137 million tonnes by weight, having grown to that size from about 110 million tonnes in 1990-91. It is, indeed, this large size of the total cargo that has led to the targeting of India as a market by foreign shipping companies. Since the home base is crucial to establishing a competitive industry,[8] India's cargo generating capacity is an important advantage for Indian shipping from the viewpoint both of building a substantial merchant fleet and of bargaining.

Second, though wages of maritime manpower have risen strikingly in recent years and Indian vessels are overstaffed, India still has a relative advantage in lower labour costs, provided there is rationalization of personnel employed on Indian ships. Third, India can be said to possess a "vigorous shipping milieu", which is believed necessary for success in competition in shipping. Stromme Svendsen has defined shipping milieu as "the network of qualified men and women working in the cluster of shipping activities, private and governmental".[9] The presence of such a milieu is evident as much in the rapid expansion of the merchant fleet from almost scratch to 6 million grt in the 1960s and 1970s as it is in the export of maritime manpower from India to other flags. It is also apparent in the resilience of the Indian shipping industry. For, while the industry received a devastating blow from the structural break and structural change in the 1970s, and was severely damaged in the process, it did not completely go under.[10] Besides, the industry has thrown up several international-sized firms; apart from the public sector giant of SCI, these include Great Eastern Shipping and Essar Shipping. Even in respect of the container trade, where India suffered the most, there have been signs more recently of renewed activity. Behind its shipping milieu, there lies, of course, the maritime tradition of many centuries, which sadly was broken by imperialism and the colonial state.

On the other hand, the Indian shipping industry is at a severe disadvantage compared to foreign shipping. Several aspects of its disadvantaged situation--such as over 37 per cent of the world's tonnage being under "flags of convenience" where shipowners pay no taxes and face no government controls, or elsewhere governments providing open and hidden subsidies and protection to their shipping--can be explored, but it seems best to focus on two decisive ones, which are interrelated.[11] The single most fundamental constraint to the expansion of Indian tonnage is the high cost of capital, in an industry which is highly capital intensive, compared to the access to low-cost finance available to foreign shipowners. Interest rates in India are twice as high as abroad, and as a consequence dividend expectations are also very high. This feature depresses the incentive to invest, especially in view of low rates of profitability to begin with in the world shipping industry as a whole. What is more, even if sufficient capital were forthcoming, there is literally a wall against expansion because of the foreign exchange constraint--the second decisive aspect.

There is an argument of old in the world shipping industry, of course, that maintains that developing countries, suffering as they do from shortage of capital and foreign exchange, should leave shipping to the capital-surplus traditional maritime nations and put their meagre resources to better use elsewhere. Apart from strategic reasons which make a merchant fleet mandatory, this is a prescription that would seem to be worse than the disease. For, it would aggravate the problem through the drain of the very capital and foreign exchange that are in short supply. Take 1993-94, when the share of Indian shipping in the country's trades was 33.6 per cent, while the net operating surplus in foreign exchange earnings or savings was Rs. 29.9 billion. Since Indian shipping tends to get largely lower-value cargo, the NCAER formula on apportioning the freight bill as between Indian and foreign shipowners in the ratio of 30:70 seems reasonable. That would mean the net operating surplus of foreign shipowners from their Indian trades was Rs. 69.8 billion. Suppose India had been able to exert itself more so as to earn 50 per cent of the net freight bill, rather than the 30 per cent it actually did, its foreign exchange earnings would then have been Rs. 49.9 billion (half of the sum of Rs. 29.9 billion and Rs. 69.8 billion) instead of Rs. 29.9 billion that was actually earned. That is, it would have been able to staunch the outflow of Rs. 20 billion of capital in foreign exchange.

In other words, the argument on account of the capital constraint and foreign exchange constraint is, on analysis, stood on its head so as to conclude that India cannot afford to neglect building its merchant fleet sufficient to carry 50 per cent of the cargo in value, not just weight, or to earn the equivalent from a combination of participation in national trades and cross-trades. To rely on others for shipping services, it is apparent, is very consumptive of capital and foreign exchange. This element emerges even more sharply when it is remembered that what is needed in the acquisition of tonnage is, not the entire price, but the initial down payment of 20 per cent for new constructions, with the rest obtained as loan abroad at foreign rates of interest, and that the capital cost of a vessel is recovered out of its own earnings in five to six years for secondhand ships and in six to eight years for new constructions, while the economic life of the vessel is generally about twenty years.

How can India break out of the impasse where it is constrained by the shortage of capital but the capital constraint itself urges investment of capital in shipping? Essentially, there seem to be two ways: one, to lower the cost of capital for the Indian industry to make it competitive with foreign shipowners; and, two, to provide it the custom for the capital invested. In terms of supply of capital, traditionally the state had supported the industry directly with interest-subsidized concessional finance through SDFC until the mid-1980s and through a development rebate in taxation until the mid-1970s. Opinions differ on the wisdom of the cessation of the two programmes. Given the budgetary constraints, direct subsidies seem implausible, and would probably undercut the incentive to be competitive. On the other hand, a higher depreciation allowance of 40 per cent on the pattern of what is made available to other transportation industries, or at least 33 per cent instead of the current 20 per cent, should be helpful to the industry in reducing its capital costs. This mechanism has the advantage of avoiding involvement of the bureaucracy in administering assistance to the industry on a case-by-case basis. From the perspective of the budget, it would have the advantage of reducing revenue only temporarily since it would widen the base of collection in the future.

Since ships cannot be acquired without foreign exchange, at least for the initial 20 to 30 per cent down payment, the longstanding demand of the industry for a special pool or fund--constituted from a part of its annual foreign exchange earnings--for the purpose of purchase abroad of tonnage deserves sympathetic consideration. Perhaps the fund could be administered by a public financial institution, such as SCICI, so as to enable the state to focus on larger policy issues and not on financial detail. In the alternative, shipping companies could be allowed to retain a certain portion of their actual foreign exchange earnings as an entitlement for the purchase of additional tonnage, on the pattern of what is allowed to export-oriented industries for import of inputs. Perhaps more favourable treatment could be extended in these programmes to areas of shipping where India has lagged behind seriously, such as container shipping.

Although many states provide cargo preference for their shipping, this is most likely to encounter stiff resistance in India from the shippers lobby and the ministry of commerce. Two reasonable possibilities exist, however, to assure greater access to cargo for Indian shipping. One is to enforce strictly the guidelines on FOB and CIF terms for imports and exports in all government contracts and to channel all government cargo through the relatively efficient chartering operations of Transchart. Since Transchart conducts its business on a globally competitive and transparent basis, it should not affect the incentive to efficiency for Indian shipping companies. Perhaps the coverage of cargo for Transchart needs to be broadened to include cargo supported through public financial institutions, such as the Export-Import Bank. The other possibility is to provide financial incentives to Indian shippers--instead of employing coercive mechanisms as had been proposed in the past--to ship through Indian lines. These incentives may include enhanced import entitlements, over and above what shippers already get in pushing exports, or 15 to 20 per cent reduction in customs duty when cargo is carried by Indian ships.

A final, but crucial, requirement relates to an area that lies outside shipping as such but without which shipping cannot function--infrastructure. The poor nature of the infrastructure has been a serious handicap for the Indian shipping industry. Since a home base is important to the development of a competitive industry, rapid upgradation and expansion of the infrastructure, particularly port facilities, require urgent attention. No shipping industry can flourish if it is blocked by an insufficient and inefficient port structure.

All this, no doubt, will cost money, but not to invest is far costlier through the drain of economic surplus. It was precisely such a drain in respect of the overseas freight bill that evoked horror in Prime Minister Nehru in 1959, leading him to declare that it would have been enormously preferable to have built the country's tonnage through increased investment rather than paying vast sums to foreign shipowners in freight charges. Those remarks inspired a series of policy initiatives which led to the rapid expansion of tonnage in the 1960s and 1970s. The issue still remains the same: whether it is more costly to invest or not to invest in Indian shipping.

NOTES

1. See Peter J. Katzenstein (ed.), *Between Power and Plenty: Foreign Economic Policies of Advanced Industrial States* (Madison: University of Wisconsin Press, 1978).

2. I discuss the debate in reference to the aviation sector in "Regimes, Power, and International Aviation", *International Organization*, vol. 49, no. 1 (1995), pp. 139-70. On the basis of an in-depth study of the postwar attempts at regime formation in international aviation, I underline the robustness of realism.

3. Stephen D. Krasner, *Structural Conflict: The Third World Against Global Liberalism* (Berkeley: University of California Press, 1985).

4. John Gerard Ruggie, "International Regimes, Transactions, and Change: Embedded Liberalism in the Postwar Economic Order", in Stephen D. Krasner (ed.), *International Regimes* (Ithaca, N.Y.: Cornell University Press, 1983), pp. 209-14.

5. UNCTAD, *Review of Maritime Transport 1993*, p. 29.

6. K. Dabrowski, "Internal and External Shipping Policy Measures", *Maritime Policy and Management*, vol. 6, no. 2 (1979), pp. 81-92.

7. On the benefits of domestic rivalry, see Michael Porter, *The Competitive Advantage of Nations* (New York: The Free Press, 1990), pp. 143-44.

8. On the importance of the home base, see Porter, pp. 19-21.

9. A. Stromme Svendsen, "Shipping as Human Achievement and Culture in Economic and Ecological Context", cited in Gunnar K. Sletmo and Susanne Holste, "Shipping and the Competitive

Advantage of Nations: The Role of International Ship Registers", *Maritime Policy and Management*, vol. 20, no. 3 (1993), pp. 243-255.

10. On the damage to African shipping, see O.C. Iheduru, "Merchant Fleet Development by Legislation: Lessons from West and Central Africa", *Maritime Policy and Management*, vol. 19, no. 4 (1992), pp. 297-317, and "The Limits of Public Sector Reforms: Evidence from the Maritime Sector", *Journal of Developing Areas*, vol. 28 (April 1994), pp. 393-424.

11. Apart from the demands made intermittently by the industry through INSA, two rather extensive lists of measures recommended for assistance to Indian shipping appear in Asian Institute of Transport Development, *Indian Shipping Industry: Critical Issues in Global Context* (New Delhi: 1993), pp. 36-43, and National Council of Applied Economic Research, *Indian Shipping Industry: Retrospect and Prospect* (New Delhi: NCAER, 1993), pp. 90-107.

SELECT BIBLIOGRAPHY

Allison, Graham T. *Essence of Decision: Explaining the Cuban Missile Crisis.* Boston, Mass.: Little, Brown and Company, 1977.

Apter, David E. *The Politics of Modernization.* Chicago: University of Chicago Press, 1966.

Asian Institute of Transport Development. *Indian Shipping Industry: Critical Issues in Global Context.* New Delhi: 1993.

Associated Chambers of Commerce and Industry of India. *Indian Shipping, Shipbuilding and Ship Repair Industries: Problems and Prospects.* Prepared by G.B. Sundriyal. New Delhi: 1991.

Borsa, Giorgio. "Recent Trends in Indian Ocean Historiography 1500-1800", in Giorgio Borsa (ed.), *Trade and Politics in the Indian Ocean.* New Delhi: Manohar, 1990.

Broeze, Frank. "Underdevelopment and Dependency: Maritime India During the Raj", *Modern Asian Studies,* vol.18, no.3 (1984), pp. 429-457.

Cafruny, Alan W. *Ruling the Waves: The Political Economy of International Shipping*. Berkeley: University of California Press, 1987.

Canada. Transport Canada. *Task Force on Deep-Sea Shipping: Report to the Minister of Transport.* Ottawa: 1985.

Carlisle, Rodney. *Sovereignty for Sale: The Origins and Evolution of the Panamanian and Liberian Flags of Convenience*. Annapolis, Maryland: Naval Institute Press, 1981.

Chandra, Bipan. *The Rise and Growth of Economic Nationalism in India: Economic Policies of Indian National Leadership, 1880-1905.* New Delhi: People's Publishing House, 1966.

Couper, A.D. *The Geography of Sea Transport.* London: Hutchinson University Library, 1972.

Dabrowski, K. "Internal and External Shipping Policy Measures", *Maritime Policy and Management,* vol. 6, no.2 (1979), pp. 81-92.

Dalal, P.T. "Indian Shipping in Different Sectors of Foreign Trades", *Indian Shipping,* vol. 21, no. 5 (1969), pp. 15-19.

______. "Indian Shipping in Relation to Long-Term Export Strategy", *Indian Shipping,* vol. 26, no. 3 (1974), pp. 11-17.

Desai, H.B. *Current Issues in Indian Shipping.* New Delhi: Commonwealth Publishers, 1989.

______. *Indian Shipping Perspectives (Critical Reflections).* New Delhi: Anupama Publications, 1988.

Franklin, Philip Earle. *The Economic Impact of Flag Discrimination in Ocean Transportation.* Ph.D. Dissertation. Washington, D.C.: American University, 1968.

Fukuyama, Francis. *The End of History and the Last Man.* New York: Free Press, 1992.

Ghandhi, R.K.S. "Role of Public Sector in Development of Indian Shipping", *Indian Shipping,* vol. 36, nos. 4-5 (1984), pp. 11-15.

Gilpin, Robert, *The Political Economy of International Relations.* Princeton: Princeton University Press, 1987.

______. *U.S. Power and the Multinational Corporation: The Political Economy of Foreign Direct Investment.* New York: Basic Books, 1975.

Gordon, Leonard A. and Philip Oldenburg. Eds. *India Briefing 1992.* Boulder, Colorado: Westview Press, 1992.

Hutchins, Francis G. *India's Revolution: Gandhi and the Quit India Movement.* Cambridge, Mass.: Harvard University Press, 1973.

Iheduru, Okechukwu C. "Merchant Fleet Development by Legislation: Lessons from West and Central Africa", *Maritime Policy and Management,* vol. 19, no. 4 (1992), pp. 297-317.

______. "The Limits of Public Sector Reforms: Evidence from the Maritime Sector", *Journal of Developing Areas,* vol.28 (April 1994), pp. 393-424.

India. Commerce Department. *Report of the Reconstruction Policy Sub-Committee on Shipping.* New Delhi: Government of India Press, 1947.

India. Director General of Shipping. *Seminar on Containerization: Bombay, December 1968.* Bombay: 1968.

India. Lok Sabha. Committee on Public Undertakings (1964-65). *Third Report: Shipping Corporation of India Ltd., Bombay.* New Delhi: Lok Sabha Secretariat, 1965.

______ (1971-72). *Twentieth Report: Shipping Corporation of India Limited.* New Delhi: Lok Sabha Secretariat, 1972.

______ (1981-82). *Forty-Third Report on the Shipping Corporation of India Ltd.* New Delhi: Lok Sabha Secretariat, 1982.

______ (1987-88). *Forty-Fourth Report: Shipping Corporation of India Limited.* New Delhi: Lok Sabha Secretariat, 1988.

______(1990-91). *Fifth Report: Shipping Corporation of India Ltd.* New Delhi: Lok Sabha Secretariat, 1990.

India. Lok Sabha. Estimates Committee (1956-57). *Sixty-Fifth Report: Ministry of Transport: Shipping.* New Delhi: Lok Sabha Secretariat, 1957.

______(1958-59). *Thirty-Eighth Report: Ministry of Transport and Communications: Department of Transport.* New Delhi: Lok Sabha Secretariat, 1959.

India. Lok Sabha. Public Accounts Committee (Third Lok Sabha). *Seventh Report.* New Delhi: Lok Sabha Secretariat, 1963.

India. Ministry of International Trade. *Report of the Sub-Committee Appointed by the Board of Trade to Study the Problems of Transportation of Bulk Cargoes by Indian Vessels.* New Delhi: 1963.

India. Ministry of Transport and Shipping. National Conference on Shipping, Shipbuilding and Ports, December 1967. *Recommendations, Agenda Notes and Contributed Papers.* New Delhi: 1967.

India. Ministry of Shipping and Transport. *Report of the Working Group on Containerization.* New Delhi: 1971.

India. Planning Commission. *Eighth Five Year Plan 1992-97.* New Delhi: 1992.

______. *First Five Year Plan.* New Delhi: 1953.

______. *Fourth Five Year Plan: A Draft Outline.* New Delhi: 1966.

______. *Fourth Five Year Plan 1969-74.* New Delhi: 1969.

______. *Indian Shipping in the Time Perspective of 2000 AD: Report of the Planning Group on Shipping, September, 1987.* Chairman: L.M.S. Rajwar. Bombay: 1987.

______. *Papers Relating to the Formulation of the Second Five Year Plan, 1955.* Delhi: Manager of Publications, 1962.

______. *Report of the Steering Committee: Perspective Planning for Transport Development.* New Delhi: Planning Commission, 1968.

______. *Second Five Year Plan.* New Delhi: 1956.

______. *Seventh Five Year Plan: 1985-1990.* New Delhi: 1985.

______. *Third Five Year Plan.* New Delhi: 1961.

Indian Institute of Foreign Trade [IIFT]. "Entitlement Voucher Scheme: A Case Study of Cargo Support to National Ships" (typescript). New Delhi: IIFT, 1986.

______. *Role of Shipping Policy in the Export Strategy of India.* New Delhi: IIFT, 1977.

______. "System Approach to Shipment and Carriage of Export Cargo" (typescript). New Delhi: IIFT, 1976.

Indian National Shipowners Association [INSA]. *Annual Review 1994-1995.* Bombay: INSA, 1995.

Indian National Steamship Owners Association. *"Indian Ship": Why Shipowners Oppose Indo-Foreign Combine for Shipping.* Bombay: INSOA, 1958.

Indian Shipping [monthly journal], 1960-1995.

Indo-American Chamber of Commerce. *The Role of Shipping in Indo-American Trade: Issues and Challenges--Report of the Seminar held on January 16-17, 1971.* Bombay: 1971.

Jain, N.C. "Indian Shipping and Future Development" (project paper; typescript). Cardiff: Department of Maritime Studies and International Transport, University of Wales, 1993.

Jantscher, Gerald R. *Bread Upon the Waters: Federal Aids to the Maritime Industries.* Washington, D.C.: The Brookings Institution, 1975.

Jog, N.G. *Saga of Scindia: Struggle for the Revival of Indian Shipping and Shipbuilding.* Bombay: Scindia Steam Navigation Co., 1969.

Juda, Lawrence. "The Reagan Administration and United States Maritime Policy", *Journal of Maritime Law and Commerce,* vol. 19, no. 3 (July 1988), pp. 323-48.

______. Ed. *Shipping Nationalism and the Future of the United States Liner Industry: The UNCTAD Code and Bilateralism.* Wakefield, Rhode Island: Times Press, 1984.

______. *The UNCTAD Liner Code: United States Maritime Policy at the Crossroads.* Boulder, Colorado: Westview Press, 1983.

Katzenstein, Peter J. Ed. *Between Power and Plenty: Foreign Economic Policies of Advanced Industrial States.* Madison: University of Wisconsin Press, 1978.

Kennedy, Paul. *The Rise and Fall of Great Powers: Economic Change and Military Conflict from 1500 to 2000.* London: Unwin Hyman, 1988.

Khanolkar, G.D. *Walchand Hirachand: Man, His Times and Achievements.* Bombay: Walchand & Co., 1969.

Kilgour, John G. *The U.S. Merchant Marine: National Maritime Policy and Industrial Relations.* New York: Praeger, 1975.

Kim, C.K. *An Innovation in Liner Shipping: The Round-the-World Service as a Global Strategy.* Bremen: Institute of Shipping Economics and Logistics, 1987.

Knudsen, Olav. *The Politics of International Shipping: Conflict and Interaction in a Transnational Issue-Area, 1946-1968.* Lexington, Mass.: Lexington Books, 1973.

Krasner, Stephen D. Ed. *International Regimes*. Ithaca, N.Y.: Cornell University Press, 1983.

______. *Structural Conflict: The Third World Against Global Liberalism.* Berkeley: University of California Press, 1985.

Lawrence, S.A. *International Sea Transport: The Years Ahead.* Lexington, Mass.: Lexington Books, 1972.

Lee, Tae-Woo. *The Growth of Korean Shipping, 1962-1981: The Advantages of Combining a "Backward" Start with Imported Ideas.* Ph.D. dissertation. Cardiff: Department of Maritime Studies, University of Wasles, 1989.

______. "Korean Shipping Policy: The Role of Government", *Marine Policy*, vol. 14, no. 5 (1990), pp. 421-37.

Lindblom, Charles E. *Politics and Markets: The World's Political-Economic Systems.* New York: Basic Books, 1977.

Maru, A.H. *Indian Shipping Since Independence August 1947.* Bombay: A.H. Maru, 1969.

Marx, Daniel, Jr. *International Shipping Cartels: A Study of Industrial Self-Regulation by Shipping Conferences.* New York: Greenwood Press, 1953.

Master, M.A. *So I Rest On My Oars: Collection of Writings and Speeches, 1947-1970.* Edited by K.V. Hariharan. 2 volumes. Bombay: M.A. Master Memorial Trust, 1977.

McFaul, Michael. "State Power, Institutional Change, and the Politics of Privatization in Russia", *World Politics,* vol.47, no. 2 (January 1995), pp. 211-43.

Mehta, N.P. "The National Shipping Policy: Relative Roles of Private and Public Sectors in Indian Shipping Development", *Indian Shipping,* vol. 12, no. 5 (1960), pp. 11-19.

Mohile, S.P. "Competitiveness of Manning of Indian Ships", *Indian Shipping,* vol. 45, nos. 1-2 (1993), pp. 13-19.

Morris, Morris D. *et al. Indian Economy in the Nineteenth Century: A Symposium.* Delhi: Delhi School of Economics, 1969.

Mukerji, Radha Kumud. *Indian Shipping: A History of the Sea-Borne Trade and Maritime History of the Indians from the Earliest Times.* Bombay: 1912.

National Council of Applied Economic Research [NCAER]. *Indian Shipping Industry: Retrospect and Prospect.* New Delhi: NCAER, 1993.

Nayar, Baldev Raj. *India's Mixed Economy: The Role of Ideology and Interest in Its Development.* Bombay: Popular Prakashan, 1989.

______. *The Modernization Imperative and Indian Planning.* New Delhi: Vikas, 1972.

______. *The Political Economy of India's Public Sector: Policy and Performance.* Bombay: Popular Prakashan, 1990.

______. "Political Mainsprings of Economic Planning in the New Nations: The Modernization Imperative versus Social Mobilization", *Comparative Politics,* VI, no. 3 (April 1974), pp. 341-66.

______. "Regimes, Power, and International Aviation", *International Organization,* vol. 49, no. 1 (Winter 1995), pp.139-70.

______. "Self-Reliance versus Marginalization: [The] Case of India's Overseas Shipping", *Economic and Political Weekly,* XXX, no. 17 (April 29, 1995), pp. 941-54.

______. *The State and International Aviation in India: Performance and Policy on the Eve of Aviation Globalization.* New Delhi: Manohar, 1994.

Nehru, Jawaharlal. *The Discovery of India.* New York: John Day Company, 1946.

______. *Planning and Development: Speeches of Jawaharlal Nehru, 1952-56.* New Delhi: Publications Division, n.d.

North, Douglass C. *Institutions, Institutional Change and Economic Performance.* Cambridge: Cambridge University Press, 1990.

Oppenheimer & Co., Inc. *International Research: Indian Shipping Industry.* New York: April 10, 1995.

Panikkar, K.M. *A Survey of Indian History.* London: Meridan Books, 1947.

Parthasarathy, S. "Financial Aid to Shipping Industry", *Indian Shipping,* vol. 41, nos. 6-7 (1989), pp. 9-14.

Peters, Hans Jurgen. *India's Growing Conflict Between Trade and Transport: Issues and Options.* Working Paper 345. Washington, D.C.: World Bank, 1990.

Porter, Michael. *The Competitive Advantage of Nations.* New York: The Free Press, 1990.

Raj, Dev. *Shipping and Shipbuilding Industry in India.* Delhi: H.K. Publishers, 1990.

Rajwar, L.M.S. "Indian Shipping--Need for New Policy", *Indian Shipping,* vol. 35, no. 7 (1983), pp. 11-21.

______. "The Liner Code: Its Philosophy and Approach", *Indian Shipping,* vol. 36, no. 6 (1984), pp. 29-31.

______. "Trends in Indian Shipping", *Indian Shipping,* vol. 38, no. 5 (1986), pp. 15-21.

Rapkin, David P., "The Inadequacy of a Single Logic: Integrating Political and Material Approaches to the World System", in William R. Thompson (ed.), *Contending Approaches to World System Analysis.* Beverly Hills, Calif.: Sage Publications, 1983.

Rao, T.S. Sanjeeva. *A Short History of Modern Indian Shipping.* Bombay: Popular Prakashan, 1965.

Ruggie, John Gerard. Ed. *The Antinomies of Interdependence: National Welfare and the International Division of Labour.* New York: Columbia University Press, 1983.

______. "International Regimes, Transactions, and Change: Embedded Liberalism in the Postwar Economic Order", in Stephen D. Krasner (ed.), *International Regimes.* Ithaca, N.Y.: Cornell University Press, 1983, pp. 195-231.

Sanklecha, S.N. *Economics of Shipping and Other Papers.* Bombay: Bhandarkar Publications, 1982.

______. *Tramp Shipping in India.* Bombay: University of Bombay, 1966.

______. *Tramping to Success: Story of the Great Eastern Shipping Company Limited.* Bombay: Popular Prakashan, 1994.

Shipping Corporation of India [SCI]. *Annual Reports.* 1980-81 to 1993-94.

______. *The SCI Story.* Bombay: SCI, [1986].

Simai, Mihaly. *The World Economy of Our Age and the New Multilateralism: New Challenges for Hungary.* Budapest: Hungarian Scientific Council for World Economy, 1991.

Singh, Nagendra. "India and the Technological Revolution in Shipping", *Indian Shipping,* vol. 19, no. 12 (1967), pp. 17-20.

______. *The Legal Regime of Merchant Shipping.* Bombay: University of Bombay, 1969.

Singhal, N.C. "Indian Shipping: Past, Present and Future--Financial Aspects", *Indian Shipping,* vol. 40, nos. 3-4 (1988), pp. 13-17.

Sletmo, Gunnar K. and Ernest W. Williams, Jr. *Liner Conferences in the Container Age: U.S. Policy at Sea.* New York: Macmillan, 1981.

Sletmo, Gunnar K. and Susanne Holste. "Shipping and the Competitive Advantage of Nations", *Maritime Policy and Management,* vol. 20, no. 3 (1993), pp. 243-255.

Srivastava, C.P. *Lal Bahadur Shastri, Prime Minister of India, 9 June 1964 - 11 January 1966: A Life of Truth in Politics.* Delhi: Oxford University Press, 1995.

Strange, Susan, "Cave! Hic Dragones: A Critique of Regime Analysis", in Stephen D. Krasner (ed.), *International Regimes.* Ithaca, N.Y.: Cornell University Press, 1983, pp. 337-54.

Sturmey, S.G. *British Shipping and World Competition.* London: The Athlone Press, 1962.

______. *Shipping Economics: Collected Papers.* London: Macmillan, 1975.

Takahashi, Hiroshi. "Facing the Future", *Containerization International,* June 1992, pp. 48-49.

Thanopoulou, Helen A. "The Growth of Fleets Registered in the Newly-Emerging Maritime Countries and Maritime Crises", *Maritime Policy and Management,* vol. 22, no.1 (1995), pp. 51-62.

Tilly, Charles. Ed. *The Formation of National States in Western Europe.* Princeton, N.J.: Princeton University Press, 1975.

Trivedi, H.M. *Indian Shipping in Perspective.* New Delhi: Vikas, 1980.

______. "Indian Shipping--Some Basic Issues", *Indian Shipping,* vol. 33, no. 5 (1981), pp. 19-21.

______. "Integrated Policy for National Shipping", *Indian Shipping,* vol. 34, no.5 (1982), pp. 7-12.

United Nations Conference on Trade and Development [UNCTAD]. *Review of Maritime Transport.* 1968-1993.

Vaghul, N. "Indian Shipping Industry--A Provocative Evaluation", *Indian Shipping,* vol. 39, no. 12 (1987), pp. 5-6.

Wadiyar, Jaya Chamaraja. "Indian Shipping Under the Five-Year Plans", *Eastern Economist,* November 4, 1960, pp.828-32.

White, Lawrence J. *International Trade in Ocean Shipping Services: The United States and the World.* Cambridge, Mass.: Ballinger Publishing Company, 1988.

INDEX